TO THE STARS

TO THE STARS

• THE AUTOBIOGRAPHY OF •
GEORGE TAKEI
STAR TREK'S MR. SULU

POCKET BOOKS

New York   London   Toronto   Sydney   Tokyo   Singapore

POCKET BOOKS, a division of Simon & Schuster Inc.
1230 Avenue of the Americas, New York, NY 10020

Library of Congress Catalog Card Number: 94-67660

ISBN: 0-671-89009-3

First Pocket Books trade paperback printing December 1995

10 9 8 7 6 5 4 3 2 1

POCKET and colophon are registered trademarks of Simon & Schuster Inc.

Cover design by James Wang
Cover photo by Kelly Campbell

Printed in the U.S.A.

Photo insert credits:

Page 1: courtesy of Fumiko Emily Takei; Page 2: Top photo is a gift of Dr. Toshio Yatsushiro and Lily Koyama, and the Japanese American National Museum/ Bottom photo is from the collection of Yukio Nakamura and the Japanese American National Museum; Page 3: courtesy of Fumiko Emily Takei; Page 4: courtesy of Fumiko Emily Takei; Page 5: Top photo from CBS, Inc./Bottom photo from the Everett Collection; Page 6: Top photo from Culver Pictures Inc./Bottom photo from the Everett Collection; Page 7: Top photo from the Everett Collection/Bottom photo from Culver Pictures Inc.; Page 8: Globe Photos; Page 9: courtesy of Stephen Edward Poe; Page 10: courtesy of Stephen Edward Poe; Page 11: courtesy of Paramount Pictures; Page 12: courtesy of Paramount Pictures; Page 13: courtesy of Paramount Pictures; Page 14: Top photo courtesy of Fumiko Emily Takei/Bottom photo courtesy of Paramount Pictures; Page 15: courtesy of Paramount Pictures; Page 16: courtesy of Paramount Pictures

To Daddy

... ...

Thank You

The idea of this autobiography first sprang from a lunch I had over a year ago with Tom Kagy, the publisher of *Transpacific Magazine*. We were on the terrace of an ocean-view restaurant in Santa Monica when he suggested that the story of my life as an Asian American actor/activist would make an interesting chronicle. A week after that, my agent, Steve Stevens, proposed the notion of recounting my almost thirty years with the STAR TREK phenomenon as an autobiography. I had been demurring on all such suggestions, claiming that I was much too young to be writing about my life. But I realized that when two people whose judgments I respect come up with the same idea only a week apart, I couldn't continue to pretend that I was a blooming adolescent. My time had come.

But as I began grappling with the notion of putting my life down on paper, the growing awareness of the scope and complexity of my experiences began to loom formidably. I have vivid, real memories from my days of incarceration in America's internment camps, but I felt the imperative of placing the child's recollection in a larger, historic context. For assistance in the recounting of those years spent behind barbed-wire fences, I am deeply indebted to many people: from the Japanese

THANK YOU

American National Museum—curator Dr. Kaoru Oguri, microfilm manager Clement Hanami, and Legacy Center manager Chester Hashizume; from the Japanese American Citizens League, Carol Saito; and from the Japanese American Cultural Community Center, Kango and Katsumi Kunitsugu. I am also appreciative of the help on my family's background provided by Dr. John Kashiwabara and Ken Wakabayashi.

To nail down the details from the STAR TREK years of my life, I owe a great debt of gratitude to Richard Arnold, TREK consultant extraordinaire, ably assisted by Phil Burrill.

My thanks to Ana Martinez-Holler, publicity director of the Hollywood Chamber of Commerce, for assistance on the history of Hollywood.

My special appreciation to journalist Brad Altman, who was indefatigable in providing advice and research assistance. Without the constancy of his support, this effort would have been less joyful.

Contents

CONTENTS

The Trek Begins

Life After Cancellation

STAR TREK Lives

Live Long and Prosper

PROLOGUE

Silver Anniversary

A QUARTER CENTURY. TWO AND A HALF DECADES. IT WAS AN undreamed-of anniversary. STAR TREK was twenty-five years old. The television show first aired in September of 1966, and now, in what seemed like only a shimmer of the transporter, it was 1991. From cancellation to revival, from blockbuster to disappointment, from fictional space battles to real-life Trek wars, we had persevered through ecstatic highs and utter discouragements for twenty-five years. We had lived an unexpected lifetime. Never in our wildest dreams could we have fantasized all that actually happened. And now, we had reached a rare and unimagined milestone. In 1991, STAR TREK celebrated a glorious silver anniversary.

The centerpiece was the release of STAR TREK VI: THE UNDISCOVERED COUNTRY. But the day before the opening of the film, on December 5, 1991, all seven of us—Bill Shatner, Leonard Nimoy, DeForest Kelley, Nichelle Nichols, Jimmy Doohan, Walter Koenig, and I—gathered at a historic landmark on Hollywood Boulevard, the Chinese Theater, for a fantastic ritual ceremony.

The Chinese Theater was the most glamorous film showcase in town, built in 1927 in a "Chinese" architectural style that cannot be found anywhere in all of China. It is singularly Hollywood-style "Orientalia." And the concrete squares in the forecourt of this theater contain the autographs and handprints of the great luminaries of motion picture history.

This was the theater that my parents took me to as a kid on special occasions. I remember putting my hand in the huge palm prints left by Gary Cooper, Gene Kelly, and Clark Gable and getting goose bumps at the thought that my hand was occupying the very same space that had held the hands of those magical heroes of the screen. Now, we of the STAR TREK cast were gathered in the same forecourt, to add ours to that exalted collection. We were joining those legends of movie history!

But before the ceremony, in an informal briefing inside the theater, we were instructed to write only our autographs in the wet cement and nothing else. Space in the block was limited, and we had to get seven names in. It was emphasized repeatedly that only our names could be written in the square. Then, we were hustled out the back way and loaded into convertibles for the parade down Hollywood Boulevard.

The cheering crowd, the rousing marching band, the congratulatory speeches from officials, and finally, the moment for Hollywood's version of an investiture ceremony came. Bill was the first to walk down the red carpet and get on his knees. He picked up the writing stick and, with bowed head, dutifully inscribed his name in cement—only his name, as instructed. Then Leonard followed suit and completed his act of inscription into the hallowed forecourt. De was next. He seemed a bit nervous. I didn't blame him at all. It was an awe-inspiring experience. He got down, wrote his name, and got up. Somebody whispered, "He's misspelled his name." Bill heard that and yelled out, "De! You misspelled your name!" We looked down at his autograph. There in concrete was written D-e-F-o-r-e-t Kelley. De had left out the *s* in his name! Grinning with red-faced embarrassment, De got back down and squeezed the missing *s* into his autograph. The flashbulbs were blinding. De's public shaming made the rest of us very cautious.

When my turn came, I carefully wrote my name on the

viscous surface, crossed my *T*, and prepared to dot the final *i*. But suddenly, an awesome sense of responsibility struck me. I realized that I was the only native Angeleno in our group. Leonard was from Boston, De from Georgia, Nichelle was from Chicago, and Walter from New York. Bill and Jimmy weren't even Americans—they were from Canada! None of them could be expected to know the history and tradition of the Chinese Theater. But I had grown up here with it. I had a responsibility as the sole Angeleno! Then I remembered, we had been strictly instructed—only our names, nothing else.

But, I deliberated, what could they do? They wouldn't dare erase it! I dotted my *i*, put my stick down, and, with mind heavy with the obligation to the tradition that I alone bore, I opened my palm wide and sank it firmly into the wet cement. There was shocked silence. It was broken only when Bill gasped, "George put his hand in!" I felt the stillness of accusatory silence, but I continued pressing down. Then Bill cried again, "I want to put my hand in, too!" He dashed down the red carpet and with a loud "splat" slapped his palm right down by his name. The floodgate was opened. All the rest ran down to their respective names and started slapping their hands into the now drying cement. But ever-aware Leonard, always in character, sank his hand in solidly, forming his Vulcan salute.

STAR TREK VI: THE UNDISCOVERED COUNTRY was a triumph. The critics raved, the box-office exploded, and our silver-anniversary showpiece was another gleaming achievement in our twenty-five-year trek.

Two months after the opening of the film, Majel Barrett and the rest of the cast gathered again, this time on the opposite coast, at another landmark institution, the National Air and Space Museum of the Smithsonian in Washington, D.C. This was another premiere, but of a totally different kind. It was the grand opening of a museum installation titled *The Twenty-Fifth Anniversary STAR TREK Exhibit*. This, too, was an unanticipated distinction.

We were assembled onstage for the press conference prior to

the opening festivities. It was a huge, hangarlike hall packed with representatives from the print and electronic media. A reporter got up and addressed this question to the curator of the exhibit, Mary Henderson:

"The National Air and Space Museum here is the most distinguished repository for our civilization's achievements in air and space exploration. We have the original *Spirit of St. Louis* that Charles Lindbergh flew in the first solo flight across the Atlantic. We have astronaut Neil Armstrong's space suit that he wore on the moon. We have a genuine chunk of the moon rock here in the collection of the Smithsonian. Why should a television and movie series, a piece of entertainment, be honored with an exhibit alongside these genuine artifacts of our space achievements here in this museum?"

"Yes," Mary Henderson responded. "We do have the genuine artifacts you mentioned here. But this museum is not just a repository for these pieces from history. Our collection is here to teach young people about our achievements. They are here to stimulate their thinking. To encourage and arouse their curiosity about the universe beyond.

"STAR TREK very much has a place in this museum, because over the last quarter century, the show has sparked the imaginations of not just youngsters, but so many people. STAR TREK inspired many to a life of inquiry and exploration. School teachers, engineers—indeed astronauts—have been touched by the ideals of the show. STAR TREK over the last twenty-five years has generated a vibrant excitement about the exploration of space. *The* STAR TREK *Exhibit* most certainly belongs here, right in our nation's capital, because STAR TREK, with its ideas, has galvanized a powerful sense of adventure for the challenges of our future and for the great conundrums that we face here today." Mary Henderson was confident and eloquent. She filled me with a pride that soared through that vast hall.

The exhibit was scheduled for a three-month run. I don't think the Smithsonian people really knew of the enormity of our audience base—or of its determination. From the opening day on, the museum was encircled by an endless line of people

4

patiently waiting to get in. The schedule was extended. Then, it was extended again. Then again. People flew in from all parts of the world to view the exhibition. *The Twenty-Fifth Anniversary STAR TREK Exhibit* ran for a record-breaking eleven months and finally had to be closed because another exhibit couldn't wait any longer for the space. The Smithsonian had never before had such a response to an exhibit. For STAR TREK, it was another precedent-setting distinction.

The Silver Anniversary STAR TREK Convention in Los Angeles was the biggest ever held. The gargantuan Shrine Auditorium was packed beyond its capacity. STAR TREK was now a worldwide phenomenon, and fans flew into Los Angeles from throughout the world—Europe, the Americas, Asia, and Australia. The metaphor of Starship Earth had become stirring reality, and the assembled fans buzzed with anticipation in a myriad different accents and a multitude of languages.

The convention, befittingly, was a tribute to Gene Roddenberry, the creator of STAR TREK. The entire program was dedicated to Gene as an expression of gratitude and affection for an artist-visionary who had touched so many in such incalculable ways.

All of the actors were again gathered to honor the man who had drawn the international legion of fans here. We, who were blessed to know Gene as a friend, spoke from the vast stage of the Shrine. Fond memories were shared, amusing anecdotes related. Our admiration of Gene was expressed with appreciation and affection.

But throughout our speeches, there was a hint of melancholy. For Gene had been ill for a long time. Over the past year, we had watched him assaulted by a series of strokes. First, his speech had suffered from a slight slurring. Then another attack took from this giant of a man, a former police officer, his firm, purposeful steps. From then on, he walked with a cane and a quivering, timorous shuffle. By the time of the great convention, Gene was in a wheelchair. But that puckish smile and the twinkle in his eyes could never be taken from him.

Gene was the last to be introduced. He had been waiting in the darkened wings of the stage, seated in his wheelchair. His smile, as he listened to all the accolades, beamed out at us onstage.

"Ladies and gentlemen, the man of the hour, the man for all seasons—Gene Roddenberry." The master of ceremonies' voice reverberated through the tremendous space of the auditorium. Gene's wheelchair, pushed by his son Rod, began rolling across the stage. The lights came up on the entire house. We were lined up in front of the back curtain. As one body, the entire auditorium exploded in thunderous applause. The sound grew and grew as Rod pushed his father's wheelchair to the center of the stage. Like one giant tidal wave following another, the massive ovation continued roaring in.

I looked over at Gene's hunched figure in his chair. And a flash of alarm shot through me! Gene's arms, pressed on the armrest of the wheelchair, were trembling furiously. I looked at Rod questioningly. Why wasn't he doing something? Then I noticed Gene waving off Rod's concern with his head. Gene didn't want help. He was forcing his body up with the muscles in his arms. His legs may no longer have been able to support him, but he was determined to rise up on his own to acknowledge the great sound of tribute that continued rolling onto that stage. It was heart-stopping to watch. Gene's arms shook and wavered perilously. But with sheer willpower, he was pushing his stocky frame upright to receive the endless sound of gratitude and love. With the fierce determination that had characterized his life, he commanded every resource within him. Slowly, agonizingly, he rose up, tall and smiling. Standing proudly, he whispered to the world, "Thank you very much."

That Silver Anniversary Convention at the Shrine Auditorium will remain for me the shining highlight of an extraordinary year glittering with the laurels, trophies, and mementos of an undreamed-of twenty-five years.

That this quarter-century association with STAR TREK should even be a part of my life is the most unexpected miracle. As inextricably identified as I am now with soaring galactic voyages, to a boy in Los Angeles more than fifty years ago, gazing up to the stars and dreaming, the idea would have been the sheerest of fantasies. For that Japanese American boy and his family were on another, quite different, journey. Their world was collapsing around them in a chaos of cataclysmic events. I was that boy. And my personal journey began in the turmoil of World War II.

AN
AMERICAN
BEGINNING

1

Journey to Arkansas

A GUST OF HOT, DUSTY WIND BEAT AGAINST THE WINDOW AND JUST
as quickly blew away. The train was moving at top speed, but in
the empty vastness of the desert landscape, only the occasional
dust billows and the lonely saguaro cactus that sped by defined
any sense of movement. That and the steady, monotonous
rocking of the train. The scene outside remained the same.
Hour after hour, day after day.

I was four years old and sensitive enough to feel the tension.
There was a strange solemnity in the leathery faces of the old
folks as we swayed together in unison. Some of the women had
cried when we left Los Angeles, but now they just stared out at
the silent emptiness, impassively swaying, their dry tear stains
leaving lacy patterns on their cheeks. All of us wore numbered
identification tags attached with soft wire firmly twisted into
our clothes. I was No. 12832-C. Occasionally, the Military
Police, standing like statues at parade rest at both ends of the
railcar, would thump their rifles on the floor to break their
tedium.

Our father had told us—my younger brother, Henry, and my
baby sister, Nancy Reiko—that we were going for a "long

vacation in the country." I believed him. I thought it would be a wonderful adventure. I just assumed that this was the way people went to the country for a long vacation. I only wondered why that sick lady at the far end of our car, who kept up a constant onslaught of hacking and coughing, had to go on this vacation with us. Our father told us we were going to a camp called Rohwer in a faraway place called Arkansas. When I asked him what it would be like there, he said he wasn't sure and didn't say anything more.

The trip seemed interminable. It was the second day, and Camp Rohwer felt no closer. The rocking and the swaying was never-ending. The hard, upright wooden seats were torturous. The dull heat, relentless. Everybody was numbed into a muzzy lethargy.

Suddenly, the tedium was broken. For no discernible reason, the train came to a roaring, huffing, squealing stop in the middle of the desert. Immediately, everyone was alert. What was happening? My mother tightened her hold on my shoulder and drew me toward her as she held my sister in her arms. She looked at my father, who was fixed on the MPs. Alarm flashed in everyone's eyes.

"All right. Everybody out for exercise. Outside. Outside." Both MPs were gesturing for us to leave the car.

"Outside?" "Here?" There was confusion. "Why are we stopping in the middle of nowhere?"

"Outside. Outside for exercise," the MPs barked.

The younger people began explaining the situation in Japanese to the bewildered old folks. A few young men staggered up from their seats and sluggishly began the hurly-burly of leaving the train. Tired, rumpled people who had been sitting in the same place for two days and a night started to gather themselves up. My mother hurriedly arranged on her head her new Sears Roebuck straw hat and handed my father his Panama hat. All three of us kids had white cotton caps placed on our heads.

The high railcar steps seemed like a series of small cliffs to me. My father held my hand, and I was dangled down. Henry was hanging from my father's other hand. It felt great to be outside.

As soon as I was put down, I grabbed a handful of warm sand and flung it at my brother. He yowled and started toward me. I grabbed another handful and started to run away. Just then, I felt a firm hand grab my arm. It was the quiet man who sat across the aisle from us. He stopped Henry with a gentle point of the finger. "You have lively boys, Takei-san," he said smilingly as he handed me over to my father.

"Thank you." My father was strangely subdued as he took our hands. My father looked down at us, and for a moment I expected a frown of disapproval. But instead I saw sadness in his eyes. They seemed to linger on us. He repeated softly to himself, "Lively boys." Then he gazed off into the desert void. As if asking the empty horizon, he murmured, "What am I taking them to?"

After the railcar was cleared of those who wanted to stretch their legs, the MPs planted themselves again at parade rest at the foot of the car steps. The one closest to me was idly singing the tune, "Shoo fly, don't bother me. Shoo fly, don't bother me." Most of us who got off the train milled about near the car, but a few young men wandered farther out into the hot sand. Others were bending down inspecting the underside of the train. One young man ducked between the cars and urinated on the train wheels. There was a steamy sizzle when the liquid splashed onto the hot steel. I thought my father saw him, too, but he pretended not to notice. Henry and I looked at each other and giggled.

"All right, everybody, back on board. Everybody back." The MPs roamed about, shouting. "Exercise break's over. Back on the train." The tumult and congestion getting back on was worse than getting off. Some old folks had to be carried back up the steep steps. Our "shoo fly" MP planted himself beside the steps, offering a hand to anyone who needed it. We were standing right beside him waiting our turn up. His rifle was slung smartly on his shoulder. I reached up and touched it. The gunmetal was hot from the heat of the desert sun. I yelped, more out of surprise than pain. The MP smiled down at me. "Ya won't do that again, will ya." He bent down, picked me up, and set me down on the upper step. "There ya go, kiddo." My father struggled up, dangling Henry by the hand. My mother was already up in the car with my sister, Nancy Reiko, in her arms.

Our brief exercise break in the middle of the desert was over. Our family's long journey across America with hundreds of other Japanese Americans to a barbed-wire-enclosed camp in Arkansas had another night and day yet to go. And, for an inquisitive and energetic four-year-old boy, a great adventure was just beginning.

Memory is a wily keeper of the past, usually true and faithful, sometimes elusive but, at times, deceptive. Childhood memories are especially slippery. Sweet and so full of joy, they can be as much a misrendering of the truth as the fondly remembered taste of candy at a funeral. That sweetness for a child, out of context and intensely subjective, remains forever real. I know that I will always be haunted by the larger, vaguely remembered reality of the surrounding circumstances of my childhood.

I remember my father's melancholy and my mother's obsessive concern for our basic well-being. But they are dusty, peripheral remembrances. My bright, sharp memories are of a joyful time of games, play, and discoveries.

I remember my mother bought each of us kids our own individual water canteens at Sears for our trip. We thought that was great. She had actually bought them because she was worried about the quality of the water supply on the trip. But no matter how great my mother's anxiety, my own more vivid memory is of the fun of taking those wonderful little sips of lukewarm water that we were periodically treated to from our very own canteens.

For my father, Takekuma Norman Takei, that long, hot trip through the southwestern desert was more than the end of all that he had built of his life. It was a journey into uncertainty with a wife, three small children, and nothing else. As the desolation of the desert flew by his window, a myriad thoughts must have rushed through his mind. Memories of his coming to America from Japan at age thirteen with his older brother and his widower father, so full of hopes and dreams. Of growing up in the vibrant Japantown community of San Francisco. As the arid landscape swept past him, his thoughts must have drifted back to memories of the cool San Francisco Bay Area that he traveled as a member of the Japantown Seals baseball team. Memories tumble on top of memories. How stinging it must have been to think of the buoyant plans he had made for the future when he graduated from Hills Business College of San Francisco. Of his move down south for the opportunities in the booming, young city of Los Angeles. Of starting up a lucrative cleaning business in the Wilshire corridor. There, he met Fumiko Emily Nakamura of Sacramento, and in 1935 they were married by the city clerk on the twenty-seventh floor of Los Angeles's stunning new City Hall. Then he would remember the pain at the loss of their firstborn child at only three months.

But they knew joy again at the birth of a healthy boy on April 20, 1937. This baby, so precious after the loss of their firstborn, became the center of their lives, the most important being in their world. He needed a fitting name. To them, this baby was as great as a prime minister, even a king. As an Anglophile, an admirer of things English, my father therefore had a choice between Neville and George. He and Fumiko Emily—whom he had decided to call "Mama" from then on, and she would call him "Daddy"—settled on the royal choice. The baby was named George, for King George VI of England. They chose Hosato, Japanese for "Village of the Bountiful Harvest," for his Japanese middle name. A year later, another boy was born—a healthy, chubby baby—as fat as King Henry VIII. He was named Henry, of course. Two years later, another baby arrived —this time a girl. She was named Nancy Reiko—Nancy for a remarkably beautiful woman they knew and Reiko, Japanese for "gracious child."

Then a terrible war had broken out, and my father's whole world was blown away. All people of Japanese ancestry in

15

America were to be immediately removed to internment camps, leaving everything behind. So much was irretrievably lost. The business—abandoned. The rented house on Garnet Street—hurriedly vacated. The car, sold for the best offer, five dollars—better to get something than leave it behind. But the new refrigerator got no offer. It nearly killed Mama to have to abandon it to the vultures. Everything other than what we were allowed to carry—all abandoned. All memories now. All as fleeting as the sand blowing past the window. All gone.

My father's memories of that train ride are so different from mine. How I wish I could have shared some of his anguish. How it grieves me now that I could not do anything to have somehow lessened his pain. But time and a generation separated us on that desert voyage—our shared and yet so different journeys to the camp called Rohwer.

My mother's background is the transpacific reverse of my father's. He was born in Yamanashi, Japan, in the shadows of Mount Fuji. She was born in the United States on my grandfather Nakamura's farm near Sacramento, California, in a town called Florin. My father came to America as a young teenager and was educated here. My mother was sent to Japan and educated there. They traded countries and experiences in their youth, but fate brought them together in the city of the angels, Los Angeles.

My grandfather Nakamura grew hops, strawberries, and grapes by sharecropping the land of a man named Cransarge, and he was quite successful. My grandfather was one of the first to own a Model T Ford in Florin. When my mother was five years old, he bought a grand piano for her, and she began her lessons. He could afford not to have his children educated in the inferior and segregated rural school of the Sacramento delta of the time. All seven of his children were educated in Japan. When my mother, the third child and first daughter, was seven, she was packed off to be schooled as a proper Japanese lady. So although American-born, my mother was and is quite traditionally Japanese. But she was always traditional in her own unique way.

16

As the train rattled on, Mama was constantly preoccupied. The baby had to be fed. Henry got carsick, and his mess had to be cleaned up. George needed to go to the bathroom, and there was the constant long line at the end of the car to contend with. Yes, we all faced an unknown future, but the reality before us had to be dealt with. She was not going to surrender to the angst of our condition. She was determined to make her own certainly out of our collective uncertainty. As certain as the rice balls she had wrapped in seaweed and packed in her hand luggage to supplement the cold train box lunches. She was not going to yield to the monotony that others accepted as inevitable. She had stuffed into her limited luggage space special treats for the children; a few lollipops, packages of animal crackers, and Cracker Jack boxes that contained little surprise toys. She packed story books for Daddy to read to us. Boredom was a foe she was determined to fight.

She was not going to allow anything, not even the United States Government, to affect the well-being of her family. She had packed a potent arsenal in the hand baggage she hauled on board that traincar. That memory of my mother's huge, shapeless, wonderful bag, I can now share with her. I have glowing recollections of her bag so full of goodies that made the journey an unforgettable train ride. But even that shared memory was from two very different journeys—one an adventure of discovery, the other an anxiety-ridden voyage into a fearful unknown.

It was the third day, and we were finally out of the desert. We could see trees now and an occasional billboard. As we approached a small, rural east Texas town, the MPs ordered us to pull down the window shades, as we'd done at every little ramshackle station we'd passed through. The townspeople were not to know that Japanese Americans were being transported on the train. We rumbled in slowly. Gradually the train came to a hissing, coughing stop. We were ordered to keep quiet and still in the dim light that filtered in through the olive drab shade. I could hear sounds of things being loaded and unloaded outside. I could hear loud shouts flying back and forth between the men on the work crew. I could hear clanging sounds, rolling sounds, heavy scraping sounds. I could hear people laughing. It was the sounds of life just outside, tantalizing me beyond the tightly drawn canvas barrier. It was unbearably alluring. I lifted the bottom of the shade the tiniest little bit and peeked out. Right in front of me—in full, bright sunlight that made me squint—I saw something I had never seen before. There on a long, splintery wood bench sat a row of old black men. I had seen black people before in Los Angeles, but I had never seen people so deeply and purely black in color. These weathered old men, looking like they had been charred by the scorching Texas sun, sat there in their baggy, shapeless clothes all lined up as if they had been there waiting forever. In their eyes I saw wearied, stoic patience. It was fascinating. I thought I recognized something. There in the eyes of these pure black old men, people who looked so different from us, I saw the same distant, drained look that I saw in the eyes of the old folks who sat in our train car.

Henry noticed me peeking out through the bright sliver of sunlight and tried to force his face next to mine. Suddenly, my narrow little view of the outside world blacked out. Mama had noticed us, too, and quickly slammed the shade closed before the MPs could catch us.

A low rumble, the squeal of tired steel on worn-out tracks, a huff of strenuous exertion from the engine car up front, and we were moving again. Slowly, laboriously, we began our final stretch to Rohwer, Arkansas.

2

Rohwer Remembrances

"ROHWER!" THE MPS' BELLOW HAD REVIVED ENERGY. "EVERY-body get ready to leave. This is Rohwer!" Their lusty voices sounded as if they were shouting "roar." They sounded like a pack of guard lions. We could hear them roaring out in all the other cars, like bouncing echoes fading with distance. "Roar!" "Roar!"

The train sidled up right beside the barbed wire fence. The camp had been built along the west side of the tracks of the Missouri Pacific Railway. On the other side, to the east of the tracks and running parallel to them, was a gravel-covered dirt country road incongruously, but officially, named Arkansas State Highway No. 1.

Camp Rohwer—or Rohwer Relocation Center, as it was called in the formal governmental euphemism—was the east-ernmost of the ten internment camps hurriedly thrown up by the War Relocation Authority created by President Franklin D. Roosevelt's Executive Order 9102. An earlier order by the President, Executive Order 9066, authorized the internment itself. Milton Eisenhower, brother of the future President, was the National Director of the War Relocation Authority.

Rohwer was located in the southeastern corner of Arkansas,

about seven miles west of the Mississippi River and roughly forty miles north of the Louisiana border. One of the internees, Eiichi Kamiya, later gave a vivid description of the camp as "far enough south to catch Gulf Coast hurricanes, far enough north to catch midwestern tornadoes, close enough to the river to be inundated by Mississippi Valley floods, and lush enough to be the haven for every creepy, crawly creature and pesky insect in the world." For me, it was to be a great, paradisiacal adventureland.

"Rohwer!" the MPs continued bellowing. We rolled slowly alongside the barbed wire fence—so slowly that it seemed the train was forcibly impressing upon us each detail of the place to which it had brought us. In the bright sunlight, we could see each and every barb glinting and flashing like sharp, deadly gems strung out along the new wire fence. We passed tall guard towers with armed soldiers staring down at us. Beyond the fence, a distance away, we could see internees who had arrived earlier lined up and waving forlornly. Beyond them were rows upon rows of black tar-paper-covered Army barracks aligned in military parade precision. Mama recognized a friend among the people out to greet us, and she managed a wan smile and a wave. Daddy just stared out the window in intense silence. With a final lurch, the train came to a stop. Our grueling three days and two nights were finally over.

I jumped up from our hard wooden seat. I couldn't wait to run out of the car. But Daddy grabbed me, made me sit down, and said we had to wait our turn. In as orderly a fashion as a trainload of exhausted, unwashed and nervously apprehensive people could muster, we gathered our luggage from the overhead shelves and under the seats and filed out in silence. Only the commands being shouted by the guards could be heard over the scuffling and the thumping of the mass exodus.

We waited beside our train car in the blistering Arkansas sun for quite a while before we finally heard someone shouting, "Takei family of five." A guard with a clipboard was calling out our name. "Takekuma Takei and family."

"Right here," Daddy shouted back. The guard strode over

and began to tag all of us with a card that read 6-2-F. We were told to continue to wear the ID number card that had been attached to our clothes at the beginning of the journey. Daddy seemed to stiffen as he was being tagged.

"What is this?" he said. It was more a demand than a question.

"That's where the driver's gonna take you," the guard with the clipboard answered, "6-2-F." It was the address of the single room that was to be our new home. Block 6, barrack 2, unit F.

All of the Block 6 people were loaded onto an open truck with their luggage, and after another quick check by the guards at the gate, we were driven through the camp entrance and past the waving group of early arrivals. Mama waved and nodded politely to the face she recognized. "It's Imai-san," she whispered. Daddy didn't say anything. "Mrs. Imai. From North Hollywood," she emphasized. Daddy remained impassive.

The camp had a huge, sprawling layout. We drove past block after similar block of black tar-paper barracks all the way to the southern edge of the camp. Every block was set up exactly alike. There were twelve barracks to a block, with six units of rooms to a barrack. Each block had six barracks lined up on each side with the toilet-shower-wash building and the mess hall in the center. A dirt road and a drainage ditch surrounded each block. A block was planned to house about 250 people. Rohwer had 33 blocks in all and, at its peak, a population of almost 8,500.

The driver unloaded us by the Block 6 mess hall and drove off to pick up more new arrivals. Our block was at the southern border of the camp right beside the barbed wire fence. We could see a guard tower, and it could see us. Daddy went off to locate 6-2-F, leaving Mama and us kids with the luggage.

While Mama, carrying our sister in her arms, chatted with the other ladies, Henry and I sat on the luggage waiting. Beyond the fence we could see a forest of tall trees with thick, shrubby underbrush. It was dense with dark shadows. From the distant depths of the woods, we occasionally heard eerie "caw-cawing" sounds. The forest looked and sounded like a scary place beyond the barbed wire fence.

"You know what that funny sound is?" a voice asked. I looked around. A big boy about eight years old sat on a nearby pile of baggage waiting for his father to come back.

"No. What is it?" I asked.

"It's a dinosaur out there," he whispered to us confidingly. Henry and I looked at each other. We had never heard of this thing.

"A dino-what?" I asked.

"A dinosaur, dummy," he replied. "Don't you know about dinosaurs?" We both shook our heads. "They're great big monsters that lived millions of years ago and then they died."

"They died?" That's strange, I thought. "Then how come we can hear them out there?"

"Well," he said after a long, ominous pause, "the only place they didn't die is right here in Arkansas. That's why they put this fence up. To keep them caged in."

"Oh," I said. It was comforting to learn that those sharp barbs on the fence would keep the cawing monsters from attacking us.

"Okay. I found 6-2-F." Daddy was back and he had with him two young men who had volunteered to help us. They grabbed all our baggage, big and small, arranging the smaller pieces under their arms. One of the young men even tried to take Mama's big bag full of goodies, but she insisted on carrying that herself. "It's heavy, Mrs. Takei," he persisted. But that bulky cornucopia she never let anyone carry—not even Daddy. Mama brought it all the way from Los Angeles to Arkansas by herself, and she was determined to get it to our new home without help. I wondered what other surprises she had in store for us.

We tagged along after the struggling ragtag band with Daddy in the lead. It was hot and dusty, and they kicked up a golden cloud of fine Arkansas dirt. The black tar paper, instead of absorbing heat, seemed to radiate shimmering waves of hotness. Thankfully, Barrack 2 wasn't too far off, and Unit F was the room at the near end of the barrack. Daddy stamped up the three raw-lumber steps in front of 6-2-F and opened the door.

22

The heat that blasted out was enough to almost knock him over. If it was hot outside, it was a roaring furnace inside. Black did indeed absorb heat.

Daddy asked the young men to set our baggage down outside and thanked them for their help. Then he plunged into the baking-hot room to open the windows. He came staggering back out panting and drenched in perspiration. Half-cooked and florid from the ordeal, he gasped, "Let fresh air get in for a while, and then we'll go in." From her goody bag, Mama produced a big white cotton handkerchief and wiped Daddy's brow.

When we finally went in, the air was still heavy and warm. The room was a bare sixteen-by-twenty-foot space with raw-wood plank walls, three windows, and a floor of wooden planks. And sitting in one corner like a big, fat practical joke was a solitary piece of furniture—a black potbellied stove. "Don't touch it," Daddy warned us kids. "It might still be hot."

Mama stood near the door silently appraising the room. She was still carrying her goody bag. "What we sleep on?" she asked.

"They're distributing Army cots at the other end of the block," Daddy said. "I'll get some people to help me bring them here."

Just then, we heard voices and stamping and thumping from the other side of the wood plank wall. It was our next-door neighbors moving in.

"Holy jeez, it's hot in here," a male voice said. Some loud thumping could be heard and then, "Thanks very much."

"Anytime. Don't mention it," another male voice replied.

"Yell when you need help," the first voice said.

"We hear right through wall," Mama whispered, distress knitting her brow. "We not have privacy."

"*Shikata ga nai.* It can't be helped," Daddy whispered back. "I guess that's the way it's going to be." He went out to bring in our baggage. I couldn't understand why they were whispering with such concern in their voices. I thought it was fun to be able to listen in on the neighbors talking.

When Daddy got all our baggage inside, Mama finally set her bulky carryall bag down on top of the pile of suitcases. I had a feeling the moment had arrived. Mama looked at all of us smiling and announced, "I show you something."

She reached in and hefted out a heavy rectangular object wrapped in her beige sweater decorated with pretty flowers made of yarn. The object had weight, I noticed, so it probably wasn't something to eat. It must be something to play with. She carefully unwrapped her sweater from the mystery thing. It had still another layer of wrapping—my sister's pink baby blanket. This was the heaviest and biggest thing in Mama's bag. So I knew this had to be the reason she didn't let anyone else carry it. This treat had to be the best of all the surprises she had produced from that well-worn carryall. She pulled a corner of the baby blanket off to reveal something metallic. It must be a toy for us, I thought.

The pink cloth slipped off easily to reveal a rectangular, mahogany-colored metal box with a dark blue inset on top with a slot in it. She slipped her fingers into the slot and pulled. Up popped something I had never expected. It was Mama's portable sewing machine! We were speechless. We stood there looking at it in puzzlement.

"You brought that!" Daddy gaped, dumbfounded.

"I not want to leave it behind," she said simply. "And children going to be needing new clothes." There was a long silence.

Finally, Daddy said in a low whisper, "You knew this was forbidden."

"I know," she answered. "But children be needing new clothes."

Daddy stared at the contraband we now had before us. Then suddenly, an astonishing thing happened. Daddy burst out laughing. Laughing out loud. The sound erupted from the bottom of his stomach, rising up through him and shaking his whole body. He shook so much, it looked as if he was trying to throw off some invisible thing that had been clinging onto his body for a long time. He held onto the sewing machine and laughed and laughed. With tears rolling down his cheeks, he choked out to Mama, "And you knew this was forbidden." Mama, politely covering her mouth, joined in his laughing. We giggled, too, because they looked so funny.

We hadn't laughed together like that in a long time. I didn't really understand then the full resonance of all that laughter filling the small, bare room on the first day of our arrival at Rohwer. I do remember, though, that to us kids that sewing machine of Mama's was the biggest, heaviest, and most crushing disappointment of all the wonderful goodies she pulled out of her old, worn-out bag.

Setting up our new life in Rohwer immediately became a full-time occupation for both Daddy and Mama.

Mama began the daunting work of making a home for us out of that rough-hewn single room. With her portable sewing machine, she ran up window curtains made from government surplus fabrics. Using strips of rag, she braided together colorful foot mats that she placed by the steel Army cots that were distributed to us. She brought in interesting tree branches and tall weed stalks and artfully arranged them in painted coffee cans. And, of course, there were the never-ending tasks of the washing and mending and the hundred other necessary chores that three young children required. But because the mess hall crew provided the meals, cooking was the only thing she didn't do for us. To Mama, however, this was not a relief, but another deprivation of a precious personal responsibility—a cherished family charge taken from her life. Another loss.

Almost as if to make up for it, she went about creating new tasks for herself with fierce determination. I remember Mama was always busy doing something. Certainly, the curtains, foot mats, and rustic plant arrangements were expressions of love for her family. But I can't help wondering now if they weren't, like her sewing machine, her own private statement of defiance against our circumstances. The government may have taken her home and placed her family in this raw single room in a tar-paper barrack, and it may have taken her freedom and put us in this barbed wire enclosure. But it could not take her family from her nor her ability to care for us. Not as long as she could sew and braid and create beauty out of fallen branches and dried wild foliage.

Daddy, too, was confronting the challenges of our new life. He scoured the campground for scrap lumber and loose nails left by the construction workers and made shelves for storage and little stools for us kids to sit on. But more importantly, Daddy, who on our journey to Rohwer seemed tortured by personal anguish and the uncertainty of his family's future, here in camp came to grips with the blunt certainty and the necessity of a shared existence with a great number of people confronting common difficulties. From the outset, he threw himself into helping other families move in, carrying luggage, distributing beds, and volunteering for whatever brigade was being organized. And as Daddy worked to help settle people, he became more acquainted with the varying needs and personal histories of the folks who were thrown together in Block 6.

There was tiny, sparrowlike Mrs. Takahashi, with four children, whose husband had been arrested and taken away by the FBI solely because he was a Buddhist minister. And there was Mrs. Yasuda, with two children and an elderly mother, whose husband was taken by federal officials because he was a Japanese language schoolteacher. Both were separated from husbands, who had been taken without trials or even formal charges—their only crime being that they occupied positions of high visibility in the Japanese community.

Then there were Mr. and Mrs. Mamiya in the barrack facing ours. She was a tall, white-haired Caucasian lady, whom Mr. Mamiya was always fretting over because she was so sickly. He said she worried herself ill out of self-consciousness as the only white person in our block.

And there was an elderly couple from Lodi, California, whose only son refused to be interned, citing his constitutional rights, and thus was arrested and separately incarcerated.

There were people from many different communities up and

26

down California and a few from Hawaii. There were farmers from Fresno and fishermen from San Pedro, professionals from Los Angeles and shopkeepers from Stockton. There were old immigrants and old Nisei, American-borns. There were young immigrants and many young Nisei and even Sansei, third-generation Americans. We were so diverse. All so different. And yet, we were the same. We were all Japanese Americans and we were all in Block 6 at Rohwer. That was our common denominator. Daddy felt keenly the need for this diverse group somehow to be able to live together. We had to forge a community.

But problems and complaints were inevitable, and they immediately started cropping up. The women objected to the lack of privacy in their lavatory facility. It was a long, open row of toilet seats and nothing else. Partitions to ensure some semblance of privacy were needed.

Beef brains had been served at one of the first meals in the mess hall. It was a delicacy unknown and unpalatable to most Japanese tastes. A request had to be made to the camp administrator for meals appropriate to the Japanese palate.

The need for someone to work on these problems and be a representative of the people with the camp administration was evident. Daddy's name was put forth as the block manager, and he was elected.

Although Daddy didn't particularly think of himself as a leader, under these circumstances he was uniquely equipped to serve in that capacity. He was fluent in Japanese and English and so was able to communicate with the Japanese-speaking immigrant group as well as the English-speaking American-born generation. His age also bridged the gap. Daddy was thirty-nine—right in between the elders in their fifties or sixties, thus old enough to have some credibility with them, and the young American-born Nisei group, which was composed mostly of people in their teens and early twenties. Most of all, he felt acutely the needs of those with whom he shared a common circumstance. He willingly accepted the urgency of serving. As block manager, his role became a combination of mayor of the block, liaison with the camp administration, arbitrator of disputes within the block, and—to some—even a marriage counselor.

While Daddy and Mama were consumed with starting up our new life in camp, Henry and I had a brand-new world to explore. The camp itself was boring in its geometric symmetry and rigid uniformity. But the areas near the barbed wire fence became a place of never-ending discoveries.

We were city kids, and although we had seen butterflies back in Los Angeles, never had we seen such large and colorful ones as those that flitted along the barbed wire fence. But these were dumb butterflies. If I quietly approached one resting on the wire and then moved swiftly, I could snatch it up with two fingers before it knew what happened. They were beautiful but dumb. Catching them was too easy. I threw them back up into the air, and as they gratefully fluttered away, I would find beautiful powder patterns left on my fingers.

The more interesting of the flying exotica were the dragon-flies. These crimson or electric blue animated torpedoes, buzzing and darting about the fence, would alight briefly on the wire as if to tease us by showing off their bright luminescent tails in full stationary glory. And they would reveal their wings to be, not really invisible blurs, but actually strong transparent propellers shimmering with changing iridescent colors. I had to catch these creatures. But even before I could get close enough to snatch one of them by its stilled wings, it would dart off, mocking me triumphantly in its fancy zigzag flight pattern.

One day, when Henry and I were playing near the fence, two big boys, brothers who lived on the other side of the mess hall, came up to us. I knew that the older one, about thirteen, was named Ford and his chubby brother, a few years younger, was Chevy. I had heard Daddy pointing them out to Mama during lunch in the mess hall and telling her that their daddy named them after cars because he bought those cars the year each boy was born. Daddy thought that their daddy must have been very proud of his cars.

"Hey, kid, you want to learn a magic word?" It was Ford talking to me.

"What kind of magic?" I asked.

"You can have power over the guards in the tower."

"Power over those soldiers with rifles? Really?" It did sound like something awesome. "Okay," I said, somewhat tentatively. A decision like this was not to be rushed into rashly. "What's the magic word?"

Ford started to explain. His brother, Chevy, the one with the round, dumpy face, hung back and giggled for some unknown reason.

"With this magic word," Ford began, "you can get the soldiers to give you anything you want. First, you shout at them all the goodies you want. Then you yell out the magic word real loud. And if you say the word right, then they'll give you everything you shouted at them." This sounded simple enough, I thought. But I was becoming aware of something else—Ford had a crazy kid brother. While Ford was telling me about the magic word, Chevy covered his mouth like some loony, stupidly trying to suppress his giggles.

"Well, what's the magic word?" I asked.

"Remember, you've got to say it right, or it won't work," Ford emphasized.

"Okay, I'll say it right. What is it?" I demanded.

"All right, here it is," Ford said. He began pronouncing the words very slowly and deliberately. "Sakana beach."

"Sakana beach?" I was puzzled. What's so magical about sakana beach? I thought to myself. *Sakana* means "fish"—so, fish beach. What's magical about that?

"Remember, you have to say it right," Ford said.

"Well, how do I have to say sakana beach?" I asked.

"You have to say it real fast, and you have to say it real loud. It's real important you say it fast."

By now, Chevy was convulsing uncontrollably in a silent fit, his arms wrapped tightly around his shaking body, struggling to contain the giggles about to burst from him. That nitwit brother was getting on my nerves. "Okay, so I shout at the guard all the things I want, and then I yell 'sakana beach' real fast, right?" It sounded so easy.

I told Henry to stay where he was, and I started toward the guard tower. "Get bubble gum," Henry yelled to me.

"Remember," Ford emphasized again, "if you don't say it right, then the guards get real mad and they might start shooting. So if you don't say it right, you better run like hell."

They might start shooting? Why did he add that part after I started out? That's a whole different story. But it was too late. I was on my way. I wasn't a coward. I kept walking toward the guard tower.

The guards were just changing shifts, and the one who had been up in the tower had come down. Both guards were on the ground chatting. I approached them and stopped about fifty yards away. I yelled out, "Bubble gum!" That was for Henry. The guards glanced at me startled, then smiled. I took a few more steps and shouted, "Popsicle!" That was something I remembered from Los Angeles that we didn't have in camp. The guards just smiled and shrugged their shoulders. A few more tentative steps and I shouted, "Tricycle!" Nothing. They were now ignoring me. I thought I had better not get too greedy.

I took a couple more steps toward the chatting guards, then a deep breath, and shouted at the top of my voice as fast as I could, "Sakana beach!" They turned to me, stunned. I waited. How were they going to produce bubble gum, Popsicles, and a tricycle, I wondered. But they just stood there glowering at me. Maybe I didn't say it quite right. I took another breath and yelled out even louder and faster, "Sakana beach."

"Why you little rascal," growled one soldier. And he started to bend down to pick up a pebble. It wasn't going well. I hadn't said the magic words right. Maybe I could undo the mistake by saying it a bit slower. But just as I got out my third—and as it turned out, my final—"sakana beach," the guard flung a pebble at me. I turned and ran as fast as I could.

Behind me I could hear the other guard call out, "You little snot!" Another pebble skittered past me. They were really mad!

This was a disaster. They could start shooting at me with their rifles next. I grabbed Henry's hand, and we ran as fast as our legs could carry us. From the corner of my eyes, I saw Ford and Chevy hiding behind a barrack. They were rolling in hysterics, laughing their heads off.

Back home, I asked Mama what was so magical about "sakana beach." She couldn't figure out what I was talking about. "*Sakana*" mean 'fish,'" she said. "And 'beach' mean *kaigan*. No magic. Just Japanese and English all mixed up." We knew that. She was no help.

That night we told Daddy the whole story and asked if he could solve the riddle of sakana beach. He sat there repeating it at varying speeds over and over. Sakana beach fast. Sakana beach medium, and Sakana beach slowly. Finally, he stopped and smiled. He said it again, "Sakana beach," and started to chuckle. Sakana beach, he told me, sounds like very bad words in English that he didn't want us using—and certainly not shouted at the guards. He said Ford and Chevy Nakayama were bad boys for teaching me those words, and he did not want us playing with them anymore. Good, I thought. I didn't like those crazy brothers anyway. But the power of the words "sakana beach" remained a mystery to me. It wasn't until I was much older that I realized that sakana beach, said in just the right way, sounds like "son of a bitch."

I wasn't always getting into trouble like some kids. But the times I did, I remember well. In one such experience, I could have gotten into serious trouble, but ultimately it turned out wonderfully. Henry and I became friends with the boy who had told us about the dinosaurs in the woods on our first day in camp—his name was Paul, and he lived two barracks away from us. One day we bumped into him walking along the dirt road by the drainage ditch. He had a coffee can filled with yellowish water from the ditch.

"You wanna see what I caught?" Paul said boastfully. He let us peer into his can. There were little, wiggly black fishlike things swimming around.

"What are they?" I asked.

"Pollywogs," he bragged. "They turn into little frogs."

Paul was older than me for sure, but he really acted like a big know-it-all. I looked at him suspiciously. I knew what frogs looked like, and in no way did these wiggly fish look like little baby frogs.

"You're lying," I challenged.

"Yeah. You're lying," Henry echoed, backing me up like a good kid brother.

"You don't believe me? Well, look at this one then," he said, pointing to one lying still at the bottom of the can. "See? Can you see the tiny legs growing out on the sides there?" It was an amazing thing to behold—a fish with two miniature frog legs sticking out of its side. "Well," Paul continued, "the legs get bigger, and the tail gets smaller, and finally it disappears. By that time it's got two front legs, too, and then it becomes a frog and hops out of the water."

With a little imagination I could see the fat, round shape of a frog in the body of the pollywog with the legs. If what Paul was saying was true, what a fascinating thing to watch happening right before one's eyes. "Can I have some?" I asked.

"Go catch your own," he said with a proud grin.

"We don't know where to catch them. Will you show us where?" I pleaded.

"Well, okay," he relented with exaggerated reluctance. And we were off on our great pollywog expedition.

Late that morning before lunch call, Henry and I came home each with our own coffee can of freshly caught wiggly pollywogs and excited tales of the magic that was about to unfold before our eyes. But before we could finish the story of our adventure, Mama burst into hysterics. "What! You playing at drainage ditch by fence? Oh, *abunai*." She started repeating *"abunai"* uncontrollably. *"Abunai.* It so dangerous. *Abunai,* you could get hurt." We didn't think it *"abunai"* at all. Why do mothers always make such a big fuss over all the things that are fun? Just then, Daddy came home from the block manager's office to have lunch with us. Mama immediately let loose with another flood of alarm, liberally punctuated with more "*abunai*," on a startled Daddy.

Over lunch in the noisy mess hall, Daddy soberly told us about schools of venomous snakes called water moccasins that disguise themselves as floating sticks to bite poison into little boys. And in the woods, he told us, live dangerously beautiful snakes with copper-red bodies called copperheads and another family of snakes that carry rattles on the tip of their tails that they sound as a warning before they eat little boys. I didn't want to be eaten, but it sounded fascinating—both scary and intriguing. Snakes that float like sticks on the water and snakes with rattles as dinner bells. The unknowns that lie hidden in the dark of the woods seemed spellbindingly exotic and that much more alluring. "Daddy, will you take us into the woods with you so we can see it safely?" I asked. Mama immediately launched into another chorus of "*abunai.*" But Daddy pondered for a moment and then said, "I'll see what I can arrange."

That evening after his block manager's announcements at the mess hall, Daddy seated himself with us. Then he told us about a special treat he had arranged for us. He was able to borrow a Jeep from the motor pool and get us clearances "to go outside" for a few hours tomorrow afternoon. Daddy was going to get us outside our barbed wire confinement! It was great having a daddy who could make wishes come true.

It seemed like forever before "tomorrow afternoon" actually came. I told all the kids Henry and I knew, including Paul. They all said we were lucky, but I knew it was because our daddy was the block manager.

After lunch, Henry and I waited, sitting on our front step. With us were Paul, Eddy—the Buddhist minister's son—and another kid named Tadao, with his little brother Akira. Suddenly, in a cloud of yellow dust and rubber tires crunching gravel and dirt, Daddy drove up from the road behind the mess hall. He looked great driving that Jeep. Uniformed guards were the only ones we ever saw driving Jeeps—never Japanese. But this time, Daddy was the driver. He was wearing his white short-sleeved shirt and Panama hat and was driving like he owned that Jeep. In an enormous billow of dust, the Jeep came to a crunching stop. He honked the horn twice, stood up, and waved us over.

"Mama! Mama! Daddy's here. Hurry up," we yelled and ran over to Daddy. Henry and I clambered onto the backseat and began chanting, "Mama, Mama, hurry up. Mama, Mama, hurry up." It seemed a full eternity before the barrack door opened and Mama stepped out leading Reiko by her hand. Mama had on her usual white cotton blouse, but she was wearing a new skirt made of some tan-colored Army surplus cloth and a scarf made from the same material on her head tied under the chin. And Reiko was outfitted in a matching scarf and overall pants made from the same fabric. It was mother and daughter in coordinated Army surplus. So that's what she was sewing in such a frenzy all last night and this morning, I thought. I guess Mama knew this was a special occasion, too. "Hurry up, Mama. Hurry up," Henry and I chanted, losing our patience. We asked Daddy to give another beep on the horn. They came running and climbed on beside Daddy.

We waved good-bye to the envious faces of Paul, Eddy, Tadao, and Akira and drove through the camp to the main gate. Daddy stopped and handed the guard a form sheet he had filled out earlier and signed his name on a clipboard—and we were out. The guard towers and barbed wire fence were behind us for the first time since our arrival many months earlier. Once Daddy picked up some speed on Arkansas State Highway Number 1, the dust was behind us, too, and it was only clean, fresh wind that caressed our faces. The rush of air made Daddy take off his Panama hat. His hair was starting to thin, and Mama didn't want him bareheaded in the Arkansas sun. She was prepared with his old baseball cap, which she placed on his head with the brim in the back like a catcher.

Daddy drove through open fields and over bumpy bridges spanning murky swamps. He drove through lush, shaded forests and along placid pools. And he took us to visit a farm in the depths of the woods.

There I saw something I will never forget. At the time, I

thought it had to be the dinosaur in the woods that Paul had told us about. It was colossal in size and awesomely ugly in appearance—more than twenty times the size of Henry and me both put together. But the sounds it made were strangely not the cawing we had heard on that first day. This massive creature made obscene grunts and snorts, and an occasional, frighteningly loud bellow. And it was not running wild in the woods as Paul had suggested dinosaurs were, but was cooped up in the muckiest, smelliest, foulest pen I had ever come across. But, without a doubt, it was the most terrifying monstrosity in the world. I thought surely this had to be the creature Paul told us was a dinosaur. But Daddy and the farmer called it a hog. Daddy said that the Spam that was occasionally served for dinner in the mess hall was made from this huge animal. If Daddy said so, then it must be, I thought, but undoubtedly, anything this awesome had to belong to some family of monsters.

Mama and Reiko wanted to stay on the Jeep, so Daddy, Henry, and I wandered around the place with the farmer. We saw chickens—lots of them—some in cages and others strutting around loose. Animals were everywhere—dogs sleeping and mangy cats stalking about. I didn't know people lived like this, surrounded by so many wonderful animals. I envied the farmer.

On the drive back, Daddy pointed out likely places where snakes lived. Sunny, open areas like dirt patches and warm rocks for rattlers and copperheads; calm, quiet pools for water moccasins. Daddy wanted us to learn about snakes so that we'd know how to avoid getting bitten by them. But we saw no water moccasins, no copperheads, and no rattlesnakes—only the most monstrous creature I had ever come across in my life. And rather than being devoured by it, I learned instead that we ate it.

The sun was starting to set. For some reason, Daddy was driving very slowly—so slowly that an exhausted Henry fell asleep in the backseat. Mama looked back and noticed. She touched Daddy on the shoulder and pointed at my sleeping brother. They smiled and looked at me with a finger held to their lips. Then they pointed to Reiko on Mama's lap, who also had fallen fast asleep. Daddy and Mama looked so happy. For once, the perpetual worry on their faces had been blown away by the soft evening breeze. I was getting sleepy, too, but I didn't want to miss any of this wonderful trip. I was determined to stay awake for the whole ride all the way back. I'm glad I did because, as we neared home, the western sky turned a brilliant orange. The clouds seemed to glow with a luminous yellow halo. As our Jeep approached the guard towers, they turned into little black silhouette cutouts against the spectacularly blazing Arkansas sunset. I finally fell asleep as Daddy was checking us back in with the guards at the gate.

Childhood memories come rich with sensations—fragrances, sounds, colors, and especially temperatures. The fondly remembered memories radiate glowing warmth. That's the way I remember that golden afternoon when Daddy took the family on that wonderful Jeep ride.

Even memories that might have frost covering them glow with that same toasty warmth—like one chilly morning that following winter when we woke to discover everything blanketed in white. From the eaves of the tar-paper barracks hung rows of glassy icicles. Overnight, the landscape was transformed into a wonderland in pristine white and tar-paper black.

Mama dressed us in our warmest clothes for our breakfast trip to the mess hall while Daddy stirred the fire in the big, black potbelly stove. As soon as we were bundled up, Henry and I dashed out into the soft white powder. It scattered before us, light and weightless like dust. But this dust was cold. It had no taste, only the smack of cold. It could be shaped into a ball, and it left our hands tingly. It had weight now and could be thrown at a person but without hurting, leaving only a sharp, icy sting. The feeling of cold—something that we had felt only in the air—was made tangible overnight in the form of this white dust covering everything. We had never experienced such chilly wonder before. It was magical.

Henry and I already were covered with snowball fragments

when Daddy, Mama, and Reiko came outside. I hit Daddy with my snowball, and Henry got Mama with his, and we ran helter-skelter, yelling and laughing, for the mess hall. Just when I thought we had made it into the safety and warmth of the big building, I felt Daddy's big snowball hit me squarely on my back. His baseball-pitching arm was still strong and accurate.

After breakfast, Daddy showed us how our little snowballs could be rolled in the snow to make great big snow boulders. These were lined up in a row to create a wall. Then medium-sized ones were placed on them, building higher with each layer. Every new row of snowballs was of diminishing size, until we had built a tall snow fortress with a strong, solid base tapering up over our heads—a sturdy building made entirely of snow. It was amazing what we could make from this cold dust. It was a great feeling of accomplishment.

We could see our excited, exhausted breaths, white and frosty each time we exhaled. Daddy and Henry both had pink cheeks and rosy nosetips. We were cold and tired outside, but inside we were filled with a happy, warm glow.

Our first Christmas in camp came not too long after the snowfall. Mama put up homemade decorations in our room. In the mess hall, volunteers strung long paper banners that read "Merry Christmas" in big red-and-green letters. The banners were hung from one beam and reached all the way across the mess hall to another beam.

The highlight of Christmas was supposed to be the visit from Santa Claus. Everybody told us he was coming to our mess hall, but nobody knew when. Well, I knew the one person who knew everything, and that was Daddy, the block manager. I asked him. He answered, "We don't know whether he could come for Christmas Eve dinner or Christmas morning breakfast." I asked him why Santa was so slow, when he had his sled and reindeer and all this good slippery snow. Daddy answered that Santa wanted to visit the children in all thirty-three blocks at Rohwer, not just the ones in Block 2. "Why can't he visit all the children on Christmas Eve?" I asked. Daddy answered that Santa liked to spend some time with each boy and girl. To me, it was an unsatisfying answer.

Christmas Eve dinner finally came. It was a special menu— roast chicken, sweet potatoes, rice, and chocolate pan cake. The families with young children were seated near the door. I had a feeling deep inside that Santa Claus might come to Block 2 tonight. We finished dinner, but no Santa. We sat waiting. Some people killed time by having a second helping of chocolate cake. Then a group of grownups got up and sang Christmas carols. I couldn't understand why they were singing "I'm dreaming of a white Christmas" when everything outside was already completely white with snow. All this time was being wasted when Santa Claus could be here with us right now. I had almost given up on his making a Christmas Eve appearance when, without any warning, the mess hall doors banged open, and a gust of cold wind rushed in. We heard the jingling of bells, a loud "Ho, ho, ho," and in waddled a short, puffed-up, over-jolly Santa Claus in a wrinkled red suit.

Henry and Reiko sat wide-eyed with surprise and wonder. This Santa "ho-ho-hoed" an awful lot and then started to move from kid to kid asking them their names and whether they had been good or bad. Some were dumbstruck. Those that spoke up said they had been good. Nobody confessed to doing anything bad. Not even Ford and Chevy Nakayama. Most kids just stared in awe or puzzlement, but they got presents anyway from the gigantic sack he carried. A few burst out crying, so their presents were given to their embarrassed mothers. Henry and Reiko, staring transfixed at Santa, nodded when asked if they had been good, and they received their presents.

But when he asked me, I nodded and shouted, "Yes." And I looked at his face good and hard. At the same time I pressed my hand firmly on his stomach. Just as I thought! The suspicions I'd had since his blustery entrance were confirmed. I felt newspapers crinkle under that red suit where his stomach should be. And his beard looked like ratty cotton layers taken from some quilt. But the final, unassailable evidence was in the face of this

Santa Claus. He was Japanese! This Santa was a fake. I knew what Santa looked like. Mama had taken me to visit him the previous Christmas at May Company department store in downtown Los Angeles. I met him. I sat on his lap. I talked to him. And he wasn't Japanese! This "ho-ho-hoing" Santa in front of me was a fraud! But, just to be polite, I accepted my present from him anyway. I saw that Henry and Reiko believed in this one, and Mama and Daddy also acted as if they had been fooled. In fact, everybody seemed tricked into believing in his overjolly "ho, ho, ho." I didn't have the heart to break it to them.

I guessed that the real Santa probably couldn't get past the barbed wire fence. So somebody here in camp dressed up as this fake Santa to make everybody's Christmas a little bit merrier. They all seemed so happy. I decided to keep my discovery my own private secret.

These are the memories that glow in my heart. Even over the years, they radiate a pleasant warmth. But I also have recollections of Rohwer that are sharp—chilly to the core. And I remember them with a shiver.

The most terrifying camp memory I have is of an Arkansas spring thunderstorm. It was after dinner, and we were back in our barrack room, except for Daddy, who was out at another block meeting. Mama was quietly mending some clothes, and we were playing with our toys. Suddenly, there was a bright, soundless flash, and everything in the room turned electric white: the walls, the floor, the bed, everything. Even Mama's startled face was lit in ghost white. Then it was gone. It was there just long enough to shock us, and it was gone. But even before we could say, "What was that?" the terror began. With a colossal bang, the sky began to tear apart. The room shook, the beds rattled, and my little toy truck went skittering away. Reiko shrieked in fright, and Henry screamed as if he had touched the hot potbelly stove. Just as Mama came rushing over, an even more violent explosion ripped the sky. Mama's tin sewing box on the shelf high above came crashing down, scattering scissors, thimbles, rulers, and spools of thread all over the floor.

She gathered us up on Daddy's bed in the center of our room and huddled over us.

But the thunderclaps were unrelenting, one after another. Just when one seemed to settle down to a deep, rolling grumble, another gigantic clap would shatter the heavens like a horrific explosion. It was as if the world was going to end.

And Daddy wasn't with us. That was when I began to cry. Our family had always been together in crisis. Daddy and Mama said nothing could ever break us apart. And now with the world ending, Daddy was somewhere out there in that dark, hellish night. I couldn't stop crying. Even when the thunderclaps stopped and the rain started, I couldn't stop. Mama kept stroking us gently, but I could feel the fear in her, too. We'll never see Daddy again. It rained long into the night.

Then, I heard stamping on the front steps. The door rattled, and in walked a thoroughly drenched Daddy with a soggy *Life* magazine held over his head. The shock, the joy, the relief and love I felt at the sight of him I will never forget. He took his wet jacket off and gave us all a warm, damp hug. The sky threatened with another ominous grumble, but I wasn't afraid anymore. Daddy was with us, and we were together again in our big family hug.

Memories are our most precious possessions. They are the ultimate connective links to our past. My Rohwer remembrances may be only a child's fragments of history, incomplete, disjointed, and simplistically intense. But I treasure every piece and broken shard, every brief and unfinished wisp of memory I have. Especially of that strange and dreamlike night when something woke me up—a sound, a discomfort, or perhaps intuition. I don't know what. Something stirred me from my sleep.

I woke and I saw a dim light glowing from the far side of our room. It was the kerosene lamp placed on the low chair Daddy had built for Reiko. Daddy and Mama were seated over it whispering. His voice was hushed, thoughtful, sober. Mama sat ramrod straight. There was something strong and determined about her posture. Her face was expressionless, but the light shone in two shiny wet streaks down her cheeks. She looked like she had tears streaming down.

There was a long, silent pause, then Mama whispered something slowly and deliberately. She didn't talk like she was crying. But when she breathed in, the tears in her nose made a soft sniffling sound. It was strange. Mama sounded like she was crying without acting like it.

"Mama, don't cry," I said in a drowsy murmur. They both looked over at me, startled. "Don't cry, Mama," I repeated. They tiptoed over in their stocking feet, Mama quickly wiping her face.

"Everything's all right," Daddy whispered to me. "Go back to sleep. Mama and I were talking about grownup things."

"Shhhh," Mama said softly. "Don't wake up Henry and Reiko. Everything fine." And she tucked me back in. Reassured by that, I must have drifted back to sleep. That's all I remember of that momentary waking. It wasn't a dream. It really happened.

Over the years, I have come to cherish that breath of consciousness that I was somehow granted. Because of it, I can claim witness to a discussion on a devastating event that again set the Japanese American internees reeling with confusion, shock, and anger. That sleep-fuzzed memory is my only connection with a wrenching decision Daddy and Mama had to make. Their decision was again to have us packing for another arduous journey—this time for a camp back in California, so poetically named Tule Lake.

By early 1943, the political winds of America were charged with the racist rhetoric of opportunistic politicians like Earl Warren, the attorney general of California. He became governor of the state riding on a fear campaign of potential Japanese American sabotage. The already volatile war climate was inflamed by Warren with his charges of possible Japanese American spying—what he called fifth-column subversive activity.

41

In actual fact, there was not a single case of treason by Americans of Japanese ancestry. The only American citizens arrested for espionage against the United States during the entire war were two Caucasians. Yet, disregarding the facts and blind to the pain, injury, and anguish inflicted in pitiless succession on an already incarcerated people, the desk-bound bureaucrats of Washington responded with alacrity. They devised a program of astounding cruelty. It was a plan to document the loyalty of Japanese Americans held behind barbed wire. As the ultimate proof of fidelity to the United States, all male and female internees aged seventeen and older, regardless of citizenship, were required to respond to a Loyalty Questionnaire. The questionnaire listed dozens of questions. The two most crucial questions were Number 27 and Number 28:

No. 27. Are you willing to serve in the Armed Forces of the United States on combat duty wherever ordered?

No. 28. Will you swear unqualified allegiance to the United States of America and faithfully defend the United States from any or all attack by foreign or domestic forces, and forswear any form of allegiance or obedience to the Japanese emperor, to any other foreign government, power, or organization?

When Pearl Harbor was bombed in December 1941, many young Japanese American men, like most American men of their age, had rushed to their recruitment offices to volunteer for service. These genuine acts of loyalty were answered with a slap in the face. The men were summarily rejected and classified 4C, the same category as enemy aliens. Those already in the military at the time of Pearl Harbor—and there were approximately five thousand young Japanese American men in uniform at the outbreak of war—suffered the humiliation of being stripped of their weapons. Some even had to endure the outrage of being thrown into the stockade like common criminals. The fever pitch of anti-Japanese hysteria was epitomized by General John L. DeWitt, the commanding general of the Western

Theater of Operation. DeWitt stated, "A Jap's a Jap. . . . It makes no difference whether he is an American or not. Theoretically he is still a Japanese, and you can't change him."

But with the war effort consuming manpower, President Roosevelt made a swerving, 180-degree turn in policy. He declared in February 1943, "No loyal citizen of the United States should be denied the democratic right to exercise the responsibilities of his citizenship regardless of ancestry." Japanese Americans could now volunteer to serve in the military.

The substance of American citizenship—most vitally, freedom and justice—was torn away from us, but now we were not to be denied the "responsibility" of citizenship. Japanese Americans had the right to be killed for a country that had humiliated them, stripped them of property and dignity, and placed them behind barbed wire. That was the sticking point of Question Number 27.

Question Number 28 was as subtly insidious as Question Number 27 was blunt. The stealth of this question was in the single sentence asking respondents to "swear unqualified allegiance" to the United States and in the same breath "forswear . . . allegiance . . . to the Japanese emperor." If one answered yes, intending an affirmative to the first part, it was also "forswearing" a presumed existing loyalty to the Emperor of Japan. If one were to answer no to deny any such preexisting loyalty to "forswear," then the same no also rejected allegiance to the United States. It was perceived by many as a trap question. The two questions became an incendiary combination that exploded in turmoil in all ten internment camps, from Manzanar, California, to Rohwer, Arkansas.

When the dust finally settled, it is remarkable that so many internees answered "yes-yes" to the two questions. This paved the way for recruitment officers to sign up young men for military service. The large number of men who signed on is a tribute to their extraordinary determination to make true the ideals of the flag to which they had pledged allegiance daily in their classrooms, even in camp.

For my parents, the struggle to answer the Loyalty Question-

43

naire was torturous. My father was raised and educated in America. He had chosen this country as his home. Until the war broke out, his plan for himself and his family had been to build our future here. But he had been born in Japan, and U.S. law denied naturalized citizenship to Asian immigrants, though their children born in the U.S. would be citizens. Question Number 27 asked if he would be willing to serve in combat for the United States, a country that not only rejected him for citizenship but had incarcerated him because of his race. At forty years old, with a wife and three children all interned by that government, he was being asked to go on combat duty for such a country.

Question Number 28, in essence, asked him to be a man without a country. My father felt no particular allegiance to the Emperor, but Japan was the country where he was born. It was the place where he still had relatives and memories. This question asked him to discard all that and swear allegiance to a country that would not have him. For my father, this was ultimately the point where he had to say enough—no more! It was now no longer a question of any citizenship but of simple dignity. He answered "no-no."

For my mother, Question Number 27 was almost laughable in its preposterousness were it not so anguishing. She answered no. The most tormenting question for her was Question Number 28. She was an American citizen, born in Florin, California. Her children were all Americans and knew only this country. But she was married to a man her country rejected for naturalization and now considered an enemy alien. Her native country uprooted her family and brought us all here to this crude one-room barrack in Arkansas. And now this inquisition, this insult piled on top of injury. Question Number 28 was asking her to choose between her country and her husband, her birthplace or her family, one or the other.

It was this scene that I had witnessed in that brief waking moment in the dark of that kerosene-lit night. I saw the moment when Mama was making the decision to answer no-no on her Loyalty Questionnaire. It was an act that was going to have her categorized "disloyal" by the U.S. government and the beginning of Mama's eventual loss of her American citizenship.

My final memory of Rohwer, like my first, eight months before, is framed by a train window.

At breakfast in the mess hall that morning, I said my good-byes to Paul, Eddy, Tadao, and Akira. I didn't say good-bye to Ford and Chevy Nakayama because they were going on the train with us. The ladies were sniffling as they bowed their final farewells to each other. Some of the teenage girls were embracing and openly crying out loud.

At the train by the main gate, Daddy shook hands somberly with everybody lined up to see us off. Then we got on. From the window, all I could see was a sea of sad faces—faces of people who had become our friends. Paul, Tadao and Akira, Mama's friends Mrs. Imai and Mrs. Yasui, our neighbors the Mamiyas, the Yasudas, and the Takahashis. Mama said we will never see them again. The black barracks that seemed so stark in their uniformity when we first arrived now had identities. They had become the homes of friends. The guard towers were no longer ominous sentinels but simply a part of the landscape. And even the barbed wire fence had become just my familiar playground enclosure. All this now we were leaving forever.

The lurch of the train as it started to move was the tug that broke the emotional grip. The sorrow was uncontainable. Some ladies wept as if there were no bottom to their grief.

The train quickly picked up speed. I kept looking back at the crowd of people as it got smaller and smaller. Soon, our friends who were lined up at the railroad siding became just a cluster of colors. The low-lying barracks became nothing but a dark line on the horizon. The tall guard towers were the only structures I could see distinctly. As they got smaller, the sounds of crying, too, seemed to fade into soft sniffles. I kept on watching until a fly buzzing on the window glass began to look bigger than the towers. Then the train turned a bend in the tracks, and the guard towers disappeared. They were gone. Rohwer was now only a collection of memories.

45

3

Chill Wind of Tule Lake

TULE LAKE WAS—(AND IS)—A COLD, WINDSWEPT, DRY LAKE BED near the northern California-Oregon border. It was the bleakest opposite of Rohwer. Where the southern Arkansas air was lush and sultry in the summertime, while crisp and invigorating in the winter, Tule Lake's higher elevation, at four thousand feet above sea level, always made the air sharp and biting, with a cold that in winter could plunge down to bone-chilling frigidity. Instead of the soft dust of Rohwer, here there was gritty gravel and cutting little shards of hard fossils and rocks. From verdant Rohwer, we had come to a harsh landscape barren of any foliage except for the spiny tumbleweeds that rolled aimlessly around the stark, flat surface. The only landmark was Castle Rock, a great brown abalone shell of a mountain that loomed bleak and solitary to the east.

Camp Tule Lake was an internment camp converted into a maximum-security segregation camp for "disloyals," those who had responded no-no to the key questions on the Loyalty Questionnaire, or those who had applied for repatriation or expatriation to Japan, or those whose loyalty was questionable "in the opinion of the Project Director." The barbed wire fence

46

and guard towers were here, too, but unlike Rohwer, the fence was heavy wire mesh and "man-proof." The guard towers were turrets equipped with machine guns. The outer perimeter was patrolled by a half-dozen tanks and armored Jeeps. The guards were battle-ready troops at full battalion strength. All this bristly armament was positioned to keep imprisoned a people who had been goaded into outrage by a government blinded by hysteria. Half of the 18,000 internees in Camp Tule Lake were children like me.

I liked our barrack in our new Block 80. It was right across the way from the mess hall. To an always-hungry six-year-old, it was great to be just a short dash through the cold to the noisy warmth and comfort of food. But Mama hated it. She didn't like the loud clanging and banging from the kitchen that began in early morning with the preparation for breakfast and continued on until the last cleanup after dinner. She didn't like the idea of people lining up just outside our windows three times a day, every day. But most of all she complained bitterly about the smell that blew across from the kitchen—the lingering aroma of mass cooking, combined with detergents and other chemicals from the dishwashing and the acrid smell of disinfectants from the hosing down of the floor after dinner. "Stink terrible," was Mama's simple summation of the problem.

Daddy was philosophical. He said that was the trade-off. Here at Tule Lake, we had two rooms. Each room individually was smaller than the one we had at Rohwer, but combined, we had more space. We now had what we could call a bedroom and a living room.

"What trade-off?" Mama persisted. "Now toilet so far away. Children can't go so far in cold." She was right about that. Sometimes it was sheer torture dashing through the wind, muscles tightly held, to the latrine. There were occasions when I didn't think I could make it in time. I would barely get there, frenzy in my eyes, jumpy with tension, just on the verge of bursting. Fortunately, I never had an accident, though Henry

47

did. That was when Mama started collecting big coffee cans, which she kept in the bedroom for us kids.

There was another reason I liked being across from the mess hall. Life in camp was usually boring and monotonous. But the mess hall was the social focal point and cultural center of the block. We were closer and had better access to those great special events.

Sometimes, after dinner, movies were shown in the mess hall. A big white sheet would be hung up at one end and a bulky, black projection machine set up at the opposite end. Because we were right across the way, we always had the best seats. I saw Paul Muni in *Scarface*, Bette Davis in a movie where she suffered a lot, and the *Gangbusters* serials. Of them all, I remember Charles Laughton most vividly as the tragic monster in *The Hunchback of Notre Dame*. The movie was a transporting experience. I empathized with, of all things, this love-starved, deformed cripple whom people scorned and insulted. I discovered the fascinating world of old Paris through his pathetically misshapen eyes. I ached when he pined. I hurt when he agonized. And his final plummet down the tower of Notre Dame with the bells banging and clanging was unforgettably terrifying. I discovered the mind-expanding, world-extending, emotion-exhausting joy of the movies in the mess hall across from our tar-paper barrack.

At other times, we saw old Japanese movies about samurai and ninja and tear-jerking contemporary stories about long-suffering mothers and widows. Apparently, the sound track on some of these Japanese movies was missing. When that happened, a man from another block who specialized in these things would come and sit at the bottom of the screen. He had a dimly lit script in front of him, and he would narrate in Japanese what we were seeing on the screen. Not only did he narrate, but he played all the speaking roles as well. He would do the deep voice of the gruff samurai, then immediately become the crystalline-voiced princess, then the cackling old crone—all matching the fast-moving drama on the screen.

At exciting high points in the movie, like a sword fight scene, he had bamboo clappers that he would slap rhythmically and his assistant would crash small cymbals. The cymbals made drama-heightening "chang" sounds and the clappers a rippling "bara-bara" sound, matching and energizing the swordplay on screen. The old folks called all samurai sword-fighting epics "*chambara*" movies, and I could see why. Whenever the swords started to fly, the "chang" and "bara-bara" sounds filled the mess hall.

I found the performance of the narrator completely mesmerizing. With his voice alone, he became so many different people; he suffered anguish, experienced joy, provoked fear, and stirred so many emotions—wonderfully. After the movie, I asked Daddy how one man could become so many people and experience so much. He told me these people are called *benshi*. In the old days in Japan when movies had no sound, these *benshi* provided the aural dramatic accompaniment, making the silent movies talk. He told me that a good *benshi* in those days was considered an artist equal to actors. I said, "I think the man we saw tonight is an artist." Daddy agreed.

Daddy was again elected block manager of our new Block 80 at Tule Lake. And again we lost him to meetings, pressing matters, and crises. And Mama again began the work of making a home for us—this time from two rooms. The living room windows got new curtains, of course, but now we had an extra bed in the living room, for which Mama made matching cover and pillows. It became our sitting couch. And she found beauty even in the tumbleweeds that rolled around outside. Mama brought them in and made austerely elegant arrangements.

Cold wind would blow up through the spaces in the floorboards and the open knots in the wood planks. Daddy covered the knotholes using lids from empty tin cans. The one luxury appointment of the living room we owed to the cracks between the floorboards. To cover them up, Daddy and Mama went to the camp canteen many blocks away and bought a square of blue linoleum spangled with white stars. It was so shiny and smooth. Henry and I loved sliding on it in our stocking feet, and

Reiko shrieked with delight when Daddy pulled her around on the slippery linoleum floor.

In the limited space of the other room that became our bedroom, there was no possibility of esthetic arrangement. It was jammed with five beds lined up side by side. But Mama made absolutely sure of one thing. None of the beds were *kita makura*—pillows to the north. This was bad luck. In Japan, dead people were laid out with their heads to the north, she told us. All of our pillows were laid to the south. Daddy was farthest away, then Mama, then a little space for entry from the living room, then in reverse birth order Reiko, Henry, and me. I was oldest so I was the farthest away from Daddy and Mama. And I had the window over me. I could stand on my bed and look out on the back side of the next barrack. The curtain over Daddy's window on the opposite side was always drawn closed. That was the side that faced the mess hall.

One afternoon after our naps, Henry and I were playing in back of the mess hall kitchen. From behind a pile of empty vegetable crates came a shaggy, black dog with brown paws and brown streaks on his side like peanut butter smears. Over his sad-looking eyes were two dabs of peanut butter eyebrows. We petted his head, and he whined piteously. "He must be hungry," I said. "Let's get him something," Henry suggested. We went in the kitchen back door and asked Mr. Kikutani, one of the mess hall workers, for something to feed the dog. He gave us a half wienie from the wieners teriyaki that were being prepared for dinner. The dog gobbled it up ravenously.

We went back in for another, but this time Mr. Kikutani wouldn't give us any more. "Hey, I gotta feed people here, you know. Not stray dogs, you know," he said. But while I was pleading with Mr. Kikutani, Henry reached up behind him and took another half wienie and slipped out quietly. I thanked Mr. Kikutani anyway and left the kitchen.

When I got outside, the dog was already eagerly throwing the small morsel of wienie into the back of his throat. He licked his chops and looked up at me with a big doggy smile and wagging tail. He was too cute to leave hungry. Maybe Mama might have something for this dog to eat. We ran home yelling, "Mama, Mama." The dog bounded happily behind us with reinvigorated, wienie-fed energy. I opened the door, holding it clear for the dog, and Henry ran in yelling, "Mama, Mama," with the dog leaping after him.

Then I heard Mama shriek as I'd never heard before. It sounded as if somebody were trying to kill her. Looking inside, I saw the dog skidding and sliding in panicked helplessness. He scrambled vainly to regain his balance on the slippery linoleum floor. His paw nails tapped uselessly on the highly polished surface as he struggled desperately to the edge of the linoleum. With terror flashing in his eyes, the panic-stricken dog finally fled back out the door, and Mama's screaming stopped. I stepped in to find an equally terrorized Mama suffocating poor Henry in a tight embrace against her breast. "Not hurt?" she asked, her voice quavering with fear. She quickly moved to the door to secure it. "Oh, *abunai* dog." She let go of Henry, who was coughing and gasping for air.

"Mama, that's a hungry dog," I informed her.

"I know. Chasing Henry, that dog. Oh, *abunai*."

"No Mama, that's a nice dog that's hungry," I insisted.

"Yeah, Mama, it's a nice dog," gasped Henry, trying to regain his breath. We explained to her about the poor hungry dog we found behind the mess hall kitchen. "Mama, do we have anything to feed it?" we asked.

Reassured and a bit embarrassed, Mama thought. "I have cookies," she offered. These were the snacks she kept for us. "But dogs not like cookies," she said skeptically.

"Let's see," we both chimed. "Can we have a cookie?"

When we came out, the dog was keeping a wary distance from our door. But when he saw Henry and me, he came up wagging his tail and wiggling his body with happiness. Then, when Mama followed us out, he stopped short in his tracks and cowered with mixed emotions. "He thinks you're a scary lady," Henry said to Mama. She smiled and broke the cookie she had in her hand into three pieces, handing a piece to me, a piece to

Henry and keeping a piece. I offered my piece first, wondering whether he would eat it. He came up, sniffed, lapped it from me, and crunched it with gusto. He accepted Henry's piece immediately. Now it was the scary lady's turn. Mama held out her piece. He wanted to take it, you could see. But he held back. He was afraid of starting up the frightening sound she made. I could see the conflict going on in that dog's poor, sad eyes. But hunger ultimately won out. He looked up at Mama warily and wagged a tentative tail. She didn't make that horrific noise. Approaching her carefully, he quickly lapped the piece of cookie from her finger. It was gone in one crunch.

And that's how Blackie came to be a part of our family at Tule Lake. We built him a shed behind our barrack, right under my bedroom window. We always got a little bit more food than we could eat at each meal so that we could bring something home for Blackie. And Blackie became our playmate and constant companion wherever we went—everywhere, that is, except into our living room. He was afraid of that room with the treacherously glistening floor. Blackie absolutely refused to venture in there, even if we pushed him. Daddy said he was a smart dog. "He learns fast. No living thing likes to have his world suddenly turned unstable," he said. "Let's give him a good home." And Blackie didn't have to worry about his world turning unstable. At least not while we were at Tule Lake.

For us, though, Tule Lake was a very different world from anything we had ever experienced before. I would be wakened at daybreak by the distant sound of large numbers of young men exercising. *"Wah shoi, wah shoi, wah shoi, wah shoi."* I would lie there listening as the sound came closer and closer and then faded back into the distance. *"Wah shoi, wah shoi, wah shoi."* These young men were counting cadence in unison as they jogged in military formation around the blocks in the cold dawn air. They all wore *hachi-maki* around their heads—white headbands, some with the rising sun, the military insignia of Japan, painted on them. These were the young men who had turned radical in their disillusion and their sense of betrayal by America. If America was going to treat them like enemies, then they resolved to give America adversaries it would have to take seriously. They would become the enemies that America would be forced to reckon with from within. They would harden their muscles and their spirits. They would prepare to rise up when the Japanese military landed on the West Coast, as these men fervently believed, and join the battle.

Tule Lake was a camp seething with political tension. Although the camp population was predominantly composed of those generally categorized as "disloyal," there was within this group the full spectrum of beliefs and political positions, from those who responded no-no to the Loyalty Questionnaire in dignity-sustaining protest all the way to genuine radicals who were newly and fiercely committed to Japan's victory. Among the latter group was Joe Kurihara, a former pro-America patriot and a World War I veteran. In his bitterness at the betrayal by the America that he had trusted, he openly swore to "become a Jap one hundred percent."

The Camp Command, however, viewed all internees as adversaries and, in its clumsy attempt to maintain control, exacerbated an already volatile situation. There were midnight raids by guards to pick up those suspected of being radical leaders, and often the wrong individuals were arrested. Whole groups of people suspected of being radicals were dismissed from certain work crews, thus causing disruptions in essential services such as the delivery of foodstuffs and fuel. These acts, in turn, would incite protests and demonstrations.

In this turbulent climate, rumor-mongering within the internee population proliferated. Those that were retained on certain work crews where people were dismissed were suspected by other internees of having curried favor with the Camp Command. These suspects would be accused of being informers or *inu*, the Japanese word for "dog." There were violent arguments, even beatings, which then brought on even greater repression from the Command. Curfews were imposed, bringing heavier guard presence. The internees retaliated with hunger strikes and even riots.

"Keto!" That's the word I remember hearing over all the yelling and shouting. *"Keto, keto!"* Over all the chaos. "Goddamn *keto!"* *"Keto* go to hell!" It was screamed at the guards roaring around in their Jeeps at the scattering crowd. The people were running in every direction. The Jeeps with guards aiming weapons were chasing them, rumbling around in billowing dust clouds, swerving in threatening curves and circles.

Daddy and I were far from those Jeeps, but he held my hand tightly, and we ran as fast as we could. We ran for many blocks before we got back home. I don't remember why we were so far from home. In fact, I can't recall why we were a part of that chaos at all. But the yelling, confusion, and terror were unforgettable.

This isolated childhood memory burned onto my mind like a random spatter on the skin from a boiling pot of liquid. It seared me, but with time it left only a barely noticeable scar.

I can still remember how frightening the day was. I can still call to mind that chaos and confusion. But I cannot remember what I was a part of. I can't recall the substance of that unforgettable terror.

It wasn't until I was much older that I asked Daddy about this vivid but somehow disconnected memory. He told me that we were there to demonstrate in protest against the arbitrary arrest of somebody suspected of being a radical. That's what he told to an adult many years later. But the essence of the experience had wafted away like the dust kicked up by those wildly circling Jeeps.

What I do have fixed in my memory is the answer that Daddy gave me to a question I asked him when we were safely back home in our barrack. "What does *keto* mean, Daddy?" I asked. He told me it was an angry word that people fling at white people. "But why?"

"It's a bad word meant to hurt people."

"But the guards didn't look hurt," I said.

"That's because they don't understand it."

"But what does it mean, then?"

"It means 'hairy breed,'" my father answered.

"Well, white people do look hairy. Look at the guards' arms."

"That may be. But it's a word meant to be insulting and hurtful. I don't ever want to hear you using that word."

"Even at the guards?"

"At anybody. Ever. It's a bad word," Daddy said with a tone of finality. I presumed that *"keto"* must be another one of those mysterious words like "sakana beach."

By mid-1944 Tule Lake was a fractured community of anger, suspicion, and confusion. Rumors ran rampant. Neighbors suspected neighbors. The simplest disagreement could erupt into angry exchanges and oftentimes violence. Into this volatile situation, Congress threw another incendiary device. It passed the so-called "denaturalization bill." This legislation, Public Law 405, provided that an American citizen could renounce his or her citizenship on American soil in time of war. The relentless tide of anti-Japanese hysteria had produced another explosive and constitutionally indefensible piece of law.

With the war's end becoming more likely by the day, politicians from the West Coast were beginning to agitate against the probable return of Japanese Americans to their former homes. Congressman Clair Engle of California, later to be elected United States Senator, declared, "We don't want those Japs back in California. The more we can get rid of, the better."

The scenario envisioned by Washington seemed to entail getting American citizens of Japanese ancestry to renounce their citizenship under the pressure-cooker conditions in the camps, so the legal path would be cleared for their eventual "deportation" to Japan as "aliens." This would be an especially useful tool to rid the country of those nettlesome radical activists of Tule Lake. The result was another convulsive wave of anguish and turmoil that swept up not just the radicals but all internees in Camp Tule Lake.

The activists wanted to get as many to renounce with them as

possible, and they launched a campaign of aggressive prosely-
tizing. They staged wildly stirring "banzai" rallies. The Camp
Command responded with more midnight raids, again frequently taking the wrong people. There was fury and discord.
Tule Lake was turned into a boiling-hot cauldron of conflicting
passions.

Mama was targeted by these fervently pro-Japan militants as a
likely prospect for renunciation. She was a no-no respondent to
the Loyalty Questionnaire and married to an immigrant from
Japan, albeit one educated in America. "America treats you like
garbage," the militants argued. "Why keep taking their racist
outrages?" "Take some pride in our own racial heritage." All
compellingly persuasive arguments.

But Mama resented the high-pressure militancy of the radicals. And she was irritated when some of them tried to affect
her decision through Daddy. This was her decision that she had
to make privately with Daddy for herself and her family. She
was not going to be coerced by zealots. *"Hito wa hito. Uchi wa
uchi,"* I remember her always saying. "Other people are other
people. Our house is our house."

Then Washington, in its amazing capacity for unrelenting
cruelty combined with consistent clumsiness, did something
that played right into the hands of the zealots. In December
1944, without any warning or prior indication, officials abruptly
announced the closing of the camps. In six months to a year,
maximum-security Camp Tule Lake was to be closed.

This was an astounding new development for the internees.
Terror swept through the camp like an electric current. We
were to be thrown "outside"—out to the wolves. White boys
were still being killed by the Japanese in the Pacific war. The
firestorm of anti–Japanese American paranoia raged at full
pitch on the West Coast. Radical nativist organizations were
intensifying their "exterminate the Japs" campaign. The
barbed wire fence that kept us incarcerated was ironically our
protection as well. And now, that would be gone.

The militants seized this gift from Washington with relish.
"Go back out there and get shot up? Hell no, not me!" They

argued that if enough people renounced their citizenship, then the government would be forced to keep Camp Tule Lake open. The psychological pressure was unbearable.

Mama's sole concern now became to keep her family safe and together. It wasn't the radicals' pressure. It wasn't any notion of doctrine anymore. For Mama, her greatest anxiety was for the safety and well-being of her family. She decided to force Washington to keep Tule Lake a safe haven for us. She renounced her American citizenship. Mama became a "denaturalized citizen."

While all these things that a seven-year-old boy could hardly understand were swirling around me, half a world away events that would have been even more incomprehensible were taking place. These distant developments, unknown to me at the time, were to be of profound and historic importance to my future.

In far-off Europe, brothers and cousins of the young men wearing the rising sun *hachi maki* were wearing the very same uniforms as the guards in the gun towers watching over us. In fact, they were fighting on the same side as those guards manning the machine guns aimed toward us. These young men with faces that America saw as that of the enemy were spilling their blood carrying the Stars and Stripes. They were Japanese American men who had signed on to serve in the United States Armed Forces despite the most surreal of circumstances.

GIs, it is said, were fighting to get back to the proverbial "Mom's apple pie." But the young Japanese American GIs were fighting literally to get their moms out from behind American barbed wire fences. They were in combat to assert, under the most incredible of circumstances, their faith in the fundamental ideals of a country that had itself betrayed those ideals. In their determination, some called it crazy trust, they jolted America into a reappraisal of their citizenship and the very notion of patriotism. And with the boldness and extraordinary courage that they demonstrated on the battlefields of Italy, France, and Germany, they firmly established not only their reputation as fighting men but, beyond any doubt, their Americanism. Through their heroism, these Japanese American GIs revitalized the ideals of this country and brought added dimension to the definition of American citizenship. But it came at high cost.

The all–Japanese American 442nd Regimental Combat Team, in its first action in Italy in the Rome-Arno campaign, lost roughly one fourth of its total troop strength. To gain 40 miles, the outfit suffered 1,272 casualties. In the Rhineland campaign in France, its heroic rescue of the 1st Battalion of the 141st Regiment caught behind enemy lines—"the lost Texas battalion"—resulted in 800 casualties to save 211 men. At the end of the war, the 442nd Regimental Combat Team had compiled an outstanding battle record and emerged as the most decorated unit of World War II. It also suffered the highest casualty rate of any unit its size. In July 1946, President Harry Truman received the Japanese American soldiers on the White House lawn and stated, "You fought not only the enemy, but you fought prejudice—and you have won."

There were other events from far-off places that affected us in Tule Lake.

I was near the laundry building when I heard about one. A solemn-faced group of men were standing around talking. I wandered over and heard the man with the bald head saying, "He's not really dead. It's a trick. Just leave it to them to try a thing like that."

But Mr. Takeda, our neighbor, insisted, "No, it's got to be true. I was by the Camp Command office this morning and they got the flag at half-mast."

A slim young man then said, "No kidding? Really? Then Roosevelt really must be dead. Well, whadda ya know."

But the bald-headed man kept insisting, "It's a trick. I tell you, it's a trick."

I ran home to tell Mama a man named Roosevelt died, but they're worried it might be a trick, so they put the flag at Camp Command at half-mast. At dinner that night in the mess hall, Daddy officially announced that President Roosevelt had passed on.

The far more devastating news to internees came about a year later on a summer day in August. A new bomb, more destructive than anything previously invented by man, had been dropped on Japan. The news came crackling over contraband short-wave radio reports. No one knew who first heard the news, but everyone was talking about it. This fearsome weapon, an atomic bomb they called it, had been dropped on the southern Japanese city of Hiroshima. The devastation from this bomb was gruesome, but the firestorm that followed was catastrophic. Tens of thousands of people had been killed in the conflagration. Then, three days later, another atomic bomb was dropped—this time on the city of Nagasaki.

The people of Tule Lake were stunned. The quick succession of events was overwhelming. The two bombings, as ghastly as they were, were also deeply personal tragedies to many. A considerable number of internees had families and close relations living in the two cities.

Our family was one of them. Our grandparents, Mama's father and mother, had returned to Japan before the outbreak of war. They had gone back to Hiroshima.

Mama was frantic with worry. Every shred of news on the bombing was desperately sought. Any bit of information gleaned from someone's short-wave radio was seized upon. Even rumors were pursued to their inconclusive, distressing end. But nothing reliable was available. The certitude of knowledge, as fearful as it was, would have been more bearable than the torture of this uncertainty. It drove Mama insane with anxiety. Daddy finally said to Mama, "It was a devastating bombing. An incredible number of people were killed. But you've got to go on living. You've got to give yourself some peace. For your sake, for your own well-being, let's consider your parents at rest."

It was not until much later, long after we were out of camp, that we learned that, by some miracle, our grandparents had survived the atomic bombing of Hiroshima. But one of Mama's younger sisters, our Aunt Ayako, died with her baby in the fiery holocaust.

The war was over. Japan had surrendered. "It was inevitable," Daddy said. "I knew it would come to this. But there are some who can't accept it."

When Daddy gravely made the announcement at lunch in the mess hall, a group of older men silently got up and left without eating lunch. Later, when I went to the latrine, that bald-headed man was standing by himself shouting at whoever passed by, "It's a lie. Don't believe it. It's another trick." But he was a lone voice. There was no hysteria. A strange calm prevailed over once-turbulent Tule Lake.

Now we faced a new anxiety, the unknowns of a life outside barbed wire confinement and stripped of everything. There was only one certainty—Camp Tule Lake was closing. February 1946 was announced as the target date. We now had six months to plan for a new home outside in a hostile America.

Then another thunderbolt hit. It was announced that the renunciants of American citizenship were to be "deported" to Japan. November 15, 1945, was the date the first ship was to sail. Mama was scheduled to be on that ship. Her daring sacrifice for our safety had backfired terribly. Daddy and Mama were consumed by this new threat. I remember nights when something would wake me. I'd lie still in the dark and listen to Daddy and Mama engaged in intense, whispered conversations. Henry and Reiko were asleep. I only pretended to be. In the daytime, they would go on long walks far from our barrack to get some privacy. Mama often came back distraught and dabbing at her bloodshot eyes with her handkerchief.

Mama and the others in the same situation needed legal representation. A terrible chain reaction had been set off by a desperate act taken under great duress. But who would represent them? Why should anyone take on such an unpopular cause? Mama and the other renunciants were pariahs. They were despised Japanese Americans who, even more despicably, had renounced their American citizenship. And now they were pitted against the full might of the United States Government. It was an impossible situation.

I frequently wonder about turning points in life. They are usually major historic junctures such as war and peace, the great inevitable flow of events that determine one's destiny. But, as a small pebble can sometimes alter the direction of a river, in the rush of circumstances sometimes a single individual can change the course of another human being's life. I wonder what my life might have been like—indeed, who I might have become—if one brave man had not stepped forward at this crucial and seemingly hopeless point in our lives.

Wayne Collins, a brilliant San Francisco attorney and a passionate crusader for the fundamental guarantees of the Constitution, took on the bleak cause of the Japanese American renunciants. He said, "You can no more resign citizenship in time of war than you can resign from the human race." In court, he argued that "Renunciation was not the product of free will but forced upon them by the unlawful detention and the conditions prevailing at the Tule Lake Center, for which the government alone was responsible."

The November 15 "deportation" date came. The ship that Mama and we were to have been aboard sailed with a full manifest. But we were still in Tule Lake. Wayne Collins had gotten Mama a mitigation hearing just days before the ship sailed. He saved us, literally, in the nick of time.

It was to take many anxious years of tireless dedication by Wayne Collins for Mama to have her United States citizenship restored. But in the meantime, he got her clearance to "relocate" anywhere in America. And with that, Wayne Collins kept Mama here on American soil. He also determined the course of my destiny.

Daddy and Mama now had another life decision to make— where to resettle. One of my uncles, Daddy's older brother, had chosen Salt Lake City, Utah. The Mormons there, he reported,

61

offered a hospitable climate for Japanese Americans. Two of Mama's cousins were in Chicago, one studying medicine at the University of Chicago. It was a big city with many job opportunities, they wrote. Some of their friends had moved to far-off Seabrook, New Jersey, where there were jobs in the vegetable freezing industry. Each option presented certain attractions for a new home, and each had its drawbacks. Los Angeles was always there on their minds. It was where they came from. And it was the city they knew and loved.

But the West Coast was still prickly with anti-Japanese passion. To ease the return of the internees, the government was now very publicly showcasing the heroic deeds of the Japanese American GIs of the 442nd Regimental Combat Team. But Daddy knew of reports where returning Nisei veterans with war wounds were not only insulted but actually thrown out of restaurants and barbershops. Mayor Fletcher Bowron of Los Angeles, one of the most inflammatory leaders calling for the removal of Japanese Americans at the beginning of the war, was still the mayor.

And yet my parents loved Los Angeles. Despite everything, Los Angeles still drew them. Part of it, I suspect, was a challenge—to take back something that used to be theirs. To struggle to regain something they valued. To win back their memories and their dignity. I remember Daddy's final, decisive words, "Let's start all over in Los Angeles." We were going to return to the city where we had started.

They didn't want, however, to risk the safety of the children. The climate there was too uncertain. Daddy would leave first to test the temperature of postwar Los Angeles.

This was to be the first time our family would not be together. But it had to be done. Daddy left Camp Tule Lake on December 22, 1945—just three days before Christmas.

I have fond memories of my Christmases in camp. But for some strange reason, I have no recollection of that one Christmas of 1945. Mama says she decorated a tumbleweed with fruits and candies. She says we opened presents on Christmas morning, and she made hot chocolate for us. I remember none of that. I don't even remember the fact that we had a Christmas without Daddy. Somehow, Christmas 1945 has completely vanished from my memory.

It was night, March 6, 1946, our last few hours in Tule Lake. The February closing date of Camp Tule Lake was extended to March 20, 1946. We were almost the last people left in Block 80. The car would be coming soon to take us to the railroad station at Klamath Falls, Oregon, where we were to board a Los Angeles–bound train. Mama had us all dressed, warm and ready, for the long journey. While she was attending to last-minute packing and fussing over Henry and Reiko, I wandered over to our old mess hall across the way. It had been closed and unused for the last three weeks. Camp officials had consolidated us into the mess hall at Block 79 because so many people had left Block 80. Some internees had been "deported" on a second ship bound for Japan, others had left to resettle outside.

I touched the old weathered door that we looked across at every day. It seemed so worn, tired, used up. I pulled at it, and it creaked open. The mess hall was completely empty. Everything was gone—tables, benches, even the serving counter. Everything. Only a vast emptiness remained. This huge hall, always so noisy with the racket of trays, utensils, pots and pans; chatter and laughter; crying children and scolding parents; this space that had been so full of the sounds of life, was now ghostly still. The big hall, which was always pungent with the savory aromas of food or acrid with the sting of detergent and disinfectants, was devoid of any smell. Only a scentless nothingness remained. Just cold, empty air. I gazed at this vast space that had once thrilled me with the adventures of samurai and ninja, anguished me with the plight of the poor hunchback of Notre Dame. Now it was only a silent, lifeless vacancy. The announcements Daddy had made here at mealtimes, happy news and grave developments, were now only echoes of memories. Even Daddy was gone.

I stood alone in the immense emptiness for a long time. Then, I heard Blackie bark outside. I took one final look. Then I stepped outside and closed that creaky door for the last time.

Blackie was waiting for me with his big doggy smile. He didn't know that we were forbidden to take him with us to Los Angeles. He wagged his tail, not knowing that we couldn't find anyone to take care of him. He looked up at me with those big trusting eyes, not ever suspecting that his world would again suddenly turn unstable. I hugged him tightly. I couldn't bear the thought of leaving him here. But there was nothing else we could do. I stayed with him in the cold night air until the guards finally came to pick us up. Even in the car far from Block 80, far from Blackie's frantic barking, I couldn't stop my tears.

4

Home Again

WE ROCKED AND SWAYED, DOZING AND WAKING ON THE TRAIN ALL night long. But with the coming of daylight, no one seemed tired. There was restless anticipation throughout the car. We were nearing Los Angeles.

Ken Wakabayashi, a family friend from Block 80 whom Daddy, when he left camp, had asked to look after Mama and us kids, sat with me. In his soft, gentle voice, Ken told me all about this wonderful place, Los Angeles. It was warm and sunny there all the time, he said. We would no longer need the heavy clothes of Tule Lake. Cars and streetcars would take us wherever we wanted to go. No curfews, no guards, no fences. Nothing to keep us from going wherever we pleased. There were big, tall buildings and nice little homes with green lawns. Ken told me everything about this paradise. But, to me, the most important thing about Los Angeles was that it was the place where Daddy was waiting for us.

As we approached a big, green mountain, our train slowed down. There were many tracks around us now, and trains were everywhere. I had never seen so many—some just sitting there, others going back and forth as if they couldn't make up their minds where to go. Our train slowly made its way amongst them, somehow managing not to bump into any of the others. The big, green mountain was tapering down to an end. The track seemed to follow the curve of the foot of the mountain. It was as if the mountain were a curtain pulling back to reveal the spectacle behind it. Gradually, slowly, it appeared as we rounded the bend. Right before our eyes, I saw tall, magnificent buildings reaching for the sky just as Ken had told me—some had ornate, richly carved stone crowns on top, others had giant signs on them mounted on thin, weblike supports as big as the buildings themselves. And soaring far above them all loomed a sleek, tapered white tower radiant in the late morning sunshine. "That's Los Angeles City Hall," Ken told me. "It's the tallest building in the city. Nothing taller can be built." I was awestruck. It was the most beautiful building I had ever seen.

Mama nudged me and said, "That where Daddy and Mama married." So, we ourselves had some connection with that majestic structure, I thought. That made it even more impressive. Mama pointed to one of the upper floors. "See floor up there?"

I really couldn't tell which one she was pointing to, but I nodded anyway and said, "Yes."

"Oh, I have so nice memories there. So nice." I realized then that this was where Mama had left her memories. She was coming home to her life before me. Then this wonderful, exciting, new place was also part of my history. This city where I was born eight years ago, this place where Daddy was waiting for us, this place of my dreams was now right in front of me. I couldn't wait for the train to stop.

Daddy was standing there on the station platform smiling and waving. He looked exactly as I remembered him. Even after the ten long weeks that we hadn't seen him, he wasn't changed at all. He was wearing the same gray suit he had on the day he left us, and on his head, the same well-worn Panama hat. He was standing there beaming with his arms outstretched. We all ran up to him and assaulted him from all sides with hugs. We knocked his hat off, but he kept laughing and laughing. We were so happy that we couldn't speak. All we did was laugh and laugh. Then we noticed Reiko holding Mama's skirt and shyly hiding behind it. Ten weeks had taken its toll on her. Daddy had become only a vaguely familiar acquaintance. Daddy laughed and very formally offered his hand. Only after energetic cheerleading by all of us did she bashfully, so very tentatively, shake his hand. We were a complete family again.

We walked through a long tunnel, thunderous with the echo of a hundred hurrying footsteps. I lugged a small suitcase; Henry struggled with another. Daddy carried three suitcases, the smallest one tucked under his arm. Mama led Reiko by one hand and in the other she carried the big carryall bag containing her portable sewing machine. She had brought that machine full circle back to Los Angeles.

Suddenly, we were in a space so vast its sheer size stopped me in my tracks. The walls were decorated with beautiful Spanish tile. "This is the waiting room of Union Station," Daddy announced. It was a hundred times bigger than all our mess halls at camp put together. Mama prodded me to move along. Stumbling in amazement, I gaped at the tall, elegant windows, turning around and around as I walked, and gawked at the great decorated beams high up in the ceiling. I had never experienced such a monumental expanse of space. And to think that human beings had built this grandeur. This was a wondrous achievement. I was dizzy with awe.

And people were everywhere, completely ignoring this magnificent space. So many people in such great variety. So many faces that weren't Japanese. So many so nicely dressed. All rushing in a great hurry, going in one direction or the other. And the soldiers in Los Angeles didn't carry rifles. In fact, they were just a part of the river of people rushing somewhere in the same hurry as everybody else. Black people in different uniforms rushed about carrying other people's luggage. It was too much to take in all at once.

When we stepped out into the bright sunshine, there again, even whiter and more glorious than before, stood Los Angeles

City Hall. Daddy led us to the street. As if it were waiting for us, there stood what Daddy called a streetcar—a yellow-and-green streamlined smaller version of a train car. We climbed aboard, and with a loud "ding-ding," we were moving.

From the window, I saw one incredible sight after another. The street was crowded with cars in an amazing variety of styles and colors. Blues, greens, yellows, black, and even a red one. But there were no Jeeps. I saw signs with gigantic pictures of strikingly beautiful Caucasian men and women smoking cigarettes or drinking soda pop or liquor from elegant glasses. Suddenly, a huge red truck screamed by, sounding a frightening wail and blaring its loud horn threateningly. The clamorous "rat-tat-tat" of workmen breaking up the street surface using powerful mechanical devices sounded almost gentle after the red truck had gone.

The streetcar turned a corner at First Street and Alameda Street. Daddy whispered, "Now we're going to go through old Little Tokyo." Daddy and Mama had told me so much about this Japanese section of Los Angeles, I was anxious to see what it was really like. I looked up at Mama to watch her reclaim another memory. But instead of the happy anticipation I had expected, she looked shocked. I heard her whisper to Daddy, "So many black people here now." We were rolling through a section of old brick buildings with shops and restaurants, and, just as Mama noted, lots of black people were standing around.

Daddy whispered to Mama, "They called Little Tokyo Bronzeville during the war. But Japanese are coming back now. Look, Nisei Sugar Bowl is back already. Still the best cup of coffee and apple pie in town. And see, there's Kyodo Drug Store. We're coming back."

Before we knew it, we were rolling past a block with an impressive building facade fronted by a lush green park. Daddy nudged me. "This is City Hall." We were now actually in front of the tallest building in Los Angeles. I craned my neck to see the top of the soaring tower, but the streetcar window wasn't big enough to accommodate the full height of this imposing skyscraper. So City Hall is this close to Little Tokyo, I thought.

Then we turned another corner, and all at once the street was ablaze with brilliant colors and dazzling lights. This was Broadway, Los Angeles's premier street of movie palaces and big department stores. In broad daylight, giant marquees flashed zigzag neon, colored lights, and white hot bulbs. Each marquee flamboyantly showcased its current presentation, commanding and competing for attention. Interspersed between theaters named Million Dollar, Roxy, Palace, Los Angeles, Lowe's State, and Orpheum were the glamorous show windows of stores, bearing names like Bullock's, Desmonds, May Co., and, quite appropriately, Broadway. Where the marquees blazed and jigged and danced with unrelenting movement and light, the show windows were the quintessence of frozen grace and serenity. And on the street, people, people, people everywhere. All rushing with somewhere to go in such great hurry.

Los Angeles in 1946 was an amazing place—an electrifying city and an overpowering new experience. Going from the barbed wire confinement, monotony, and confusion of the internment camps to this explosive activity and bewildering variety was a revelation. I may have been born here, but I had no recollection of any of this. It was all so new. I felt like an immigrant in my own hometown.

We got off at Broadway and Fifth Street and started walking east on Fifth. After one block, the street's character changed. We crossed a tree-shaded street of tall and imposing granite office buildings. There were many stylishly dressed men and only a few women. Daddy told us, "This is Spring Street, the financial center of Los Angeles. This is where men make the big money, and Broadway is where women spend the big money."

Another block and another change. Here, there were more casually dressed men, and the women wore dresses much tighter than anything I had ever seen before. They had on high-heeled shoes made even higher by thick platform soles. There were lots of soldiers in many different uniforms—Army, Navy, and Marines. But these soldiers weren't like the guards at camp. These were happy, laughing, relaxed soldiers. In fact, some of them were downright loose. They lurched about and leaned on each other's shoulders. This street was vibrantly honky-tonk.

From open doorways I heard the sound of jukebox music wafting out, together with the rich, heavy aroma of alcoholic drinks. Neon marquees blazed on this street, too, but in front of these theaters were towering cutout posters of statuesque women with not a stitch on except for sparkley bits of ornaments placed on three strategic points of their bodies. Mama hurried us past these theaters. *"Hayaku, hayaku,* hurry up, hurry up," she urged.

Another block farther and there were more changes. I was shocked to see people lying on the pavement, reeking of alcohol. A few more blocks, and we turned the corner onto a messy, crowded street called Wall Street. Disheveled men with bleary eyes stood leaning on building walls. I had never seen people like this before. They were weird—pitiful and scary at the same time. We rushed past a row of garbage cans, some overflowing onto the sidewalk. There was a stench of rotten food, and the smell of urine assaulted us from the dark, narrow recesses between the buildings. *"Hayaku, hayaku."* Mama's whispered exhortations to us now were almost frantic. But her face remained expressionless. We came to a grimy, three-story brick building with a deep orange neon sign that sizzled and flickered. It read, "Alta Hotel."

"This is it," Daddy announced. "We're here. There are lots of other families from camp here," he said reassuringly. Mama stopped for just the briefest moment, staring at the building, utterly stoic. Then she followed Daddy in.

We staggered down a darkened corridor behind him. Then Daddy started up a flight of stairs. A loud stamp emphasized each rising step he took. We kids were terrified. We had never been in a two-story building before. We had never gone up stairs in our lives. Was I expected to go up to that frightening height at the top of the stairs by myself? And carrying this suitcase to boot? Henry and Reiko flatly refused to go up. So, Mama stayed with us at the foot of the stairs.

We held our breaths as we watched Daddy stomp up and

down the stairs, carrying a few pieces of luggage with each trip. After he had delivered them upstairs, he came down, and we all held hands. But Reiko absolutely refused to go up with us. She may have been five years old now, but she insisted on Mama carrying her. Only after Mama pleaded exhaustion did Reiko agree to let Daddy carry her up the stairs. With Daddy carrying our sister and holding my hand, and with me tightly grasping Henry's hand and Mama holding his other, we started up. Warily, we took step by tentative step. I kept my eyes glued on each tread, but Mama's were fixed upward. She seemed more apprehensive about what waited for us at the top. Daddy kept saying, "Carefully now. One step at a time. Up we go." A fearful but reunited family worked its way up to a new home in a skid row hotel.

For Mama, again it was the noise and the smells—just like at Tule Lake. But it was stinkier and noisier here—constantly, not just at mealtimes. Even I didn't like it.

Daddy had found for us two connected rooms, with a hot plate for light cooking, at the derelict Alta Hotel. The walls had brown stains so old that they were starting to fade to a fuzzy beige. The linoleum on the floor was cracked and torn. Everything about the rooms was tired and worn out. "It's not the Biltmore," Daddy joked, "but, remember, it's only temporary. I promise."

"Only temporary," Mama repeated. I knew she really believed that because all during the time we were at Alta Hotel, she never made any effort to unpack her sewing machine.

For us kids, it wasn't so much the grimy rooms or the noise or even the stench of urine that wafted up to our window from the alley below—our hardest adjustment to life at Alta Hotel was the stairs. Each trip up and down those stairs became a dreaded journey. Going down filled me with even greater trepidation than climbing up. I hugged the railing for dear life while feeling for the next precarious tread with my foot. My eyes were closed to keep from looking down that frightening height. When I sensed solid footing, I would shift my weight down, never letting go of the railing, then feel for the next solid footing below. I still recall the feeling of great accomplishment and even greater relief at the end of each harrowing descent.

Reiko never traversed the stairs by herself. She insisted on being carried. But even while being so royally transported, she kept her eyes tightly closed.

When Daddy returned to Los Angeles from Tule Lake, his most daunting challenge was to find a job. It was the immediate postwar period, and unemployment was starting to creep across the country. Finding a job in Los Angeles was next to impossible. To make matters worse, the hostility toward Japanese Americans was still at fever pitch. The only place where Daddy and his friends could find work was in Chinatown. Daddy had celebrated Christmas 1945 and the New Year's Eve following in the kitchen of a chop suey restaurant in Chinatown washing dishes.

Even so, he had to consider himself fortunate. He had a job. There were others who were totally bereft. Many couldn't speak English. Others were fearful for their safety and paralyzed with apprehension. These people appealed to their old block manager for help. So, Daddy found himself spending all his time off from his dishwashing job trying to find employment for others who were coming back from the internment camps. For the men, he found positions as gardeners, heavy laborers, or janitors. He placed the women as household domestics, kitchen helpers, and garment workers. Anything for survival.

By the time we joined him in Los Angeles, Daddy had left his dishwashing job in Chinatown and had opened a small employment agency on East First Street in Little Tokyo. I remember Mama and us kids walking from Alta Hotel on Wall Street all the way over to Daddy's little office to help out. While Mama dusted and cleaned and arranged papers for Daddy, we sprawled on the floor and drew pictures on the back side of used employment forms.

Daddy was always either on the phone talking in English or talking in Japanese while handing slips of paper with job leads to the people who were seated in his office or waiting in the corridors outside. I remember wondering why the people were so profuse in their thanks to him. They bowed more deeply and longer than any Japanese etiquette required. Others clasped his hand with both hands, tighter and longer than a normal handshake. Some even had tears in their eyes.

Mama told us that these people were grateful because Daddy sacrificed so much to help them. But she herself didn't sound too grateful for Daddy's sacrifices. One day, she told us he had been sacrificing too much for too long. He would have to quit this business. It wasn't until we were much older that we learned Mama had made him close up the employment business because Daddy was not collecting the commission for his services. He understood too achingly well the circumstances of the people he was assisting. He simply could not bring himself to ask for his fee from these desperately poor people just out of camp. Mama understood, too. She, however, could bring herself to demand of Daddy that he sacrifice for the family instead. Most of the returning internees by this time, she insisted, had found some kind of employment, however temporary. Somehow they were eating. Now, she said to Daddy, it was time to work at something that could have us eating as well. Mama insisted he make some money.

That money-making pursuit was to be the dry cleaning business, familiar to Daddy from before the war. He borrowed some money from his older brother and a few friends, putting together the necessary capital. Mama said she could contribute with her sewing.

Daddy found an established dry cleaning store on North Soto Street in East Los Angeles with a small one-bedroom apartment attached in the back. We could live in that apartment; Daddy and Mama would save time and money on transportation getting to work, and the family would be together. It was an ideal arrangement. So, after six weeks on skid row in downtown Los Angeles, we moved again, this time into the largest Mexican American barrio in the United States.

GROWING UP DIFFERENT

5

Tacos and Mariachis

FROM THE NOISE, STENCH, AND THE TERROR OF THE STAIRS OF ALTA Hotel, we moved into a seemingly boundless environment in East Los Angeles, to our modest new home at 1400 North Soto Street. The sprawling yard to the side had wide-leaf banana trees, fruit-bearing kumquat trees, and a big, old, gnarled apricot tree in which Henry and I built a secret tree house. A wide bed of ice plants tumbled down the side embankment from the yard to the sidewalk. Across Soto Street we had a sweeping green municipal park named Hazzard Park, so named not as a warning for the kind of activities that took place there, but after a long-forgotten city father, a councilman named John Hazzard.

We now had the space to have pets again. Our first dog was a frisky, short-haired stray the color of peanut butter. We named her Skippy after the brand name of our favorite food. But, abruptly, she was taken from us by an auto accident on busy North Soto Street. As if by fate, another dog came into our lives—a dog we just could not turn away. She was a mongrel that had the bearing of a pedigreed breed. She had the long coat and bone structure of an Irish setter, but she was black with streaks of brown on her side. And over her soulful eyes, she had two brown dots the color of peanut butter. She was the spitting image of Blackie, our dog in camp!

Henry, although he was seven years old and should have known better, really believed that this dog was Blackie and had followed us all the way down from Tule Lake. But Daddy, Mama, and I could see that this dog was a bit younger and smaller than our old beloved pet. We all tried to think of a name for this new addition to the family, but, despite our best efforts, we always found ourselves calling her Blackie. We decided to accept destiny: She became our new Blackie.

Almost as if to make up for all the years before Blackie with no pet, Daddy and Mama let us continue to add to our growing menagerie. For Easter, they bought us a pair of bunny rabbits. A neighbor gave us a giant land turtle. Our uncle, who had relocated in Salt Lake City after camp but had subsequently moved back to Los Angeles, gave us a pair of ducklings. We even added two baby sparrows that Daddy rescued when a windstorm brought down their nest. We kids took turns feeding their voracious appetites. We had just been taken to the Clyde Beatty Circus when the two baby sparrows joined our family, so we named our two birds Clyde and Beatty. Rather than a circus, we could have named our little menagerie the Takei Family Zoo.

Daddy and Mama tried to create as normal an environment for us as they could. But "normalcy" was, for us kids, a constant series of new discoveries. When Reiko was given a nice, yellow banana and told it was a delicious treat, she bit into the whole, unpeeled fruit and decided she didn't like it. Cheerios breakfast cereal, "shaped like little letter O's," as the radio commercials touted, was as fascinating to play with as it was good to eat. Henry and I pasted them onto some of our school assignments, and Reiko made edible bracelets and necklaces out of them.

The chore of creating yellow butter out of white margarine by mixing the reddish-orange liquid from tiny cellophane packets was something we were all eager to volunteer for. And the wonder of all "normal" wonders was that goodies were brought right to the front door by vendors in trucks, some of them musical.

I remember how anxiously we looked forward to the tinkle of the music from the Good Humor ice cream truck or the cheery whistle of the Helm's bakery truck carrying treats like chocolate cupcakes and flaky raspberry tarts. The iceman actually came stomping into the kitchen with a giant block of ice balanced on his back held by a big steel tong, always seeming to know when the old block in the icebox was almost melted down.

An extra special treat of "normalcy" was Sunday morning. That was when Daddy and Mama didn't have to get up early. They stayed in bed, and we all got to crawl in with them. Daddy read the funny pages of the *Los Angeles Examiner* to us. Then, while Mama got breakfast ready, Henry and Reiko walked on Daddy's back. Henry was small for his age, even smaller than Reiko, so he got to walk on Daddy with her. I didn't, because Daddy said I was too big and too heavy. Daddy would lie there on his stomach, grunting and groaning in pleasure with each wobbly step they took. After the "walk on Daddy" ritual, it was a Sunday breakfast of pancakes with syrup poured from a tin container shaped like a little log cabin. I remember those Sunday mornings so fondly. I know they were Daddy's and Mama's efforts to get us back to normal living, but to me those Sunday mornings were abnormally special.

But try as they might to create a "normal" environment for us, we knew that we were different. When we enrolled at Murchison Street School, we were the oldest ones in our grades. All three of us were behind in our schooling because of camp—I was almost nine years old and in the second grade.

We were the only Japanese—in fact, the only Asian—family in a practically all Mexican neighborhood. My friend across the street and down a ways was named Onorato. In the house across the empty lot from him lived the three brothers Chi Chi, Lata, and Pelon. The Gonzales family lived next door to us. We shopped at a neighborhood grocery store called Venegas'. We heard Spanish spoken all around us. To be normal in our neighborhood was to be Mexican.

I loved this normalcy of our new barrio neighborhood. Every experience was a constant procession of new sensations and wonderful discoveries. Once, walking home from school with Onorato, I was invited over to his house to be shown his collection of dog cards. These were cards of various breeds of pedigreed dogs that came wrapped in each loaf of Langendorf bread. "I got one that looks just like your Blackie," he said. "You wanna see?"

Onorato's house was only half a block away from ours, but I'd never been in it. I followed him to the back of his house, and he held the screen door open for me. He ushered me into a kitchen warm with enticing aromas. We were greeted in Spanish by a short, plump lady. I knew she was his mother because he called her Mama—the same name we called our mother. But unlike us, he said "Mama" with the emphasis on the second "ma." Then he pointed to me and said something in Spanish that ended with "George." I guessed that he had introduced me, so I extended my hand and said, "Hello, Mrs. Moreno." Wiping her hand on her apron, she chortled and said something that sounded happy and welcoming and shook my hand.

The kitchen was redolent with the comforting smell of food cooking, something made of corn, I guessed, and something else more savory. Onorato brought out his cards and spread them on the red Formica table. "Here," he said, pointing to one card. "Don't he look like your Blackie?" He did, but he was the wrong color. It was a picture of a silky-haired dog like Blackie, but it was completely reddish brown, not black.

"He's not black like Blackie, but, yeah, he sorta looks like him," I agreed.

"The card says 'Irish setter,'" he noted. "So that means Blackie's part Irish. *Eee ho,*" Onorato exclaimed, singing out the last part slowly, almost lyrically.

"Eee ho" was an expression I heard frequently among my new friends. From the way it was used, I guessed it suggested

something impressive or admirable. *"Eee ho wale,"* I learned, was an even stronger version.

Then his mother said something I couldn't understand. The way she spoke sounded so melodic. The words just rolled off her tongue as if she were singing.

Mrs. Moreno set down a plate in front of us containing a single steaming pancake. But this wasn't a pancake like my mama made on Sunday mornings. It was steamy with the fragrance of corn. This must be what I had smelled when we walked in. *"Tortilla,"* Onorato informed me. Then his mother dipped a big spoon into a bowl containing a thick brownish paste. *"Frijoles,"* Onorato announced. I realized that, actually, he was repeating for me what his mother had already said in her musical, accented Spanish.

She plopped a spoonful of the pale brown paste on the yellowish pancake and spread it around. Then she dropped on a dollop of red liquid. *"Salsa roja,"* Onorato repeated. Two words in Spanish this time. This red liquid chili, this *salsa roja*, smelled pungently spicy. Then she rolled up the pancake and with a knife cut it through its plump middle. A little bit of the brown paste oozed out both ends. With a genial smile she held up the plate with her exotic creation. I took one piece and waited so I could watch Onorato manage his. He bit down with gusto and with a deft contortion of his tongue caught the overflow oozing from the opposite end just as it was about to drop off. I wasn't as quick, and the overflow dribbled onto my fingers.

The taste was fantastic! The soft earthiness of the *frijoles* was delicious with the spicy-sweet tang of the *salsa roja*, all wrapped in the warm corn flavor of this wonderful pancake called "tortilla." Onorato told me this delicious concoction was a "burrito." I loved it, and I couldn't wait to tell my family about it. Better yet, I had to get my mama to cook like Onorato's Mamá.

It wasn't long before our kitchen was exuding the same earthy aromas that I first came across in Onorato's mother's kitchen. And Mama became a wonderful cook of various

Mexican dishes. Her tacos became our favorite. Henry, Reiko, and I had contests to see who could eat more of Mama's tacos than anyone else. I usually won with four.

The discovery of the flavors of our new community was easy and pleasurable. But the melodic mystery of the language that surrounded us was a bit more challenging. The three of us kids used to mimic the sounds that we thought we heard. "Pilino parano, pilino parano" was the rollicking phrase we made up when we wanted to pretend we were speaking Spanish to each other.

Daddy, however, was way ahead of us. He was learning the actual Spanish words. When his customers came to pick up their dry cleaning, he was using words like *pantalón* for pants, *camisa* for shirts, and *abrigo* for coats. I decided then that I was going to get past "pilino parano" and start learning the real words. Here was a rich, fascinating world around me that I could see, hear, smell, and eat. Yet, I had an invisible wall of language keeping me from participating fully. Daddy was already starting; I wanted to, also. But learning to speak Spanish was going to take some effort.

The joy of Mexican music required no effort at all. A friend who lived down the street, Danny Sandoval, had an older brother in his early twenties named Cesar. I thought Cesar was a little strange. He rarely spoke. He had an enormous black mustache and wore his shiny black hair long, almost down to his shoulders. Danny said Cesar's hair was long because he was a musician. Cesar lived by himself in the Sandovals' garage facing the back alley behind their home.

Danny would occasionally take Onorato and me to visit Cesar in his tiny converted garage apartment. These were special experiences, and, for me, more exotic revelations. I vividly remember the first time we went there. The walls of Cesar's garage room were completely draped with boldly colored serapes. Thick wall-to-wall orange shag carpeting concealed the concrete floor. The only bed in the room was covered with a red-and-black serape-like blanket and a half-dozen pillows made from serape cloth. Candles glowed in little red glass containers placed throughout the room. Brightly colored giant pillows were strewn over the carpet.

Cesar didn't say much. Barely nodding when we followed Danny in, he acknowledged us with a muffled grunt. We sat on the floor pillows, and Cesar sat on his bed, taking his guitar and idly fingering the strings for some time. When he was ready, suddenly he struck a loud, resonant chord and started singing. Cesar's voice was like nothing I had ever heard before—rich, deep, and lyrical. I didn't understand the words, but I felt his emotions right down to my core. The sad songs were achingly sorrowful. When he went into a wail, he made his voice thin, crystalline pure, and high beyond belief, holding that note forever. I dared not gasp for breath until his wail was completed. I thought Cesar must have experienced some unbearable grief in his life to sing so tragically.

Then abruptly, he struck another chord, trembled his fingers rapidly over his guitar strings, and then began a lively, bouncy, joyful number. Suddenly, his whole body seemed to spring to life. His shoulders undulated, his toes tapped, his head rocked in rhythm. The Spanish words bobbed and trilled and rolled off of his lips to the beat of the strumming of his guitar. Cesar had transported me musically from one emotional extreme to another.

Then, when he finished just as abruptly as he began, he took out a pack of cigarettes, lit up, drew deeply, and sat silently smoking. Danny reached over and took the pack of cigarettes, put one in his mouth, and offered one to each of us with a friendly "Smoke?" Onorato took one. I wasn't sure I wanted to. I had heard that smoking could stunt one's growth. But this first time, just to be polite, I took one. Danny lit his and brought the match up to Onorato's. I was surprised to see Onorato puff away easily like an experienced smoker. Then Danny brought the match to my wobbly cigarette, perched unsteadily in my mouth. I drew in deeply just like Onorato. An acrid, burning sensation pushed into my nose and mouth. I felt like I was breathing in the exhaust from a car. I burst out hacking and coughing and blew out Danny's match. It was awful. I never did that again.

But I went back as often as Danny would invite me to hear his brother Cesar's music.

As it turned out, Cesar's wonderful artistry was my introduction to the full splendor of Mexican music and culture. One day, Danny told me that Cesar would be playing with a mariachi group at a fiesta called Cinco de Mayo. I had never heard of mariachis or Cinco de Mayo fiestas. But I certainly knew and admired Cesar's music. I wanted to go.

The fiesta was to be held at a housing project called Ramona Gardens, located just beyond Venegas' grocery store. I was familiar with Ramona Gardens because a lot of my friends from school lived there. Daddy and Mama knew it wasn't too far away, and they knew how much I loved Cesar's music. I got permission from them to go with Danny and Onorato to the Cinco de Mayo fiesta after school. But I had to promise that I would be home no later than five o'clock.

When we arrived, people were jammed into the green, parklike center of the Ramona Gardens housing project. Banners and flags and crepe paper streamers flapped vigorously in the strong spring breeze. Vendors all over the place were selling from tables, carts, and big, wide trays strapped onto their necks. *"Churros!"* shouted one as he sold long, sugared, deep-fried dough. *"Dulces!"* called out another on whose tray were arranged sweet, sticky candies. *"Taquitos, taquitos,"* sang out another, standing by a cart with a white cloth covering a mound of what I knew were little rolls of meat-filled tortillas.

Daddy had given me fifty cents for spending money. It was enough, but I had to plan carefully because he told me to buy my friends the same treats I bought myself. I decided on the five-cent *churros* and eight-cent Nehi soda pop. That left me eleven cents in change.

The focus of the crowd's attention was on a fat, sweaty man in a white embroidered Mexican shirt standing on a makeshift stage in the middle of the green lawn. He was speaking in rapid-fire Spanish over the loudspeaker. Occasionally, he mixed in some English words like "crazy" and "movie star" and "best in the West." When he finished there was a ripple of applause, and then a fast-paced music started to blare from the loud-speaker.

Like a pair of energetic colts, a boy and a girl dressed in bright Mexican costumes came stamping and prancing onto the stage. They looked like they were about my age—ten years old. The boy, who wore a huge Mexican hat, was dressed in a white cotton outfit with a colorful serape draped over one shoulder. He held his hands behind him as he stamped in rhythm with the music. The girl pounded her feet in unison with him, but she was much more spectacular. Wearing a full, voluminous skirt embroidered with beautiful designs, the girl flounced and swirled to the bounce and the beat of the music. The boy took off his giant hat and threw it down on the stage. The hat then became the focus of the dancers' energies. They circled it, stamping and pounding. The tempo of the music picked up. The dancers reversed directions, and their feet picked up the quickened rhythm. The music got faster, and the stamping picked up. The girl flounced around the hat, and the boy jumped over it. The tempo got even faster, and the dancers' feet now were thudding at breakneck speed. Just when it seemed impossible to go any faster, they stamped out a breathtaking flurry, and—with a loud, dramatic thud of finality—it was over. I was exhausted just watching them. But the dancers beamed brightly as they bowed and bounded offstage.

"Pretty good, huh?" Onorato asked, smiling at me. I was speechless. All I could do was try to applaud with at least the same energy that the dancers displayed onstage. And they were only about our age!

"Nah, that was nothing," Danny, our cultural authority, opined. "That's why they came on first. Just wait. The dancers get better."

I was astounded. They get better than what we had just witnessed?

"Just wait," Danny assured me. As the afternoon moved on, I discovered how right he was.

As the other dancers, all of whom were adults, were introduced, I realized that the artistry wasn't just in the stamping. It also was in their bodies—in the dips and sways of their shoulders and in the proud poise of their torsos as they glided along on their thudding feet.

We all agreed that the best couple brought another element —sexiness. Their bodies undulated in unison, almost seeming to caress but never touching. Their eyes, playful and teasing at first, became ardent, hungry, burning. As the pounding feet intensified, their eyes blazed with passion, building up to flashing, ecstatic rapture. Their stamping got not only louder and faster, but sensitive and nuanced. Suddenly, their feet appeared to stop pounding, but quickly we realized this wasn't true. Their feet were actually still moving, almost imperceptibly vibrating, gradually becoming audible again, swelling and growing and pounding to a voluptuously explosive climax of staccato stamping. The dancers were sound and motion in elegant control and wild with abandon simultaneously. They were fantastic!

"Sexy, huh?" Danny smiled. He was finally impressed. He clapped with the same enthusiasm as the rest of us.

We were having a great time, but I was getting worried. It was past four-thirty, and Cesar hadn't performed yet. "When's your brother coming on, Danny?" I asked. "I've got to be home by five."

"*Eee ho,* you're so antsy," Danny said. "Keep your shirt on." This was a slightly different usage of *eee ho,* I thought. I guessed that it must also mean something like "golly" or "gee" or maybe even "shut up." Danny seemed a little irritated, but nevertheless I knew I would have to leave soon.

Just then, the bright, loud blare of trumpets cut through the hubbub of the crowd. Three trumpet players were poised to the left of the stage. Magnificently arrayed in black-and-silver spangled outfits, they ascended the stairs playing an aggressively spirited melody. Their flamboyant pants, skintight at the hips, gradually flared out at the bottom. They wore jet-black short jackets. Running down the sides of the arms and legs and across the fronts of the jackets were shiny, silver disks that gleamed and sparkled in the sunshine.

Then, the clear sound of the trumpets was joined by the sweet lyricism of violins. Offstage to the right were three violin players dressed just like the trumpeters. They climbed the stairs to the stage playing the string refrain to the same lively tune. The violins and trumpets joined their sounds in harmony.

Then came a dramatic break. Instantaneously, we heard the vibrant sound of guitars. Three guitar players in the same resplendent costumes and a fourth musician playing a resonant giant instrument that looked like a big, pregnant guitar rose from the back of the stage. Their playing gave the same refrain a richness, a deep-toned solidity. Cesar was the guitarist at the far left.

"There's Cesar," Danny whispered, nudging everybody excitedly. With dramatic precision, the trumpets and violins joined in—luxuriant and thrilling. I had never heard music like this before. I was absolutely enchanted. No, it was more than enchanting—it was transporting.

But it was now almost five o'clock. I knew I would be late getting home. I whispered softly to my friends, "I gotta go."

"*Eee ho*," was all Danny said.

Onorato whispered back, "I'll go with you."

As the spirited mariachi music played on, Onorato and I maneuvered our way out of the crowd and started trotting home. I was still heady with this Cinco de Mayo fiesta—the dancing, the music, the jubilant merrymaking. I couldn't wait to tell my family all about this wonderful afternoon.

We lived in a fantastic community, I thought. I felt lucky to have friends like Danny who introduced all this splendor to me. It was great having a good friend like Onorato who invited me into his home to share the tastes and sounds and intimacies of the people who were our new neighbors.

"You know, Onorato," I said as we hurried home, "I like living in our barrio."

87

"Yeah? How come?"

"Well, it's so special," I gushed.

"How come?" he repeated.

"Well, the Cinco de Mayo fiesta. It's fantastic!"

"Oh yeah. I know," he said rather matter-of-factly. "It happens every year, you know."

I was stopped in my tracks. "You're kidding! Really?" I couldn't believe something so spectacular was an annual event. Even Christmas wasn't like what I had just experienced.

"Yeah," Onorato said with an amused smile.

"Really!" I said, still incredulous. It was going to be wonderful living here.

As we started jogging again, Onorato asked, "Where did you used to live before?"

I kept moving, but that question sent a chill down my back. For some unknown reason, a vague sense of shame crept over me.

"Oh, we lived far away," I answered indifferently.

"But, where?" he persisted.

This was getting uncomfortable. "Oh, a place far away called Arkansas," I said, hoping he would quit asking. We trotted along for a while in silence. Then he broke it.

"What did it used to be like there?" he asked. We were almost home now. Onorato's house was across the street, and mine was half a block farther.

Without looking at Onorato, I said, "I forgot." I picked up speed, running ahead of him. "I'll see you tomorrow," I shouted and ran home as fast as I could.

When I came huffing and puffing into the cleaner shop, Daddy looked over from the steam presser and, with a reassuring smile, stated the obvious: "You're a little late."

"I'm sorry, Daddy," I apologized. "I ran back all the way with Onorato."

"Watch time better," Mama reprimanded from her big new sewing machine.

"Must have been lots of fun," Daddy said expectantly.

"Yes, it was nice," I answered, and moved quickly back to our apartment. That was all I was able to tell Daddy and Mama about one of the most memorable afternoons in my life.

We were different. There was always something to remind me of that fact.

I remember the apprehension I felt when my second-grade teacher, Mrs. Lewis, started to take attendance on my first day in her class. She took great pleasure in pronouncing each name with care—with emphasis on accurate pronunciation.

"Bobby Corral," she read out, rolling the *r's*. "Martha Gonzales," she called, pronouncing the *z* with an *s* sound— seeming very familiar with Mexican names. "Ofelia Gutierrez" just rolled off her tongue. She was taking the roll in alphabetical order. After calling out "Mario Silvera," she stopped and gazed silently at her roll book. I knew she was looking at my name.

"George, how do you pronounce your middle name?" she asked as she spelled out H-O-S-A-T-O. She had called out all those other names so easily, I thought. My name was pronounced exactly as in Spanish. It was so simple. Why did she have to make such a big thing of mine?

"George Hosato Takei," I recited. I gave her my complete name so she wouldn't next ask for the pronunciation of my last name as well.

"Hosato," she repeated slowly. "It sounds so poetic. It's lovely," she complimented.

I answered, "Thank you," but I wished she had not commented at all.

At recess, some kids approached me, saying, "You have such a lovely name."

"It's so poetic."

"How do you pronounce it?" I felt like punching them.

Mrs. Lewis seemed to like everything about me. She liked my drawings; she said I was artistic. She liked the way I sang our school anthem, "Oh, Murchison, Dear Murchison." And she liked the way I recited the rhymes we had to memorize. In fact, she cast me in my first acting role.

* * *

I learned the meaning of stage fright in our Thanksgiving skit. I played the lead role, the part of the head Pilgrim. I had more words to speak and memorize than anyone—even more dialogue than Bobby Corral, who played the Indian chief.

My biggest fear was a single line I had to say in an Indian language, welcoming the Indian chief. In addition to all my dialogue, I had to memorize Indian! Bobby had it easier because he repeated the same greeting after I said it.

The more I practiced and rehearsed, the more nervous I got. I had the line down pat, but the fear of forgetting onstage had me paralyzed. The performance was scheduled the afternoon before Thanksgiving vacation. I was a wreck. All I could think about was that one line of Indian.

When the curtain rose, a little zombie Pilgrim leader, dressed in a black crepe paper costume, marched out leading his people onto that stage. My voice quavered, my hands trembled, and I dropped my Pilgrim rifle. A girl Pilgrim forgot her cue to stand up, so I accidentally stepped on her gray crepe paper skirt, causing it to tear. But, by some miracle, when Bobby Corral made his entrance—splendiferous in his paper feather Indian chief bonnet—I got my full Indian greeting out to him. Bobby stuttered, repeating the greeting after me. Thank goodness that wasn't me, I thought. That fearful moment had passed. Then my mind went blank. I couldn't remember my next line. I stood frozen, sheer terror gripping me. I could feel everybody's eyes staring at me.

Mrs. Lewis came scooting out in front of the stage, bent over like a hunchback. Did she think nobody could see her? She was gesticulating frantically and trying to whisper something to me hysterically. I could hear nothing. Her silent, panic-stricken pantomime continued on and on. Suddenly, the forgotten lines came back to me, and my voice returned. Somehow, the rehearsed order of things started to move forward again.

Before I realized it, the skit was over. I was drenched in perspiration, my T-shirt stained black from the color of my wet crepe paper costume.

To my surprise, Mrs. Lewis appeared backstage full of praise.

She thought our skit was the best of the presentations given by all the classes. And she singled me out for particular praise. She pointed out to the other little thespians the cool, controlled way in which I kept my composure when I forgot my lines. Instead of breaking, she observed, I calmly and naturally maintained some believability until I remembered my words again—then continued on. She showered me with accolades. I was stunned. Couldn't she see I was too paralyzed to break down? Too traumatized to be believable as anything but a boy who had stuck a wet finger into an electric socket? But Mrs. Lewis's raves continued. My stage debut was heralded as a giant success.

Only I and my black-stained T-shirt knew the truth. After a few washings, however, the black stain came out. But to this day, my mind still retains that absolutely unforgettable Indian greeting. I think it will be etched in my brain forever. *"Yo hay, yo hay, mee tah koo lah nah hum poh, om neechi ni chopi."* I have no idea what it means.

Mrs. Lewis thought I was brilliant at everything. She gave me a straight-A report card and skipped me a year. I went from her second-grade class to Mrs. Rugen's fourth-grade class. I graduated from a teacher who liked everything about me to a teacher I came to hate.

Mrs. Rugen was a short, stout, rosy-cheeked lady who wore her steel gray hair in a round bun on top of her head. The reddish color in her cheeks was not from a healthy blush; a fine web of red veins gave her face that florid ruddiness. It was a face that never smiled. There was something no-nonsense and hard about her.

I felt an air from her as chilly as Mrs. Lewis's was warm. Whenever she asked a question and I raised my hand to answer, she always picked someone else. When I was the only one to raise my hand, she waited a long while for someone else to respond, deliberately overlooking me. If, finally, no one else raised a hand, she very reluctantly called on me. I soon stopped raising my hand.

In addition to teaching the fourth-grade class, Mrs. Rugen

also had afternoon recess yard duty. She was assigned to watch over the playing children. In the school yard, she was the very opposite of the classroom teacher trying to brush off a student. Rather than ignore me, she watched me like a hawk. When playing dodge ball, if I crossed the line of the circle a little too often in the heat of enthusiasm, she would grab my arm with brutal suddenness and yank me back with a reprimand. If I shouted too loudly while playing tetherball, she would blow a shrill, scolding whistle at me for making too much noise. She was never as attentive or as concerned with the other kids' behavior, and I knew she hated me for some reason.

During recess one afternoon, Mrs. Rugen was standing chatting with another teacher. I was playing close enough to hear them talking, but I wasn't really paying attention. Then something Mrs. Rugen said shot out at me like a bullet. She referred to me as "that little Jap boy." I felt shock, pain, rage, and shame all at the same time. Those words stung me more than any of the other hurtful things she had done to me. But I found myself looking away from Mrs. Rugen, pretending I hadn't heard her. I just contained that terrible hot feeling inside. To this day, it angers me that I looked away. I didn't speak up. I swallowed my hurt.

Even when we returned to the classroom, I felt a churning inside. She might be my teacher, but I couldn't help glaring at Mrs. Rugen sitting at her desk in front of the classroom. I hated her. But when she stared back at me with that innocent, "What are you looking at?" expression, I avoided meeting her eyes again. Somehow, shame dominated my anger. I had the queasy feeling that her calling me "Jap" had something to do with our having been in camp. And camp, I was old enough by now to know, was something like jail. It was a place where people who had done bad things were sent. I had a gnawing sense of guilt about our time spent in camp. I could not fully understand it, but I thought perhaps we had it coming to us to be punished like this. Maybe we deserved to be called this painful word, "Jap."

Jap is only one syllable—the word "Japanese" shortened. A

clipped-off, rather-too-spare sound. Yet, this simple syllable has come to acquire over the last century the curious power to lacerate. History forged a neutral sound—hammered by the blunt hatred of racists, fired by the hysteria of political and economic opportunists, and finally by the searing red heat of war—to a fine razor edge. It can just graze—and still open wounds. It can slash and dehumanize. To a Japanese American, "Jap" is a sound that vibrates with threat, an epithet sonorous with menace. Only a sound, an abbreviated word. Yet, the pain it can inflict and the injury it can cause lie in the force that history has hammered into it. "Jap" has become more than a word. "Jap" is an assault weapon.

I understood then what Daddy had told me about words meant to hurt—words like "keto" and the ones that sound like "sakana beach." What Mrs. Rugen called me hurt. It hurt too much for the pain to have faded by the end of the day. Even on the way home from school with Onorato, it still hurt, but I didn't tell him. It was still lingering when I walked into the cleaner shop. I didn't tell Daddy and Mama what Mrs. Rugen had called me. I was coming to understand that they, too, were uncomfortable talking about our years in camp, and "Jap" was a word that inevitably was associated with those years.

Daddy and Mama were suffering pains of their own. Something that I never remembered from camp began to happen; Daddy and Mama started to fight.

Quietly, before we realized it, a chilly tension had grown between them. Their conversations became strained. Sometimes there were long stretches when they didn't talk to each other at all. But their silences were taut with emotion.

It first erupted one afternoon after we had come home from school. I was reading in the living room, Henry was listening to the radio, and Reiko was playing in the bedroom. Daddy and Mama were out front in the cleaner shop. We heard the steady rhythm of Daddy's steam presser stamping down, hissing for a few seconds, thumping back up, then repeating the pattern again. Mama, I guessed, was seated at her sewing machine.

Suddenly, the stamping and the hissing of the steam presser stopped, and we heard them talking loudly to each other. I stopped reading, and Henry looked up from the radio. Reiko appeared silently at the bedroom door, her eyes wide. Daddy was shouting, and Mama came rushing into the apartment, cold with anger. The steam presser started up again, this time going at a furious pace. Mama remained in the back, stony and at a loss for something to do. Then she strode into the kitchen muttering to herself. We heard her slapping down plates on the counter and clattering stacks of dishes, all the while keeping up a steady stream of barely audible mutters. The sound of the steam pressing stopped.

"What did you say?" Daddy bellowed back from the shop. Mama became silent, but the air was charged with tension. I was paralyzed with fear. When the sound of the pressing resumed again, our relief, too, was almost audible. Mama started clattering again in the kitchen. Daddy's presser answered back with hot hisses. It seemed to turn into an argument between hisses and clatter; clatter and hisses. Then Mama's challenging mutters again joined the fray.

"Mama, please don't do that," I wanted to say to her. But I was too petrified to speak up. Thankfully, the presser continued, stamping and hissing lividly.

Then, Mama said in Japanese loudly enough for all of us to hear, "If only he had some spine." The sound of the pressing stopped. I was frozen in terror. There was an excruciating silence.

"What!" Daddy barked. Silence. He stomped straight back to the apartment and into the kitchen. "What did you say?" Daddy bellowed. Mama remained silent, then tentatively began rattling the plates again.

"You think I didn't hear that?" Daddy roared. The clattering continued. "You think you're the only one who can rattle plates?" I heard Daddy yell. Mama gasped, and then I heard a plate crash onto the floor.

"You break plate," Mama screamed as she ran into the dining room.

"And I can break more, too!" Daddy yelled as he followed her out with a large plate in his hand.

Mama rushed into the bathroom, but just before she slammed the door closed, she screamed back at Daddy, "Spineless man!"

The large plate shattered with explosive force on the door. Reiko shrieked and started to cry. Daddy banged furiously on the bathroom door, demanding it be opened. We all ran up to him pleading, "Please, Daddy, please, please, please, stop." The banging and our crying continued for some time.

Finally, Daddy stopped, hugged us, and said, "It's all right. It's all right. Don't cry anymore." Then he closed the shop and drove away.

There were more confrontations after that between our parents. To tell the truth, they happened too often. Home became a tense and uncomfortable place. More and more, after school, I started to stay at Onorato's or Danny's house. My friends' homes were such happy, friendly places. I hated coming home to our sour, tension-filled dinners.

Henry began wetting his bed. It became a regular occurrence. Mama made him take out his yellow-circled sheet and hang it on the laundry line. She thought this exercise in humiliation would cure an eight-year-old bed wetter. It didn't. Henry's bed sheet just acquired more overlapping yellow rings. Mama finally had to bleach it, and Henry started all over again with a whitened sheet.

Reiko was the only one of us who seemed to benefit from Daddy's and Mama's sense of guilt over their fighting. They showered her with what Henry and I thought was excessive love and attention. If any goody had to be divided among the three of us, Reiko always got the largest third. If there was only one goody, she got it. She became the princess of a guilt-and-anxiety-laden family.

A constant air of unease permeated our house. It made me nervous when Daddy and Mama were silent for any stretch of time. But I hated even more the end of those silences. Whenever I heard a sharp sound from the shop out front—a pair of scissors put down with force on the front counter, a ruler slapped down on Mama's sewing machine, or even the soft thud of a bundle of laundry dropped on the floor—I would flinch. Was this going to be the beginning of another traumatic argument? Thankfully, most were false alarms. The only reassuring sound to come from the front was the steady rhythm of Daddy's steam presser.

I believed there could be nothing more terrible than our parents' fights. One busy Saturday night, however, I learned there were worse terrors. The shop was open late, and the three of us kids were in back in the living room. As I read I could hear the comforting rhythm of Daddy's pressing and hissing. Suddenly, I thought I heard Mama stifle a gasp. The pressing stopped. A chill stabbed my back. I heard loud voices and then the sound of heavy, thudding footsteps coming our way. Mama staggered into the apartment shielded by Daddy, who was being shoved by a young Mexican man. Then, I saw the glint of a gun he held right next to Daddy's head. I froze.

"Please, I've got kids back here," Daddy said.

"Where you keep the big money?" the man growled.

"Mama, get it," Daddy ordered urgently.

Mama ran back to the bedroom. The man's dark eyes flashed all over our apartment as he stood with Daddy in the doorway between the apartment and the shop. Daddy's eyes were fixed on the gun.

"What she doing?" the holdup man snarled.

"Mama!" Daddy shouted.

She came back from the bedroom clutching a crumpled brown paper bag. As she passed by me, I saw her surreptitiously slip a wad of money held in her right hand under a sofa pillow. She hurried over to the man and thrust the paper bag toward him.

"Take all money," she said. He glared at the rather airy brown bag.

"That's all?"

"That all," she answered.

"Please, that's all," Daddy affirmed.

The man stared at Mama menacingly, then grabbed the bag, and he was gone. Like a quick, horrible nightmare, it was over. Only stunned silence remained. Then, Reiko started to cry.

Daddy and Mama rushed back to the shop.

"Be careful. Be careful," Mama was whispering. I peeked from the doorway into the shop. Daddy was outside looking down the street.

"They drove away to the north," Daddy said. As he came back in the shop, he said, "There were two of them. One was waiting out in the car." Daddy immediately locked up and called the police.

When they came back into the apartment, Mama went straight to the sofa and retrieved the wad of money she had hidden.

"What's that?" Daddy asked. "I take money out bag and hide," she answered, holding out the thick roll of bills.

"What! You mean you didn't give him the whole thing?" Daddy was incredulous. "You held out on that guy?"

"We work hard. This hard-earn money." And with that, Mama put the money on the table.

My mother is a strong woman. I was starting to realize how strong. Her strength, though, was made up of equal parts quick-thinking mixed with simple greed; courage combined with a good portion of foolhardiness. Because of Mama's swift shuffle, the holdup man got less than half the money in the bag. He took several small bills, quarters, and dimes in the change box under the front counter and about three hundred dollars that Mama handed him in the brown paper bag. Later, Daddy and Mama counted the wad of money that Mama had hidden from the robber. It totaled almost five hundred dollars.

About half a year after the holdup, Daddy and Mama were at a hospital visiting a sick friend. As they were leaving, Mama heard a voice she thought she recognized. It was a deep, drink-ravaged growl. She looked down the sidewalk and saw the backside of a man pushing someone in a wheelchair. Instantly, she recognized the hulking figure of the man pushing the chair. It was the holdup man.

"Daddy, that him," she whispered. He glanced over quickly and agreed.

"Hurry, let's get to the car," he said.

They drove around the block to reconfirm what they had seen and then went straight to the police station. The man was immediately arrested.

Mama's avarice had stiffed the holdup man when he committed the crime, then her sharp ears sent him to prison for it.

Mama was observant about many things. She was becoming especially perceptive about the way my friends dressed and wore their hair. She didn't like Danny Sandoval's long, ducktail haircut. She didn't like it at all. She felt uneasy about the wide, draped-at-the-ankles trousers he wore. And she detested his thick-soled shoes with the noisy horseshoe-tapped heels.

"Danny only ten year old. Why he dress like little *pachuco?*" she would complain to me. I was surprised Mama knew what *pachucos* were. I had thought the day might be coming soon when I would have to explain to her that *pachucos* were the grownup boys in high school and older who hung out together and dressed in the sharpest, most stylish ways. Not only did she know all this, but she thought they were gangsters. I tried to explain to her that Danny dressed the way he did because he had older brothers and he was just wearing their hand-me-downs. She seemed reluctant to accept that reasoning.

Mama became alarmed when Onorato started to wear his hair in a heavily greased ducktail. When she saw Onorato's new haircut, she scowled. Without comment to him or me, she went straight to Daddy and began a frowning, whispered conversation—all the while glancing over at Onorato's shiny, slick head. I was embarrassed. Onorato's parents never made comments about the way I dressed. I resented Daddy's and Mama's doing that to my friend.

* * *

Beyond their big fights, I was beginning to sense other, more subtle, changes happening in my parents. Their great drive for normalcy in our lives began shifting more toward defining our differences from the community we were living in. It wasn't just in the clothes we wore or the style of hair. It was in their thoughts about our education, their feelings about our culture, and their hopes for our future.

They didn't want us to lose the Japanese we spoke at home. In fact, they wanted us to get better. They enrolled us in Saturday Japanese language classes. When we protested that we went to school five days a week and our friends got to play on Saturdays, Mama would just recite her old maxim, *"Hito wa hito, uchi wa uchi."* "Others are others, our house is our house." When we noted that it was expensive and we should save the money, Mama and Daddy responded that we would be grateful later in life that they spent this money now. We grumbled that we didn't feel grateful right now.

Even at regular school, our parents nudged us to be better. They bought us a set of the voluminous Encyclopedia Brittanica when they could ill afford it. Many evenings, Daddy would sit with us on the living room sofa and read to us from it. It was fun learning about the miscellanea of the world connected only by their common beginning letter. One evening, he was reading to us from the *S* volume of the encyclopedia. This was when I first learned about William Shakespeare.

Three months after the Cinco de Mayo fiesta, our parents took us to Little Tokyo in downtown Los Angeles for the Nisei Week Festival. This was a festival of Japanese American arts and culture held every August. It was a colorful combination of traditional Japanese arts, crafts, and martial arts, with such singularly American components as talent shows, baby contests, an outdoor carnival, and a beauty pageant. The highlight of this week-long festival was the Ondo Dancing parade on the final evening. The streets of Little Tokyo were full of folk dancers—male and female from old folks to tiny tots, anyone wanting to participate, all dressed in their cool, summer kimonos, called *yukata*. The dancers belonging to classical dance schools were clad in showy, matching silk kimonos. It was a beautiful sight—a sea of dancers stepping and swaying to the lilting melody of the samisen, a kind of Japanese guitar.

None of the formally trained dancers—as exquisite and lissome as they were—were as memorable as a giant black man, an old-time Little Tokyoite that Daddy told us was affectionately called "Little Joe." He wore a *hachi maki,* the white cotton headband, around his shiny, shaved head and a crisp, white-and-blue cotton summer *yukata* wrapped around his huge body. His towering six-foot-plus height and massive physique made all the other dancers around him look downright diminutive. But his great bulk gave the surprising grace and ease of his movements a charming grandeur that made him a crowd favorite. Excited shouts of "Here he comes," "Hey, Little Joe's coming" were heard when he approached.

"It's just like before the war, with Little Joe back," I heard one man saying to his wife nostalgically.

"Look how he's aged, though," the woman observed.

As Little Joe gracefully glided by, I heard the husband say to her, "Yeah, but look at you. No change." She gave him a hard punch on the shoulder.

Daddy and Mama started a new activity on Sunday afternoons—family drives looking at houses for sale. They emphasized that we were only looking, not really buying. We still had to save up more money, they told us. It was great fun, but I wondered why, if we were only looking, we were driving around only in areas like the Crenshaw district or Culver City or the San Fernando Valley. It was more interesting driving around beautiful neighborhoods like Beverly Hills and Bel Air where the houses were the biggest and the grandest. If they wanted us to do our best in school, then on our Sunday drives we should ride through only the best neighborhoods, I insisted.

So Daddy began driving us through the entire Los Angeles basin. He drove us down the great boulevards of the city; Wilshire, which cut right through a shimmering lake in

MacArthur Park; Sunset Boulevard, with its lush, sinuous stretches of palatial mansions; and Ocean Boulevard in Santa Monica, with its panoramic vista of the Pacific Ocean.

Daddy made a particular point of driving us through the campuses of the great universities of southern California: UCLA and USC.

"These are two of the treasures of America," he told us. Pointing out the students reading in the shade of ancient trees, he would say, voice loaded with implication, "See how hard they're studying? They have to study real hard in college." We got the point. But, nevertheless, these insinuating commentaries seemed to become his automatic reaction to the sight of every college student studying outdoors.

"See how hard they study in college?" he would repeat. Such heavy-handed observations stopped only after Henry and I started our counterattack.

"Look, Henry," I would say soberly, pointing to a student napping in the shade of a campus tree. "Do you think you can be like him?"

"I don't know," he would respond in mock awe, "I'm only a kid. I'll have to work much harder on sleeping back home."

It was on one of these Sunday drives that I made my own serendipitous discovery—what became for me another of the treasures of Los Angeles—the fantastic world of the movie studios. Driving down Melrose Avenue, I glanced up Bronson Avenue and caught sight of the fabled wrought iron gates of Paramount Studios.

"Daddy, Daddy, go back. I just saw a movie studio."

He turned around and drove us up to Marathon Street and right to the studio gate. Here, right in front of us, was the gate that I had seen in so many movie magazines—the very gate that luminaries like Alan Ladd, Lizabeth Scott, Gary Cooper, and Barbara Stanwyck passed through every day on their way to some glamorous movie set.

"Daddy, Daddy. Park the car. I want to get out and look around."

On Sunday there were plenty of spots to park on the street. I peered through the ornate gate to the deserted street between the soundstages. A lone security guard dozed in the booth just inside the gate, but I was free to fantasize cowboys, plumed harem girls, and foreign legionnaires ambling around that empty street just on the other side.

We walked along the high studio wall down Marathon Street. Beyond the wall, we could see a gigantic block of pale blue sky painted on a towering structure looming up over the entire backlot. It looked more beautiful than the real one surrounding it. I thought I recognized the sky from so many Paramount movies. Magic was made on the other side of this wall. It was hard to believe that this wonderful place, this factory that produced such dreams far surpassing reality, was actually here in the city where we lived—that Hollywood was so close.

From that Sunday on, Daddy started to include a movie studio drive-by whenever we were in an area that had one: Republic Studio in the San Fernando Valley; 20th Century-Fox in West Los Angeles; and M-G-M when we were in Culver City. Empty movie studios, devoid of life on Sunday afternoons— and yet they became magical places swarming with the glamorous hustle and bustle of my fantasies—and yes, my first glimmerings. Hollywood was just on the other side of a fence.

These Sunday drives—rides of hope, discovery, and, for me, of dreams—took us, after many years, to their announced destination. Daddy and Mama bought a house. We found a sprawling white stucco in the Wilshire district, the old neighborhood where we had lived before the war. It was a quiet, racially mixed residential neighborhood of primarily white and black professionals. We would be the first Asians on the street.

Again, we had to move. But this time, the change was eagerly anticipated. We were moving to a nice, big house with a backyard filled with fruit-bearing orange and peach trees. We kids were excited about the Punch and Judy Ice Cream Shop two blocks away and the beautiful Uptown movie theater just another block up. Our parents were enthusiastic about the schools that we would be attending. For me it was to be Mt.

Vernon Junior High and for Henry and Reiko, Wilton Place Grammar School. But most importantly, for Daddy and Mama it was a move charged with significance. This was a decision made on their own. They alone had decided to buy this house. It was not an order from the government sending them to some unknown place at the point of a gun. It was a move back and a move up. They were regaining something they had lost—control over their lives.

We moved out of East L.A. in the summer of 1950. Our four years in the barrio had come to an end. I was thirteen years old—a teenager now. We were moving to a new home and to a new life. But I was also leaving people and a life I had come to love. Onorato and Danny, Cesar's music and the color of Cinco de Mayo, Mrs. Moreno's cooking and the flavor of a good, messy East L.A. burrito.

I may have left the barrio, but my years there had given me appetites and appreciations that became a good part of me. More than I realized then, I am a product of the barrio of East L.A.

6

Mt. Vernon Days

MT. VERNON JUNIOR HIGH WAS ACROSS TOWN AND A WORLD APART from Murchison Street School in East Los Angeles. A lush, green lawn led up to a row of elegant pillars fronting a three-story building. The facade replicated the architecture of the home of the first United States president—hence, the name Mt. Vernon. Here, the student body was as different from that of my old school as the architecture—predominantly white with a sprinkling of kids born in European countries such as England, Russia, Germany, and Czechoslovakia. The black kids were the children of professionals. There were few Asians—and those were mostly Japanese—and practically no Mexicans. I had to adjust to another new environment.

But I didn't want to lose my link with the life that we had just left. In junior high school, we had a decision to make about which foreign language we wanted to study. I chose Spanish.

Our teacher, Mrs. Woods, despite her English surname was Mexican and a passionate proponent of language studies as a relevant part of life. She made learning Spanish come alive, calling us all by the Spanish translations of our names. I was Jorge. The girl across the aisle from me, Nancy, became Anita, but Mrs. Woods told us that the diminutive of the name was Anitita and that an even fonder form was the last two syllables of Anitita alone, the playfully affectionate "Tita." I liked that name. My sister's English name was Nancy, so I found a way to incorporate Spanish into my own family. Reiko has been Tita to me ever since.

A clique of guys in class called themselves the "Oddballs." But to Mrs. Woods and all the rest of us, they became *"Las Pelotas Curiosas,"* a hilarious translation of "Oddballs" that they themselves adopted.

She asked us to name famous nearby landmarks with Spanish names, such as La Brea Tar Pits or San Gabriel Mission, or street names like Pico Boulevard or Figueroa Street, or the names of surrounding cities such as El Monte or Santa Monica or even our own Los Angeles. Mrs. Woods taught us that they weren't just exotic sounds to which we had become accustomed. They all had meaning and a dense, fascinating history. And in southern California, this was in great part Mexican. From Mrs. Woods I learned that Spanish not only gave me access to the people around me but also unlocked the whole saga of the surrounding world.

Daddy and Mama didn't let up on the self-improvement program they had begun with us. In fact, they expanded it.

Of course, our Saturday Japanese language classes continued. They enrolled us at the Jefferson Gakuen Language School in the Crenshaw district not too far away from our new house.

They bought us a grand piano for the music room. We thought it would be fun to bang on, but we didn't realize that they intended us to play it properly. Every Tuesday after school, with the regularity of a metronome, our piano teacher, Miss Kawakami, would appear at our doorstep, her metronome in hand. While it ticked away and she wagged a rhythmic finger at us, we would pound out the finger exercises. We thought that if we hammered on the keys loudly enough, the constant battering on Mama's nerves would bring an end to the lessons. We didn't realize how high Mama's tolerance was for the racket that passed as our piano lessons. The lessons continued, and eventually we started to sound not too bad. At the annual recital, we even received hearty, if not unbiased, applause.

Our parents signed Henry and me up with Boy Scouts Troop 379 at Koyasan Buddhist Temple in Little Tokyo. There, our piano-playing fingers became quite deft at tying sheepshanks, slipknots, and whatnots. But even with the Boy Scouts, we didn't escape music. Troop 379 had a drum and bugle corps that was fabled from before the war. It had been founded in 1932 and had rebuilt its reputation since the return of the Japanese American community to Los Angeles. Membership in the troop meant becoming a part of the drum and bugle corps. Henry became a bugler, and I was assigned the bass bugle, a larger and lower-register instrument. And so Thursday nights and weekends became our bugle lesson times. But this was group activity with a sense of common purpose—it was fun. We eventually became acceptable buglers.

The corps was invited to participate in parades and festivals throughout southern California, including the New Year's morning Tournament of Roses Parade in Pasadena. The cheering crowds, rousing music, and the bracing festival atmosphere were all elements that stirred my now not-so-dormant thespian yearnings.

As we were changing, so was the world that surrounded us. And far away, Washington, D.C., also was beginning to reflect that change. The government that had been so virulent in its hostility toward Japanese Americans passed—in an act both of healing and of conscience—a landmark bill, the Immigration and Naturalization Act of 1952. Sponsored by Congressman Francis Walter of Pennsylvania and Senator Pat McCarran of Nevada, the act made all races eligible for naturalized citizenship. The passage of the bill by Congress, however, was not an unalloyed victory. Underscoring the still-extant attitudes toward us, President Harry Truman vetoed it. But both the House and Senate overrode the veto, and the bill became law. Daddy could now become a citizen.

Daddy had sold the cleaner shop in East Los Angeles and bought a grocery store on Western Avenue not too far from our new home. Running the store meant long hours of hard work, but somehow, Daddy was reenergized by the passage of the bill that would grant him citizenship at last. Getting home from work after dark, he would grab a quick dinner and then bury himself in his books late into the night.

I remember watching him studying by that lone lamplight at his desk and thinking about this strange thing called citizenship. This invisible thing that I had never thought about—something I was born with that I just took for granted, yet that Daddy valued so greatly and Mama rejected with such passion years ago. What power did this intangible thing possess that it could compel such determination from Daddy and such anger from Mama?

I didn't mean to interrupt him, but Daddy noticed me watching. He smiled, took off his glasses, and pinched the tension strain on the bridge of his nose. He gestured to a chair, so I sat down. "You look like you have something on your mind," he said. I knew it was late and he was tired, but I had to ask him what citizenship meant. This is how I remember his reply.

Daddy explained that citizenship is to be a member of a country or a city or a community; but more than that, to be a citizen is to subscribe to a set of values. When I asked why he wanted to be a member of this country when he didn't have to, he answered, "Citizenship is a choice. Some people are born with it but never do anything about it. That's not real citizenship. That's only paper status. You have to consciously decide to give it meaning. Your mama felt so strongly about her citizenship and what it stood for that when it was violated, she acted. She made her citizenship meaningful and made a strong statement. And because she values it, she's fighting hard to get her citizenship back.

"For me, there was a great struggle to make my citizenship possible, by people who wanted to give me that choice, by people who believe in America's best ideals. America is where

I've lived most of my life. You kids are Americans. My future is here—in this country. Now that I have the choice, my decision is to become an American citizen."

"But America has treated us so badly," I persisted. "There's no justice in this country. What made you decide to become a citizen of a country like this?" Daddy closed his book and pondered. "America is a strange country," he began. "Despite everything, it's still a nation of ideals. Yes, justice here is neither blind nor fair. It only reflects the society. But this is an open society where people who want to can become a part of it. The system here is called a participatory democracy, where the important thing is to participate. If people like me aren't willing to take a chance and participate, America stays that much farther from its ideals. My choice is to be in there with good people like Wayne Collins, the lawyer who is helping Mama with her legal battle. My choice is to help America be what it claims it is."

That night, as I listened to Daddy's fatigued but resolute voice, my understanding of the meaning of American citizenship became as solid as the book lying on his desk. By the light of the lamp shining on that well-used American history book, America and its ideals were eloquently explained to me by an immigrant, a wartime "enemy alien," a concentration camp internee, the husband of a renunciant of her American citizenship—my father.

It was in my midteens that I discovered newspapers. We had always had the *L.A. Times* coming into our house, but, like so many things that we kids took for granted, only part of it—the comics and movie ads—had had any interest for me. I just flipped through the other sections. But Daddy frequently brought up current events for discussion at the dinner table, and I soon found that the *Times* had photos illustrating what he was talking about. From there came the realization that the text offered more details and even contrary views. Out of this grew genuine interest in the news. I began devouring the newspaper from the front page to the back. The war in Korea was almost always on the front page.

One morning, in the middle of the front page, there was a big photo of a field of rotting strawberries. It was a shocking picture. I loved strawberries. It was so wasteful to let good, ripe fruits decay in the sun. The accompanying article talked about an "Operation Wetback," the banning of workers from Mexico. It said that "braceros," a term for farm workers from Mexico who went from farm to farm picking produce when it was ripe for harvesting, were to be kept from coming into the country. Unless American pickers could be recruited to replace these braceros, this labor shortage meant that the strawberry crop for this season would be lost and a significant part of California's agricultural economy would be devastated. The article said this would make the price of strawberries skyrocket.

I decided to do something about the situation. It was vacation time. A lot of my friends had time on their hands. We usually were lazing the days away on the beach. We could instead go to the farms and save the strawberry crop. The more I thought about the idea, the more my fourteen-year-old idealism became fired up. Here was a cause that we could put our energies behind and maybe eat some great strawberries to boot. Daddy heartily endorsed the idea. I got on the phone and started calling my friends. Their responses were a revelation. Ken was busy. Fred had something else to do. Billy was going away. When it came to work, there was no group of people more busily occupied than teenagers on vacation. Only Earl Gravely, my black friend, would join me.

The morning that we were to report for work, we got up in the middle of the night, and Daddy drove Earl and me to the East Los Angeles Farm Labor Station. It was still dark when we got there. A fleet of large trucks were gathered to take the drowsy volunteer pickers to various strawberry ranches. We joined a horde of people, most of whom were Mexicans. Many were experienced farm workers, but a good number were Mexican Americans who, like us, were first-timers. They were there simply to help save the crop and make a few extra dollars. For me, it was also an opportunity to practice my growing command of the Spanish language.

Once Earl and I were loaded onto the designated truck, I hunkered down and immediately engaged the Mexican man next to me in conversation. All during the time we chatted, however, he eyed me searchingly. Finally, he asked the question that quite obviously had been bothering him. He asked in Spanish, "What tribe do you belong to?" I was puzzled. What did he mean by tribe? He repeated the same question. It dawned on me finally that he thought I was a member of some Spanish-speaking southwestern Indian tribe.

I was a teenage sun-worshipper. Almost every weekend I was at Will Rogers State Beach turning as brown as the proverbial berry. My deep copper tan and my Spanish had deceived the man next to me into thinking I was an Indian! When I revealed my Japanese ancestry to him, he widened his eyes in disbelief and covered his mouth in embarrassment. Then he nudged the man next to him, exclaiming, *"Este japonés como indio habla español."* "This Japanese that looks like an Indian speaks Spanish." There was great commotion, much laughter, and a lot of pointing at me. I became the prime curiosity on the truck.

We were taken to a strawberry farm in Orange County, southeast of Los Angeles. A vast field carpeted with endless rows of low-lying strawberry plants, each heavy with big red berries, reached all the way to the horizon. We hopped off the truck and were given our picking orders by several Japanese American men. Evidently, they owned and operated the ranch.

The picker's job was to go out in the field with wooden trays, already lined with empty individual cartons, and fill them with the ripe berries. Our line bosses sternly emphasized we were to select only the ripe ones. There would be a later harvest as the other berries ripened. Simple enough, I thought. Why the big fuss? Of course I'll pick only the ripe ones.

After about an hour, I became aware of a few of the verities of strawberry picking and of life. My first discovery was the remarkable capacity of the human body to adapt to almost any kind of task. The experienced Mexican farm workers were moving along at an amazing clip, straddling the row of plants and nimbly picking the plumpest of the fruits. In that uncomfortable, hunched-over position, they had grace and economy of motion combined with remarkable productivity. They were at least five hundred yards ahead of me after the first hour.

The next thing I realized was that we use the word "backbreaking" too loosely. I had never experienced such pain, such agony, as those merciless shooting stabs that began attacking my back. The pain became progressively worse as the day wore on. It became almost paralyzing. No one can claim to truly understand the meaning of the word "backbreaking" without having spent a day picking strawberries. By afternoon, I was crawling on all fours down that muddy row of strawberry plants, too crippled to keep from crushing any berry that happened to come under my knees, ripe or not. By the end of the day in the field, I came to the excruciating understanding that the line between idealism and delusion can be filament-thin. My vision of "saving" the California strawberry industry had completely destroyed my back. But my romantic idealism was still somewhat intact. That became the next victim of assault.

Exhausted, bedraggled, and bent over, we lined up at the pay window. I was moaning and complaining in Spanish to my fellow farm workers about my aches and pains. There were two Japanese American paymasters behind the window calculating the amount each picker earned. The highest earners, of course, were the experienced Mexican farm workers, most of whom spoke little English. When they were being paid, I noticed something odd. The paymasters spoke to the workers in good—in fact, forceful—English. But, periodically, they broke into Japanese among themselves. They were speaking openly in Japanese, obviously taking me, like my Mexican friend on the truck had, for a suntanned, Spanish-speaking non-Japanese of some kind. They seemed oblivious to my presence. I listened closely when they broke into Japanese, the language they thought no one there understood.

What I heard made my blood boil. They were shorting the pay of the non-English-speaking workers! I elbowed my way up to the window and irately told them in Japanese that I was on to what they were doing. The paymasters were stunned speechless. I threatened that if they didn't make restitutions to the people they had cheated, I would report them to the authorities. The look of astonishment on their faces was followed by rage that turned into a flustered shuffling of papers. Shortly thereafter, an announcement was made in English that there might have been some slight miscalculations in some of the pay and that adjustments would be made. This was quickly translated into Spanish by one of the Mexican American workers.

That day on the farm, I saved neither the California strawberry crop nor the soundness of my back, nor even my idealism untarnished. In their place, however, I gained an aching understanding of the very real world. I learned, sadly, that people who have been exploited, even Japanese Americans with whom I shared a common history, are not immune to exploiting others in turn. And most importantly, I learned that an individual can count. One person can make a difference. I knew now how strenuous it was to pick strawberries. I saw how hard the Mexican workers labored. Because I spoke up, I made the difference between their being paid the money they had worked so hard to earn and their being taken advantage of. My back hurt, and there was a crack in my innocence, but deep inside, I felt good.

Despite the blemish on my idealism from the day in the strawberry field, I still reacted to the photos of each new disaster on the front page of the newspaper. Perhaps it was because of my memory of Daddy in camp, actively throwing himself into the work of the community. Perhaps it was because of the warm, good feeling I got by helping to make a difference. Maybe it was because it was just good fun working with kindred people. Whatever the reason, volunteerism became a part of my life. I began doing a lot of work with the Junior Red Cross. Every report of a flood or a tornado or a firestorm sent me hurrying to the Red Cross headquarters on Vermont Avenue not very far from home, where I stuffed informational packets, first aid kits, and relief packages.

It was the biggest rage of 1952. Everybody at school was wearing them, socks in luminous chartreuse or bright fluorescent pink. It was the "cool" way to dress. They turned the ankles into eye-riveting moving neons. I had to be "with it," too. Half of my sock collection was in the new fluorescent colors. Mama complained of almost going blind every time she did my laundry.

To a teenager, a sense of belonging and being accepted, of being a member of an "in" group, is the most intensely important thing in life. And to look cool was vital. I had my socks fluorescent. I had my shoes—blue suede, like Elvis. And for dressing up, I had my charcoal gray suit with a pink shirt. When I could filch one, I would even add a pink carnation. For me, living with the muted memory of the camps, then the feeling of being a passionate outsider to the exciting life of the barrio, to be "in" became a great teenage compulsion.

Working with the Junior Red Cross, both at the headquarters and at school, buttressed my idealism and fulfilled my need to be a part of something larger. It also fed another hunger—the prospect of popularity. When I was elected president of the Junior Red Cross at Mt. Vernon Junior High, the event sparked the hope of another possibility. This would be a good stepping-stone to an office in the student cabinet.

When I mentioned this idea at the dinner table, Daddy thought my plan to seek a higher student office was great. He suggested, however, that before I shared my goal with friends, I help others get elected to office. So I got behind my friend Everett Van Vlear's campaign to become boys' athletic commissioner. Daddy bought the poster board, and I made an artfully designed poster for Everett. I buttonholed everyone and urged them to vote for Everett. At the assembly where candidates made their speeches, Everett did well. He spoke thoughtfully and persuasively. But when his opponent, a pleasant enough kid, spoke, he started playing musical spoons, utensils that he held between his fingers and rhythmically slapped against his thighs, elbows, and even against his head. He played them quite cleverly, and the audience cheered with delight. Against those syncopated spoons, Everett didn't have a chance. He suffered a landslide defeat.

The next semester I ran for health commissioner and gave away souvenir Red Cross buttons. My opponent didn't give anything away, so I won by a landslide.

It was a strange and wonderful feeling accepting congratulations after the election. Strange because the campaign was fun. I always felt that congratulations should come after a hard struggle, after much sweat and strain, after overcoming some kind of adversity. My campaign was full of laughter and whoopee with a lot of friends. Most of all, I thought it was strange to be congratulated for getting to do what I wanted to do. But at the same time, I made a surprising self-discovery. I was becoming addicted to this postelection wave of congratulations. It felt great. And I wanted to feel it again. As health commissioner, I was now on the student cabinet. Any other office would be merely a lateral move. The only office left for a vertical move was student body president.

As the end of the semester approached, and the time neared for the candidates for student body offices to declare themselves, it looked as though the only other likely person to run for student body president was my friend and the current boys' vice president, Lee Young. I used to kid him by calling him my Chinese friend because of his name. He was actually black, and his full name was Leonidas Young, Jr. Lee had an easy, engaging personality, and he was very popular, making him tough competition.

Sure enough, on the day of filing as candidates, Lee declared for student body president. Why did it have to be a good friend? Why couldn't someone I didn't like be an opponent? It would make it so much easier, I thought to myself as I filed my papers.

Nevertheless, as the student photographer from the journalism class snapped pictures, I shook hands with Lee and said with a bright smile, "Lee is a good friend of mine. But politics makes strange bedfellows." The journalism students immediately scribbled my unoriginal quote into their notebooks. Lee, ever the swift politician, nimbly countered with, "Whatever George's position may be, I am not getting into bed with anyone." The journalism students eagerly jotted down that quote. The campaign was off and running.

Lee was a great wit and clever storyteller. I noticed he was campaigning on his personality. I had my secret weapon, though. Of course, I couldn't use my Red Cross buttons again. But Daddy could get me little hard candies at wholesale. So as I campaigned, the students discovered that every one of my handshakes had a little sweet something in it.

The real showdown was at the assembly. I wrote and rewrote my speech. I wondered what Lee would do with his. Surely he wouldn't stoop to the level of playing musical spoons. Then it hit me like a lightning bolt. Lee's father was a musician with the Duke Ellington Band! And I didn't know if Lee himself played any musical instrument. Or if he did, would he? Certainly, I wouldn't play the piano or blow the bugle during my speech. I wouldn't go that low. Besides, I wasn't that good. My playing would probably lose me votes. But did Lee have a secret instrument? That became my big worry.

When Daddy asked me, "How's your campaign speech coming along?" my answer was, "I don't know what Lee's going to play." Daddy sat down and said to me, "Don't worry about Lee. He's a good boy, and so are you. What you have to do is to tell the other students who you are, what you stand for, and why you want to serve as student body president. And tell them that you will do the best you can. That's all. Then let the students decide." I knew he was right. I decided to go with his advice. I wasn't going to worry about Lee's secret weapon anymore.

On the day of the assembly, the auditorium was abuzz with excitement. There was a long list of offices with an even longer list of candidates vying for the various positions. The only two candidates for student body president spoke last. Because speeches were assigned in alphabetical order, I spoke first. I spoke concisely, sincerely, and perhaps a bit dramatically. Then I sat down. I thought I did well. The applause was enthusiastic.

Then Lee spoke. The anxiety that I thought I had suppressed came prickling up uncontrollably. Would he play a musical instrument? Maybe even sing? Perhaps dance? Or play musical spoons?

Lee began by telling a joke. There was light laughter. When was he going to play his secret saxophone? I worried. Then he told a funny story. More laughter. He was going to sing next, I was convinced. Then he told another joke. Now he's going to start dancing, I thought. He told another story. He must have Duke Ellington himself in the audience, and he was going to introduce him from the stage, I anguished. Then he concluded and sat down. That was it. I almost felt cheated. All Lee did was tell funny stories. And the audience enjoyed it. So that was his ace in the hole, and now it was up to the voters.

When the vote was all counted, we were told that it was very close. Close, but I had won. I was elected student body president of Mt. Vernon Junior High School.

My senior semester, like all senior semesters, was heady and memorable and flew by much too fast. I have memories of presiding over the student cabinet, of dances with girls wearing puffy poodle hairdos and full skirts with layers of stiff petticoats underneath, of singers like Johnny Ray and his hit song "The Little White Cloud That Cried," and Joni James and her "Teach Me Tonight." Before we knew it, graduation was upon us. High school was waiting for us next.

The capper of those three years at Mt. Vernon was the awards assembly. I was recognized for academic and service achievements with the coveted American Legion Award. As honored as I felt, I didn't realize at the time how much this recognition meant to Daddy and Mama. Only a little more than a decade before, the American Legion had been one of the most virulent voices for the removal of Japanese Americans from the West Coast. Now I was standing onstage as the outgoing student body president receiving the highest award given to a member of the graduating class—from that same organization, the American Legion.

7

To Be or Not to Be

LOS ANGELES HIGH SCHOOL HAD A STRONG SENSE OF HISTORY AND tradition. Founded in 1873, it was the oldest high school in the city, with a distinguished alumni that includes prominent business, civic, and cultural leaders. The building's imposing English Tudor architecture made a statement of solidity and establishment. A stately clock tower chimed melodiously on the hour. The overall look was more like an Ivy League college campus than a high school. The school was one of the primary reasons that Daddy and Mama sacrificed so much to buy our house. They were realizing another of their dreams. Their son was now a student at L.A. High.

I was excited, too, but, at the same time not just a little discomfited. I was sixteen now. The move from Mt. Vernon to L.A. High symbolized matriculation into adulthood. There were decisions to be made. A direction for my course of study had to be determined.

I was acutely aware of my parents' dreams—of their hopes for their children's futures. But I also had the growing sense that Daddy's and Mama's hopes were becoming transformed into expectations. They expected us to go to a university—

ideally a distinguished one—then to enter a profession, and then to be "successful." Quite typical, really. But I felt the weight of their all-too-typical aspirations. I was their oldest son. At Mt. Vernon, I had fulfilled some of their dreams, but that only heightened their expectations—and increased their sacrifices. I was grateful for their investment in us kids. I knew keenly how hard they worked and how much they gave up for us. But that awareness only intensified my inner conflict. I harbored my own secret aspiration. I wanted to be an actor.

What is this fascination with acting that starts from childhood and by steady degrees grows into passion? Henry and I grew up only a year apart, in the same family with the same shaping influences. Yet we were so different. Henry was a sports nut, and things mechanical fascinated him. But Henry had no interest in the arts, literature, or the theater, while I had little interest in any of his activities.

To me, the theater was life, its artists, the chroniclers of human history. By my midteens, I had already memorized a good number of the famous soliloquies from the plays of Shakespeare. But whenever I began reciting "To be or not to be" to Reiko, this ungrateful and unappreciative audience accused me of bothering her. "Mama," she'd yell, "he's starting his 'To be or not to be' at me again. Make him quit!" Pearls to swines.

I saw traveling Broadway plays for free by ushering at the old Biltmore Theater downtown. I saved to go to the movies as often as I could. Actors personified for me the whole of theater, movies, and the new rage, television. They were demigods—glamorous, powerful, witty, and heroic. It was crazy of me even to think of wanting to be one. Such a wild, farfetched fantasy. But I thought it anyway—without giving voice to my covert yearning.

Daddy knew of my love of the theater and actors, and he approved.

"Everyone should have culture in their lives," he observed. "It enriches them."

But I knew he didn't mean culture as a career choice. He

meant it as a hobby. As my life's work, he envisioned a "serious" profession, one that would require a college degree. I knew that. And I didn't want to disappoint Daddy and Mama. Despite my own hidden dream, in spite of the inner conflict, I chose a college preparatory course of study at L.A. High.

Daddy sold the grocery store on Western Avenue and then went into selling real estate. Japanese Americans were now recovering from the internment years and buying homes and businesses. Some were even making investments. It was an opportune time for Daddy's new business move.

With the sale of the grocery, Henry and I lost our after-school jobs as stock boys helping out at the store. In that job, Henry was the better worker. I spent a lot of time back in the stock room reading newspapers and magazines—but when the boss is your dad, the work rules get a bit relaxed. Now, we had to get real jobs.

I found a job as a temporary stock boy at Orbach's. This was a stylish new department store on the Miracle Mile, a retail stretch of Wilshire Boulevard lined with sleek, streamlined art deco buildings. It was conveniently only a couple of miles from L.A. High and an easy bike ride away. I now had a real job that paid real money and required real work.

But I found nonpaid volunteer work much more satisfying. My work with the Junior Red Cross continued at L.A. High. We organized drives to collect used clothing and canned foods to aid people struck by disasters. We gathered volunteers to help stuff and pack the goods at the headquarters on Vermont Avenue. But most of all, I remember the fun and camaraderie of these activities. I was elected president of the Junior Red Cross chapter at L.A. High and, subsequently, chairman of the Western Regional Council, an assembly of all the Junior Red Cross chapters in western Los Angeles. This service with the Junior Red Cross presented me with an unforgettable experience—my first air travel—to Colorado Springs, Colorado, to attend the Junior Red Cross Leadership Training Camp.

* * *

Unconsciously I pulled up on the armrest, as if to help lift the trembling plane off the runway. I peeked out the porthole-like window at the swiftly rushing scenery that seemed to be descending. It was an exhilarating feeling tightly laced with anxiety. Within seconds, the rushing shifted to a lifting sensation. The illusion of descent became clear ascent, and the view from the window turned into a quickly miniaturizing landscape far down below. The row of giant oil tanks in the beach city of El Segundo now looked like small bolts holding down the coastline. I was flying. For the first time in my life, I was off the planet earth.

I tentatively thumped the floor with my foot. It was firm. It felt secure. But it sounded hollow. We had thousands of feet beneath that thin, light floor. My sweaty hands gripped the armrest firmly.

"First time flying?" A portly businessman sitting next to me smiled.

"Yes. I guess it shows," I responded. "I'm loving it, though. I think it's great."

"Isn't it amazing," he chortled. "I flew a bomber in the Pacific during the war, and here I am still flying. This time on business. Progress in aeronautics is amazing."

Then, without any indication of interest on my part, he proceeded to tell me how amazing he thought this progress had been.

The man was a garrulous raconteur who rambled on and on to a captive audience tightly strapped in the seat. I kept an obliging but nervous smile on my face. I soon discovered that his favorite topic was his wartime air exploits. My smile froze in place, then slowly faded. He continued regaling me with his adventures. It was nerve-racking enough flying for the first time. Of all passengers on this full flight, why did I have to get for my seatmate an ex-bomber pilot who loved talking about bombarding Japanese?

Then, out of the clear blue, he said, "I suppose you were in one of those Japanese camps here during the war."

I gripped my armrest—gripped it hard to restrain my welling

emotion. To him, I thought, I'm probably still the same as those enemies he fought in the war. I felt like ignoring him and looked out the window. Immediately, the memory of Mrs. Rugen, my fourth-grade teacher who called me Jap, came rushing back into my mind. No, I won't look away this time. I will confront him.

With a tight smile, I turned to him slowly. As cool and as controlled as I could be, I answered, "Yes, I grew up in an internment camp in Arkansas. But, as a matter of fact, it was an American camp for American citizens of Japanese ancestry." I got it out. It felt good.

He sighed and looked down, shaking his head. "A terrible thing. A terrible thing," he said, and sat there, silent for the first time, only shaking his head. I was puzzled. What did he think was terrible?

"It was a terrible thing that was done," he began slowly. "You know, during a war people do crazy things. One of my neighbors in Denver is a Nisei—Jack Ishihara. Sweetest guy you could know. Veteran of the war in Europe. Fought for old Uncle Sam while his family was behind barbed wire. Terrible thing. Terrible." He sat there, mutely shaking his head.

He knew. He understood. He wasn't the man I had girded myself against. Suddenly, my unclenched muscles let loose a flood of emotions. I excused myself to go to the lavatory. I locked the door, and the pressure broke. Uncontrollably, the tears began to flow. There are people who know about us. There are people who understand. It took me some time to regain my composure. Then I washed my face and returned to my seat. The nerves had eased. I felt much lighter. Even the flight seemed smoother.

My fighter pilot seatmate, too, was back in his chatty mode.

"Did you know that the two most critical points in flying are the takeoff and then the landing?" he asked.

Before I could answer his question, he was saying, "The landing is actually the tougher of the two." Automatically, my fingers gripped the armrest again. I braced my foot. We were now descending.

He nattered on and on about the various dangers involved in the landing process—wind shears, updrafts, downdrafts, atmospheric instability, and other ominous-sounding pilot jargon —as my grip got sweatier. The plane dipped. Then violently, it jounced and trembled.

"Whoops," the man exclaimed, as my stomach seemed to surge up into my throat. But he seemed to take all of the turbulence in stride. I was a tight ball of nerves as the tarmac of Denver's Stapleton Airport began rushing up at us. We could hear and feel the vibrations of the landing wheels reaching out for the ground. A hard bounce, and, for just a moment, the wheels touched solid earth, then again, and again. Then we were rolling on the runway. The entire plane burst out in relieved applause.

I grinned at my loquacious seatmate as we joined in the clapping. But my applause was not only for the pilot of this aircraft. It was also an appreciative hand for the lesson my fighter pilot seatmate had unwittingly taught me. Amazing advances may have been made in aeronautics, but remarkable progress was being made in people as well.

Colorado Springs was a glorious setting for a group of young student leaders to gather and commune—with each other and with nature. The air was crisp and stimulating; ancient cedar trees rose up into the heavens. The exchange of ideas was animated and the participants' optimism soaring. Our anthem, written by a black songsmith, Evelyn Burwell, said it all:

> In hearts too young for enmity,
> there lies the way to make men free.
> When childish friendships are worldwide,
> new ages will be glorified.
> Let child love child and
> wars will cease.

We were going to change the world. The older generation had despoiled everything with its wars, pollution, and greed. We were the ones with the ideas, the energy, and most of all, the will to make things better. I returned to Los Angeles fired up.

Idealism can have a grim underside. Youthful idealism especially is vulnerable to it. Its shine can become dulled by arrogance, an insidious self-righteousness. To this day, I deeply regret a painful conversation I had with Daddy on arriving home from Colorado Springs. I want to wish it away somehow.

It was after dinner, and everyone else had left the table. Only Daddy and I remained sipping tea. He wanted to know all about my Colorado experience. I could sense his pride in my exuberant recounting of my summer adventures. His son was fulfilling more of his expectations.

I told him about our discussion sessions, the campfire singing at night, the beauty of the scenery, the dynamism of the city of Denver, and I told him about the terror and exhilaration of my first air travel experience. Then I shared with him the insight I had gained from my fighter pilot seatmate. I said to him, "People change, Daddy. This man was bombing Japanese during the war, and now he's living next to a Japanese American. He understands the distinction, and he knows that what was done to us was wrong."

And then I asked pointedly, "Daddy, why did we go to camp? Why did you comply with what was fundamentally wrong? Why did you take us to those camps?"

He thought silently for a moment forming his response, then he answered, "You have to know what it was like back then. All the forces were against us. I had you kids to consider."

"But it was wrong, Daddy," I interrupted. "By your going, you acquiesced to the wrong. You passively consented."

He gazed at his teacup and took a sip. "Then what is it you think I should have done?" he asked calmly.

"I would have protested. It was wrong—period! And the decent Americans knew it. With an appeal to the consciences of good people, I know it could have been stopped." Then I added vehemently, "The trouble with the Japanese is, we're too passive. We don't speak up. We can't raise our voices. I would have protested!"

Daddy sat there listening to my gush of passion. When I finished, he remained silent. Then, with a patient tone that angered me even more, he said, "The circumstances were different then. It was a very different time. You'll understand one of these days."

"When I grow up? Is that what you're suggesting?" I retorted heatedly. "Well, I am grown up now. And I do understand a lot. I understand that you took us like sheep to slaughter into a barbed wire prison!"

Daddy was quiet for a long time. He stared at his teacup and took a sip. Then he said with melancholic calm, "Maybe you're right." Then he got up and went into his bedroom.

I was a young Japanese American who could speak up. I could speak up righteously—and foolishly. It still pains me today to think of that impetuous boy's outspoken bluntness. His arrogance inflicted on his father, who knew the anguish of those dark internment years so much more keenly than that boy could ever understand, was a second torment. My father suffered in silence the self-righteous condemnation from the son in whom he took so much pride—in whom he held so much hope. For both of us, Rohwer and Tule Lake were still not history.

L.A. High had many clubs—the Drama Club, Glee Club, Stamp Club, Chess Club, and a host of others. These were hobby clubs, and anyone who was interested could join them. I was a member of the Drama Club and the Glee Club.

Then there were the elite clubs—the Barons, Nobles, and Cardinals. The most popular guys, the brightest guys, and the best athletes belonged to them. Just by virtue of their club memberships, they became envied members of the select "in" crowd of L.A. High.

Some of my friends were members of these clubs. But how one became a member was a mystery to me. When I asked anyone, the only answer I got was a vague and evasive, "You have to be invited." How the invitation was extended or by whom was never explained. It was shrouded in secrecy. But it wasn't long before it dawned on me that an invitation would never be forthcoming to me. These clubs were all white. I became further aware of the fact that the Cardinals was all Jewish and that the Barons and the Nobles were white Anglo-Saxon Protestants—that stinging acronym, WASP.

Although I felt very much a part of L.A. High, I was becoming conscious of the subtle distinctions that were drawn in certain sectors in the life of the school.

I sang with the Glee Club and performed with it at student assemblies. But when Lerner and Loewe's *Brigadoon* was announced as the big musical production of the school year, I was made acutely aware of the Scottish locale of the play. Casting, it was emphasized, would be based on creating the look of authenticity. I may have thought I had talent, but I knew I didn't look like a Scotsman. I didn't bother auditioning.

Brigadoon was a radiant production, and the two guys who played the leads, Jerry Cottone and Dennis Daily, were terrific. They sang entrancingly and danced superbly. They and the entire company transported me to the misty, mystical Scottish highland village of Brigadoon. They were friends and classmates, and still they were able to work their magic on me. And they did something else. They enlivened in me again my suppressed theatrical yearnings. It would be wonderful to be an actor—to be the creator of all this magic. That dream gnawed at my insides.

But I was a math-science student and got good grades. I was on the track team during the spring semesters and ran cross-country in the fall. I busied myself with student service activities and ignored my growing awareness of the invisible but nevertheless clear lines of distinction that existed around me. I held in check my personal aspiration and applied myself to fulfilling Daddy's and Mama's expectations of me. I studied hard to be accepted by a great university.

* * *

There are certain moments in a movie that seem to have resonance directly for one's own life. Marlon Brando in *On the Waterfront* struck me profoundly.

I knew nothing about the life of a longshoreman. The New Jersey waterfront was another country to me, and the drama of a power struggle in the labor movement was a totally new revelation. Yet, the movie was a shatteringly personal experience.

The Brando character, Terry Malloy, had been a promising young prize fighter. He knew he was good. His dream was to win the title. But because of his brother Charlie's ties to the mob-run labor organization, because he loved his brother, because he asked him to, Terry Malloy compromised himself and took a dive. He gave up a fight to an opponent he knew he could beat. And that one compromise became the turning point that haunted the rest of his life. He had a cushy position with the labor organization now. His brother became ensconced in a position of power. Life was good. Yet, somehow it was hollow.

Brando's famous scene in the backseat of the car with his brother Charlie was wrenching. Still remembering that long-ago event, Terry intones, "I did it for you, Charlie. I did it for you." He gave up his dream for his brother, and life since had become blandly purposeless. Then the devastating lament, "I could've been a contender. I could've been somebody." It was a powerful scene that resonated directly through to me. "I could've been a contender. I could've been somebody." Those phrases haunted me long after the movie was over.

The clock tower's mellifluous bells marked the hours, the days, and, before we knew it, the years at L.A. High. Soon, the carillon was pealing the ebbing days of our senior year.

Tommy Wolver, a star basketball player, was student body president. I was Senior Board president. That fall, the L.A. High basketball team placed in the championship games, and Tommy was a leading player on our team. Our cross-country team ranked lowest in our league, and the best that could be said of me as a runner was that I was tenacious; I never gave up.

Some people may read parallels between Tommy Wolver's and my athletic exploits with our offices in student government. I prefer to think that Tommy ran for student body president and won. I ran for Senior Board president and I won.

The big suspense, the most urgent concern of the senior year was our acceptance by the colleges of our choice. It was on everybody's mind. The anxiety was palpable.

I had decided to study architecture. It was an interest of mine that was acceptable to my parents. One of the great schools of architecture was at the University of California at Berkeley. Daddy was delighted and urged me to send my application there. The expectations now were becoming sharply focused. As it turned out, Tommy had applied for U.C. Berkeley as well. At least we had one anxiety that we could share—would we get in?

When I got home from school one afternoon, Mama was waiting for me expectantly. An envelope had arrived from the University of California's admissions office. I wanted to open it immediately. But Mama suggested that we wait until Daddy got home.

"We open envelope together," she said.

"But," I protested apprehensively, "we don't know what it says. What if it's a rejection?"

"We open envelope together," she repeated.

Mama knew how to heighten suspense more keenly, more cruelly than even Alfred Hitchcock.

It seemed an eternity before Daddy's big, green Buick finally drove up the driveway. I opened the front door and waved the envelope at him.

"The envelope from Berkeley's arrived!" I yelled.

"Did you get in?" he shouted back from the car.

"I don't know. We haven't opened it yet. Hurry in so we can."

The second Daddy stepped through the door, I ripped open the envelope. I was in! I had been accepted. It was an indescribable joy—and great relief! I would be entering Berkeley for the spring semester of 1956.

The next day, Mama went downtown to Little Tokyo and

bought a large chunk of fresh tuna, white radishes, cucumbers, and all the necessary fixings for a sashimi dinner—one of my favorite dishes. "College cafeteria not serve sashimi. Boarding house not serve sashimi. Eat lots sashimi before you go Berkeley," Mama insisted. She talked about Berkeley as if it were some foreign country that had never heard of Japanese restaurants.

I had to admit, though, that Mama's celebratory sashimi dinner was wonderful—the hot, steamy white rice with the cool, red meatiness of the raw tuna, perked up with a bit of wasabi, the pungent green mustard of Japan. It was delicious—and very special.

Mama, in her singular way, was sending her first son off to be a student of architecture at a great school. Her son would become a designer of buildings that would soar up into the heavens. She was letting go of her child now. Her boy, no longer little, was going off to the famous academic institution—a goal for which she and Daddy had worked so hard and so long. This was their dream; their expectations and aspirations were about to be realized.

I tasted that dream and their love in the warm, steaming bowl of rice. And I tasted it in the sting of the green wasabi as well. I was off to face newer, higher expectations.

8

Separate Dreams

RISING TALL OVER THE WOODED HILLSIDE CAMPUS OF THE UNIVERsity of California at Berkeley, lean and austere like an obelisk of learning, loomed the tower of the Campanile. This classic column of gray marble was the dominant architectural presence over an eclectic collection of buildings, ranging from the vine-covered Victorian of North Hall in its immediate shadows, to the neoclassic pomposity of Wheeler Hall to its south, to the darkly aging shake-wood Craftsman of Wurster Hall on the far north side of the campus. This rustic structure was in distinct contrast to the formality of the rest of the campus architecture and was an incongruous home for the School of Architecture.

Of all the structures on campus, the School of Architecture's was the least impressive. Its low-lying frame structure was almost hidden in the embrace of a dense forest of spruce trees surrounding it. The well-worn wood floor of its corridors creaked as the students hurried from lecture halls to drafting rooms, with their fishing tackle boxes filled with drafting tools and other equipment. The surface of the corridor walls was pocked with scars from a long history of displaying student project renderings, posters, "roommate wanted" notices, and

130

other such miscellanea. But it was also the most relaxed of all the buildings on campus—as comfortable and popular as a well-used common room in a dorm.

The first few days were dizzyingly hectic. Moving into my dorm at Collegian Hall. Registering for classes. Buying the books and drafting tools. Opening a bank account.

Occasionally, I bumped into friends from L.A. High, like Tommy Wolver. Yes, Tommy had made it here, too. It was good to see familiar faces in a bustling new environment, but they were quickly engulfed by the swirl of new people that came into my life. At Collegian Hall, my new friends were Joe Avakoff from faraway Alaska, unique also in that he was in the top scholastic percentile; Richard Clarke, who was on the G.I. Bill, a veteran of the Korean War with a full life experience behind him; and George Romero from Santa Rosa, working his way through school by "hashing" in the dorm dining room. Larry McCoy in my architectural design class told me he was "following in Dad's and Grandpa's footsteps," the third generation in his family to be attending Berkeley. These people, each in their own way, were impressive. I knew the competition was going to be intense here. And I was determined to meet the challenges.

Yet, whenever I was alone, whether studying in the great reading room of Doe Library or walking back from class through the cool glade along Strawberry Creek, a twinge of melancholy would creep into my mind—a bittersweet feeling of something ebbing away, a quiet sense of loss. As quickly as it came, the feeling would flee. The slightest of disturbances—a resonant echo from a chair being pushed back in the vast silence of the library, a cheery greeting from a friend hurrying to class through the glade—would chase it away like a frightened cat. But it would creep back again, quietly and persistently. I might hear Pat Boone singing "Love Letters in the Sand" on the radio, and I would be filled with a saccharine melancholy. I might pass a poster announcing a production of Shakespeare's *The Tempest* on campus, and I would be consumed by a wistful longing. No matter how much I tried, I could not keep suppressed this pining for a fading dream—my muted yearning to be an actor.

The first summer back from Berkeley, I got a job installing venetian blinds working for a small company run by an entrepreneurial young couple, George and Betty Filey, in West Los Angeles. I was their sole employee. A garage down an alley was the production factory, and their living room served as their office. But their customers came from the lush commercial buildings along Wilshire Boulevard or the beautiful homes in Santa Monica, Brentwood, and Beverly Hills. So, even with my summer job, there were chance occurrences that served as sparks to rekindle my yearning.

I remember keenly getting job assignments to install blinds in the homes of actors—no, not just actors, but movie stars—like Eva Marie Saint, Jeannette MacDonald, and Gene Raymond. I couldn't believe it. I was actually being sent to work in the private sanctums of these dream figures. As I put in the blinds, even their window frames seemed to cast a special, palpable enchantment. Eva Marie Saint would be gazing wistfully through these blinds I've hung, just as she did in *On the Waterfront*, I daydreamed. Jeannette MacDonald might be singing "Indian Love Call" as she gracefully opened my blinds, I fantasized—I was getting ridiculous.

I decided I had to cast this now-bothersome infatuation out of my system once and for all. I would do this, I resolved, by taking a summer-session acting class at Berkeley's sister campus, UCLA. Then, cleansed of this lunacy, I would return to Berkeley in the fall.

I sat down to dinner one evening and announced my decision to Daddy and Mama. With this class, I promised them, I would expiate myself of an adolescent fascination with acting. This was going to be my farewell gift to my teenage years, and then I could move on to serious adulthood and architecture.

After I made what I thought was a momentous announcement, all Daddy said was, "That's all right. But keep your day job. They should have evening classes at UCLA." There was no long, thoughtful discussion. No resistance. No opposition. I was taken aback. I had fully expected a veto. But Daddy didn't express any objections to my studying acting! So before he could have any time to rethink, I quickly followed through. I kept my venetian blind job, and I enrolled in my first formal acting class in the summer evening session at UCLA.

By the end of a day of lugging stacks of venetian blinds and drilling, screwing, and hanging them, I was physically exhausted. But somehow, I found renewed energy for my three-evenings-a-week class at UCLA. A quick dinner on the run and the prospect of the challenging acting class always wiped away the exhaustion, and I was reenergized.

I plunged headlong in the class—examining the tortured psyches of Eugene O'Neill and Tennessee Williams, then manifesting them in muscular contortions, anguished convulsions, and a good, resounding, cathartic howl. The class wallowed luxuriantly in emotions. It was wonderful. I was reveling in this final present to my teens. I didn't know that this summer was to hold in store for me an even greater surprise gift—a real, paying job in a movie.

I got home from class one night, spent but exhilarated. It had been another full day and night. Daddy was in the living room reading the Japanese community paper, the *Rafu Shimpo*.

He looked up and said to me, "I circled an ad here in the *Rafu* that might interest you. Here, take a look at it."

He pulled out a sheet from the English section and handed it to me. There, near the bottom of the page, was a big pencil circle around an ad that began, "Casting for voices to dub film." It gave no details other than a name and a telephone number to call. But that was all I needed. I tore out the ad and folded it into my wallet.

"Thanks, Daddy," I said. "I'll check it out first thing tomorrow morning."

What I found out was that a film, imported from Japan by an independent Hollywood company called King Brothers Productions, was to be dubbed onto English from the original Japanese for the American audience. It was a science fiction piece about a gigantic prehistoric flying monster, brought back to life after some millennia of hibernation by modern-day radiation, which terrorizes the people of contemporary Tokyo. The title of this preposterous epic was *Rodan*, the name of the monstrous creature. But even more unbelievably, when I auditioned, I was cast! The movie was the most farfetched of science fictions, but my brief adventure with giving English voice to this interlingual fantasy epic was to be almost as bizarre.

I was making more money installing blinds than I would be dubbing *Rodan*. I knew also that I would be aggravating George Filey's business during his busiest summer period. Yet, I begged George to let me off for the three days required for the movie work. I promised eternal gratitude to him if he would. He didn't question my rationality. He didn't grouse about the inconvenience to his business. I guess he understood who I was. He gave me those three days off without a hassle, and to this day, I am grateful to George Filey for his indulgence of an aspiring actor's madness.

Daddy noted dryly, on the other hand, that I was doing scenes from O'Neill and Williams and Arthur Miller at UCLA at night. "Why would you want to take off from a well-paying job during the day and great theater literature at one of the finest universities in America in the evenings to rant and rave in a monster movie?" He still didn't understand his son. Didn't he know that I was actually getting paid to do a real movie inside a genuine Hollywood soundstage?

That soundstage was on the lot of the legendary Metro-Goldwyn-Mayer Studio in Culver City—one of the studios that I had peered into so longingly as a youngster on those Sunday afternoon drives long ago. Now, I was checking in with the guard at the gate, actually finding my name on the list on his clipboard and being waved through as if this were the most normal of occurrences.

What was quite abnormal, in fact downright surreal, were the three days I spent on that soundstage. The two brothers of the King Brothers independent production company, producers of the epic, turned out to be awesome behemoths of men. Both brothers were colossally, unbelievably fat and almost always stayed seated. But when they got up and moved, the deep, labored wheezing sounds they made were more like some primeval animal noises than human panting.

They perspired profusely. When they reached up to their brows with a damp handkerchief that they always carried in their hands, they grunted like irritated beasts. They completed the image with gargantuan black cigars that protruded out of each of their mouths like some phallic prods. They spoke very little. They just sat in the gloom at the back of the darkened recording studio snorting and grunting.

There were four actors, all cast for their varying vocal qualities—three males, mature, middle-aged, and youthful, and one female. We were each assigned eight or nine different characters to do. With oversized earphones that made us look like science fiction characters ourselves, we stared up at a gigantic screen on a wall across which passed silent images: the prehistoric monstrosity, Rodan, soundlessly swooping down on panicked crowds, fleeing noiselessly; close-ups of bug-eyed faces in mute, open-mouthed terror; shots of sober-faced officials gravely moving their wordless lips. We listened for three clicks in our earphones, which were coordinated with a flickery line that danced across the screen. The third click sounded just as the flickery line reached the right side of the screen, and that was our cue to speak the line—when the lips started moving or the chest heaved for the gasp. The sounds we uttered had to match the movement on the screen precisely, or else the lips would continue moving silently or our dialogue would persist over a closed-mouth face.

The director was a big man also, but, in contrast to the King brothers, he was merely husky. He also chewed a cigar, but, again in proportion to his bosses, his was not outsized—just big. Unlike the King brothers, however, the director was always in motion. He kept jumping up from his seat as if he sat on springs—to change a word here or rewrite a line of dialogue that didn't seem to work there. He paced about chewing his cigar, searching for inspiration. But most of all, he was constantly jumping up to run to the portable telephone that was set up to the side of the recording stage to check with his bookie. He was on that phone almost every fifteen minutes. He would hang up, more often shaking a fist in angry frustration but sometimes grinning broadly, his cigar dancing up and down in his clenched teeth.

The joy for me in this unusual dramatis personae was in meeting and working with Keye Luke, a distinguished Chinese-American actor whom I had grown up watching in such films as *The Good Earth* and *Keys to the Kingdom,* and as Charlie Chan's obedient number-one son. Keye was the very personification of professionalism, dignity, and good humor. His lip-syncing was crisp and precise, and he managed to find a unique voice for each character he was assigned. During the breaks, he was warm and friendly. He was my anchor of sanity, the stabilizing personality in a strange environment, which looked to my novice eyes like some manic cartoon of Hollywood.

I watched Keye work, and I learned from him to individualize my characters. As the image of the bright young scientist on the screen silently moved his lips, I studied the movements closely, just as Keye would; I gave him an astute, analytical voice. As the young honeymooner seemed to whisper sweet nothings into his bride's ear, I gave him audible passion in sync with his heavy breathing. As the image of the man terrorized by the enraged monster mutely opened his mouth, I gave him a series of blood-curdling screams that matched every tremble of his tonsils. With earphones over my head and intensely focused on the silent images, I stuttered, cried, pontificated, and shrieked. No, this was not some madman's asylum. It really was the modern-day equivalent of the *benshi,* the men who narrated the Japanese films I remembered from my boyhood back in the internment camps. I thought, I've got to tell Daddy about this connection.

At the end of the third and final day of work on the dubbing, Keye gave me a hearty congratulatory handshake and a slap on the back. "Fine work, George. You make me proud," he said, smiling broadly.

I was hoarse from all the screaming I'd done, but somehow I was able to croak out, "It was really a treat working with you, Mr. Luke. Thank you very much."

The director embraced me in a tight bear hug that reeked of his big, black cigar. Then he held me by my shoulders at arm's length and beamed at me, wiggling his cigar up and down. I guessed that this silent accolade from a man who had spent the last three days searching for just the perfect word for each scene was his expression of the epitome of acclaims—praise beyond words.

I hurried for the exit before I could receive whatever form of acknowledgment for my work the King brothers might make. I was relieved to see that they had no intention of getting up. From their regally ensconced positions, they waved their giant cigars in unison and growled out, "Good work, kid. Thanks."

My enchanted summer was over before I knew it. My dreams had been fulfilled beyond my expectations. I had taken acting lessons at UCLA. I had the serendipitous joy of working on a real movie in a recording studio at the fabled M-G-M studios and getting paid for it to boot. My youthful passion had been indulged. Daddy and Mama believed that I had finally gotten the acting bug out of my system. Now I had promises to keep, my word to honor. I returned to Berkeley determined to become a great architect.

The more I studied architecture, however, the greater became my quandary. Because, perhaps of all the arts, the work of an architect has the largest, weightiest, most lasting consequence. A building is a dominating presence in society that can enhance the quality of life, or it can degrade it profoundly. I felt keenly the enormity of that accountability. I was only too aware of irresponsible architecture, which seemed to surround and diminish us.

And I learned just how much inspired architecture could contribute to the enrichment and health of a people.

My architectural hero is Frank Lloyd Wright. His philosophy of organic architecture is based on the notion of harmony—the balance between people, structure, and nature. The architect's task is to serve that balance. Wright manifested his philosophy in an astonishingly wide variety of environments, from the urban setting of Los Angeles with the Hollyhock House, to the arid desert of Arizona with Taliesen West, to the tumbling river and lush forest of Pennsylvania with Fallingwater.

The one seeming violation of Wright's notion of harmony with the environment is in probably his most visited work, the Guggenheim Museum in New York City. This gracefully spiraling white edifice is the elegant individualist on the gray row of ennui that lines Fifth Avenue. It is the hallmark of Wright's genius. A master knows when and how to break the rules. To harmonize with the genteel mediocrities that align themselves along Fifth Avenue would be polite but, like so many polite people, deathly dull. The Guggenheim is hardly that. It is a gloriously iconoclastic work of art proudly standing alone like the sculptural promontory of an urban rock outcropping overlooking the great natural expanse of Central Park. It is an extraordinary edifice that defines and ennobles the land—as does its master builder.

I met Frank Lloyd Wright the semester I returned to Berkeley. He was to be the guest lecturer at a special evening event. There was much anticipation of the great man's visit. On the night of his address, the sizable lecture hall was completely packed. I arrived early and was comfortably set in a good seat in the center section of the hall. Architecture students were supposed to have had priority seating, but many arriving later couldn't even get in. There was confusion and much pushing and shoving. People were still trying to squeeze into the aisles when the hour arrived.

Suddenly, with no introductories, the door to the speakers stage banged open, and in swept a figure dressed completely in black—a black wide-brimmed hat, a voluminous black overcoat flung over the shoulders like a cape, and a loose, old-fashioned black suit. He carried a black cane, but his brisk, firm steps immediately signaled that it was an unnecessary but dramatic prop. From under his black hat, a full mane of snow-white hair cascaded down to his shoulders. Frank Lloyd Wright had arrived. This was one of the most spectacularly theatrical entrances I had ever witnessed.

Wright was well into his eighties, but he was a forceful, passionate, absolutely mesmerizing speaker. He spoke eloquently on his ideas of organic architecture. He railed against the mediocrity he had to fight. And he was impassioned about the need for an architect's total commitment to a project. When he finished speaking, he responded rather imperiously to a few questions from the audience, and then, as abruptly as he had entered, he swept out. Without ceremony. Frank Lloyd Wright was there one moment, and then he was gone. There was a stunned silence before the assemblage broke out in thunderous standing ovation to an empty stage. He had left a powerful impression. As Wright the architect had graced the land with his work, he as a man singularly personified all that it took to be a great architect.

I was profoundly inspired by Frank Lloyd Wright. He gave me renewed understanding of the importance of architecture. I was impressed by his strength and passionate dedication to his vision of the world. And I was troubled by his strong advocacy of a total commitment to architecture.

Frank Lloyd Wright's words haunted me the rest of that year. I would hear echoes of Wright in the speeches of professors. "An architect designs for individuals, but an architect's design also speaks of his time," I remember one saying, and I would think of the responsibility an architect carries. I would roam about the Berkeley hills and find buildings by the great Bernard Maybeck. His complex craftsmanship, the intricate details in his work, and the quiet delight they evoked only reminded me of the unreserved dedication such artistry demanded. The more I exposed myself to the great achievements of architecture, the more conscious I became of my divided commitment. I could imagine myself ten years later working as an architect —suppressing a nagging regret. I couldn't make a complete and unreserved commitment to architecture.

It was Easter vacation, 1957, and I was back home in Los Angeles. On my agenda for this brief holiday at home was a serious talk with Daddy. But I felt ill at ease. I couldn't find the words, or the right occasion to say what I wanted. I couldn't do it at the dinner table. Too many people. I couldn't do it when Daddy was relaxing with the papers after a hard day at the office. He had been investing in hotels and apartments lately, and the stress on him was considerable; he deserved to unwind. The short holiday week would be over soon, and I would have to be heading back to Berkeley. I felt the anxiety of time slipping away. Would I be able to have my discussion with Daddy before I had to go back?

One relaxation Daddy enjoyed was to water the back lawn in the nocturnal calm of late evening. He would sit on the steps of the back porch gazing up at the night sky as he held the hose spraying a soft mist over the lawn. One evening, I spied him from the kitchen window sitting there alone. I watched this solitary figure for a long time. This man who had worked so hard at so many jobs for his children, this father who gave so much to us and who wanted so much from us. As I watched him gazing up at the stars, I felt I knew what he must have been dreaming about. And I ached over what I had to tell him.

I slipped out of the house and sat beside him. The spring night air was soft and balmy.

"Daddy, I've been giving my future a lot of thought," I began tentatively, "and I'd like to share it with you." I told him of my love of architecture but also of my anguish over my divided feelings. I told him that I didn't want to live my life always harboring a regret. I told him that, ultimately, I had to live my own life, and although I was deeply grateful for all that he and

Mama had done for me, I had to be true to myself. Then I said in one breath something that I had never before said aloud.

"Daddy, I want to go to New York and study acting at the Actors Studio." Only the soft hiss of the nozzle as it sprayed the mist could be heard. "It's where Marlon Brando and James Dean studied," I explained earnestly. My father only stared out, still and silent. "Daddy, I want to be an actor."

My father gazed down at the lawn pensively and continued watering in silence. All I could hear was the soft sound of the mist. A quiet heartache tightened around me. I knew the pain I was causing him. Then Daddy spoke, and I was taken aback. He said thoughtfully, "I knew that we would eventually be having this discussion." He had expected this! Such a revelation was the last thing I had anticipated. He told me in his measured words that he had sensed my distress and that he was troubled by it. He said that what he and Mama wanted was for their children to be happy. Then he said the words for which I had steeled myself.

"You love acting, and you think becoming an actor will give you happiness. All you know, though, is the glamour you see on stage and on screen. But you don't know the real difficulties of making a living as an actor. There's no security. There's no continuity. And as a Japanese, the kinds of roles available to you will be limited. The truth is, there's no dignity in that kind of life. We want you to be happy. But we don't think you'll be happy with the kind of life an actor has to live."

I said to Daddy that I knew there were no guarantees for an actor. But I said that what was guaranteed for me as an architect, no matter how successful I might become, was a lifetime of needling regrets. With impassioned words I said to my father that I would be going into this with my eyes wide open, that I was mindful of all his concerns, but that I was strong and I was determined and that I would not disappoint him. I asked him to have the same faith in my decision to pursue acting as he had in me as a student of architecture.

Daddy twisted the nozzle closed, and the fine hissing stopped. He turned and faced me directly.

"You're determined, are you?" he asked.

"Yes," I answered.

"Then do it," he said. "Do what you are so determined to do. Become the best that you can be. We want you to be happy."

I was stunned. But before I could respond, he continued, "But there is an alternative I want you to consider. The Actors Studio is a fine acting school. But when you finish there, they won't give you an academic degree. UCLA, as you know, has a distinguished school of theater. Study theater and acting there, and when you finish, they will grant you a bachelor's degree. It will make your future a bit less perilous. Your mother and I would like you to have that."

I didn't know what to say. I had been prepared to press my cause, to press it as vigorously as I could. But I hadn't expected Daddy to turn the tables by accepting my cause before advocating his. No wonder he was successful at selling real estate. He continued.

"You ought to know that New York is a tough place, a really merciless place, and a very expensive place. If you go to New York," he said, "you had better be prepared to do it on your own. On the other hand, if you study acting at UCLA, which your mother and I would prefer you to do, we would be happy to cover your expenses."

There it was. The deal. New York on my own at the Actors Studio, versus UCLA with subsidy. It was the classic offer you couldn't refuse. I was pitted against a professional deal maker. Daddy knew I was a practical kid; he knew I wouldn't be able to resist the subsidy. As Daddy might have put it, "It's a win-win deal."

I went back to Berkeley and began preparing to wrap up my three terms as a student of architecture. I also took out the transfer papers for my shift to UCLA. And I readied myself to become an actor.

TO
BE AN
ACTOR

9

Wild Luck

WILD CHOICES SOMETIMES PRODUCE IMPROBABLE RESULTS. IF MY determination to be an actor seemed quite unrealistic that summer of 1957, then what happened even before I began my first term at UCLA was like catching lightning in a bottle. I landed a plum role in the most prestigious live drama on television, *Playhouse 90*.

It began when I looked up an agent I had met on the M-G-M studio lot when I was dubbing *Rodan* the summer before. He was a Japanese American man named Fred Ishimoto. He had given me a card that I secreted away among the mementos of my theatrical dreams. I never thought I would actually be using it. But now I was going to be seriously pursuing an acting career, and I needed an agent. After all, I was now a student of acting in Hollywood.

Fred greeted me cordially in his Sunset Boulevard office. He revealed to me that he knew my father from his grocery store days, when Fred was a beer salesman. Fred genially told me that he had been impressed with what he saw of my performance on the dubbing stage. But when I asked if he would represent me in "the business," he said, "George, go to school and get your degree first. If anything should come up in the meantime, I'll be happy to let you know."

He sounded like my father, supportive but not wholly enthusiastic. At least he said he would call if anything right for me should come up. I concluded this was not yet the time for me to be shopping for an agent, so I went back to my old summer job with George Filey and his venetian blind business.

But about a month later Fred called.

"George, something interesting has come up that you might want to check out," he began. "It's a *Playhouse 90*."

He might have heard my gasp over the phone. *Playhouse 90* was the most critically acclaimed dramatic anthology series on television and my favorite show. I never missed it on Thursday nights.

"Now don't get all worked up over it," he cautioned. "There'll be a lot of competition for this one, but I thought the interview process might be a useful experience for you to have."

This is the man I wanted to represent me? Interviewing merely for the experience? Is that all the confidence in me he could muster? I was a little irritated, but I tried to hide it. He, after all, was the one who was opening this door to *Playhouse 90* for me.

"Tell me the place, and I'll be there," I responded. But inside myself, I thought, "I'll show you how I interview. I'm going to go out there and get that part. I'll show you."

The place was the sprawling, modern new facility at Fairfax and Beverly that CBS had grandly dubbed Television City. Giant, stark white blocks with black panels housed the multilevel studio facilities. Artfully placed high up on a corner of the largest white block was the familiar logo of the CBS eye. The offices were in the glass-walled block at the eastern end of the complex.

This was where the interviews were held. First I read for the casting director. Fred called a day later with their request for another reading. A callback, he termed it. I was pleased by the slightly obsequious tone he now had in his voice. This time I

146

was to read for the director, Herbert Hirschman—a name I remembered from some of the credits for *Playhouse 90*.

"Give him a good reading," Fred urged. "Even if you don't get this one, he'll be casting other projects. It'll be good to have him know what you can do."

Fred still didn't think I could actually get the part. That just fired my determination even more. I'd show him.

CBS had delivered a scene from the script for me to look over and prepare. My part was that of a young Japanese soldier returned to a devastated postwar Japan only to discover that his betrothed had fallen in love with an American G.I. When she is killed in an accidental fall from a bridge during a lovers' quarrel with the G.I., the embittered Japanese soldier becomes the prime suspect. The test scene was between my character and the defense attorney in a grim jail cell. It was a strong, dramatic scene, the kind I would have loved doing in my acting workshop. But I now was to read this scene before a distinguished director for *Playhouse 90*—just the thought was overwhelming. I hungered for the part, but my fervor was not unmixed with anxiety.

I was a bundle of nerves as I was ushered into a compact, sun-flooded conference room to read for Herbert Hirschman. The room was filled with many people, all of whom looked like assistants. None looked like a powerful director of *Playhouse 90*. Seated at the head of the table was a smiling elfin gentleman, spectacles perched on the tip of his nose and with a salt-and-pepper hairline that began near the back of his scalp. He was in shirtsleeves with his tie loosened. He looked like the jovial right arm to some high-ranking producer. It wasn't until a collegiate-looking young man referred to him as "Mr. Hirschman" that I realized he was the distinguished director.

We chatted briefly, and then he announced that the college student assistant would read the defense attorney's role with me. The young assistant started out in a flat monotone, reciting the words that I had practiced so much at home that they were now as familiar to me as a monologue from Eugene O'Neill or

Tennessee Williams. But I resented his emotionless reading. That resentment just increased the tension I already felt. My reading was bitter, ironic, spiteful. As he continued to drone on, an uncontrollable anger began to well up impotently inside me. It made my reading that much more hostile and sullen, I could do nothing about the way this assistant's colorless reading was stealing from the most important test of my life. Then, quite unexpectedly, I felt hot tears of frustration brim up into my eyes. As I read my final biting lines, the tears overflowed and streamed down my cheeks. There was a long, eerie silence when I finished. Then Mr. Hirschman said softly, "That was very nice, George. Thank you." I walked out quickly from the room, wiping my face.

When Fred called a few anxious days later, it was to tell me that I was doing *Playhouse 90*.

"Well, young man, it looks like we're starting out from the top. I'm really proud of you, George," he crowed. Fred sounded as though he'd known I would get the part all along. I felt like reminding him of the gossamer-thin confidence he evidenced in me before, but I thought the better part of valor was in biting my tongue.

This episode, he told me, was titled *Made in Japan*, with a script by Joseph Stefano starring Dean Stockwell, E. G. Marshall, Harry Guardino, Robert Vaughn, Dick York, and lovely newcomer Nobu McCarthy, whom Fred also represented. It was an impressive cast and very heady to think I would be part of it.

Playhouse 90 was an hour and a half of the best live original drama on television. The scripts were by some of the most talented young dramatists in America, including writers like Rod Serling, Paddy Chayefsky, and Reginald Rose. Exciting young actors such as Paul Newman, Joanne Woodward, Jack Palance, and Geraldine Page shone brilliantly on the series. And the show possessed the one great essential of drama—the immediacy of danger. It was live television.

What this meant was that the show was telecast as it was played, not recorded on film or tape. It had the dramatic sense of the moment of live theater without the need to project out to the second balcony. There was no opportunity for retakes, as in films. But, unlike the stage, the camera provided maneuverability to gain the intimacy of extreme close-ups. Live television combined the best and the worst of both film and theater: The enormous potential audience of television could enjoy the excitement of drama as it was happening in the present tense; but there was the ever-present possibility that disaster would be witnessed by millions. To an actor this could mean both great fulfillment and sheer terror. I felt the two extremes with the *Playhouse 90* production of *Made in Japan*.

The great luxury of live television was the two weeks of rehearsals that was not possible with films. And for a young aspiring actor, those two weeks with a distinguished cast that gathered every day in the spacious new facility at CBS Television City was the best internship that I could have been granted.

Dean Stockwell was a child film star who had matured into a fine actor on the Broadway stage. E. G. Marshall was a highly respected veteran of stage, screen, and live television. Nobu McCarthy, in contrast, was a model from Japan whose only other credit was a Jerry Lewis comedy. She spoke English with charming hesitancy, but I noted her drive and abundant discipline. Robert Vaughn was a self-confident and charismatic personality, and Dick York was a relaxed and rather reserved working film actor.

Harry Guardino was cast as the passionate defense attorney with whom all my scenes were played. He was, I had been told, what actors here in Hollywood referred to as a "New York actor." What that term suggested was a breed of actors who were serious, intense, and more committed to the theater than to films.

"Nah, don't believe it," he told me during a rehearsal break. "This town likes to categorize people. I'll do a good film any day. I pass on a lot of bad theater all the time. George, it's all in the quality of the material."

He shattered one part of the myth and reinforced others. I saw that Harry was indeed an actor who was serious and intense about his art. During the course of the rehearsals, I also noticed something else about Harry. He was having difficulty retaining the words to a lengthy, rather convoluted courtroom speech at the climax of the drama. His problem didn't seem to be with any particular part of the speech. Sometimes he would get past the part he had forgotten in the last run-through, only to "go up," or have his memory fail him, on another. Or he would get the whole speech out without a lapse, but the next time around go up again on a completely new portion of the speech. It was quite unpredictable. As we neared the air date, the concern we had for Harry grew into anxiety for the show. I overheard E. G. Marshall whispering an old actor's tip to Harry.

"Why don't you carry the script pages of that scene around with you like some prop notes on a clipboard you could refer to?" he suggested.

Herbie, as everyone called our director, also implied to Harry that he was not averse to hiding slips of clippings from the script around the set as he orated around the courtroom to help him out.

To all these suggestions, Harry's reply was, "Nah, don't worry. Those tricks only take away from my concentration. If I go up, I know what I can do." But he never let on what he had in mind.

We moved from the rehearsal hall to the actual sets two days before the air date. All of the many different locales were constructed on one enormous soundstage. It was awesome. There was a whole Japanese village street running the length of the stage. There was the high, gracefully curved bridge from which Nobu was to fall during the quarrel with Dean. Tucked into a corner of the huge stage was the smallest of the many sets, my jail cell. And there was the pivotal set for the climax of the drama, where Harry was to make his impassioned, and now to us, quite suspenseful, summation speech—the military courtroom.

When the extras were added at dress rehearsal, the sets came to life. The street teemed with bicyclers, noodle hawkers, merchants, shoppers. The courtroom was crowded with onlookers, adjutants, and sober-faced judges. The movement of the crowd of extras on and off the floor, swiftly and silently as the live action played, had to be orchestrated. The drama was not just before the camera but in the noiseless, fast-moving activity behind as well. The tension was becoming electric, as were my opening jitters.

I watched the dress run-through of Harry's courtroom oration on my dressing room monitor. The old pro sailed through this final rehearsal without "going up." It was a great sign, I thought.

But out in the corridors of the dressing rooms, E. G. told me that in the theater a good dress rehearsal foreboded the very opposite: a bad dress rehearsal was a good omen, and a good dress rehearsal was an ominous portent. I thought it was a crazy superstition and chose to ignore it. Harry did fine, I'll do fine, the show will be wonderful, I kept repeating like a mantra in my mind. Then, I remembered the proverbial whistling through the cemetery at night, and with a shiver, my jitters returned. I realized, then, that in this precariously uncertain world of show business, so fraught with the unpredictable, superstitions become a cozy security blanket, an irrational but calming solace to jittery nerves. Anything to hang on to. Especially on live television.

Airtime was announced with a flashing red light. Millions of viewers throughout America were now listening to the lush overture as the title, *Playhouse 90*, came on the screen. The same music I had listened to every week on my living room television set I now heard as I sat watching a tiny monitor screen in my brightly lit dressing room. I watched as I waited to be called to the huge soundstage floor next door. This was going to be my professional acting debut. It was indescribably thrilling.

The drama moved from one scene to the next with breathtaking swiftness. Before I knew it, the assistant stage manager was knocking on my door with the call for my first scene. I went out onto the stage floor. Everyone—cameramen, technicians, actors—moved briskly to a silent choreography. Any mishap would be sent immediately into millions of homes throughout America. I walked quickly to my cell set and waited.

Soon two dark cameras converged on me like voracious mechanical beasts. A beat after the Cyclops eye atop one of the cameras lit up bright red, Harry walked in. He was wary, probing, calculating. I felt insulted by his suspicion—defiled. There was so much I felt inside me. The dishonor of defeat in war and in love. The injustice of the victorious Americans. The despair in the helplessness of my situation. None of which I would discuss with this prying foreign official. Cold bile welled up inside me. This lawyer's trickle of compassion for me seemed degrading and patronizing. My rising anger boiled over in hot, stinging tears. They dropped down my cheeks bitterly. I spat out my defiance. Then the scene was over. The cameras quickly turned away to the next set and rolled on.

I hurried back to my dressing room. A swift traffic flow had to be maintained; actors merely got in the way after the scene was done. On my monitor, the drama rushed from one scene to the next with spine-tingling speed. Before I knew it, I was returning to my cell for my next scene. The cameras alighted on me briefly, stared intently as Harry and I played out our scene, then they raced on to the next. Back in the dressing room, I watched as we rapidly approached the final courtroom scene and Harry's big speech. I was glued to my monitor with my fingers crossed.

When the scene came, Harry seemed in perfect command. He began slowly, methodically building his case. He paused, and I held my breath. Harry continued; it was a dramatic pause. His speech began to build in force and passion. Suddenly, of all times, the sound on the monitor went on the blink. Harry's lips continued moving mutely on the screen. I rushed out to see the action live on the floor. In the corridor, other actors popped their heads out of their dressing room doors whispering, "Something's happened to the sound on my monitor. You too?"

I got out on the floor just in time to catch Harry in the last few seconds of using his much-vaunted secret weapon. He was earnestly, passionately pleading his case before the military judges—in pantomime! Not a sound was being made by his fervently moving lips. Then, as suddenly as he had lost his voice, Harry was talking again. His voice, but more crucially, his memory, had returned. Harry had cloaked his memory lapse with the illusion of a technical glitch. But even without sound, Harry's performance was brilliant. He had voicelessly maintained his concentration, emotional core, and his command of the audience.

"And . . . we are off the air. Thank you, ladies and gentlemen, for a wonderful show." Herbie Hirschman's voice boomed over the loudspeaker from the control booth high above. Immediately, people came pouring on to the stage floor to envelop Harry in wild, congratulatory embraces. E. G. was already jubilantly slapping him on the back. As I watched this mad, joyous hubbub from a distance, I couldn't help thinking to myself, "I love this. I love being an actor. I love being a part of all this."

I knew, then, I had made the right decision. It was crazy, but it was right.

After *Playhouse 90*, the rest of summer was something of an anticlimax. Hanging venetian blinds became the buildup to the next act, beginning my studies as a theater arts student at the great university of my parents' dreams. Each blind I hung, I imagined was a letter on the marquee of a movie theater announcing the next attraction. They spelled out U.C.L.A.

Although Berkeley and UCLA are both parts of the great University of California system, the two campuses are as different as north is from south. While the air of Berkeley is usually cool and crisp, UCLA's is almost always warm and balmy. While the campus style in the mid fifties at Berkeley was the traditional white buck shoes and khaki trousers, the look of the UCLA arts students was shaggy early-beatnik black. And my move down to the southern campus had transformed an unsure architecture student into a resolutely single-minded young actor.

I was now a veteran of live television and sci-fi dubbing, eager to take on the challenges of academic theater. UCLA meant returning to lecture halls and libraries, seminars, and writing papers. But what was markedly different here were the project assignments. Every student in the Theater Arts Department had to serve on a work crew of a production.

My first semester, I was assigned to the stage crew of the Royce Hall main stage production of Edmond Rostand's romantic classic, *Cyrano de Bergerac*. It was like beginning a serious meal with a big portion of high-caloric confectionery dessert—extravagantly delicious.

Bill Wintersole, the most dashing student actor on campus, was electrifying as the rapier-witted and heartrendingly heroic Cyrano. The massive sets—whether rococo theater or combat-ravaged battlement or serene nunnery—which I pushed around in the semigloom of the scene shifts, seemed to float magically on air. I watched the clangor and the smoke of the battle scenes from the darkened wings, transfixed.

Best of all, for the first time I tasted something I had only read about—a "thunderous ovation." It is amazing how sweetness can sound so loud. It really wasn't for me; I knew that. I had only shoved the sets around. And yet I felt I, too, had contributed in my way to the total theatrical experience for the audience. The ovation was partially mine. And it was there for the taking. Scrunched in the dark crevice of the nunnery wall, as the smiling actors strode by me in their lace collars and plumed hats to bask in the glory of their curtain calls, I vicariously bathed with them in the gorgeous warmth of the sound. Indeed, it was "thunderous." Indeed, it was sweet. I was transported—there at the footlights bowing and smiling with the actors. Hidden in the dark behind the nunnery wall, I beamed. It was wonderful.

But the morning after the applause and the glory and the splendor, we had to be in our seats for the nine o'clock lecture of Theater History 101. Bill Wintersole sans nose, chevaliers sans rapiers, and me, tired and yawning. It was all very egalitarian. This was what Daddy wanted for me. To do theater but to also learn about its history, its place in civilizations, and the ideas that shaped it. I was discovering, though, that I found this aspect of theater engaging also. New doors were being opened up, new concepts that piqued my curiosity. Daddy was right after all. I was grateful for his good guidance.

In fact, I was beginning to realize how special my father was. His counsel was so unlike the stern dicta of Japanese American fathers of my friends. I couldn't imagine any of them supporting their sons' desire to go into a venturesome career field, whatever it might be. My father understood and encouraged the individual aptitudes of his children. The guidance he gave was benevolent, and it was enlightened. He widened rather than restricted our horizons, stimulated rather than demanded. He subsidized my choice instead of throwing me to the wolves.

Nevertheless, I was grateful that I had a brother and a sister going into more "respectable" fields. A bit of the pressure was lightened. Henry was studying to be a periodontist at the University of Southern California, and my sister, Tita, was going to join me at UCLA to become a schoolteacher. I was the black sheep of the family. I knew it; Daddy knew it. But he wanted me to be the best black sheep out there in the pasture. I felt the weight of that responsibility. But it was a different kind of weight from the one I felt up in Berkeley. This one fed my determination not to let him down.

I worked hard. Being a theater student at UCLA was fun and engrossing, but I worked hard too. I also recognized that I was lucky. When I started at UCLA, I was the only Asian student in the Theater Arts Department, and I was lucky in the good casting opportunities that I enjoyed. I was also lucky in receiving the esteem of my peers. In 1959, for my portrayal of an American Indian in an original play by James Hatch, *Tallest Baby on the River*, I was named the Best Supporting Actor of the Year at UCLA. The following year, I won the same recognition for my role as Mr. Shu Fu in the Bertolt Brecht classic, *The Good Woman of Setzuan*.

I look back on my UCLA years as a halcyon time of rare opportunities and good challenges blessed by lady luck. But luck is not some whimsical caprice of fortune that flits about touching this one and arbitrarily ignoring another. Luck is something that one can make. Hard work and being prepared to seize opportunities create the chance for luck to grant her gentle encouragement. I've found that the harder I worked, the luckier I seemed to get.

That luck, however, didn't seem to carry over from the theatrical stage to my involvements in the arena of politics. My streak of bad luck in politics started when I volunteered to help in Adlai Stevenson's 1960 presidential campaign.

Daddy was a great admirer of Adlai Stevenson, the former governor of Illinois. He had cast his first vote as a newly naturalized American citizen, back in 1956, for Stevenson for President of the United States. Stevenson didn't win, but the eloquent campaigner was again a candidate in 1960. The Democratic Party's nominating convention this time was to be held in our hometown, Los Angeles. It was a fortuitous opportunity to experience the American electoral process firsthand.

Daddy and I went downtown one Saturday morning to the old Paramount Theater Building across from Pershing Square. This was where the headquarters of the Stevenson for President campaign were located.

The place was a beehive of activity. Earnest young coordinators were organizing the volunteers into various task forces. Frantic messengers scurried about. Telephones jangled, and typewriters clacked incessantly. The air was intense with a driving sense of purpose. And there was urgency. The Democratic National Convention and the struggle for the presidential nomination was going to begin on July 12.

Daddy was able to help only until noon, so we were assigned the task of stuffing envelopes with campaign literature. This was essential work in spreading the word on Stevenson's issue positions and winning supporters, we were told. We pinned on our name tags and joined a group of people seated at a long table piled high with neat stacks of folded campaign literature. The other volunteers greeted us cheerfully as we sat down and quickly became a part of their efficient assembly line. Once we got the rhythm of the task, we were able to chat while we worked.

What impressed us was the diversity of the volunteers and the singleness of their commitment to the ideals personified by Mr. Stevenson. There was a gray-haired high school teacher in suit and tie who liked the Stevenson educational reforms. There was a black legal secretary who felt Stevenson was the best man on civil rights issues. There was a housewife from Glendale with two teenaged sons who were enamored of Stevenson's oratorical eloquence. Most of the people at the table were college kids like me. There were political science students, foreign policy students, and journalism students. And then there was me—a theater arts student.

When I revealed this fact, the assembly line perceptibly slowed down. "Oh, really?" some said, exaggerated friendliness barely disguising their curiosity. Again, I was the oddity. The shuffling of paper continued, but I could sense the next question silently poised on everybody's lips.

There were a few beats of a polite waiting before the most nosy person asked, "What will you do for a living?"

"Well, I'm going to be an actor," I answered.

"Oh . . . how nice," and there was more shuffling of paper. The envelope stuffing continued, but the group's curiosity was palpable.

"And what kind of films do you like to do?" The paper shuffle resumed, but everybody's ears were cocked to hear my answer.

"Well," I began thoughtfully, "I plan to be very selective about the films I do. I'll be looking for scripts with Academy Award potential." There was an indulgent ripple of laughter. I could tell they were thinking, "Poor thing."

Then Daddy helpfully announced, "Actually, I see him making a good drama teacher." And with that, everybody chorused, "Ah, of course." "Yes, a teacher indeed." "I'm sure he'd make a fine drama teacher."

The old rhythm resumed. Everything now made sense. They

didn't have to sympathize with the pathetic plight of a nice young man condemned to a life as an actor. The task of the assembly line could carry on.

Daddy said he had to leave, but I decided to stay the whole day. I was sorry he didn't, too, because late in the afternoon, something extraordinary happened. Like an electric current rippling across the room, excitement spread throughout the vast office. "She's coming," they whispered. "She's supposed to be on her way right now." Then, "She'll be here in ten minutes," followed shortly by, "Five minutes. She's going to be here in five minutes."

I looked up and saw flinty-eyed men in dark suits filter in from the front door. Then to a spatter of applause that grew and grew, the legendary lady stepped through the door. With a dark straw hat crowning her loose gray hair, Eleanor Roosevelt entered radiating her famous toothy smile. She waved at everybody in the room, then turned and began shaking every volunteer's hand as she graciously worked her way around the huge room. I stood with the others at my table and waited. When she took my hand, she looked right into my eyes with her sparkling crinkly ones. "Thank you, George, for all that you are doing for Adlai. I so appreciate your work."

This renowned woman, this fabled former first lady, was personally thanking me! I was incredulous. And she called me by my name. She was amazing. I was too euphoric to realize I was wearing my name tag. I watched her move through the room from one volunteer to another, connecting with each, touching every person with her charm and appreciation and thus energizing the campaign for Adlai Stevenson. This is American politics, I thought. People connecting with people from all walks of life in a common cause. Eleanor Roosevelt certainly buoyed our support for Adlai Stevenson that afternoon, but, in a much larger sense, she also strengthened my commitment to our democratic process.

At the dinner table that night, I shared my excitement over meeting Eleanor Roosevelt. I told Daddy that it was too bad that he couldn't have stayed a few hours longer, and he repeated something about being too busy. It wasn't until much after the campaign that I discovered that Daddy, in fact, knew that Mrs. Roosevelt was coming that afternoon and chose not to meet her. He was there to support Adlai Stevenson's presidential campaign but not to meet Mrs. Roosevelt. I remembered, then, what the name Roosevelt had meant to him so many years ago.

I continued to go back to the Stevenson headquarters and became a regular volunteer for the campaign. I was given the job of coordinating the "spontaneous" rallies. I organized the Stevenson demonstrations at the Biltmore Hotel, which served as the hotel headquarters of the Democratic Party, and at the Los Angeles Sports Arena, where the convention was being held. Back at the headquarters on the night of the nominations, we were moved as we watched on the television screens Senator Eugene McCarthy's impassioned speech placing Adlai Stevenson's name in contention. Our work as volunteers was now done. The rest was in the hands of the delegates.

In the turbulence of the campaign, I experienced the sweat, the messiness, and the exhaustion, but most of all the fervent commitment, of the people involved in the electoral operation. I was surrounded by savvy, dedicated idealists. And I saw that the fuel of our democratic process is very American: It is a compound made up of ideas, spirit, potato chips, and soda pop. I was exhausted, but proud to have been a part of the noble effort to elect Adlai Stevenson as our President. Alas, luck would not be with us. The nominee of the Democratic Party in 1960 was John Fitzgerald Kennedy.

10

Burton and Guinness

As indispensable to an actor's career as a key to a locked door is that one crucial person we call an agent. I had him now in Fred Ishimoto, who agreed to keep his eyes open for projects right for me while I was still at UCLA.

The labyrinthine corridors of Hollywood, however, have many locked doors, and an actor requires more than one friend with a key to open them. Another such friend now was Herbie Hirschman, my *Playhouse 90* director. Herbie liked what I had done on the show, so when he began work on his next project, he asked for both Nobu McCarthy and me. The production was the popular television series *Perry Mason*, starring Raymond Burr. Again, Nobu and I were teamed as ill-fated lovers. This time, the story involved the theft of a rare "blushing" pearl— and murder.

A less-macabre production introduced me to another important key bearer who was to help open many doors for me in my journey through the maze of Hollywood. This person was a casting director who saw me in a UCLA summer theater production of an American theater retrospective entitled *Portraits in Greasepaint*. The presentation was a sweeping saga told

160

in vignettes of representative scenes from plays throughout our theater history. I played a variety of roles ranging from Uncle Tom in *Uncle Tom's Cabin* to the Captain of the *H.M.S. Pinafore* in the Gilbert and Sullivan classic. The eagle-eyed casting director in the audience at one performance was Hoyt Bowers from Warner Brothers Studio. He was the gatekeeper who was to open the door at many important junctures in my career, the first of which was a role in a major feature film.

The day after he saw *Portraits in Greasepaint,* Hoyt Bowers left a message with the Theater Arts Department office for me to call him at the studio.

It seemed half the department knew about the call before I got the message. The set design class was just breaking up when a friend told me she heard people at the office talking about a call for me from a movie studio. As I was hurrying across campus to the office, another classmate yelled out, "Hey, George, I heard Warner Brothers wants you to call. It's urgent!" I'm sure others within hearing simply assumed this was another silly theater-arts student joke. When I arrived breathless at the wooden bungalow that served as the Theater Arts Department office, a chorus of voices again assaulted me with the same urgent information. "Call Warner Brothers Right away!"

I could feel a dozen pairs of eyes looking over my shoulder when I was handed the note. I read it, then asked the secretary if I could use her phone to call my agent. I could feel those eyes turn silently to each other with the expression, "He's got an agent?" Fred had counseled me always to contact the studios through him.

"Fred, this is George. I've got a message here from a Hoyt Bowers at Warner Brothers. Could you check it out for me?" And I gave him the number in the message.

"Thanks for the phone," I said to the secretary as I hung up. I strolled out as nonchalantly as I could, knowing that I left in my wake a crowd of nonplussed faces. But inside, I prickled with an excitement that coursed through me like an electric current. What could this be about?

I learned that Hoyt Bowers was casting *Ice Palace,* a film

161

adaptation of Edna Ferber's epic three-generational novel about a powerful dynasty in Alaska. He was calling me in to read for the role of a young Chinese cannery worker, Wang, who ages from eighteen to eighty. Most of this character's scenes were in his youth, so Bowers was looking for a young Asian actor who could also play the later scenes credibly.

"Here's the actor who had me believing he was Uncle Tom one moment and then the Captain of the *Pinafore* the next." Hoyt Bowers greeted me cheerfully in his modest office at Warners. "I hope you can convince me you can be an eighty-year-old Chinese man as well." With that mild challenge he handed me a few pages from a script. I read one scene from the character's youth and another as the old man Wang.

"Not bad . . . if I keep my eyes closed," he said smiling. "But you look so blooming young. Let's go see what Mr. Sherman thinks."

This was Vincent Sherman, the director of the film. We walked from Bower's office across a garden courtyard to a spacious bungalow office. Mr. Sherman was a courtly, gracious gentleman with a deep, strong voice. After I read the same scenes again he concurred with Hoyt Bowers. "Young man, you're a fine actor. But I'm just a bit concerned about the old-age makeup. Could we ask you to do a screen test for us?"

I hoped my dropping jaw wasn't too noticeable. He's asking me to do a screen test? I was incredulous—I would have killed for such an opportunity. I must have been speechless, because Hoyt Bowers broke the silence by saying that he would set it up with my agent. As we walked out of Mr. Sherman's office, Bowers said, "I'd better settle this with Fred real quick. I suspect maybe you're one of those difficult actors who are above doing screen tests." And then he winked at me.

It was at this interview that I learned the leads were being played by Richard Burton and Robert Ryan, actors I admired. The teaming of the two was intriguing, a classic British actor with a rough-hewn American ideal. The contrast and the conflict would be sharp and strong. It would be fantastic working with this team. I had to be in this film; I had to convince them I could play eighty.

On the morning of the screen test, I was instructed to report directly to the soundstage before I went to makeup. I wondered what this was all about. When I arrived at the soundstage, Mr. Sherman greeted me genially.

"Good morning, George. It's very kind of you to stop by before makeup. We just wanted to get you on film first as you are. Please make yourself comfortable there in front of the camera."

With that, I was ushered to a lone stool set in a pool of light. Mr. Sherman seated himself on a stool right next to the camera and whispered something to the operator. It started to whirr softly. It was all very casual and relaxed, but I knew my screen test had now begun.

"Now then, George," he began smilingly, "tell me something about yourself." Mr. Sherman asked me a series of questions about my feelings on school, on movies, and on my hopes for the future. I responded as honestly, and, I hoped, as interestingly as I could. Mr. Sherman chortled at my attempts at wit, frowned gravely at the serious points.

"Thank you, George. Now I think the makeup people are waiting for you." The soft whirr stopped. Mr. Sherman got up from his stool and shook my hand, and with that, this part of the screen test was over. The real test was about to begin.

George Bau was a balding, rotund man who came from a family of makeup people that had worked at Warner Brothers studio practically from its beginning. The makeup man was an old hand at aging actors. He studied my face through sternly squinted eyes. He pinched my skin and frowned. He rubbed my forehead and scowled. He silently analyzed my face as if it were some insensate lump of flesh, with no regard for the living human being inhabiting it. There was no conversation, no chitchat. Only a wordless evaluation of the youthful challenge that sat in his makeup chair. Then, he began assembling his materials—liquid latex, powder, various shades of base, and makeup pencils. He cut a small square of foam rubber, and with it, he started dabbing the liquid latex on my face. Suddenly, as if he had been struck by a flash of inspiration, he stopped.

"Al!" he shouted out into the corridor. "Al Greenway! Can you come in here and help?" A large, hulking man with tightly curled steel gray hair and a genial smile came in.

"Can you hold the skin here stretched real taut while I dapple it with the latex?" he asked, pointing to my forehead with the square of foam rubber in his hand. "I want it stretched real tight," he emphasized.

"With pleasure," replied the hulking man. And with his powerful fingers, Al gripped, then stretched the skin of my forehead until it felt as if it were about to tear apart. My head reared back and my body extended straight in the chair. It was excruciating.

George Bau proceeded to dab the liquid latex on the now agonizingly smooth skin surface. Each dab felt as astringent as the touch of an ice cube on sunburned skin.

"Sorry about this, young man. I know it's uncomfortable," Al said. Uncomfortable was hardly the word, I thought. At least Al knew there was a living, traumatized being down here. But George Bau just continued dabbing in silence. When he had covered my forehead with his dabbings, he turned around and reached for something. I heard the sudden drone of a hair dryer. Then, a blast of cool air was blowing furiously on my forehead. As the latex started to dry, I felt my tightly stretched skin begin to contract even tighter. Al's hard grip struggled to hold firm. Just as suddenly as it had begun, the blowing ended. Next, George Bau took a powder puff and began to softly powder my forehead still held taut. This gentle act had to be the most torturous part of the whole ordeal. I could feel every pore on my forehead starting to pucker up and shrivel.

"Okay, Al. Let go," George commanded. Instantaneously, like a venetian blind suddenly yanked up, the skin of my forehead violently closed on itself into a wrinkled, shrunken mass. It was jolting and unbearably painful. Tears welled up in my eyes.

But the two makeup men were looking down at me, smiling happily and patting each other on the back.

"That is gorgeous, George. Just beautiful," Al beamed. He was talking to the makeup man—not me.

"Thank you. Thank you." George Bau smiled back. "Now, Al, if you'll hold the skin next to the eyes for the crow's feet. . . ." And they continued on in small painful patches, repeating the process all over my face.

When they finished, my forehead was numbed, the sides of my face were prickly, my cheeks smarted, my whole face hurt, and I really felt eighty years old. When I looked into the mirror, I was stunned. I saw a pitifully wizened old man's face resting on a youthful body. My watery eyes just stared in amazement, while over my head, Al continued to shower George Bau with effusive congratulations.

I returned to the soundstage in costume as well as my new prickly makeup to continue with my screen test. George Bau followed behind me with his makeup box in hand. When I stepped back into the pool of light in front of the camera, the crew broke out in spontaneous applause. I started to break into a slow, painful smile to acknowledge the accolade, but immediately it froze on my face. The eyes of the people clapping were not looking at me. The applause was being directed at George Bau, smiling and nodding in the gloom behind the camera. Only Mr. Sherman seemed to give me some credit for my suffering for art.

"You look amazing, George. Well done," he said, directing his approving smile at me. Then he added, "Now, don't try to play the age. You already are old. Just play the scene." And with that guidance, he whispered, "Action!" The camera started to whirr, and I played the scene I knew so well. The pain of the makeup made me talk and move so much slower. I felt like I had arthritis of the face.

When the scene was done and Mr. Sherman had shouted, "Cut!" there was stony silence. No audible sign of any verdict. But I noticed there were a lot of smiling faces. I saw Hoyt Bowers was smiling in the gloom with the crew. So was Mr.

Sherman. I overheard him whispering to George Bau, "That was masterful, George. The watery eyes are a stroke of genius. A wonderful touch."

"Thank you. Thank you," he was repeating almost robotically.

George Bau was claiming the compliments even for my tears of pain! It seemed more his screen test than mine. And quite obviously, he had succeeded with flying colors. I was merely the model wearing his wrinkled, painful creation.

The suspense of my casting, however, was to linger for another week. When I finally got the call from Fred, he told me to start packing for a two-week location trip to Petersburg, Alaska, and then two more months of filming back at Warner Brothers studios. I was doing *Ice Palace* with Richard Burton and Robert Ryan.

The vista from the window of the small twin-engine plane that was ferrying us from Vancouver, British Columbia, to the location site at Petersburg in the lower panhandle of Alaska was as heart-stopping as the turbulence of the flight. The awesome majesty of the snow-streaked mountain ranges only made me grip the armrest harder. The lushness of the black-green primeval forests took my breath away as much as the sudden bottomless drops of the tiny plane. And the almost surreal blue of the rivers that laced the pristine landscape looked to my traumatized eyes like parts of the sky visible through cracks in the beautiful landscape.

This was my second flight since the trip to Colorado Springs years ago, but it was my very first in a flimsy twin-engine propeller plane. Only a thin, trembling metal wall separated me from the hair-raising grandeur of Alaska. I was so grateful when we finally splashed down on the waters of what the Alaskans call "the narrows," though we were bobbing around on what to me looked like the widest river I had ever seen. I could barely see the other shore from the pier where the small aircraft alighted. I was traveling with two stuntmen who were to double for Burton and Ryan. I'm sure the driver who picked us up thought I was talking about the scenery when I kept repeating, "It's so good to be alive."

As soon as I unpacked at the hotel, I thought I'd wander around the village. The midsummer air was breezy, bracing, and as clear as crystal. Petersburg was a quaint little fishing community of wood-frame cottages built into a steep wooded hillside. The main street, made up of the hotel, a general store, a café, a barbershop, and a couple of saloons, ran parallel to the narrows. It would have looked like a frontier town in a western except for the great body of water that flowed by the village and the giant cannery standing on stilts in the water with its piers jutting out into the narrows. This huge, weather-worn structure, pungent with the smell of fish, was the major employer and only industry of the village.

I walked out on the long pier alongside the cannery. At the far end I could see a lone man looking out across the narrows. As I walked farther out, the soft breeze turned sharper, chillier, a gale that slapped my hair briskly on my face. I walked more forcefully against the wind. Then I recognized the man at the end of the pier. It was Robert Ryan. I approached the lean, craggy figure standing tall in the wind, intending to introduce myself. I guess he sensed my advance toward him. He moved away, turning his back to me, and shifted his gaze downstream. I stopped. He probably didn't want to be bothered by a fan. I just stood near him and gazed out across the wide expanse of water to the immense range of wooded mountains on the other side. We stood there for a long time silently communing with the vast beauty of Alaska.

Then I heard that famous, raspy voice say, "What do you catch here?"

I wasn't sure he was talking to me. But there was nobody else around. "I beg your pardon," I answered hesitantly.

"What kind of fish you catch around here," he drawled again.

"Oh, I . . . well . . . um," I faltered. "I'm an actor. I just arrived from Los Angeles, and I'm afraid I can't tell you a thing about the fishing here."

He looked at me with those crinkly eyes. He studied my face

silently and then broke into a slow-building chuckle. "Of course. You're playing Wang, aren't you," he laughed. "I took you for one of the locals here. Sorry."

I introduced myself and began to tell him how much I admired his work. I had recently seen him in a professional production at UCLA of Eugene O'Neill's *The Iceman Cometh.*

"Yes, O'Neill. Great playwright." He nodded. Then, smiling, he turned his face across the narrows again. "Beautiful country," he declared, fixing his eyes on some distant object.

"Magnificent," I agreed, and joined him in his silent reverie. He obviously didn't want to chat about his career with an enthusiastic neophyte actor. But I stood there with him at the end of the pier, pretending to scan the entire vista but actually stealing glances at him from the corner of my eyes. He looked strong and rugged, his eyes squinting enigmatically. . . . Was it a smile or the bright, clear sunlight? The wind flapped his collar against his sinewy throat. I stood there with him for a long time as we wordlessly communed with our new environment.

Finally, he turned to me and said, "Well, I'll see you on the set." And with that, he walked off. I watched his lanky old frame amble down that long pier until he reached the end and turned when a cannery building blocked him from view. Robert Ryan was very much like the characters he played—the strong, silent type. And I sensed that he didn't like talking about his acting career.

The town barbershop was commandeered by Warner Brothers as the actors' makeup facility. I reported there at 7:00 A.M., bright and early in the morning, although morning in midsummer Alaska seemed not appreciably brighter than night. The sun shone practically twenty-four hours a day in the summer and then gave way to the moon during the winter months. I had slept listlessly with an eerie golden glow filtering in through the window shades all night long.

The two stuntmen, Sol and Eddy, were already there in the barbershop, standing with steaming cups of coffee in their hands.

"Good morning, George," the assistant greeted me. "You're in the first shot, so we need you made up right away." With that, I was immediately hustled into the first chair. Thank God, I wouldn't have to get into that painful old-age makeup for another six weeks.

As soon as I was made up, I was to rush over to the cannery, where, the assistant informed me, the company was setting up. Although it was only a short three-minute walk away, he had a car waiting for me outside. I thought it was a bit absurd, but I accepted and rode the short distance in the car. They must be in an awful hurry, I thought. I was to learn otherwise.

I was made up, dressed in my cannery worker's outfit with high rubber boots, and pacing the pier, mouthing my lines. But no call came for me to go before the camera inside the noisy, smelly building. They always seemed to find some way to intensify an already nervous situation.

The shot was to be that of an exhausted Wang working at the assembly line of the clangorous fish-canning machine—so exhausted that he loses his heavy knife in the fast-moving machinery, fouling up the steady work flow. Drudging alongside Wang would be Zeb Kennedy, a fellow cannery worker who comes to his aid when the foreman lashes out at him for his mistake. Zeb was the principal character in the film—the role being played by Richard Burton.

But where was Burton? He was nowhere in sight. Sol the stuntman was there dressed as the foreman; Eddy stood around dressed as his aid; a crowd of Asian extras dressed as Chinese cannery workers lounged around in the crisp, bright sunshine of the pier . . . and me. We were all ready and waiting. Half the morning was gone. But there was no star.

"Isn't Richard Burton supposed to be in this scene with me?" I asked one of the assistants.

"Yes, but we're having some problems coordinating the camera moves with the movement of the fish through the canning machine, so we're having him wait back at the hotel," he explained to me. "Don't worry. We're in touch with him with our walkie-talkie."

Just then, I noticed some commotion at the land end of the pier. A crowd of local onlookers that was being held back at the foot of the pier burst into squeals and applause, and a figure in a yellow sweater came pushing past them.

"Oh my God, he's coming!" exclaimed the assistant, and he rushed toward the approaching figure.

"Now then, lads. What seems to be holding up the festivities?" That unmistakable stentorian voice came cutting across the length of the pier. It was Richard Burton!

The assistant and a few other people ran up to him and were excitedly explaining the situation. But he strode right past them with a smile as he continued orating down the pier, "I've read the papers, finished the crossword puzzle, and I'm utterly bored to death. Now, gentlemen, shall we get us down to work?" He turned at the huge gaping entrance to the cannery and disappeared inside. I followed.

Vincent Sherman approached him with a big smile and explained the coordination difficulties of the camera with the complex travel route of the fish through the workings of the machine. Burton walked around the ungainly apparatus listening closely as Mr. Sherman pointed out the problems.

"The essence of the scene, Vincent, is to show Wang exhausted to the point of disrupting the orderly flow of the work, isn't it?" Burton was conversing with Mr. Sherman, but even his normal way of speaking was so theatrical that he seemed to be playing to the entire cast and crew. "It seems to me," he continued in his ringing tones, "this can be done in another way without having to spend all this time choreographing a ballet with this noisome beast. Can't we have Wang show his fatigue by simply spilling a trayful of already-canned fish?" I loved listening to him, the silvery clarity of his elocution, the lyrical way in which he shaped the English language. I felt as though I were in a London theater instead of a vast, dank, stinking fish cannery.

Burton was right, of course. So the action was shifted from following the course of the fish through the problematic machine to the two of us stacking trays of cans in a neat, high pile, which the bone-weary Wang finally spills. It worked much better. It was certainly much more visually interesting with the trayful of tin cans rolling all over the cannery floor. And the scene was set up and shot in half the time.

At the end of the genuinely exhausting day, as we both trudged the pier back toward the village, I couldn't keep the fan in me contained. "Mr. Burton," I began. But he stopped me abruptly with a raised hand.

"My name is Richard," he declared. "Call me Richard, and I shall call you George. If you must call me Mr. Burton, then I shall call you Mr. Wang." And he chortled without embarrassment at his own lame wit.

A car was waiting at the foot of the pier. An assistant ran to open the door for him. Richard looked at it in puzzlement.

"And where do you propose to take me in this car?" he asked.

"To your hotel, sir," the man answered.

"My hotel is right there," Burton said, pointing to the building only a short block away. "I can literally spit at it from here. Isn't this rather silly?"

"It's the company car for your use, sir," the driver replied a bit sheepishly.

"You're so kind. Thank you, but I think I prefer to walk. What about you, George?"

I said I'd join him, and we started to stroll down the main street. But before we were more than a few yards down the road, we passed a saloon. Two blondes, dressed in their finest, I'm sure, in order to be noticed by the movie people in town, came running out.

"Richard, Richard," they cried out.

"Ah, Julie and . . . what was your name, my dear?" Richard's sparkling eyes sparkled even brighter.

"Nova," pouted the other. "I told you my name's Nova."

"Of course! Nova. Forgive me, my dear. I've had an absolutely horrific day out there in the cannery. You will forgive me, won't you, Nova?" Then turning to me, Richard said, "Carry on, George. I'll see you in the morning." Richard disappeared into the saloon with his arms around the two buxom blondes.

The breeze that blew down the road was bracing, but it was

the exhilaration I felt that quickened my steps back to the hotel.
I was working with a man who was a classic actor of the theater
and a dazzling new movie star. He was elegant and at the same
time passionate; his zest, his appetite for life was infectious; he
had grace and cultivation combined with folksy heartiness. He
was a legend who wanted me to call him Richard! I had a
feeling that this was going to be a great experience.

Anyone other than Richard would probably have considered
me a pest. In the days and weeks that followed, I peppered him
with questions about his experiences in the theater both in
England and on Broadway. "What was it like doing Hamlet at
the Old Vic?" "What were Helen Hayes and Susan Strasberg
like in the Jean Anouilh play on Broadway?" "What American
playwrights do you like?" But rather than considering me an
annoyance, Richard seemed to revel in the enthusiasm and
inquisitiveness of a stagestruck young actor. Richard, as it
turned out, was a poet raconteur.

It was during one of these talk-story sessions that Richard
made an astounding revelation. We were seated in our chairs in
the bright Alaskan sunshine on the pier while the crew set up
for another shot.

I asked him a question that I thought would prompt another
expansive and wittily told story. "How did they teach Shakespeare in England when you were growing up?"

Suddenly, his eyes seemed to blaze in mock fury. "England!
Grow up in England! Do you take me to be English?"

He may have been acting, but the intensity of the feigned
outrage was so unexpected that I was momentarily stunned.
What had I said to offend him?

"I will have you know, I was born in . . ." And he said a
strange, long, foreign-sounding name I could not quite grasp.
Was he an immigrant to England from some European country? That name sounded somewhat East European. He certainly
didn't look Nordic or Mediterranean, I thought.

"Pontrhydyfen," he repeated slowly, almost caressingly. His
eyes turned soft and wistful. "I was born in Pontrhydyfen."

"You mean, Richard, that you didn't grow up in England?" It seemed unthinkable that this quintessential exponent of the English language should not be an Englishman.

"I grew up, George, in the warmest bosom of Wales, Pontrhydyfen," he announced. "And I grew up speaking the honeyed sounds of God—Welsh."

"You didn't grow up speaking English?" I was dumbfounded. Richard proceeded to give me a taste of the honey. He started to recite something in Welsh. It was indeed the sweetest, the most lyrical, the most transcendent sounds I had heard. Sitting there on the pier, with the waters of the narrows sparkling against the rugged majesty of Alaska, Richard sang on and on. And I sat listening, spellbound by the discovery of a totally unexpected dimension to this endlessly fascinating man. So this was Richard Burton's native tongue. English was for him a second language! This great master of Shakespeare grew up speaking the strange and beautiful sounds that he was reciting before me with rapture, gusto, and such pride. I, who had grown up bilingually with Japanese and English, sat there mesmerized by his wondrous command of languages. And I felt a kind of communion with this charismatic man.

"Mr. Burton, George, we're ready for you now," interrupted the assistant. The terrific concert was over. As we got up, Richard said to me, "That was Dylan Thomas in the original you were listening to."

After the Alaskan location shoot, we returned to the Warner Brothers studios back in Hollywood. The other cast members —Carolyn Jones, Martha Hyer, Jim Backus, Shirley Knight, Ray Danton, and Diane McBain—joined us.

On the days I wasn't involved in the scene being shot, I went back to my classes at UCLA. Time seemed to fly as I shuttled from campus to studio, studio to campus. Much too quickly, the fearful last two weeks in the old-age makeup came. They were torture. I dreaded every morning that I had to submit to the painful aging process. But all too soon, the filming of *Ice Palace* was completed, and I was again a full-time student.

But now on campus, I became the object of both curiosity and envy. I found it interesting how certain people studiously avoided mentioning anything about my summer experience while others showered me with questions. "How did you get cast?" "What was Alaska like?" "What was it like doing a big feature film?" The one question I loved responding to was "What was it like working with Richard Burton?"

I usually began my answer with the word "glorious" and from there, I carried on and expanded, waxing rhapsodic. My words became luminous, shining, utterly iridescent. After all, I had been tutored by the master himself. And this, I now like to tell people, was in Richard Burton's pre-Elizabethan days— Taylor, that is.

Although *Ice Palace* flopped at the box office, Warner Brothers liked my work. Actually, Hoyt Bowers liked my work. He opened the door to a whole lineup of television series that Warners was grinding out at the time. I became practically a member of the repertory company of players on *Hawaiian Eye*. One week, I might be playing a Tibetan monk; another, a scion of a great samurai family; and another, a Hong Kong street urchin, all the while still going to UCLA. I was probably the only actor on the studio lot who, between camera setups, was reading his world theater history textbook instead of the *Daily Variety*.

Acting now was starting to pay off financially. The car that I had been driving on my commute down Sunset Boulevard between UCLA and Warner Brothers studios was an old '54 Chevy coupe that I'd bought with my venetian blind job earnings. Now, I could buy that sporty M.G. that I had always wanted. Alas, it was not to be.

My father, as in so many pivotal points in my life, stepped in with his guidance. He did this by, of all things, quoting an old show biz maxim.

"I understand that in this business of acting there is a good old cautionary saying, 'It's feast or famine.' You seem to be enjoying the feast right now," he observed.

"Daddy, I really feel good about my career. I'm building steady momentum. I don't think my career is going to be one of those up-and-down roller coaster rides. I think an M.G. sports coupe would be a good investment at this time."

"A car is not an investment. It's a moving depreciation," he retorted. "But I agree that an investment is a good idea. An investment today won't make the feast a full feast, but it also won't make the famine a real famine come tomorrow. And believe me, that tomorrow will come. If you're going to be an actor, I want you to be able to afford being an actor." And with that, he put my movie earnings into real estate investments for me. It wasn't much money, so he put it into small land parcels that he said would produce a "steady, sure return, unlike show business." My father put my first real movie earnings into mortgages on cemetery plots.

I protested bitterly then. I had my heart set on that M.G. But with the passage of time, I have come to appreciate more and more the wisdom and good counsel my father gave me. The irony of my survival as an actor being initially assured by a collection of cemetery plots also does not escape me.

My father's premonition of the famine that tomorrow might bring was yet to come true. I landed another feature film, this one starring the rising young star Jeffrey Hunter. It was titled *Hell to Eternity*. The title sounded an awful lot like *From Here to Eternity*, suggesting a cheap knock-off of the much-lauded film. Like the Academy Award winner, ours was a World War II movie. Unlike that film, however, our script was essentially an action drama, but with a unique—indeed precedent-setting—historic component.

Hell to Eternity was the first Hollywood film to deal with the internment of Japanese Americans. Jeffrey Hunter played a character based on a real person, Guy Gabaldon, a Mexican American orphan in East L.A. who was adopted by a Japanese American family. He grew up speaking Japanese and English in a warm, loving family that included his adoptive brother, the role I played. When war broke out, Gabaldon's family was incarcerated, and he went on to fight and become a war hero.

Our mother was played by a wonderful actress from the days of Hollywood's silent era, Tsuru Aoki, who was also the wife of the old-time star Sessue Hayakawa. My girlfriend was played by Miiko Taka, who was Marlon Brando's leading lady in the film version of James Michener's *Sayonara*. The set-side chitchat on this one should be great, I imagined, and it quickened my pulse to realize that my personal history, the Japanese American history in Hollywood films, and my own advance in movies were merging in *Hell to Eternity*. I didn't know, then, that Jeffrey Hunter would also play a role in my future.

The making of the film was all that I hoped it would be. The actresses were delightful. Mrs. Hayakawa, as we addressed Tsuru Aoki, was a sweet, chatty lady. She loved reminiscing about the parties she and her husband used to throw in the palacial mansion they built where today the Hollywood Freeway courses near the Hollywood Bowl. Miiko waxed rhapsodic about Brando and especially about her dream promotional tour for *Sayonara* that took her to all the glamour capitals of the world.

I found it revealing, however, that whenever Jeff brought up the subject of the internment camps, Miiko cheerfully redirected the conversation to another subject, and Mrs. Hayakawa airily announced that she had been in Japan and knew little about it. Despite the subject matter of the script we were working on, the camps were still an uncomfortable topic of conversation.

Hell to Eternity was a modest success at the box office, but it was another solid stepping-stone in my Hollywood career progression. Daddy's famine still seemed only proverbial.

My feast was prolonged again. Hoyt Bowers was there at Warners smiling and waving a shiny new key. The Broadway hit comedy *A Majority of One* was to be made into a film starring Rosalind Russell as the Jewish housewife from Brooklyn who is courted by a wealthy Japanese businessman, to be played by the

Academy Award–winning British actor Alec Guinness. Veteran director Mervyn LeRoy was to be at the helm.

I was cast to play the majordomo, or head butler, in the household of the Japanese businessman. It was a servant role, true. But this was a character with some refinement. This servant personified the restrained, formal tradition of Japanese service.

What really excited me about doing *A Majority of One*, however, was the opportunity to work with another legendary British actor. I had been deeply affected by the epic film *The Bridge on the River Kwai* and the character of Colonel Nicholson that Alec Guinness created in the film. The actor's genius had made a singularly idiosyncratic character not only understandable but tragic. What chameleon magic might this gifted English actor bring to playing a Japanese businessman? It was an extraordinary opportunity to be on the set and watch him deal with this challenge. I relished the prospect.

Equally tempting was my image of the set-side chats. I remembered with delight those dazzling vicarious journeys that Richard Burton took me on with *Ice Palace*. Any actor of Guinness's experience must have a fantastic hoard of stories to share. He belonged to an older generation of actors than Burton, and would be able to open up a whole different world for me. I couldn't wait for the great talks that we might get into.

It was my first day of filming. I was made up and in my kimono costume, ready on the set of Mr. Asano's elegant Japanese-style home. Rosalind Russell was dressed as the dowdy, salt-and-pepper-haired matron Mrs. Jacoby, but carrying on as if she were still playing the flamboyant character she had dazzled Broadway with as Auntie Mame.

"Mervyn, darling. You're looking won-derful." She greeted our director in her luxuriantly brash style. "You haven't aged a day since yesterday. How do you do it?"

"Well, my dear," responded the courtly Mr. LeRoy, "I know that under that makeup is an actress of radiant beauty. Working with you keeps my spirit young."

"That's what I wanted to hear, baby," she said, breaking into a brassy vaudeville growl. "Stick with me, kid, and I'll keep more than just your spirit young." And she laughed raucously.

Mr. Guinness, I was told, was a bit delayed in the makeup department because of the complexity of the job. I thought I'd stroll over to the building to see how his Japanese guise was applied. I hoped, for his sake, that it wouldn't be as painful as my old-age makeup for *Ice Palace*.

I had just stepped out of the dark of the soundstage into the bright California sun. As I stood squinting, a big, black car drove up. The back door opened, and out stepped a slim, middle-aged man with a strong aquiline nose. Around his neck he wore a fringe of tissue papers tucked under his collar to protect it from the fresh makeup. It was Alec Guinness. I stepped back and hefted the heavy soundstage door open for him.

"Good morning, Mr. Guinness," I greeted him.

"Good morning. Thank you so much," he said, and nodded in an exaggerated Japanese manner as he walked past me. He was attempting to get in character, I thought. But what I saw shocked me. Delicately stretched over his eyes were thin pieces of latex membrane. It was done skillfully. It was smooth and tight. But it made the eyes look cold, sinister, almost reptilian. It was grotesquely offensive, and he was supposed to be the sympathetic "hero" of this comedy.

I went up to the assistant director to ask if something might be done about Mr. Guinness's so-called Japanese makeup. I was told that some scenes had already been shot with the makeup, and therefore nothing could be done about it. Besides, I was told quite curtly, it was none of my business. I felt as a Japanese that it was indeed my business, but I decided to bite my tongue. The power of Alec Guinness's acting, I hoped, would overcome the burden of this unfortunate makeup job. However, I would be sadly disappointed.

Guinness had been working with a Japanese dialogue coach, Bob Okazaki, for the accent as well as the few phrases of Japanese he had to speak. But the slurred, oddly broken British accent he affected as Mr. Asano was like nothing I had ever heard before. His Japanese phrases were even worse. They were incomprehensible gibberish. I was chilled standing set-side, watching all this go on before my eyes. I asked Bob Okazaki if anything could be done about the embarrassing sounds that Guinness was palming off as Japanese. But all the hapless dialogue coach could do was look down and shake his head hopelessly.

"I can't tell him anything," he moaned. "He's going to do what he's going to do."

The wonderful experience that I had looked forward to was stingingly dashed. Even if I still had the desire for set-side chats with Alec Guinness, they were not to be. He retired to his dressing room as soon as his scenes were completed. He was aloof and utterly distant. Some people tried to explain him to me by saying that he was very "private" or that he was "shy." But I simply found him colorless, withdrawn, and disappointingly banal. It made me wonder how he could be so unarguably effective in so many of his roles and so disastrous in *A Majority of One.* This experience got me to thinking on the issue of the casting of actors across ethnic lines.

I obviously have a personal interest in ethnicity not being a barrier to casting. At UCLA I had played every race from black to white and everything in between. I had won awards as an American Indian and a Brechtian Chinese. But the academic world is where we try to reach for an ideal—the classic notion of casting on the basis of talent alone.

If an actor's power can create the theatrical truth onstage, that should supersede consistency with the ethnicity of the character. If a "lean and hungry" Japanese actor can compel an audience to believe he is a Roman senator, then he has succeeded as Cassius. Conversely, if a black actor cannot speak iambic pentameter with conviction, then the authenticity of his color will not save him as Othello. And therein lies the rub; the actor cast across racial or cultural lines must be keenly mindful of his increased accountability. In order to create theatrical truth despite racial inauthenticity, he bears the responsibility for crafting the verisimilitude of the character's speech, man-

179

nerisms, and very being. Makeup alone cannot do it. The essentials are the actor's talent and, most critically, his integrity. The latter was what was missing in Alec Guinness's attempt at playing an aristocratic Japanese gentleman.

Yet this ideal of color-blind/talent-based casting, if it is to be a part of American theater, must be practiced squarely and with balance. It has to be a genuine two-way street. The conceptual ideal must not be used as a euphemistic screen for the one-way traffic of white actors consistently playing Asian lead roles, simply because that singular flow courts a gridlock created by those squeezed out of the passage. I am on this road because I am hopeful that a free traffic of talent will lead to a richer, more vibrant American culture.

Graduation day, June 9, 1960. It was a bright, sunlit, perfectly cloudless day. Vespers service for students and families in the morning. Daddy hosted a luncheon in a Westwood restaurant at noon. Then came the graduation ceremony on the greens of the UCLA athletic field. It was rather uncomfortable sitting in the sun wearing the black cap and gown. I remember it all so well, but what I remember most from that exhilarating and exhausting day happened after the ceremony.

Daddy and Mama came up to congratulate me. They were beaming. This was the campus they had driven their children around more than a dozen years before. This was the day they had been dreaming about for many more years before that. Today, their son was wearing the cap and gown of academia and holding a rolled piece of document tied with a bright blue ribbon. I handed it to Daddy to examine, and Mama embraced me.

"You did it. I'm proud of you." Daddy was radiant.

"We did it," I said as we shook hands. "This belongs to you and Mama, too."

"So happy." Mama smiled. "You real college graduate now." We just stood there smiling and gazing at each other. There were groups of proud parents around us handing gift-wrapped packages to their new graduates.

"We don't have a package to hand you," Daddy said.

"Oh, Daddy, you and Mama have given me so much already," I protested. "This is the best gift you've given me," I said, holding up the rolled diploma. I genuinely meant it.

"Oh, we have a gift for you," Daddy laughed. "We just can't hand it to you." I was puzzled. What could he be talking about?

"You had your heart set on going to New York, but you came here to UCLA because we wanted you to get a degree," he said. "Well, you did it. You earned your Bachelor of Arts. Now we want you to study some more. We want you to go to summer school at the Shakespeare Institute at Stratford-upon-Avon in England. Go there and study to be the best actor you can be."

I was stunned. Stratford-upon-Avon was Shakespeare's birthplace. In England! I was speechless. They were sending me to a place I had dreamed and fantasized about for years. As the shock waned, I began to sense the profound import of this extraordinary graduation gift. It meant that they were now fully behind me. They truly believed that I could do it. Daddy and Mama believed in me! I felt a surge of joy, gratitude, and an overwhelming love. I couldn't hug them tightly enough.

11

Fly Blackbird!

THE SUMMER OF 1960 WAS MORE THAN GLORIOUS. THE SHAKE-
speare Institute alone would have been a sublime experience,
and the school was just steps away from the Shakespeare
Memorial Theater, where the fabled Royal Shakespeare Company was in residence. But I made it more than Shakespeare
and Stratford-upon-Avon. During and especially after my summer session, I roamed all over Britain. I traveled to the
medieval walled city of York for the ancient mystery play
festival, then to the Scottish capital of Edinburgh for the great
international performing arts festival.

From Great Britain, I flew to Madrid and explored Spain. The
Mexican Spanish I spoke was as distinctly different from the
Castiliano spoken by the Spaniards as my American English was
from the English spoken by the British, but they did understand
me. Then I went by train to Italy, where I got together with an
American friend from UCLA, Michael Colefax, who had been
living in Rome. We hitched a ride with a film critic friend of his,
Gugliamo Biraghi, who was driving up to the celebrated Venice
Film Festival to serve as a judge. The two-day drive up Italy with

a literate Italian eager to share his passion for his country was an unforgettable treat.

Then, the crowning jewel on a dazzling three months—Paris! To experience for the first time this most urbane treasuropolis of the civilized world was thoroughly captivating. I discovered the heady grandeur of beaux arts architecture and the magnificence of visionary urban planning; and I was completely charmed by the delightful European tradition of wines with meals. The sheer overwhelming opulence of French civilization was, for me, as for many first-time visitors to the City of Lights, much too much. I drank deeply of the culture. Paris was an effervescent and sometimes gloriously intoxicating high.

Coming home to America was the morning after the binge. It meant waking up to the cold, hard light of reality. Now, what would I do with my life? I had a nascent but unsteady acting career going. To pursue some regular employment meant potentially impacting both the career and the steadiness of whatever job I might get. Thanks to the real estate investments that my father had made for me, I had the economic cushion to explore other options. While studying for my bachelor's degree at UCLA, I had found the academic side of theater to be extremely interesting, and the history of American theater especially fascinating. The theater mirrored and was shaped by the forces and events in our country's history. I decided to go on to graduate studies in theater history at my alma mater. Daddy wholeheartedly endorsed this decision.

UCLA seemed to be the residence of serendipity for me. It was there that Hoyt Bowers from Warner Brothers studio saw me in *Portraits in Greasepaint,* leading to my first feature film role and to working with Richard Burton. My decision to go to UCLA had led to my being cast in my first television production, the prestigious *Playhouse 90,* and to working with the director Herbie Hirschman. And it was there at UCLA that my path crossed those of two people who were collaborating on an exciting musical play which was ultimately to take me to New York.

Dr. James Hatch, whom I came to call Jim, was a professor of playwriting at UCLA. He had written *Tallest Baby on the River*, the play that gave me my award-winning American Indian role. C. Bernard Jackson, whom I came to call Jack, was associated with the dance department at UCLA and had been the musical director of *Portrait in Greasepaint*. Jim was white, Jack was black, and they were working on a musical titled *Fly Blackbird!* about the civil rights movement, the drive to gain racial justice in America. Their collaboration was taken directly from the newspaper headlines of the day.

America of the early sixties was stirring from the social torpor of the Eisenhower years. Beneath the surface of smug complacency flowed a strong tide of activist energy, a current of belief that the country must come to grips with the social corrosion of racial segregation. It emerged powerfully as a movement through "sit-ins" at segregated lunch counters, "freedom ride" bus caravans of college students into southern states with racially discriminatory statutes still on their books, and, most dramatically, in the nonviolent demonstrations led by the charismatic minister Dr. Martin Luther King, Jr.

Fly Blackbird! grew out of this political and social ferment. Jackson and Hatch had begun their collaboration on the UCLA campus, but, with strong encouragement from their colleagues, the venturesome duo decided to take their production off campus and open in a commercial house, the Metro Theater on Washington Boulevard. With them came galvanized young students bringing their energy, passion, and ideals. Here was the opportunity to wed craft and beliefs to dynamic social action. A good number of the cast came from UCLA, but, in addition, the administrative, technical, and business expertise came right off the campus.

Among them was a bushy-bearded young filmmaker with whom I had made student films. He practically lived in the dusty recesses of the theater working the complicated technical side of the production. And he was madly in love with the business manager in the front office. Poor Francis, I remember thinking, always lurking up in the darkness of the grids separated from his lady love up front by a vast theater and all of us singing and dancing below. Little could I have guessed that, years later, his name—his full name yet—would be emblazoned from marquees of theaters all over the world. Francis Ford Coppola.

Fly Blackbird! depicted, in song and dance, the high-spirited adventures of a shock troop of idealistic college students, black, white, and one Asian—not so coincidentally named George—as they struggled to right old wrongs. I was cast, naturally, in the role of the Asian student, my namesake, George.

There was a big musical number titled "The Gong Song," a satire on all of Hollywood's tired "oriental" clichés. Why, it asked, do we have to be subjected in each and every movie having anything to do with "orientalia," to a reverberant bong on a gong accompanied by a melody built on a pentatonic scale? This was "my" number, although it was performed by a trio also including Big Betty, a brassy, tough-talking student leader, and Tag, a shy, demure follower in the movement.

Big Betty was played by Thelma Oliver, a multitalented singer, dancer, and actor who had also attended Mt. Vernon Jr. High School, although a bit after me. Tag was played by Josie Dotson, whom I knew from some of my theater classes at UCLA. Although she was quiet and reserved in class, I was aware of Josie from the first day because, just as I was the only Asian in the Theater Arts Department in those days, she was the only black student. But for whatever reason, I never saw her performing in any school productions. So when we met again in rehearsals for *Fly Blackbird!* it was a delightful surprise for me to discover that this sedate, modest classmate could also be a sprightly and captivating performer. In fact, I was utterly charmed by the way she used her large, doleful, fawnlike eyes. But from behind those angelic eyes, I was to learn, watched a canny and subversively creative mind.

I thought that my competition and the real scene-stealer was Thelma. She brought to Big Betty a sass and swagger that could reach out and grab an audience and never let go. As if that weren't enough to concern another actor on the same stage, I noticed that she had a way of constantly inching herself, bit by consistent bit, downstage of the original blocking. At each rehearsal, she subtly edged herself farther down until her new downstage position got to be the accepted blocking. But we were supposed to be a trio. I wasn't about to let Thelma downstage me. I kept a wary eye on her and inched downstage along with her each time she did. By the time of dress rehearsals, we were both singing and dancing our hearts out practically leaning over the footlights at the people in the orchestra. Poor reticent Josie, I thought. She was somewhere behind us obediently following the original blocking. Thelma was probably gloating while I, at least, had enough milk of human kindness in me to feel for Josie. The opening was quickly upon us, and the director froze the new positions that Thelma and I had had appropriated.

Fly Blackbird! opened to thunderous ovations and great notices. It was discovered even by distant out-of-town critics like Nathan Cohen of the *Toronto Star News*. The leads were showered with accolades, but our number, "The Gong Song," was the showstopper. They were rolling in the aisles. It wasn't, however, because of Thelma's and my energetic singing and dancing. The laughs were coming when we were at our precision best. They were coming because of something else.

Behind us, just a beat behind or a step in anticipation of ours, was Josie in a hilarious state of discombobulation. Her great, soulful eyes were the mirrors of her embarrassment. Her lashes fluttered; her lips puckered. Her prim hands were tightly clutched in hysterically demure mortification. Josie was using Thelma and me as her foils as we battled each other with our precise Kabuki high-stepping and our disciplined Hindu head swaying down by the footlights. The coup de grace in Josie's exquisite orchestration of distress was her final punctuation of a devastatingly delicate comic stumble. Josie's performance was the very quintessence of the one black person in the world who didn't have rhythm. Shamelessly, she stole "The Gong Song" from Thelma and me and shattered another stereotype with one hilarious swoop.

Fly Blackbird! enjoyed a raging good run of almost a year in Los Angeles. The production captured the energy and optimism of the times. It soared musically on the notion that America was a social experiment in the making and that changes were still happening. The audiences were huge and spanned the ethnic spectrum of the city. Over its run, *Fly Blackbird!* affected an enormous number of people.

One of them was me. I gained friends and insights that led me to a deeper understanding of this ever-changing, ever-developing new breed of humans called Americans. As a people, we may have varied histories tracing back to the *Mayflower* or to slave ships, to split-rail corrals or to barbed wire fences. But, whatever our histories, however tortured and adversarial they may have been, our destinies are bound inextricably together. We have a common future. Our challenge lies, not in carrying the weight of our pasts like anchors, but in working in concert to build that common tomorrow. With *Fly Blackbird!* we achieved this smashingly well.

During the run, I met many people who shared the ideals that we sang and danced about so lustily from the stage of the old Metro Theater. Among the many that came backstage to congratulate us was one of the people with whom I was to become forever linked as a colleague, Nichelle Nichols. It was an occasion I would have remembered even if we never met again. She was immediately striking. At a time when black women were still laboriously straightening their hair, Nichelle wore hers in an authentic and astonishingly frizzy "Afro." She was at once natural and sophisticated, straightforward and radical. From the very first encounter, I was introduced to the essential Nichelle.

A cherished gift from the run of *Fly Blackbird!* was the memory of a meeting that still burns incandescently. We were often asked to perform musical numbers from the production at various rallies and fund-raisers. The biggest and most significant of these events was a giant rally at the Los Angeles Sports Arena with the Reverend Dr. Martin Luther King, Jr.

The immense hall was packed. Dr. King was virtually the personification of the civil rights movement and the most compelling orator of the times. People had traveled from throughout the southwest to be there. We considered it a signal honor to be performing at this event.

The *Fly Blackbird!* company was seated in a specially designated section of the grandstand at the opposite end of the hall from the podium where Dr. King would be speaking. We sang the title song, "Fly Blackbird!" and the soul-stirring finale from the show, "Wake Up, the Dawn Is Breaking." Then Dr. King entered the hall. Across the vast distance of the arena, he was only a tiny moving figure. But like a single, massive organism spontaneously surging to life, the entire assemblage rose up in a great thunderous ovation. The sound continued on and on—a giant roar of love, gratitude, inspiration, and hope.

It was a long time before Dr. King could begin to talk. But when he did, immediately a dense hush fell over the crowd. There was pure silence. Only his rich, sonorous voice broke it. He began speaking in his elegantly relaxed tone of his travels across this country. He spoke of the big cities, the great plains, and of the savannas and swamps of his native South. He spoke of the reality that he saw there and of the struggle that America has had with the ideals it holds so dear. And as he spoke, his words seemed to have direct resonance for me as a Japanese American.

Then he looked out over the immense assemblage before him, and he spread out his arms. His voice took on a rolling cadence as he spoke of his hope for our country. The good people of America, he said, people like those he saw before him, of all colors, all faiths, and all backgrounds linked together by a common subscription to the ideals of this country, were the hope for the future of our nation, indeed for the destiny of the human race. His voice swelled, the rhythm building to crescendo, and the majesty of his vision became towering as his mighty oratory carried our spirits soaring up to the rafters.

The massive assemblage of people there in the Los Angeles Sports Arena was transformed into a single, dynamic entity. We swayed in unison, we clapped in concert, we shouted as one. Dr. King possessed that rare power to reach out and touch so many so personally and then to bond them together and inspire them to that most extraordinary of political acts—nonviolent action.

I was spellbound. As the audience exploded in applause around me, I understood for the first time the awesome power of the spoken word combined with the grandeur of great ideas. This was true theater. This was theater in its highest form, and Dr. Martin Luther King was the ultimate theater artist. He was the megastar of American ideals.

After the rally, the cast of *Fly Blackbird!* was taken back to be introduced to Dr. King. It seemed as if everybody in the arena was now pushing in backstage to touch him. We had to wait in a long line for quite some time for our quick meeting. Dr. King must have been exhausted, but even for my brief handshake, he had warm, gracious words to share.

"Thank you so much for your contribution to the afternoon," he said to me. "You were wonderful. Thank you very much."

They were only a few simple words, but they were words I will never forget. His handshake was easy and gentle. It was only for a fleeting moment, but I will always cherish that touch.

After ten months, *Fly Blackbird!* was closing. The irrepressible musical could have run much longer in Los Angeles. But Jackson and Hatch had sold the rights for a New York production to a Manhattan producer named Helen Jacobson. *Fly Blackbird!* was flying across the country to newer heights. It was going to the Big Apple.

The New York production was to be a completely fresh mounting of the musical with a new director, Jerome Eskow. If the actors from the Los Angeles production wanted to be considered for their roles, they were welcome to try out, we were told. They would, however, have to come to New York at their own expense and audition anew with no guarantees. New York was going to be as tough and hard as we had been forewarned.

I thought, however, that this was another stroke of luck. I knew that, somehow, I would eventually be going to New York. It was the focal point of all my fantasies. But I never dreamed that I would be going there with a tailor-made opportunity! Many of the characters in *Fly Blackbird!* were created for and by the actors that played them. Some even had the same names as those of the players . . . like George. George was really me.

I decided I would dip into my savings and chase the blackbird to New York. I had fulfilled my compact with my father. I had my degree. And, best of all, I could assure my parents that I already had a job in the big, bad city. I could tell them that I was going to New York to continue playing George.

A number of the other cast members from the Los Angeles production also decided to take a good bet and go to New York. Josie, Thelma, Palmer Whitted, Jack Crowder, Josie's stepsister, Camille Billops, and a couple of others. We were going to be the L.A. blackbirds.

It was two weeks before Christmas, 1961. I arrived at New York International Airport in the dark of a frigid night. Josie and Camille, who had left Los Angeles before me, were there to meet me. They were bundled up like Eskimos. Camille glowered at the cold with squinted eyes and huffed her steamy breath angrily as if that might scare it away. But Josie looked so vulnerable. She had a heavy woolen scarf wrapped over her head and across her face with only her big brown eyes peeking out expectantly. But glowering or expectant, it was great to see familiar faces waiting to greet me.

We rattled by subway into Manhattan to my first address in New York City, the tasteful-sounding Sloan House. I told everyone in Los Angeles that was the name of my "hotel." I didn't tell them that it was actually the 34th Street YMCA.

The brisk air of my first New York morning only sharpened

my excitement. At long last, I was in my Mecca—the capital of American theater!

I had to check out "the Great White Way." As I strode down 34th Street huffing steamy breaths in the cold, I gawked shamelessly. When I reached Broadway, I turned and started marching up the thoroughfare of my dreams. But it was puzzling. The vaunted boulevard was not what I had expected. There was incredible frenzy. That I expected. There was crushing traffic, both human and vehicular. Racks of garments trundled about. The cacophony of bleating horns, slamming steel, and shouting voices was deafening. But I saw no theaters.

I was getting close to fabled 42nd Street. That was the place where George M. Cohan sang to the waiting boys that he "will soon be there." I picked up my pace. What I saw when I got to 42nd and Broadway left me aghast. There were "boys" waiting there for sure, but they obviously weren't waiting for George M. Cohan. And the derelicts had long since given up waiting for anything. There were theaters on 42nd Street, but it was heartbreaking. Grand marquees that must have announced names like Al Jolsen and Lillian Russell in the glory days were now displaying titles of sex-and-violence potboilers. I had studied American theater out of history books, but in the meantime, the living theater had moved farther up Broadway.

At the Astor Hotel at 44th Street, I detoured west to the legendary Sardi's Restaurant and then up Shubert Alley. At last! This was the theater district I was searching for. Here was the Shubert, the Helen Hayes, and the Booth, named after Edwin Booth, the great Shakespearean actor and the brother of the assassin of President Lincoln. They were all here, including the Plymouth Theater, where the great impresario Arthur Hopkins presented the Barrymore siblings, Ethel, Lionel, and John, in the plays of Shakespeare; and the Morosco Theater, where American classics such as Arthur Miller's *Death of a Salesman* and Tennessee Williams's *A Streetcar Named Desire* had opened. This was my very first time here, and yet I felt a distinct sense of déjà vu; I felt that glow of familiarity from everything I saw—the signs, the streets, and especially the theaters. But this encounter was no longer vicarious. I was actually walking where only my spirit had roamed before. I was really strutting up Broadway!

I kept walking up to 51st Street, and finally, I stopped at the Mark Hellinger Theater. This, too, was an historic theater. But suddenly my dreamy romanticizing ended. Reality stared me straight in the face. This theater was the reason for our trip to New York. The Mark Hellinger was where, in a week, I would be auditioning for the New York production of *Fly Blackbird!* This was the place where my future was waiting to be made. I peered through the locked glass door into the front lobby, and a shiver of anxiety ran through me. My breath left two hopeful frost spots on the cold glass door.

New York is a city that will not allow undistracted concentration. My anxious preparation for the audition was rudely disrupted when Sloan House, despite its elegant name, aggressively reminded me that the maximum length of stay there was a week. Because of their long waiting list, however, they preferred that my stay be even shorter.

So I began the daunting search for an apartment in Manhattan. I was astounded by the astronomical rent demanded for the simplest places—my savings would be eaten up in a month or two. Palmer Whitted and Jack Crowder were looking for an apartment together, and they asked me if I would like to join them. Splitting rent three ways would reduce the cost for all of us. Great idea, I thought, and agreed to be their third roommate.

The apartment we found was on West 39th Street between Fifth and Sixth Avenues. It was a place that jarred all our senses in the most primitive way. Thirty-Ninth Street was the northern border of the garment district, so from early morning till late afternoon, we were treated to a rock concert of roaring trucks, slamming steel doors, the banging of bins, and the braying voices of drivers and loaders. There was a delicatessen on the ground floor that sent up a pungent bouquet of a myriad strange food aromas to our fourth-floor walk-up. On the second floor was a small hat factory that kept the air we breathed as dense as primeval atmosphere with fine felt dust. And from our window, we had a stunning view of another brick wall as craggy with alluvial markings as the glacier-hewn cliffs of Alaska. Since the building didn't have an elevator, to get to our lair we had a crude ritual stomp up three flights of stairs. But the rent was cheap. And, better yet, it would be split three ways.

But when we moved in, Jack said with embarrassment that he was a bit short. He sheepishly asked me to cover for him and said he would pay two thirds of the rent the next month. Since I assumed we would be working by then, I agreed. I should have known better since I had memorized Polonius's "Neither a borrower nor a lender be" speech from *Hamlet* way back in high school.

Jack Crowder had a powerful stage presence. He was tall, slim, and dark. His voice was a resonant baritone. At the audition, he sang "Old Man River" impressively. I thought, though, that the choice of the song was rather ironic for a civil rights musical. But it was an unquestionably theatrical piece for displaying Jack's spectacular vocal range.

When my turn came to step onto the stage of the Mark Hellinger Theater, I was immediately struck by the vastness of the space. It was challenging and just a bit scary. I had to fill all this empty air. I started to sing "Goodnight, Irene," a popular ballad that I had chosen for my audition. I was shocked. I couldn't hear my voice. It seemed to leave my mouth and fly away into the cavernous theater and disappear into the dark. In the shower, I was used to hearing the steamy reverberation of my voice instantaneously. I tried to adjust to the spaciousness. My gestures grew larger. The nuances of the song became bigger, my voice louder. When I finished, I felt like an opera singer blasting out the national anthem.

"Thank you, Mr. Takei." It was the time-honored disembodied voice from the darkness. "We are ready for Miss Dotson now."

I peered back out into the black void and said, "Thank you very much. I look forward to working with you." I knew it would help to project an air of confidence. Josie looked nervous as she approached me coming offstage. I gave her an encouraging thumbs-up gesture.

That night all the L.A. blackbirds gathered at our apartment on 39th Street. It was a "bring your own booze" party, but Palmer and I supplied the chips.

We all felt good about our auditions. The final decision on the casting wouldn't be made until after Christmas, but we were eagerly looking forward to beginning rehearsals after the new year. Everyone was there, even Jim Hatch, the producer/ director/playwright of the Los Angeles production. Everyone, except Josie. I kept looking down to the street from our window. She said she might be late, but I knew she wasn't feeling too good about her audition. Maybe she might not come. It would be good for her to be with us tonight, I thought.

It was quiet outside. There was no one out on the street that only hours before had been a riot of noise, congestion, and combative commerce. As I gazed down looking for Josie, I noticed delicate little bits of torn-up tissue paper being dropped before our window. I twisted my head up to see where the prankster might be. The white little bits were coming down from all over—they were snowflakes.

"Hey, guys! Look! It's snowing," I announced. There was a mad rush to the window to gawk. We were all southern Californians; many had never seen snow before. But the novelty quickly faded, and we were soon back in our warm tribal circle and our boozy fantasizing. "Where I'll be ten years from now" became our whimsical topic. We all fancied ourselves stars. Some of us even possessed Oscars and Tony awards by that time.

"But even ten years from now, we'll still be getting together like this, wherever we might be," I predicted.

Camille, who was really a sculptor dabbling in theater, grandly announced, "Honey, I'm going to be so busy on my big project in Africa, I won't have no time for partying. But if all my sweet darlin's are gettin' together pissin' in high cotton, well, I just might tear myself away and come. I just might do that."

"Yeah, I'll come too," chimed in Jack Crowder. "If George and Palmer are hosting with party food like this, I'll come anytime."

We L.A. blackbirds were a tribe of starry-eyed dreamers.

I drifted over to the window again to see if Josie might be coming. The snow had laid a thin fleecy blanket all over 39th Street. As if by magic, the once-tumultuous street had been transformed into a hushed oasis in white. Only the streetlamp at the corner shone cool and serene in its vigil. Then, into the tranquil pool of light stepped a tiny figure. As the bundled-up form walked through the pristine white, it left dark little footprints behind in the fresh-fallen snow. The figure wore a heavy woolen scarf wrapped over the head, but I recognized her gait immediately. It was Josie! I grabbed my coat and thudded down three flights of stairs. She was just approaching the street door as I flung it open. I rushed out and embraced the snowflake-covered bundle. Even with the wool scarf and thick, heavy coat, Josie looked so defenseless. Her doleful eyes and slight shiver made my heart melt. Then I heard the door thud behind me. I had forgotten to grab the keys on my way down!

With great embarrassment, we had to be buzzed back into the building. As we trudged up the stairwell we were serenaded with drunken choruses of "Fly Blackbird!" from the fourth-floor landing. I was sure our neighbors knew by now that actors had moved into the building.

It hit me like a blow to the chest with a baseball bat. I felt dazed. The words I was hearing could not be true! But, despite Jack Jackson's gentle voice, his words were explicitly clear.

"I'm very sorry, George. Truly sorry that it didn't work out the way we wanted," he explained. "But the New York people have their own concept, and there was nothing we could do about it. They've decided to go with another actor in the role of George."

I was stunned. George was my role. I created the character. George was me! How could they possibly cast someone else? It took me a long time to come to grips with the fact that I was not going to be a part of the New York production of *Fly Blackbird!* I was now just another unemployed actor in this big, cold city.

Palmer and Camille were not cast, either. And Josie, who was so unsure of herself but desperately wanted to repeat her role, was also out. Jack Crowder was in—cast in Palmer's role! We all ached inside, but Palmer was best at covering the hurt with a pasted-on smile and bitter humor. To the familiar tune, he sang, "There's no business in show business, for me there is no show."

We had no show, but we all had an immediate and urgent need. We had to get a job—of any kind. Josie had a salable skill. She had worked her way through UCLA doing secretarial work, so she was quickly able to find a fairly well-paying job in an office on Third Avenue. But Palmer wanted to leave his days open for auditions, so he got a job working nights.

"Well, George. It looks like I'm going to be making a lot of dough," he announced to me as he sailed into the apartment a few days later. "And I'll be making it at night." But it was not the kind he implied. Palmer got a night-shift job working at a Harlem bakery. Thanks to his job, I got first to love, then to hate sweet potato pies. As part of the job's fringe benefits, Palmer got to bring home the unsold, two-day-old pies. They were always sweet potato pies, a delectable new discovery for me at first. But even starving young actors cannot stomach sweet potato pies for breakfast, lunch, and supper day after continuous day. I varied my diet by occasionally treating myself to a nineteen-cent hot dog from a stand on 42nd Street. But those sweet brown circles of carbohydrate that Palmer brought home nightly were our basic source of sustenance for our immediate post-blackbird audition weeks.

I went from one temporary job to another. During the Christmas rush, I sold men's ties at B. Altman's department store; when that was over, I loaded trucks in Long Island City. Through Josie's connections, I got a job typing labels at a publishing office on Third Avenue. Anything that kept the cash flow going—and the hope up. Always, when the confidence started to wobble, there seemed to be those random little acting jobs to keep the dream propped up. I worked as a photo model in an insurance company ad dressed as a businessman carrying a briefcase. I did a guest role in a segment of the live television anthology series *U.S. Steel Hour*, as a Japanese American soldier with a southern accent. I got occasional work in television, but never in the theater—my prime reason for struggling in New York.

The theater, however, was still very much a part of my life. If I couldn't be behind the footlights, then I would be in front of them—in the audience. I saw every show I could afford. They were usually matinee seats up in the balcony or standing room for the big hits. Among the matinees that I caught was *A Shot in the Dark* starring Julie Harris, Walter Matthau, and a young Canadian actor named William Shatner.

I envied Jack. When *Fly Blackbird!* was in rehearsals, he would come back to the apartment bone-weary from the dancing. I envied his exhaustion. I'd see him prostrate on his bed and feel jealous. Jack sensed that, and he was gracious enough not to talk about the show with Palmer and me. But at the same time, I couldn't contain my curiosity. After the show opened, I finally broke. I questioned Jack about how it was going, what changes had been made, if anybody important had been in to see the show. But I never asked him about George. I think I was afraid to know.

One day, Jack had a tip on a casting call. There was an audition that he had heard about for an "oriental" role in a new comedy. Why don't I check it out?

I arrived at the theater at midmorning to find an already long line of Asian actors of all ages and types. An assistant was handing out "sides," excerpts from the script for the auditioner to read. I discovered that the role was that of a bumbling comic servant with a funny accent and a high-pitched laugh. It was the classic stereotype. I had played my share of servant roles, but nothing quite like this. I hadn't come all the way to New York and loaded trucks and typed labels to perpetuate this mockery. But then, it was work I had not had. It was work in the theater! And besides, the rent on our apartment was coming due. I had a decision to make. Then I thought of Daddy. I walked back to the assistant.

"I'm sorry, but I don't think this part is for me," I said, and handed the side back to him. He gave me a "who do you think you are" stare, but I turned around and walked away without saying another word. As I moved past the line of Asian actors waiting to audition, they looked at me quizzically. I looked back at them and wondered what they might be thinking. But I couldn't feel self-righteous. I knew that one of them would be selected. Someone would do the role. Without making any eye contact, I walked back out into the cold.

But I did have another job waiting for me that night. Jack Crowder had an aunt who catered exclusive parties. She had frequently hired Jack, Palmer, and me to help out as servers. Tonight she had a party in posh Sutton Place on the East Side. Jack was unavailable since he was busy at the theater. So that night, I found myself in my white jacket, little black bow tie, and polite smiles serving canapés and cocktails together with Palmer, then serving dinner, and finally cleaning up. I was in fact a servant!

But I had it all thought out clearly in my mind. This wasn't my "real" job. I wasn't "really" a servant. My "real" job was acting. And that morning I had walked out on the potential for being hired at my real job acting the part of a servant. There was integrity there. I was only "pretending" to be a servant tonight. Oh, yes, it was very clear in my mind.

But the irony in my strenuous rationalization amused Palmer no end. As he and I lugged the party leftovers back to our apartment in the breaking light of the early morning, his cynical laughter echoed through the empty streets.

It was outrageous what Jack was asking. I had covered his rent the month before. He was supposed to pay mine this

Me with my mother, Fumiko Emily Takei, and father, Takekuma Norman Takei. Between them is Toyosaku Komai, the publisher of *Rafu Shimpo,* the oldest English-Japanese daily newspaper in the United States.

My family before the war. Nancy is in my mother's arms, Henry is on the left, and that's me carrying a comic book.

The two internment camps that were our homes for the duration of World War II. *Above,* some of the "dangerous" internees changing classes at the camp in Rohwer, Arkansas. *Below,* the barracks during one of the cold winters at the camp in Tule Lake, located in northern California near the Oregon border.

My kindergarten photo taken at Rohwer.

My mother and us kids during our internment at Tule Lake. I'm on the far left.

3

Home again: Henry, Nancy, and me in front of the house our parents bought after the war.

My UCLA
graduation
photo.

My early acting career.

Above, my role in an episode of *Perry Mason* called "The Case of the Blushing Pearl." *Below,* one of my first films, *Hell to Eternity.* On the far left is Jeffrey Hunter, who would later play Captain Christopher Pike in the first STAR TREK pilot, "The Cage."

I had a small role in the Alex Guinness, Rosalind Russell film *A Majority of One.* That's Guinness on the right, whose odd makeup and very faulty accent resulted in a bizarre performance as a Japanese man.

I played alongside James Caan (center) in the Howard Hawks film *Red Line 7000.*

Me with Cary Grant, Jim Hutton, and Samantha Eggar in *Walk, Don't Run.*

I confront John Wayne in *The Green Berets.* I had reservations about the politics of the film, but I found John Wayne to be larger than life.

My introduction to STAR TREK was my role as Astrophysicist Sulu in the show's second pilot, "Where No Man Has Gone Before."

In my more familiar guise, as the helmsman of the *U.S.S. Enterprise,* Lt. Sulu.

Sulu faces off against Captain Kirk (William Shatner) in an early STAR TREK episode called "The Naked Time."

Back in action: Sulu on the bridge in STAR TREK—THE MOTION PICTURE.

Sulu is tended by Dr. McCoy (DeForest Kelley) in the often-overlooked "other death scene" in STAR TREK II: THE WRATH OF KHAN.

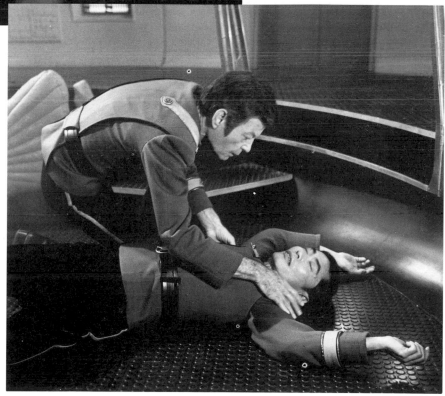

A fully recovered Sulu at the helm later in STAR TREK II.

Above, Sulu goes up against a Starfleet Security officer, and (*below*) gets the better of the much larger man. Though I was initially opposed to this sequence, I liked it when I saw it on film.

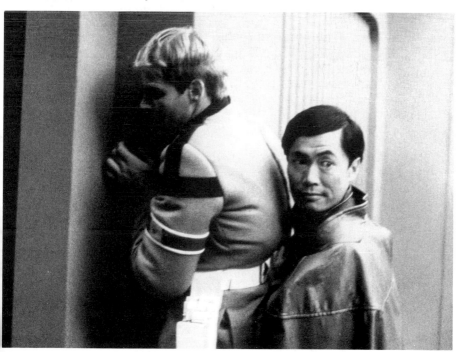

My mother takes the first step on my star on the Hollywood Walk of Fame, just prior to the release of STAR TREK IV: THE VOYAGE HOME.

Sulu "borrows" a helicopter in STAR TREK IV.

14

A behind-the-scenes look at the lost scene from STAR TREK IV, when Sulu encounters his great-great-etc.-grandfather. Here I am trying to cajole the young actor playing my ancestor into performing the scene. Both Leonard Nimoy (seated) and I did our best to inspire him, but the young man clammed up. As the day progressed, we lost the daylight and the scene.

Talking to director William Shatner on the set of STAR TREK V: THE FINAL FRONTIER. Despite our sometimes strained personal history, I found working with Bill as a director to be surprisingly pleasant.

At last! In STAR TREK VI: THE UNDISCOVERED COUNTRY, Sulu gets his first command, the *U.S.S. Excelsior.* The actual promotion scene was filmed for STAR TREK II, but cut from the final film.

month. How brazen could he be to ask me to cover for him again? He was the one who was getting paid regularly.

When Jack was refused help, he had a way of dropping into a deep, hurt silence. He took on a look of utter desolation, the face of a broken man.

"Do you think I'd ask you if I weren't desperate?" he broke his silence pleading. "I want to pay you back, man. But I had some financial setbacks." I noticed that he hadn't been sleeping at the apartment many nights lately. I also knew he had a way with women and had an idea of the kind of setbacks he was suffering.

"Jack, whatever your setbacks, you know you have an obligation with me." I was livid. "You can't ask me to cover for you again, because I haven't got it. It's as simple as that." I said that, but he knew that I had opened a savings account at the Dime Savings Bank on Sixth Avenue.

"Well, this is all I have. Take it," he said piteously. He held out a twenty-dollar bill. It hardly covered his portion of the rent for one month, much less two. But I took it anyway. And I covered for the rest of his rent again. Palmer certainly couldn't chip in more with his bakery earnings.

Jack slept at the apartment less and less. I learned that he had gotten another job singing at a small club on West 46th Street after his performance in *Fly Blackbird!* Jack was making money from two sources now! And yet, on the nights that he was back at the apartment, he made no offer to repay his debt. I seethed inside, but I wasn't going to ask him again. He was going to have to make the move himself. I wasn't going to force him to be honorable. But every time I came back in the street door, exhausted to my marrows from another frustrating day of fruitless rounds, and stared up the three long flights of stairs to the apartment, I cursed Jack. He was working. Two gigs! And I didn't have any. Every weary step up the tread became a stomp on Jack Crowder. I was raging by the time I reached the door to the apartment that Crowder was not paying for.

Josie was the great comfort. It was so good getting together with her at our usual meeting place, the Horn and Hardart automat on Sixth Avenue. She gave me her sympathy over coffee and apple pie. She always made my anger and frustrations melt away—at least for the time I was with her. Josie thought I should deal with Jack head on. He should meet his obligation or make other arrangements. It was unhealthy for me just to burn inside day after day. Deal with the problem and get on with life. Of course, she was right.

Very late one night, about the time the club would be closing, I went striding in. The room was almost empty.

"I'd like to see Jack Crowder," I said to the doorman. "I'm his roommate." He directed me to a small, curtained-off cubbyhole far in the back beyond the kitchen. It was his dressing room, and he was cleaning up after his last show.

"Oh, George!" Jack seemed startled by my sudden appearance, but he quickly put on a broad smile. "You didn't have to come here, you know. I was going to be paying you your money tomorrow. The whole thing. I just got paid tonight."

"I know," I said curtly. "That's why I'm here. I'd like the money now." Jack finished wiping his face very methodically and arranged his makeup with inordinate neatness on the little shelf that served as his table. He puttered as I stood there silently waiting. Then he got up smiling and said, "Excuse me a second. I'll go get the dough from the manager." He left the cubbyhole so quickly that I didn't fully register his last words. I thought he said he had already gotten paid. Then I noticed his overcoat still hanging on the peg. I surmised that he probably was having his money held by the manager of the club for safekeeping. Then Jack popped back in.

"Excuse me," he said, still smiling as he grabbed his overcoat. "I'll be right back." Then he was gone again. I stood there dumbfounded for a second. I rushed out into the empty club just in time to see him hurrying out the front door.

"Jack!" I shouted out across the room, and bolted after him. When I got outside, he was already halfway down the block.

"Jack, come back here!" I was raging as I started sprinting. Jack turned the corner and ran down Eighth Avenue with his long, loping strides. I charged after him bellowing at the top of my voice, "Jack, come back! Come back here! Jack!" His overcoat flapped frantically behind his lanky frame like a huge outstretched cape as I gave furious chase. "Jack! Come back here!"

The early morning sight of a tall black man wildly fleeing from an angry Asian down a deserted Eighth Avenue was a picture sure to sober up any drunken derelict who might have come upon the implausible scene.

I never caught Jack. His legs were longer than mine. And he never came back to the apartment again. His closet was filled with his clothes; he had fine taste, expensive taste. I was so angry I took his clothes and hocked them. The pawnbroker, however, did not value Jack's clothes very highly. But I sent Jack the pawn tickets at his new address anyway.

Palmer and I now had another problem. We wouldn't be able to manage the increased rent with Jack gone. My savings had been severely drained. I had just enough left for plane fare back to Los Angeles, and I didn't want to touch that. We had to find other housing.

Over coffee and apple pie at Horn and Hardart's, Josie suggested that I move in with her. I put my hand softly on hers. After the anger, the trauma, and the bile of the last few days, suddenly I couldn't keep my eyes from welling up. Dear Josie, my clever song-and-dance mate, the tender melter of my anger and my heart—my sweet, vulnerable Josie, whom I wanted to protect from this cold, hard city—was instead offering to be my guardian angel. Right there in the middle of the automat, I reached over and kissed her.

Jack Jackson was on the phone. His voice sounded diplomatic but also a little nervous.

"George, we've had a little problem with the show," he began. I wondered why he was sharing this information with me. It had been at least three months since *Fly Blackbird!* opened. Practically a lifetime. What did any problem with the show have to do with me now?

Then, very slowly, very gently, Jack explained the reason for his call. The actor who had been playing George was leaving the show. He was cast in another production. I knew the basic part, although not as redirected for the New York production. There was a big favor the producers needed.

"Believe me, I know how it must feel to you now. But they've asked me to ask you if you would consider stepping in." I felt that same flush of anger mixed with humiliation that I experienced when I was told that I wasn't cast. The shock wasn't there anymore. Instead, it was replaced by a welling indignation, a pain of a different kind. I was silent for a long time.

"I understand what you're feeling now." Jack broke the quiet. "Truly, I do, George. I would understand if you didn't want to do it." I didn't answer. I couldn't. A torrent of conflicting emotions was raging inside me. Finally I said, "Let me think about this, Jack. I'll call you back in an hour."

I walked the streets of the city for that hour. I got in lockstep with the teeming multitudes on the street. Thousands of people, all wrapped up in their own little worlds, with their own problems, their own private anguish. I walked for blocks. I reached Central Park. The branches of trees, withered gray by the cold blasts of winter, were at last starting to sprout tender green leaves. Birds were starting to sing and flit among those branches.

Finally, I walked into a phone booth and called Jack. Swallowing my pride, swallowing hard, I said to him, "Jack, I'll do it. I'll do George. When is the blocking rehearsal?"

The New York production of *Fly Blackbird!* was in its final weeks. I played George until it closed.

12

Return to Hollywood

I CELEBRATED MY TWENTY-FIFTH BIRTHDAY IN NEW YORK CITY. A quarter century. I had been in Manhattan almost a year now and had little to show for it. Nothing was happening with my career. Two television guest shots and a few photo modeling gigs. The only theater I did in New York was the last couple weeks of the *Fly Blackbird!* run. Back in Los Angeles, there had been, at least, a steady upward progression to my career in films and television. And, most of all, I missed my family and hometown.

Josie, too, had her parents in Los Angeles and was getting homesick for the space and sunshine. We both decided to go back before it started getting cold again. I closed out my account at Dime Savings Bank and bought the ticket back to Los Angeles.

The first thing we did when we got back was to drive up the coast in my father's big Buick—swooping up the Pacific Coast Highway all the way to Santa Barbara. It was sublimely liberating. After the overwhelming press of humanity, the racket and the crush of high-rises, suddenly the blue sky and the ocean, the sunshine, the breeze and open space tasted incredibly sweet.

We were Californians. We needed the freedom to ride with the wind over the tawny, rolling hills of Malibu and cruise past the marinas of Ventura. The gulls were in the sky, soaring and wheeling, just hanging out. We were back where we started, back in California. But we were no longer the same people who had left.

We had been to the twentieth-century primordial pool of Manhattan. We now knew how teeming, how competitive, and how chancy survival could be. But we also knew we could do it. If anything, our season in New York had energized us, strengthend our determination, reawakened us to the powerful potentials of the theater. We just needed some time to breathe, an intermission, then we would be ready to dive back in. As we wet our feet in the cool Pacific at the beach in Santa Barbara, we talked about our next move.

Josie knew theater could be a force in building a new America. It spoke the binding language of the "mind and the heart," and that was where the dialogue for change had to be carried on. She had been talking with Jack Jackson about a multiethnic theater where not just the performers on stage, but the policymakers, the artists, and, most importantly, the audience would reflect the entire ethnic tapestry of a community. This would be a theater literally "of the diversity of America." Josie was talking about forging a new American theater, carrying the energy of our Los Angeles production of *Fly Blackbird!* to a grander scale.

On that beach in Santa Barbara, our plans for the future soared like the gulls circling in the sky. We were back in California, where dreams still seemed possible.

Fred Ishimoto welcomed me back enthusiastically. There had been a lot of activity that I had missed out on, he told me, and he read off a laundry list of film and television projects that he was convinced I would have had—had I stayed in Los Angeles. I hated this speculating on the ifs and buts of something past.

"Fred, I don't believe in crying over spilt milk," I countered.

"But I do believe in making sure the new milk I get has plenty of cream in it. That's your job—to get me the cream."

"Boy oh boy," he exclaimed. "Send the kid to New York, and he comes back dictating orders to you. Well, yes, sir!" And he punctuated it with a snappy salute.

Within a month, Fred had me in a guest shot playing a young psychologist in a new medical series, *11th Hour*, starring Wendell Corey. This was followed sporadically by other television work like *My Three Sons*, *The Gallant Men*, and *Mister Roberts*, the most notable of which was a two-character episode of *Twilight Zone* with Neville Brand.

I also picked up where I had left off at UCLA. I had most of my credits for a Master of Arts degree. The final hurdle was the thesis. I decided to do my dissertation on Arthur Hopkins, the great producer/director, and his venturesome productions—from the classics to bold original plays—while he held the lease on the Plymouth Theater in New York from 1917 to 1926. So whenever I landed television or movie work, I was back to carrying my books with me onto the sets.

"You're such a studious young man, George. Study, study, study." It was Cary Grant commenting on the books in the pocket of my set-side chair when I worked with him on *Walk, Don't Run*, a comedy that also starred Jim Hutton and Samantha Eggar. "Why do you want to be a smart actor when all you need to be is dumb and handsome like me?"

"Well, since I'm not as handsome as you," I answered, "I thought I'd hedge my bet by trying to be a bit educated."

"Good idea. Get educated. You'll be so smart that you'll become a producer. And if you're a really smart producer, you'll be paying me millions of dollars to act in your movies. Study on, I say." Cary always got the wittiest last word in.

I received my M.A. from UCLA in 1964, but, contrary to Cary Grant's prophecy, I did not become a producer. Instead, I took a first step toward following in Daddy's footsteps. I made my first real estate investment on my own. Of course, I had guidance from Daddy, but I conducted my own search, made my own analysis, and did my own negotiating. Daddy was just there as a shadow consultant. I parlayed my cemetery plot profits into an investment in a modest eight-unit apartment building near a hospital. The hospital staff, I concluded, would be a good tenant base for the building.

This new venture, unlike cemetery plots, however, required maintenance work. So, in between acting gigs, I put on several other hats, those of painter of vacated apartments, Saturday-afternoon gardener, and all-around odd-jobs man.

Fortunately, the acting jobs maintained a regular if unpredictable flow. Unpredictability, I think, was more the hallmark of my career at this point than regularity. Certainly, I didn't expect to be working with so many Hollywood legends.

My next job was with fabled director Howard Hawks. He was sixty-nine years old, thin as a rail and topped with a bald head wearing a fringe of snowy white hair, but his eyes were still as crafty and sharp as the bird of his name. For his new film, a stock car racing adventure titled *Red Line 7000*, he had gathered a cast made up completely of young unknowns. I was cast in the role of the mechanic, who, he told me, was originally named Kelley but was changed, of course, to Kato for me. Hawks had a reputation for having a keen eye for talent and discovering young unknowns who go on to become stars, like Lauren Bacall. Again, he was boldly predicting that all seven of the young actors in his film were destined for stardom. Out of this group only James Caan emerged to fulfill his prophecy.

The possibility of stardom is an insidious virus. It can narrow vision and judgment, and it can throw values off balance. An all-consuming fever takes over. I got a touch of it back in those early years. How I sometimes suffer its aftereffects in the wee hours of the night, by the cold blue light of the late-night reruns.

It happens whenever one of two Jerry Lewis comedies I did comes on. *The Big Mouth* and *Which Way to the Front?* I lie still in bed with chills running up and down my spine. Then I convulse and heave. I've sometimes tried suffocating the nausea with a pillow. But always, I wind up staring at the screen in frozen

horror watching myself playing cartoon "oriental" characters
—outlandish cartoon wackos!

Fred, who was supposed to be my agent, the good shepherd of
my career, urged me to do it.

"Jerry Lewis is the biggest box office star in Hollywood," he
enthused. "It can't hurt you to be in a giant money-making
movie. Every one of his productions makes megabucks, and
you'll be associated with that." And then his voice turned
seductive. "George, it'll help you become . . . a star!" The scent
of stardom is a mind-addling virus, and agents are the usual
carriers. The disease runs virulent in this little town called
Hollywood.

Jerry Lewis himself was a pleasant surprise. His voice had the
same familiar nasal inflection, but unexpectedly, his real sound
was modulated and calm. There was none of that manic energy
about him off-screen but, instead, a controlled air of authority.
He was directing the movies, and everyone on the set knew who
was in charge.

I also found him to be an innovative filmmaker. I had never
seen a television playback machine on a film set until I worked
with Jerry Lewis. Rather than waiting twenty-four hours to see
the previous day's work in "dailies," with the playback machine
Jerry could check the scene just filmed immediately after
shouting, "Cut!" This eliminated costly time and labor. Any
reshooting that needed to be done could be accomplished right
then and there. Today, this system is commonly utilized, but in
the sixties, Jerry Lewis was a pioneer in incorporating this new
technology to filmmaking.

Films and television were maintaining my career as an actor,
but the theater still remained tantalizingly elusive. Los Angeles
had a vigorous theater scene. In Hollywood, there were scrappy
and venturesome little theaters, and at the acropolis of culture
in southern California, the Los Angeles Music Center downtown, there were the grand institutions: the Center Theater
Group, started at UCLA by the great John Houseman, was

presenting important works at the Mark Taper Forum; and the Ahmanson Theater presented stellar artists like Ingrid Bergman in O'Neill's *More Stately Mansions* or Richard Chamberlain in *Cyrano de Bergerac*. But as in New York, I was a part of this exciting theater scene only as a member of the audience.

One night, Josie and I went to a small theater on Santa Monica Boulevard in Hollywood to see a production of Jean Genet's prison drama, *Deathwatch*. It took place in a claustrophobic little jail cell occupied by three prisoners: a shrewd and insinuating homosexual, the muscularly handsome object of his desire, and a detached and silently brooding cell mate. The actors who played the three roles were all unknowns. Paul Mazursky was electrifying as the homosexual, Michael Forrest taunting and charismatic as the object of attention, and, in the least flashy role in the triangle but still compelling, was an actor named Leonard Nimoy. We walked out of the theater impressed by all three but predicting brilliant futures only for Paul Mazursky and Michael Forrest. The third actor, Nimoy, we thought was good as well—but he seemed too intellectual, too cool, no star quality.

It was an unusually sultry August night, one of those Los Angeles summer evenings when the dark doesn't bring any relief. People drove around just to feel the heavy air rush by their faces. It was useless. The heat was inescapable.

I can't remember why I dropped in on Jack Jackson. He had returned to Los Angeles from New York and was living in the Echo Park district. I frequently dropped by his place just to chat. It was probably to discuss the idea of the new American theater that Josie had been talking about. I don't remember for sure. But August 12, 1965, is a night I can never forget.

The picture on the television screen was shaky. It reeled and lurched from a scene of chaos to the next of conflagration. There were screams and shouts. Police sirens shrieked incessantly. The reporter's voice was breathless and staccato with alarm. A riot had broken out in Watts and was spreading to other parts of the city. Towers of flame were lighting up the night sky. Some people had been shot.

Jack and I watched, paralyzed. Before our eyes, we saw the wrenching spectacle of our city in rampage, bloodied people shaking angry fists at the camera, wild-eyed faces lit up by the flame of burning buildings. We felt the searing rage that blasted out from the screen.

But we were also watching a larger horror—we were witnessing the cataclysmic collapse of the great American illusion. The illusion that separation and equality can be maintained with doled-out tokens, that hope can be sustained on propped-up ideals, that order can be kept with assuaging promises. We were watching the terrible failure of promises too long delayed; despair could no longer be repressed. The full incendiary weight of this history was exploding before our eyes and burning up in flames.

I looked over to Jack. The blue light of the screen flickered wildly across his stoic face, staring fixed at the chaos. And I saw tears streaming down his cheeks. A paralyzing anguish gripped me. My friend was in pain, in silent, excruciating torment, and there was nothing I could do. Everything we had struggled for was going up in flames. Jack was in agony, and all I could do was sit there with him. I reached out and embraced him gently as our world was lit by the fires of chaos. And Jack broke.

"I'm angry, George," he sobbed. "I'm so angry I could be out there with them right now. I'm so angry I could pick up a brick and throw it at anything."

Jack was trembling with uncontrollable despair. This was a man of achievement, a man who moved as easily among academicians as among the power elite of New York. And yet, at his very core, I could feel the anger of a black man in America. I felt Jack's anguish break and shake through my own body, the pent-up anguish of a lifetime of subtle but penetrating slights, of deaf ears turned against whispered affronts, of exquisitely refined devaluations for no discernible reason but color. Jack's anger was no longer containable, no more than the rage

209

pouring out on the streets of the city. I felt it break and convulse through me. And I heard my sobs joining with his.

Throughout the night, Los Angeles continued to be mangled and broken and set aflame. My beloved hometown was going up in smoke. And with it went the innocence of an America that believed it could change with moral suasion.

The country passed from a time of demonstrations and protests to a period of radicalism and nihilism. Idealists disillusioned transmogrify into harrowing creatures. They become deadly zealots. My dim memory of the militant pro-Japan radicals of Tule Lake internment camp began taking on denser shape as I watched the emergence of the Black Panthers, the Weathermen, and the Simbionese Liberation Army.

The most remarkable phenomenon I watched, however, occurred with my dearest friends. Josie and Jack picked themselves up and got to work building the idea of a theater of the people. At a time of horrifying extremism—kidnappings, bombings, and radical racial nationalism—they held their original vision intact. They intensified their determination to turn an ideal into reality, to create a truly multiethnic American theater. They were joined in this effort by two Asian-American women, Elaine Kashiki and Jeanne Joe. They named the project the Inner City Cultural Center.

I wanted to throw myself into this challenge with them. I shared the vision and the goal. The idea of an American culture, strengthened by its diversity instead of balkanized by it, must not become just another experiment that was tried and then discarded as a failed notion. I was convinced that unity in diversity was at the very core of America's future. The struggle for a multiethnic theater would be hard, but nothing of worth is easily won. We had to redouble our efforts. This was the continuation of our *Fly Blackbird!* dream.

But at this point, another dream entered my life. It was a vision of that same pluralistic world, but situated in, of all places, a spaceship and shot up to the stars. This fantastical dream came into my life on a telephone call and sent me soaring into the galaxy.

THE
TREK
BEGINS

13

Meeting Mr. Rosenbury

THERE IS A COMMON, EVERYDAY SOUND AS ORDINARY AS A RINGING doorbell or a percolating coffeepot. But this simple noise seems to have as many disguises as a ventriloquist's voice. It can become a golden trumpet or a shrill alarum. It can chill with dread or sparkle with excitement. This same sound can signal an end as well as a beginning. The turning points in my life have been heralded by this multifarious noise. It is the sound of a ringing telephone. STAR TREK began for me with that chameleon ringing.

As a matter of fact, I almost missed it. Another sound intruded. I had just come in from my morning run around my Wilshire district neighborhood and was under the shower. There is something about the resonance of the shower stall and the dreamy caress of the steam that invariably gets me to crooning like Sinatra. Thankfully, the water's rush keeps me from really hearing myself. But that morning, it also kept me from hearing the phone. It must have been ringing for quite some time when I thought I heard a distant ringing. I listened. It sure sounded like the phone. I turned off the water. It was.

Dripping wet and a little annoyed, I picked up the receiver. It was my agent, Fred Ishimoto.

"Oh, you're there," he greeted with surprise in his voice. Of course I'm here, I thought to myself. Why else would he be talking to me. An irksome way to begin a conversation.

"George, I've got an interview for you tomorrow morning at Desilu Studios. Can you make it?" Fred is direct and very businesslike.

"Tell me something about it," I asked. The droplets running down my body were starting to turn cold. It was a pilot for a series, he explained. A space thing, something about the future. My part would be great. I was to meet the creator/producer, a Gene Roddenberry. I took down the information on a notepad that quickly turned wet and messy.

"Can you make it, George?" he repeated. I told him I would.

"Good, good, good. And how are things otherwise?" he added. It sounded more perfunctory than concerned.

I explained to him that I was wet, naked, and getting a little bit uncomfortable.

"Oh, that's what took you so long to answer your phone," he chuckled. "Well then, back to your beauty bath." I thanked him, hung up, and tiptoed back to the shower. The warm spray felt good. Then it occurred to me. I had forgotten to ask Fred the name of the series.

Desilu Studios was the old RKO Studios. Those letters *R, K,* and *O* stood for Radio-Keith-Orpheum, a company that started out operating a circuit of vaudeville theaters. In a town not noted for stability, this lot had seen more ups and downs than almost any other studio in Hollywood. It was in decline when Howard Hughes, the legendary billionaire, bought it in 1948 for a little less than nine million dollars. He then built it up, created stars like Jane Russell, and, true to legend, sold it a few years later to General Tire and Rubber Corporation for twenty-five million dollars.

Under this new management, inexperienced in the vagaries of show business, the studio's fortunes again ebbed. It wasn't until Lucille Ball and Desi Arnaz hit it big with their spectacularly popular comedy series, *I Love Lucy*, that this misused and frequently dispossessed film factory found a happier existence. Lucy and Desi had decided to go into the operation of a studio themselves, and the old lot got another lease on life. They had picked it up for a mere five million dollars. Fifteen soundstages and fourteen acres of prime Hollywood real estate. This was the studio where Lucille Ball had once been under contract back in the 1930s at fifty dollars a week, where Desi Arnaz had been looked upon only as another Latin singer-musician useful mainly for musical numbers. This was the studio where they had toiled as mere hired talent. Now, they were the lord and lady of their own motion picture domain—history, legend, dusty backlot, and all.

One of the first things they did was to completely repaint the great studio walls that surrounded the lot; and high above, near the corner of Melrose Avenue and Gower Street, in bright, bold letters, they painted the word *Desilu*, an acronym formed by their two names.

I looked up at that word as I walked toward the bungalow office of the man I was to meet. It can really happen in this unpredictable business, I thought. A chorus-line redhead from Jamestown, New York, and an immigrant Cuban conga drum player can rise to become modern-day movie moguls giving their own names to a studio. It's a crazy business, I thought, where dreams still come true.

I wondered what this interview with this producer could mean to my career. Fred said it was a pilot film. That meant if it sold, it would be steady employment. And I was to meet the man who could make me a regular working actor. What was his name? I pulled out the water-crinkled sheet that I had torn off the notepad by the telephone. It had gotten crumpled in my pocket, but the handwriting was pretty illegible to begin with, and the water smears on it didn't help much, either. I just couldn't make out for sure what I had written down. I tried to recall how it had sounded on the phone in my conversation with Fred the previous morning. I seemed to remember the sound better than I was able to decipher this sorry-looking squiggle I had written down. Before I knew it, I had reached the producer's bungalow. The number on the door confirmed I had reached the right place, but there was no name to go with it. So, name or no name, I walked into the receptionist's office.

A lady with a soft, welcoming smile was sitting behind a desk plate that read *D. C. Fontana*.

"Morning," I said. "George Takei here to see Mr. Rosenbury, please."

She smiled gently and corrected, "That's Gene Rodden-berry," with careful emphasis on the pronunciation of his last name. "Please have a seat."

Oh, great, I thought, I'm really starting off right on this one. I'm blowing the producer's name even before I meet the man. And this could mean a series, too. At that moment, I started to feel the first wave of nervousness.

I leafed through a few copies of *Daily Variety* and *Hollywood Reporter* lying on the coffee table. But I couldn't read a word. The possibility of regular employment in a series was increasingly tantalizing. Guest roles in episodic shows were fine, but the long, frustrating stretches of unemployment in between were killers. A running role in a series—that's nirvana in Hollywood! The more my imagination teased me, the more my nervousness increased. I flipped a page quickly, a fidgety attempt at nonchalance.

I looked up at the receptionist and smiled casually. She smiled back. Immediately, I was convinced she saw through my cover. I knew she knew. Otherwise, why would her smile seem so solicitously reassuring, so exaggeratedly encouraging. Be cool, I told myself. Be cool. I tried a wink on her. She smiled back ever so gently. This time it seemed touched with downright concern. Did she think I had a nervous twitch? I'd better stay with smiling. I smiled. "He won't be too long," she reassured. Her smile looked even sunnier and doubly unnerving. There were a lot of tense smiles exchanged before the intercom finally, mercifully buzzed. What a beautiful sound.

What a relief! She pointed to the big door. "Mr. Roddenberry can see you now." She smiled that smile again.

"Hi. I'm Gene Roddenberry." The voice had the heartiness of a host welcoming a dinner guest. The large, genial man who rose up from behind a desk and came forward to greet me had the affability of a country squire. "Why don't we sit down over there," he said, indicating a comfortable sofa in the corner of the office.

"Sorry to have kept you waiting. I hope it wasn't too long."

"Oh, no, not at all," I lied. "Had a chance to get caught up on the trade papers." My palms were sweaty.

"Oh good, I'm glad. By the way, George, how do you pronounce that last name of yours? Is it Takai?" He pronounced it "Tah-kah-ee." It is a frequent mispronunciation of my name.

"No, it is pronounced Takei," I corrected. "It rhymes with okay."

"Oh, okay. Takei as in okay. Takei is okay," he laughed.

"I might tell you, however," I added, "that Takai, as you pronounced it, is a legitimate Japanese word."

"Oh, really? What does it mean?" he asked.

"Well, it translates into English as 'expensive.'"

"Oh my God!" he roared. "I'd better make sure I call you Takei. Takei is definitely okay."

I instantly liked this man. He was unlike any other producer I had met—spontaneous, unaffected. He was comfortable. I hadn't intended to, but I found myself telling him about the problem I had with his name.

"Rosenbury!" he guffawed. "I had a feeling it might happen to me sooner or later in this business, but I never expected a Japanese to make me Jewish. Please call me Gene," he said, underscoring his folksy approach to business meetings.

He then began to sketch out for me the proposed series concept. Time: the twenty-third century. Place: aboard a huge spaceship, larger than the largest oceanliner, populated with personnel representative of the many racial groups on this planet. A spaceship earth. Format: the adventure of exploration and discovery, mankind's eternal frontier projected into the galaxies. The drama would encompass not only encounters and confrontations with alien beings and civilizations but with ourselves and our own civilizations. It would examine the familiar from fresh perspectives and explore the unfamiliar, not with fear or territorial imperative, but with open curiosity and an appetite for knowledge.

In his disarmingly amiable way, he had me dazzled. I was swept away, not just by the images but by his soaring ideas.

Then he began on the character for which I was being considered. His name was Sulu, a bright, young officer on board this ship. He was to be of pan-Asian heritage representative of that huge part of the world. There was a profile sketch of this character, but he was not yet fully defined. "What is sure is that he will be a strong, sharp, and likable character," Gene was quick to add. He seemed almost apologetic. "Believe me," he reassured, "he will be an officer carrying his weight on this ship."

I was astounded. Did he think I was somehow disappointed that the character was not yet complete? As sketched already, this character was a breakthrough role for Asian Americans. Hollywood, and especially television, had a long history of stereotypical depictions of Asian men as buffoons, menials, or menaces. I, who had agonized over taking some parts and who had lost work because I would not play certain roles, could not believe what I was hearing. This producer was sheepishly apologizing for the best opportunity I had yet come across. Then he added, "The actor who plays Sulu will certainly help fill out the character." This unassuming man was actually inviting the actor's participation in his project. It took everything in me to control my excitement.

Then, he shifted the conversation to books we had read, current events, and recent movies we had seen. As we talked some more, I tried as gracefully as I could to veneer my excitement with some semblance of professionalism. I shared with him my interest in his project and my hope that I might be on board with it; I wished him well, shook hands, and left.

This was unbelievable. This project was a quantum leap ahead of anything on the air, the role, a real trailblazer. And this was really happening to me! At twenty-seven years old, did I at last have my chance at the brass ring? I was lightheaded. As I almost dance-walked between the soundstages of this studio once owned by Howard Hughes, now owned by performers who once toiled here as hirelings, the electric charge of my excitement tingled uncontrollably. It can happen in this crazy business. I can get that role.

It wasn't until I had walked back across the studio lot almost to the Desilu sign again that it struck me. I had forgotten to ask Gene the title of the project. I still didn't know what the series was going to be called.

"Fred, what is this science fiction pilot called, anyway?" I asked my agent over lunch.

I had rushed over to Fred's office directly from the studio, just in time for him to invite me out. An unemployed actor develops an impeccable sense of timing. The Beverly Hills Hamburger Hamlet was a short stroll down Sunset Boulevard from his office. It was a new place that Fred favored for relaxing as well as for doing business. The lunchtime rush there was so crushed and noisy with people table-hopping and waving to each other that I don't know how anyone got anything done, much less relaxed. But they did serve great lobster bisque. It was while eating this savory soup that I learned the series was called STAR TREK.

"It's a good title," Fred pronounced. "STAR TREK. It's short, it sings, and, most of all, it's easy to remember."

I agreed, trying to maintain some aura of professional cool. With all the suspense involved in my finally learning the title, I told him it wasn't likely I would forget it.

"Well, let me tell you," Fred warned, "the suspense isn't over yet. As a matter of fact, it's only beginning. First, you have to cinch the part. That's still a question mark." Fred was not intentionally tactless. He was just by nature artlessly direct. He simply did not believe in dressing up an unpalatable truth.

"Then the pilot's got to sell. That's a toughie anyway," he continued. "But for something as far out as this space thing, it's really shooting craps. So maybe it sells. *That's* when the pins-and-needles suspense really begins."

He noticed that I didn't appear uplifted by this line of conversation. Quickly he added, "But you're lucky, George. Don't worry about it. I have good vibes about this one for you."

I knew he meant well. But I remembered he had had good vibes about the last television pilot I made, as well, a project titled *House on K Street*, about a master criminologist played by Academy Award–winner Dean Jagger. I played his "brilliant and trusty young assistant," according to the script. Fred had great vibes on that one too. It never sold.

"Who are some of the other actors being interviewed besides me for STAR TREK?" I asked.

"I don't know. But I would say you have a good, good chance at it." Fred was trying to be encouraging. It sounded too glib and much too on cue. I knew he knew, and I knew he wasn't telling. And he knew I knew.

It is a unique human relationship, that of an actor and his agent. It is a partnership between exaggerated opposites—one highly visible, the other anonymous. One the recipient of extravagant accolades or spotlighted ignominy, the other, nameless and holding only uncredited success or camouflaged failures. Yet these two opposites are inseparably bound together for survival, tied only by the thin, tensile nerve strings of necessity.

The strength of that bond is constantly tested. It is tested in the belief the agent must sustain in his client's talent through brutal appraisals of the actor's age, height, weight, or voice by crass casting directors. It is tested in the perspective the actor must maintain when his achievements are lauded and applauded by a capricious industry. It is tested by every compliment and hypocrisy, every rejection and duplicitous praise. It is tested by the kind of deviltry only the glamorously insecure and subversive workings of Hollywood can conjure up. Ultimately, the strength of that bond lies in the solidity of mutual trust. Out

220

of necessity, there may be some artifice involved in the dance between such opposites, but at its core, the essential element in the choreography of egos between actor and agent is trust.

With Fred and me, there was yet another bond in our relationship. We were both Japanese Americans. Although of different generations, we had a common history. While I was a boy growing up behind barbed wires, Fred was wearing the same uniform as the soldiers standing guard over us. He had gone from the internment camp at Gila, Arizona, to become a medical corpsman with the United States Third Army in Germany. He proved our Americanism on the battlefields of Europe and now was working to strengthen our image in films, as the only Japanese American theatrical agent in Hollywood. Although it remained unspoken between us, we knew we shared a mission beyond our individual careers. Our battlefield of the film business now required different maneuvers, other tactics, and a special trust. Fred, the experienced veteran of Europe, was also experienced on this field of action. So he was my agent. I trusted in him.

When we walked out into the midafternoon sunshine of Sunset Boulevard, I did something I hadn't ever done with him. I dropped the protective professional facade, that shield for the ego. I made a naked confession: "Fred, I've got to have that role. I desperately want that role."

He put a reassuring, big-brotherly arm around my shoulder and repeated, "Don't worry, George. I have good vibes about this one for you." Suddenly, that echo from *House on K Street*. At times like that, the actor-agent trust is severely tested. I slept very poorly that night.

When I'm under stress, I run. The following morning, I was running—long and hard.

I drove up to Bronson Canyon in the Hollywood Hills, parked in a leafy glen, stripped down to my running trunks, and started jogging. There was a gentle grade up a bridle path that became steeper as it neared the top and then leveled out to a long, undulating trail along the rim of a range overlooking the Los

Angeles basin on one side and the San Fernando Valley on the other. The letters of the Hollywood sign seemed to be sunbathing on the hillside. By the time I reached the rock outcropping that was my marker for the halfway point to the rim top, sweat was streaming down my body and flying off in hot little droplets. My muscles ached, and my lungs burned.

"I want that role. I want that role. I want that role." It was the only phrase that pounded in my mind. I pushed myself harder. The more the ache for the role pressed on me, the harder I pushed. "I want that role. I want that role. I want that role." It became a throbbing cadence. I was almost sprinting, and my heart was pulsating furiously. The burning sensation was almost unbearable. It felt as though my chest might explode with every gasp and every stride. The only thing I heard was my desperate heaving. The only thing that mattered now was the next searing lungful of air. Then suddenly, my mind cleared; the insistent pounding vanished, and just as suddenly, I got my second wind. My legs moved rhythmically, and my heart pumped smoothly. Everything fell into harmony with my regular, measured stride.

I reached the top. The views of the city and the valley were breathtaking. It was a clear, sparkling morning, and the air was exhilarating. I felt cleansed.

I slowed to an easy canter. The stress was gone, and I felt in tune with the world. I started trotting down the hill back to my car. But I still wanted that role—desperately.

The phone rang many times in the next couple of days. Each time, it did things to me. Anticipation, then fear. Did I get the role? Did I lose it? If I haven't heard from them by this time, does it mean I've lost it? But always, the ringing phone was from someone else. None was from Fred.

I had vowed that I wouldn't call him just to chat, something too many actors do. It is pointless and frustrating for both the actor and agent. I won't do it. This was one of my self-imposed vows.

I have a lot of them. I suppose you could say I was getting

superstitious. Another one of them is not talking about a prospective role until it is firmly set. So when my brother, Henry, called long-distance from Milwaukee, Wisconsin, where he was attending Marquette University, I didn't let on. I wanted to. I hadn't talked with him and my sister-in-law, June, for months. And this was important to me—to be up for a role as a regular in a series. I really wanted to share this with them. But I had made a vow to myself. So I didn't. Like primitive man cowering before an icon that controls the unexplainable forces playing upon him, making vows of abstinence and abjuration, there I sat with my telephone, and I didn't call my agent and I didn't tell my brother calling from half a continent away.

Faithful to my superstitions, I bided my time and maintained my vigil before this instrument, this modern-day heathen deity. There it sat, shiny, plastic, and silent. Imperiously and insolently silent, the dials looking like a gap-toothed, mocking grin. Squat, arrogant thing; a machine, a simple piece of equipment, and yet, there it sat, trying to take on the countenance of some great and inaccessible sage witholding a coveted bit of wisdom. A Buddha! A fat, smiling, silent Buddha!

And it can't bear being ignored. Just when I finally decided to walk away from it and go for another run, it suddenly sprang to life—shrill, and demanding.

So you're going to play that game with me, are you? Well, I'll just let you ring for a while and see how you like being kept in suspense. I let it continue clamoring for my attention. Finally, I picked it up.

"Hi, George." It was Fred! "What took you so long? Taking a shower again?"

"Oh, sorry, Fred." Suddenly, I felt the chill of both anticipation and apprehension. It was finally Fred with the word. Am I in or am I out?

"How've you been?" I tried feigning easy friendliness. Did it sound casual enough, or under the circumstances was it a bit too disinterested?

"Well, George, I just got the call. I thought you might like to know." I might like to know! I couldn't stand it. The torture was becoming unbearable. Speak up man, speak up, I felt like yelling. Then he said flatly, "You're doing the STAR TREK pilot." I can't remember any other word exchanged after that. I know we talked for a long while. But all I remember was Fred's flat, businesslike statement, "You're doing the STAR TREK pilot." I was doing the STAR TREK pilot! I desperately needed to go for another run.

14

Where I Had Never Gone Before

THE PILOT FILM OF STAR TREK WAS TITLED WHERE NO MAN HAS GONE BEFORE. Just the sound alone evoked adventure, something momentous—and ominous.

The pilot was to be filmed, not at Desilu's main lot in Hollywood, but at its secondary studio facility in Culver City. That did seem a bit ominous. I had heard the grapevine whispers about the extremely tight budget.

I had also been told that this was the second attempt at the STAR TREK concept. A previous pilot film, called "THE CAGE," had been made the year before with Jeffrey Hunter, my adoptive brother from *Hell to Eternity*, as the captain. That had been rejected. So, in a sense, this effort really wasn't where no man had gone before. This was the do-or-die pilot film. We had to make this one fly. Although I had nothing to do with the first, nevertheless, I felt the pressure of this project's history. We had to get it right.

But when I reported to the Desilu Culver studio, everyone gathered on the soundstage seemed upbeat and optimistic. There was the excited bustle of a new project about to be launched.

I was greeted by a scholarly-looking crew-cut man wearing an owlish pair of dark-rimmed glasses. He introduced himself as Morris Chapnik, Gene Roddenberry's research assistant. He ushered me to my dressing room, a square wooden box on wheels furnished with a couch, a floor-to-ceiling mirror, carpeting, and just enough space for a small closet. I peered in the open door and was surprised to see another person lying on the couch. He got up with a start when he sensed us looking in.

"Meet James Doohan, who is playing Scott, the engineer. He's your dressing roommate," Morris told me rather matter-of-factly.

"What! What! What's this?" The startled actor suddenly came to animated life. "What's this about a roommate?"

"We're sorry about this," apologized Morris blandly. "We have a limited number of dressing rooms so we're asking the actors to double up." The actor glared at Morris and started to get up with protest in his eyes, but I broke in with an extended hand.

"Good to meet you, James. I'm George Takei. I'm playing Sulu, the biophysicist." Then I added with a smile, "I guess when you're doing a pilot, these are the adjustments we have to make. It'll be a pleasure sharing this little box with you." He looked down at my proffered hand and tentatively took it.

"Yeah. Isn't this something," he agreed, mollified a bit. "This tiny little space, and they ask you to share it. But, you're right, I guess. I heard they have a real tight budget on this one. Real tight." He shook our clasped hands, and with a disarming smile he added, "By the way, call me Jimmy."

"Okay, Jimmy." I grinned.

While we were discussing our shared dressing arrangements, Morris had quietly slipped away to attend to other duties. Jimmy became immediately affable.

"Actually, you know," he confided conspiratorially, "I don't mind sharing with you. Back in my New York days, I've shared tiny, little closets that they call dressing rooms with other actors. Literally grungy little holes!"

"We've all gone through those days, haven't we," I agreed and started to share my own New York experiences with him.

"But!" he interrupted with stern emphasis blazing in his eyes, "we can't let them get away with this again. I mean it! Once the pilot is sold, we've got to have our own dressing rooms. That's a definite!" Of course, I thought, but before I was able to get a word out, he continued. "What do you think? Do you think this pilot will sell? Huh?" There was anxiety around the edge of his voice. And this time, he waited for me to respond.

Despite our abrupt meeting, I was charmed by this amiably forthright man. He was refreshingly down-to-earth. It would be fun working with him, I thought, hoping the pilot would sell.

"Well, Jimmy," I said, "I get a strong smell from this production."

"What! What! What do you mean?" he asked, agitated.

"I smell quality," I amplified. "I smell it in the script. I smell it in the cast they've gathered." And I told him about having seen both Shatner and Nimoy perform onstage. "And most of all, I smell quality in the concept. It's not just another knockoff of last season's hit. It's fresh and innovative. I smell quality about this entire project."

"Good. Good. Me, too," he agreed, smiling brightly. "This is a real classy project."

"But that means we're in trouble," I stated flatly.

"What do you mean?" Jimmy's expression shifted to puzzlement.

"Television has no respect for quality," I explained. "Quality is the kiss of death. Every show that I've liked was cancelled in a flash. If this STAR TREK sells," I predicted, "at best, it'll run two seasons. More likely, we'll be killed in one."

As if to put a stop to this gloomy conversation, Morris popped his head back in and asked us to get dressed right away. They would like us for rehearsals onstage.

When Jimmy and I reported to the set, it was buzzing with activity. We weren't late, but an informal rehearsal seemed to be already in progress. There was an eagerness, an anticipatory champing at the bit to get started.

The dominating voice over the cacophony was that of the director, James Goldstone. His booming baritone could be heard over all the shouts and calls and whistles. But what commanded all eyes and pulled them like some gravitational force to the blazingly lit center of the set was the single most compelling presence there, the unmistakable star of the production, William Shatner. Everything seemed to revolve around him. The director's slow, circling pacing, his keen, calculating eyes, the full intensity of his concentration, all were focused on Shatner. The camera crew, the light crew, the sound team were all converged on him. The circular configuration of the set placed his chair at the very centermost point. And Shatner fully occupied the epicenter. He commanded the hub of all activity on the set.

He radiated energy and a boundless joy in his position. He shouted his opinions out to the director; he sprang up demonstrating his ideas; he laughed and joked and bounced his wit off the crew. And the loudest, fullest enjoyment of his witticisms came also from Shatner himself—a bright, lilting, surprisingly high-pitched giggle. He beamed out an infectious, expansively joyous life force.

Standing off in the darkened periphery, I spied another face, the face from the small theater production of *Deathwatch*. I recognized the sharp eyes, the aquiline nose, and the bony angularity of the face. It was the actor Leonard Nimoy. But in the half-light of the outer edge of the set, his complexion seemed to have an eerie yellowish cast, the sides of his eyebrows arched up like the eaves of a pagoda roof. His face looked exotic, vaguely Asian. Nimoy stood there silently, wearing a terry-cloth robe, watching attentively, his chary eyes taking in everything. Then suddenly, as if he had decided he had seen enough, he turned around and stalked off into the darkness. Swiftly and as soundlessly as a cat, he was gone.

Other actors were gathering now. Two other actors sidled up next to Jimmy and me. Both were dressed in the body-hugging velour shirt of what we had been told was the Starfleet uniform. The older man was stocky, gray-haired, resolute-looking. This was Paul Fix, who was playing the ship's medical officer, Dr. Mark Piper. Next to him stood a good-looking young black actor. I knew that he, too, was cast in a breakthrough role for television, that of the communications officer of the ship, Mr. Alden. When he saw me, he smiled and moved toward me.

"Hi, I'm Lloyd Haynes," he whispered, offering his hand. "Didn't I see you in *Fly Blackbird!*? You were great!"

"Thanks," I whispered back. "Yeah, I flew as a blackbird then, and now here we are about to take off on a starship into the future. Demonstrating in the twentieth century and integrating the twenty-third. Small world, isn't it?" I laughed.

"Isn't that . . . a small galaxy?" Lloyd corrected with a smile.

"No, that isn't," Jimmy interrupted. "That's three centuries. Twentieth century to the twenty-third is three centuries. Not a galaxy." Jimmy was already fine-tuning his character of the meticulously precise Scottish engineer.

Gary Lockwood and Sally Kellerman, the guest stars of the pilot episode, appeared and joined the gathering group of actors set-side.

"All right, ladies and gentlemen, may I have your attention, please. We are ready to begin rehearsals!" The assistant director's powerful voice brought a gradual stop to all the shouting, the pounding, and the hustle and bustle. With silence and order restored, the assistant handed the set over to the director, James Goldstone.

"All right now. This is the bridge of the *Starship Enterprise*," Goldstone's deep, resonant voice began. "It is the nerve center, the brains of a great technological organism." Then he looked around at the assembled players. He craned his neck over the heads, searching, and then he asked his assistant, "Is Leonard ready to join us?"

"I am here." A voice came out of the dark. And into the light emerged not an actor, but a surreal presence. He was dressed in the same velour Starfleet shirt as all the rest of us. He was cast as an alien but looked anthropomorphic, of human form with a head, two arms, and legs like the rest of us. Yet he was startlingly exotic. His skin was the color of deep, rich cream.

His eyebrows swept up at their ends. But the most arresting thing about his appearance was his astonishing ears. They looked normal in all aspects but one. They curved to a point that rose sharply upward like the ears of an alert cat. As bizarre as they may have looked, however, they were actually quite pleasing. There was grace and a sculptural balance to them. They looked oddly genuine.

The person who stepped into full view exuded a detached, even slightly superior attitude. An air of guarded reserve. There was a curious credibility about him. Instead of seeming fantastical, he moved onto the bridge like a proud but somewhat wary foreigner placed among a group of strangers. I understood that feeling. I had experienced it myself in the past. As strange as he appeared, there was an eerie reality about him.

What a sensational entrance, I thought. To step onto the set for the first time and be completely and compellingly in character. And what a fantastic character!

On that first day, instead of meeting an actor, I first met Mr. Spock. Over the years, I was to discover how fantastically original a creation Mr. Spock would become. So intriguing, so dense, and so elevating was this character that I often had difficulty distinguishing where the shared territory with the actor began and ended—where the borders might be that finally separated Mr. Spock from the profoundly complex man who came to personify him. It was tantalizing. I wanted to get to know the actor I had met that first day as a strange but hauntingly real character. I wanted to get to know Leonard Nimoy. There was another reason now to pray that this pilot would sell.

My three short days filming the pilot episode flew by. The schedule moved at breakneck pace. The pressure was particularly intense because STAR TREK was such an unusual show. Everything was seminal. We were creating a whole new world solely out of the imagination of Gene Roddenberry, filled in with the spontaneous inventions of the actors and technical wizards on the set. God had seven days to create earth. We had eight, not only to create a new galaxy, but to film it as well. And it was done in eight days. But I was done in three.

The only actors I got to really share some time with in those hectic three days were my dressing roommate, Jimmy Doohan, and Lloyd Haynes. We talked about the challenges of a show like STAR TREK. We wondered about the prospects for such a pioneering series. And we all prayed for the possibility of steady employment. We were also treated to an extraordinary human spectacle that we happened upon only by sheer chance.

We were standing around chatting outside our soundstage. Near the entrance to the one next to ours, stood a young Asian man dressed as a chauffeur. He had his cap and jacket off and seemed to be going through a series of muscle-limbering, slow balletic movements. Suddenly, he exploded in a burst of kicks and leaps and twirls that was a symphony of speed. Our chatting ceased. We just stood there, stunned. Then he repeated the ballet. His movements had grace; his body, control and elegance. We were mesmerized. Then the flash detonation of energy and motion astounded us a second time.

Just then, an assistant poked his head out from his soundstage and called, "We're ready for you on the set now, Bruce." As we stood open-mouthed, he quietly slipped back in. It had been an amazing demonstration of what incredible feats the human body is capable of. And we had just chanced upon this extraordinary spectacle.

We later learned that the martial artist was a young actor named Bruce Lee and that he was working on a new television series that had just sold called *Green Hornet*.

A few months after we had filmed the STAR TREK pilot, I was cast in a terrific role in a prestigious anthology series called *Chrysler Theater*. My career seemed back on a roll. The episode was titled "Wind Fever," and I was playing an Oxford-educated, English-accented barrister in a former British colony in tropical southeast Asia. I would be able to use the British accent that I had added to my collection from my Shakespeare Institute summer. But best of all, and most serendipitously, the defendant that my barrister would be representing, a dedicated Dr. Schweitzer–like jungle missionary/doctor accused of malpractice, was to be played by William Shatner. I was delighted. Maybe he might have a bit of news to share about the progress the STAR TREK pilot was making. Perhaps with this production, I would get to know him a bit better. Perhaps "Wind Fever" was the omen that would have us working together for season after season. All sorts of wild fancies ran rampant through my imagination.

"Bill, how've you been?" I shouted out as soon as I spotted him on the set. He was dressed in rumpled tropical cotton clothes, and I was resplendent in my full-flowing, black barrister's gown with a tiny white barrister's wig perched on my head. He turned smiling as I rushed up to him. "Well, have you heard anything about it yet?" I couldn't restrain myself. I had dreams about the pilot night after night. They were turning into nightmares. I was hoping he had some good news. At least something to prop up hope.

He took my extended hand, smiling. Bill's smile was bright and beaming. He took my hand and continued to smile looking into my face. But the look in those smiling eyes was searching, quizzical. Instantly, I sensed it. He didn't recognize me!

"George Takei," I prompted. "I did the STAR TREK pilot with you. Sulu!" I blurted.

"Hi, George," he said without missing a beat. Bill's voice was soft and exaggeratedly affectionate. His smile remained unchangingly friendly. His eyes melted with fondness. "How are you. It's so good to be with you again." He sounded as if we had become the most bosom of buddies during the filming of the pilot. "Let's get together later. We've got to talk. But I want to concentrate on this scene here. Excuse me." He gave my arm a tight, affectionate squeeze as if to emphasize his sincerity, and then he turned away toward his dressing room.

I stood there puzzled, watching him walk away. His aggressive show of fondness was a bit bewildering. Then it occurred to me. I was wearing the British barrister's white wig. Maybe he didn't recognize me underneath it. Could he have been thrown because of the way I was dressed? That must be the reason. So he was overcompensating with excessive friendliness. I decided to be charitable with Bill.

I was informed by an assistant that Keye Luke, my old *Rodan* dubbing colleague, was also in the cast. It was getting to be like "old home week." But when I saw him, I was struck by how much he had aged. His face had become a network of fine wrinkles. His once-robust voice sounded dry and reedy. And he moved slowly with the help of a cane. Initially, I thought it was a character prop. But he told me he had had foot surgery and that he was incorporating necessity into his character. He was playing an elderly town patriarch. I realized that almost a decade had passed since we had worked together on *Rodan*.

All my scenes in "Wind Fever" were with Bill and another guest star, John Cassavetes. It was exciting working with two cracking-good actors. Cassavetes smoldered with concentrated heat as my opposing counsel. Bill was crafting a fascinating portrait of an idealist with a dark underside. It was wonderful and intensely engaging to be working with such actors. And as before, in between shots, Bill broke the tension with his jokey banter and lighthearted pranks. His silly giggles were bubbling up constantly.

But I was mystified. I wanted to talk about the pilot we had made. I thought Bill would be eager to discuss STAR TREK, too. But he seemed almost disengaged from it. He had indicated earlier to me that he wanted to talk about it later. I waited. But later never came. My work on "Wind Fever" was soon finished. But Bill never talked about a show that was keeping me, at least, sitting on needles of anxiety. I found out nothing about the progress of STAR TREK from Bill. Perhaps he was superstitious, I thought. Or perhaps he didn't know anything either. He never said.

It wasn't until January of 1966 that the phone call from Fred came. "NBC picked up STAR TREK," he shouted into the receiver. "We're a go!" The long suspense was over, and the fun was about to begin. Or so I thought.

15

The Launching

THE ROOM WAS UNCOMFORTABLY PACKED. EXTRA CHAIRS WERE crammed in. Some people had to stand against the walls. Why couldn't they have gotten a larger conference room? Perhaps this was Desilu's largest, I guessed.

But the crush only seemed to intensify the excitement. The electricity in the air was palpable as actors nervously leafed through scripts, black-suited people smiled tensely, and assistants hovered about offering pencils and cups of coffee. I waved to Jimmy Doohan across the table, and he responded with a firm thumbs-up. Leonard was concentrating on his script, scribbling notes in the margin. Bill was engaged in an animated conversation with an associate producer. I looked around and wondered why Paul Fix and Lloyd Haynes were missing. They were supposed to be regulars also. An anticipatory hubbub filled the room.

Only Gene Roddenberry seemed to be fully savoring the moment. As I watched him sitting like a genial lord at the head of a long banqueting table, I sensed in that big, all-embracing grin of his the history that had preceded this day. How sweet this moment must taste for him. The journey to bring STAR

TREK to this point had been arduous. There was the failure of the first pilot and the year-long struggle to get the second one made, then the long, anxious struggle for a decision from the NBC powers-that-be.

Now, at long last, here we were, gathered for the launching of the series itself and the first reading with the entire cast. Our audience was the studio executives and the heads of departments. With a modest clearing of his throat, Gene began.

"Well, folks, we're starting an adventure today. Let's have fun along the way." And with that, he began introducing the members of the cast: First Bill Shatner and Leonard Nimoy. Then he called out the name DeForest Kelley. He would be playing the ship's doctor, now renamed Dr. Leonard McCoy. So that's why Paul Fix was absent, I realized.

Gene introduced Majel Barret as Nurse Chapel. Then he announced that a change had been made with Sulu, the biophysicist. Gene had already told me of this, but nevertheless I couldn't help suppressing a small prick of anxiety. Sulu, he announced, had been moved up to the bridge as the helmsman, but he would still be played by me. I knew I really needn't have worried, but it was a relief nevertheless to have this change out and official. The network people, Gene stated, had expressed interest in making Sulu more regularly visible, so the decision was made to give him the helm position on the bridge.

Jimmy Doohan, Gene said, would remain the good engineer Scott. Then he introduced the woman sitting at the far end of the table, whom I had recognized and wondered about. He called out the name Nichelle Nichols and announced that she would be playing the communications officer, now named Uhura. So that's why Lloyd wasn't here, I thought. Later, I learned that Nichelle had been cast because Lloyd had landed the lead role in a new series, *Room 222*, and had asked to be released from his STAR TREK contract. Such are the quirks of fate and the capricious ways of Hollywood—had it not been for Lloyd's good fortune, the *Enterprise* might not have been graced by the beautiful Uhura's opening of hailing frequencies and raising Sulu's heartbeat. Finally, Grace Lee Whitney, a vivacious blond, was introduced as the yeoman, Janice Rand. With a grand flourish of his arm, he said, "And there we have the complete STAR TREK family." There was the patter of polite, ritual applause.

The department heads were then introduced. There were so many names to remember that, rather than try to memorize them all and get frustrated, I decided to concentrate only on those I would be working with immediately. Fred Phillips in makeup. Bill Theiss in costumes. And associate producer Bob Justman.

Then Gene introduced the person whose name I knew I had better memorize. "This is the man who will be our big chief at the studio and our link with the network, the exec in charge of productions, Herb Solow." There was vigorous applause with a touch of sycophantic fervor. One of the black suits rose up. He was a slight man, but when he began to talk, I knew immediately why he occupied his office. His speech combined enthusiasm with charm, a call to arms with optimism. He talked of the fresh and challenging project we had in front of us. He described the arid landscape of television today and the bold pioneering we as a team were about to begin. And he promised the solid support of Desilu Studios behind the project. It was a rousing, spirit-raising speech. He lit all our engines, and we began rumbling for the blast-off.

To push that button, Gene introduced Joe Sargent, the director of the first episode to be filmed, "The Corbomite Maneuver." Here was another good omen, I thought, for I had studied under Joe when he was teaching at the Desilu Workshop a few years back. My former acting coach would be directing me on the initial episode of my maiden journey into the wild unknowns of series television.

I could now confidently—and boldly—go where I had never gone before . . . my very first television series. I was in the care of many good hands. Joe was guiding us. Gene's vision primed and energized us. And we were fueled by the executive in charge, Herb Solow's promise of full backing by Desilu. It was a terrific beginning on a beautiful spring morning.

The months that followed were the most hectic, exhausting, and exhilarating work experience I had ever known. Each new episode was another fresh challenge. I hadn't been a science fiction devotee—although I had read and loved some of the works of Ray Bradbury—so the genre was an eye-opening and mind-expanding discovery. For the glimmering new world we were creating using the stark metaphors of science fiction, we received scripts that were powerful human dramas of prejudice and nobility, of war and the struggle for peace. Interspersed with these were tales of imaginative whimsy that revealed new character relationships.

As an actor, I felt for the first time the sense of being a member of a lively repertory company. Periodically the science fiction genre would allow us, while still in the body and mind of the character we portrayed, to go outside the bounds of those established Starfleet officers. We got the opportunity, rare in television, to "stretch" our thespian muscles.

I even got to stretch my running muscles as well. True to his promise, Herb Solow ensured that we had the budget to shoot some episodes on outdoor locations. So whenever we shot out at the craggy moonscape of Vasquez Rocks or a wild animal compound called Africa U.S.A., I took along my running shoes to use during the "off times" on location.

Whether on location or back on the soundstage, Leonard's presence on the set always brought another dimension to the work. He was creating a truly original character. There was no precedent for Spock. Leonard's imagination, talent, and strength of will were the only resources available to him. And from them, he created a magnetic, riveting, and original character. From the time that I first saw Leonard on the set of the pilot film, his commitment to the challenge was total. His complete dedication to building his character impressed everyone, and he enriched and elevated the work atmosphere on the set.

The doorbell buzzed stridently. It was almost nine o'clock at night, but the sound was not unexpected. I had been anxiously waiting for the delivery of the script that associate producer/ writer John Black had told me about. Two weeks ago, he had dropped by the set during the filming of "Mudd's Women." That episode, about a cargo of scantily clad beautiful women, seemed to attract an unusual number of casual visitors from the front office claiming to be "keeping an eye on the frontline action." Seated set-side next to me, John let slip a tantalizing bit of information on an upcoming script he was writing.

"How are you at fencing, George?" he asked me as he eyed a former *Playboy* centerfold rehearsing her scene. He should have known better than to ask an actor a question like that and expect a pure answer. When it comes to something that might possibly enhance a role, we actors will automatically claim to be expert at anything—and then go out and try to become one.

"How did you know that's one of my favorite sports?" I responded. "Why?"

"Just asking. How are you at samurai swordsmanship?" he continued.

"Of course I'm good at it. I grew up watching samurai movies. Why?" I persisted.

"I'm working on a script right now where you get infected by a virus that tears down all your inhibitions and you go berserkers with a sword. I'm trying to decide which way to go."

This was mouth-watering. After so many episodes of being adhered to the helm console announcing the warp velocity, this sounded absolutely delicious.

"By all means, it should be fencing," I recommended. "Samurai sword fighting is too obvious. It's too ethnically consistent. Sulu is a multi-interested twenty-third-century man, and his sense of heritage should be much broader than just ethnic. His sense of his culture should be of the greater human heritage. I'm a twentieth-century Japanese American, and al-

238

though I saw samurai movies as a kid, I actually grew up with more swashbucklers and westerns. I think it'd be more interesting to see a fencing foil in Sulu's hand."

"Sold," John responded, and we sealed it with a handshake. He got up with a final gaze at the action on the set and left the stage with a direction in mind for his script.

It was this script that I had been eagerly awaiting when the doorbell sounded. I flung open the door, and the messenger from the studio stood there smiling.

"Your script for the next show, Mr. Takei," he announced as he handed me the familiar gray envelope with the Desilu logo.

"Thanks. How come it's so late?" I asked. Actually, it wasn't unusually late. The scripts were customarily distributed at night, but my eager anticipation for this one just made this delivery seem late.

"Well, they were working on this final draft all day. I ran it over hot off the press," he explained.

I tore open the envelope and pulled out a script titled "Naked Time." I started reading immediately. When I finally put it down, I was still in the grip of a powerful story. John Black had written a drivingly tense drama. The virus that placed the U.S.S. *Enterprise* in jeopardy also revealed new aspects of all of the principal characters: Kirk's desperate fight to save his ship, his captaincy, and his soul; Spock's dual ancestry waging a galvanic internal battle; the coolly dependable Christine Chapel revealing her hidden passion for Spock; and best of all, Sulu's liberation from the helm console as a romantic swashbuckler. Freed of his shackles to the console, he was as dashing as Errol Flynn.

We were still filming the episode "Man Trap," but I couldn't get my mind off this next script. I wasn't on the call sheet for next day's filming, so I had scheduled another workout at Falcon Studio on Hollywood Boulevard for the fencing lessons I'd begun the first weekend after my set-side conversation with John Black. I went to sleep that night counting thrusts and parries.

Mr. Faulkner, my fencing instructor at Falcon Studio, was a

man in his late sixties, but he was still in great shape. His navy blue polo shirt couldn't hide his strong, brawny shoulders and hard pectorals. During the workout, I was drenched in perspiration and huffing and puffing, but he continued demonstrating a flurry of acrobatic thrusts.

"Can we take a short breather?" I pleaded. With ill-disguised amusement, he agreed.

"Fencing a little tough on a runner?" he teased.

"Errol Flynn made it look so easy and fun," I gasped. "I used to pretend I was Robin Hood after seeing him and Basil Rathbone sword fight in that movie. But I never realized it required all these new muscles."

"Flynn was good. A real fencer," Mr. Faulkner stated with authority. "But Rathbone was a wild man. Flynn didn't trust him one bit."

"Did you know them?" I asked.

"I choreographed the swordplay in *The Adventures of Robin Hood*," he revealed.

"You did?" I was completely taken off guard by this stunning remark. *Robin Hood* was one of my favorite boyhood movies back in East L.A. I had thrilled at the duel between Errol Flynn and Basil Rathbone. After the movie, I had Mama sew me a Robin Hood costume, and our backyard became Sherwood Forest.

"Oh, yes." Mr. Faulkner smiled. "As a matter of fact, I doubled for Rathbone in the fight sequences. Flynn was terrified of him."

"You mean that was your back I was watching in those shots of Errol Flynn clashing swords with Basil Rathbone?"

"All except when you saw Rathbone's face." He grinned proudly.

I was flabbergasted. This man who was coaching me in my fencing, whom I had randomly plucked out of the telephone book only because he was conveniently located, this was the very man who had swept me away with his blood-stirring swordsmanship when I was a boy. What incredible luck, I thought.

"Okay, I'm ready to go again," I announced. With new resolve and vigor, I launched into my thrusts and parries. It wasn't too hard to imagine myself as Errol Flynn now. I was crossing swords with his adversary. We clanged away with gusto until my hour was up and my energy completely spent.

At last! It was the first day of filming on "Naked Time." I got up at the crack of dawn's pale light, and instead of my usual morning run, I huffed and puffed through my fencing exercises, showered, then drove off to the studio. Nichelle, Leonard, and the actor playing the navigator this week, Bruce Hyde, were already in their makeup seats. Bill was getting the first part of his makeup done in his dressing room. I mumbled my good mornings to everyone, introduced myself to Bruce, gave my breakfast order of cereal with skim milk, a bran muffin, and a slice of cantaloupe to Greg Peters, the assistant director, and settled into my makeup chair. Marc Daniels, the director of this episode, roamed into the room to exchange a few cheering pleasantries and then roamed out. The banging and the shouting from the set was beginning to pick up in tempo and volume.

With my makeup done, I picked up a cup of coffee at the urn and strolled over to the schedule board. I wanted to check for a possible day off before my fencing scenes were up, for a final workout with Mr. Faulkner. As always, we would begin filming for this episode with the bridge scenes, all of them bunched together—the opening, the scenes scattered throughout the script, and the final tag. We had a lot of bridge scenes in this show, including one of my fencing sequences, so we were on the bridge for half of the six-day schedule.

No luck. The corridor scenes, where my other fencing took place, came right after the three days on the bridge. I'd have to dive in with only three weeks of frenetic fencing lessons. With that thought, I left the noisy pounding and bellowing of the crew on the soundstage for the peace and breakfast waiting for me in my dressing room.

As I was having my cereal, there was a knock on the dressing room door.

"Come in," I mumbled, quickly wiping the milk off my lips. It was Marc Daniels. He had directed the last episode, "Man Trap," and was back again for this one. He had a keen sense for details and was getting a fine feel for the workings of the show.

"George, I have a thought. Can you take your shirt off for me?" he asked without explanation. But immediately, I knew what he had in mind.

"Sure," I answered, swallowing my breakfast. I shucked off my T-shirt and discreetly sucked in my stomach. He appraised my bared torso as if he were shopping for a leg of lamb.

"Okay," he said nonchalantly. "Let's play your fencing scenes shirtless." He closed the door and was off. Straightaway, I got down horizontally on the floor, put my feet on the couch, and began pumping out push-ups to build up a photogenic chest.

During the next few days, people walking past my dressing room may have wondered what sort of nefarious activity might be going on inside that was making the portable structure rock with such sensuous rhythm. Whatever wild imaginings they might have had, the truth was that I was conscientiously pumping up the pectorals for my shirtless scenes of heroic swashbuckling.

Another distorted story from this episode has almost become fact through repetition and must be set straight. It is believed by many that I cannot be trusted with a sword in my hand. The story was published in *The Making of Star Trek* by Stephen E. Whitfield, and it said that I went around the set accosting my colleagues with my fencing foil, just as Sulu did in this episode. This is a highly one-sided and incomplete accounting of what really happened.

On a movie soundstage, it is not unusual to come across an actor in a darkened corner walking around talking to himself. He isn't crazy. He is merely going over his dialogue preparing for his scene about to be filmed. In this episode, "Naked Time," my scenes involved not just dialogue but fencing as well. So I found a flat in an out-of-the-way corner of the stage and began rehearsing my routine of thrusts and parries behind it. I suppose I might have been making some odd sounds—huffs and puffs, some stamps and occasional grunts.

Now, Jimmy Doohan is a man of insatiable curiosity. Nothing unusual ever gets past him uninspected. True to character, his inquiring mind was roused by the sounds I was making, tucked far away behind my flat, and he came snooping around searching for the source of the strange noises.

Another characteristic of Jimmy's is that he possesses an impeccable sense of timing, a most useful trait for an actor. So keen was his timing that he peered around my flat just at the very moment when I was lunging with my foil. I cut through the air, missing Jimmy's nose by inches. His eyes popped round with surprise. I quickly tried to apologize, but before I could, he was off and running.

A third quality of Jimmy's is that he has that wonderful Irish gift for drama, an essential for actors. But with Jimmy, it often expresses itself in inflamed and hugely magnified rhetoric. Within minutes, word was broadcast throughout the set that George had "attacked" Jimmy. Some versions even had Jimmy bloodied! Greg Peters, the assistant director, noted this in his day's report to the front office. This half-truth was picked up by writer Whitfield and published in *The Making of Star Trek*. But the verifiable whole truth is that as an actor of integrity, I was minding my own business preparing for my scene, far out of the way of others, when a nosy busybody openly placed himself, however unwittingly, in harm's way.

By the fourth day of filming "Naked Time," we were into the corridor sets. My fencing scenes were done, and Leonard's big breakdown scene was coming up next. Everyone was acutely aware of the importance of this scene. I was anxious to see how he handled it.

Leonard had already established a complex, drivingly logical, and rigorously controlled character. Alien, yet not only understandable, but strangely sympathetic. Yet in this episode, he had to reveal his seething human emotions that had been held tightly in check, a devastating break of his stern Vulcan exterior. The virulent mystery virus that had infected the crew of the *U.S.S. Enterprise* was destroying even Spock's steely capacity for restraint.

Watching Leonard craft the scene of Spock's breakdown was a rare lesson in acting. After quiet discussion with Marc Daniels, he searched the sprawling set of the starship and found a secluded, closed-off room for the breakdown. Leonard insisted that Spock would not expose such a wrenchingly private moment to others, especially to Nurse Chapel, who was in love with him. Then he asked that he be given some time to ready himself. There was no air of self-indulgence so often exercised by stars. Only pure, intense concentration.

When he was ready, he quietly stepped in front of the camera. The camera started to roll, and Marc Daniels whispered, "Action." Spock came striding down the corridor unsteadily, clearly disturbed, and quietly slipped into the room. The door whooshed closed. There was silence . . . a tremblingly hushed tension. Something was wrong with Spock. Slowly, with every muscle straining for control, he sat himself down. Almost imperceptibly, a quiver rolled across his lips. Fierce determination gripped his entire body. Then like a great, solid dam about to burst, his body began to shake. The anguish, so immense, so firmly and so long contained, was no longer bearable even by the powerful Vulcan. And he broke. The pain that came bursting out in convulsive heavings was excruciating, wrenching, and embarrassing. We felt vulgar intruding on this awful, private sorrow. But we watched, mesmerized.

"Cut." Marc's voice was barely audible, almost apologetic. For a moment, there was shamed silence. Then the entire cast and crew burst into spontaneous applause. Leonard was brilliant. Sheer, consummate artistry within the tight confines of a rigid television shooting schedule. Leonard set high standards on our set; by his example, he made all of us try to meet them.

The schedule board that doled out time in quarter pages of the script and busily kept us moving from set to set was also the dispenser of unwelcome time off. We complained about the tight schedule, but we also grumbled about furloughs from the set when the scenes being filmed didn't include us. I had too many of them, and I much preferred moaning about how the

244

studio overworked me. For the one day I had off from "Naked Time," I have a special regret.

There was another performance from this episode that I wish I had been on the set to watch. It was the day that Bill's big scene was up. My disappointment at missing his performance live became even greater when I saw the show when it was aired. Bill was brilliant.

Kirk, too, had ultimately been infected by the deadly virus, but even more horribly than the rest of us—for he was agonizingly aware of his condition. He desperately tried to maintain self-control as the terrible disease finally waged its battle inside the captain, for his ship and for his mind. There were many levels of consciousness that Bill had to play with urgent intensity. Given the stringent constraints of television, Bill's performance in that scene was an amazing display of virtuosity.

As the final credits rolled over a shot of a glistening-chested Sulu, I realized again that an extraordinary company of actors surrounded me on STAR TREK. And what an uncommon achievement "Naked Time" was, not only for television, but as a work of dramatic science fiction.

We had been laboring for months under the most intense pressure and had reached the midway point in the season's filming. The time for tasting the first fruit of our labors was fast approaching. The opening night of STAR TREK's premier season was almost upon us.

Desilu asked me to go to Chicago to promote this happy event, and I was more than pleased to go. Chicago is not far from Milwaukee, where my brother, Henry, had been doing graduate studies in periodontics at Marquette University. And he and his wife, June, had just had their first child, named Scott. This would be a wonderful opportunity to celebrate two firsts: the launching of our new series and the birth of my first nephew.

It was a happily expectant actor/uncle that found himself in

Chicago chatting on radio and television, lunching with print reporters, and anxiously looking forward to the night of September 8, 1966.

That morning, after my promotional work was finished, Henry, June, and baby Scotty drove down to Chicago to pick me up. My debut with Scotty was a warm, gurgling success. Not a cry of protest when I apprehensively received the fat, shapeless bundle from June. I cradled him halfway up to Milwaukee without a single wail of complaint. I had passed my first test as an uncle. The next as a series actor on television was coming only a few hours later.

That night, I sat on pins and needles in front of the television set in Henry and June's living room. A softly babbling Scotty was propped up on my lap. Henry looked on expectantly while June was in the kitchen preparing coffee and cookies.

"June! Hurry! It's starting now!" I shouted as the soaring theme music that was to become so familiar came on. She rushed out balancing a clattering tray as the *U.S.S. Enterprise* appeared streaking out of the star-flecked darkness for the very first time. Then in great, bold letters, the title STAR TREK. The episode was "The Man Trap." Our journey was now launched! I wondered how Gene Roddenberry must be feeling right now back in Los Angeles. The next hour seemed to zip by, practically at warp speed.

The first critical commentary came about halfway through the show when Scotty fell asleep on my lap. Then, as the final credits were rolling, June said, "That was . . . interesting. But I'm not really a science fiction buff so I really can't say. But you were very . . . interesting."

Henry waited until the commercials came on. Then he observed, "They pay you for that, huh?" After a pause, he added, "That's good." I think he meant it was good that I got paid. But I wasn't sure if that might not have been his comment on the show, too, so I left well enough alone.

The early reviews may have been tepid but weren't unexpected. Pioneering is never done in front of cheerleaders

246

urging on a roaring grandstand of popular approval. STAR TREK was venturing out into new and uncharted television space. Yet, a hardy group of viewers did discover us and began letting us know of their support. The letters started coming, first in small dribs, then larger drabs that soon turned into a steadily flowing stream of enthusiastic fan mail. Some were excited by the imaginative science fiction, others were intrigued by the speculative technology, and they all seemed to love the characters—especially the alien, Mr. Spock.

Though I had been impressed by Leonard Nimoy the actor, I never anticipated this massive reception for such a cool, dispassionate, and weird-looking character. His physical qualities certainly didn't seem to have the stuff of popular appeal, not in the usual sense. A voice too dry, a physique too gaunt, and a face more inscrutably, well . . . alien, than would normally generate such heat.

From then on, I watched Spock on screen more closely. I realized then that what Leonard the actor was projecting with his cool restraint was not the muscularity of a physique he didn't have, but the powerful attraction of a complex, agile, and strong mind. He was transmitting, right through the screen, what had impressed me in person on the set, capturing both the minds and the hearts of the viewers. Through the power of his performance, Leonard was giving intelligence the mystery and the pull of sex appeal. As a result, he was becoming the thinking person's heartthrob.

Spock's blossoming popularity, however, created unanticipated problems on the set. We already had the traditional slot of the heartthrob and classic square-jawed hero filled with Bill Shatner. But the bags holding the fan mail for Leonard were heavier. Much heavier. And the tension on the set got keener. We all discovered how keen one unforgettably long and nerve-racking morning.

Life magazine was doing a photo essay on Leonard Nimoy getting made up as Mr. Spock. Because of the time-consuming complexity of the job, Leonard was always the first in the makeup room early in the mornings. Usually, Nichelle and

Grace Lee Whitney followed. Then the rest of us came staggering in, still bleary-eyed.

By that time, Leonard's makeup was about half on, and that morning, the photographer was starting to get his rhythm. Bill walked in and was stopped in his tracks by what he saw. Then he turned around and quickly left. Shortly thereafter, an assistant rushed into the makeup room and asked the photographer to leave. Leonard's makeup and the photo record were only half complete. Even when forcefully questioned, the assistant couldn't give any reason for the dismissal, but had to insist that the photographer leave immediately. Orders from the front office, he kept repeating. Reluctantly, the photographer packed up his cameras and left, his job incomplete.

Leonard, understandably, was livid. He got up and refused to have his makeup completed until the photographer was allowed back. Until then, he announced, he would wait in his dressing room with his makeup only half done. And with that, he exited.

The rest of us sat silently listening to the drama playing out as our makeup was applied. Then we gathered at the soundstage coffee urn for our usual morning gossip fest. But this morning, our conversation was hushed, almost conspiratorial. It was whispered that Bill apparently had language in his contract that provided for his approval of photographers on the stage.

Suddenly, a covey of black suits came rushing in. It headed straight for Leonard's dressing room. We strolled over to the set with our cups of coffee and reconvened in the circle of our set-side chairs. The set was still and darkened. As we continued our furtive conversation, we saw the covey of black suits come out of Leonard's dressing room and flutter over to Bill's. We waited patiently beside a gloom-shrouded set, and we sipped our coffee. Some of us went back for refills, others stepped outside for a cigarette, as the black covey flew back and forth from one dressing room to the other. Hours passed, and the coffee was making us jittery. Morning was becoming almost midday. Greg Peters, the first assistant, came over to our circle and told us we could go off for an early lunch.

When we came back from a leisurely lunch, we were surprised to find the set lit and buzzing with activity. Leonard was at his station, his makeup complete to the very tip of his pointy ears. And Bill was in the captain's seat laughing and joking with the crew as usual. We were ready to start work. Like good professionals we all took our positions, the cameras rolled, and we commenced with the day's work as if nothing unusual had ever transpired.

A few months later, I noticed that *Life* magazine carried the complete photo story on Mr. Spock getting into his bizarre makeup. But it didn't quite carry the full story on how bizarre that process had been.

The first season filming STAR TREK was turbulent. The highs were sublime; but the hours were long and arduous, the tension was at times piano-wire taut, and the pressure to meet the schedule was always intense. We thought it was all-consuming on the set, but at least we went home to our own beds at night. Out in the front office, Gene was sometimes sleeping over on his office couch rewriting scripts. In fact, we had two Genes now guiding us as producers—Gene Roddenberry and Gene Coon. Under the high pressure of producing an episode of gripping science fiction every week, the two Genes were providing the viewers with some of the most startlingly imaginative shows that television had ever seen.

I was proud to be a part of it. But I wanted to be prouder; I wanted Sulu to be doing more. My ship may have been moving steady at warp three, but I wanted to do more than merely announce that fact. I saw that Leonard was constantly working with the directors and feeding his thoughts to the producers. So I began my lobbying campaign for Sulu. I peppered Gene Roddenberry with character-defining ideas, personal histories, plot possibilities, anything that might give Sulu more prominence. Gene was receptive and said he would devote more attention to developing my character. But the season was coming to an end, and that potential would have to be realized next season. The hiatus was almost upon us.

Almost on cue, as if some great schedule keeper up above

knew I would soon be among those actors "between engage-ments," I received an offer from Batjac Productions for a role in the feature film version of the best-selling book *The Green Berets*. Batjac, I knew, was the production company of the movie star John Wayne, who would be starring in this film. My brimming cup was now overflowing. To immediately follow the first season of STAR TREK with a feature film starring an icon! I was overjoyed.

But the excitement was mixed with some apprehension. This movie was about the Vietnam War and I knew that John Wayne was an outspoken supporter of our being there. I, on the other hand, was strongly opposed to it in a public and vocal way. But I wanted to do the film with the legendary actor. My politics and my career ambitions were colliding, and I felt I had to be honest with John Wayne.

When I met with him in his office at Warner Brothers Studio, I openly laid out my quandary. He listened attentively, his eyes looking straight at me with that slight John Wayne squint that I knew so well from close-ups. It was a curious feeling to know it was me he was looking at and not Ward Bond or Lee Marvin. He shook his head in that self-effacing way that was so John Wayne and drawled, "I respect your opinion, George. I know a lot of people feel the same way. David Janssen and Jim Hutton, who are also in the movie, feel as you do." I hadn't known that. Then he got a vulnerable look in his eyes, and he continued, "But I want you guys in this movie because you're the best actors for the job. I need your help. I'll need your ideas to make this a good movie. And I'll try to do what I can to make this a good movie." He was forthright, persuasive, and charming. After all, he *was* John Wayne.

But I also saw the John Wayne guts and fortitude in his tackling of this film. The war in Vietnam was the single most burning issue facing America. It was devastating a small Asian nation and tearing our own country apart. Yet Hollywood would not touch this conflict with a ten-foot pole. It was too controversial. Only John Wayne had the courage and the power to take on this vital, important subject, making the first Hollywood film to deal with the Vietnam War. I had to respect that, so I decided to do *The Green Berets* and hope for the best.

The production was to be filmed on location—thankfully not at the actual locale—but at Fort Benning, near Columbus, Georgia. There at Fort Benning, the explosions would be courtesy of the special effects department.

As I was preparing to leave for Georgia, Gene Roddenberry gave me a good-luck gift to take along—a wonderful, tantalizing present that sent the adrenaline shooting through me. Gene handed me a set of scripts being readied for the next season of STAR TREK. "Here's something to whet your appetite while in Georgia." He smiled as he shook my hand. I quickly flipped through them. As promised, they had much more for Sulu in them. Among the scripts were "The Trouble with Tribbles," "The Gamesters of Treskilion," and "Bread and Circuses."

I flew off to Georgia and the filming of *The Green Berets* already salivating over the next season of STAR TREK.

The Green Berets was a total John Wayne movie. It starred John Wayne. It was also directed by John Wayne, although Warner Brothers sent my old director from *A Majority of One*, Mervyn Leroy, to be on the set as backup. And, although we had a script by Clare Huffaker, and the author of the book on which it was based, Robin Moore, was always on the set, it was rewritten by John Wayne. The titular producer was Michael Wayne, his son. *The Green Berets* was not only a complete John Wayne movie, it was a John Wayne war movie. The good guys against the bad guys; "us" versus "them."

His directorial style was also very John Wayne—big, broad, and straightforward. You hit your marks, and you said your lines. All the roles were cast to visual type. Whatever nuance or color there might be in the characters, the actors had to bring themselves.

I was cast as Captain Nim—the "good Vietnamese," as Wayne referred to him. Nim was a disciplined, dedicated, and a fiercely determined man. I decided to have some fun with this character and contribute my own perspective to a very John

Wayne statement. I decided to play Captain Nim as a ruthlessly cutthroat militarist who no longer knew why he was fighting. Only that he was fighting—and that he had to prevail over the "enemy," whatever the cost. Wayne liked the interpretation.

For verisimilitude, I wanted to speak some lines in Vietnamese, so I got the studio to hire a dialogue coach for me. He was a gentle little man named Mr. Phuc from the Vietnamese language school at Fort Bragg, North Carolina. I worked long nights with him back at the Camillia Motel, where we were staying, to get the right accent as well as the hard, calloused intonation that I wanted for Captain Nim. But to get Mr. Phuc's soft, delicate voice to read lines with the brutality of the ruthless militarist was very difficult. It was like trying to get a shy Chihuahua puppy to bark like a raging Doberman pinscher.

It was, however, not half as difficult as trying to keep the cast and crew from roaring with laughter every time I needed his assistance on the set. One of the assistants would shout into his portable loudspeaker across the battlefield to summon my dialogue coach. It was not so much the sight of that sweet little man scrambling across sandbag barricades and leaping over trenches; it was the singularly American mispronunciation the assistants gave to his simple Vietnamese name. As Mr. Phuc raced across the battle-scarred landscape to the set, the cast and crew howled with laughter at the loudspeaker voice bellowing, "George needs Fuc! Get Fuc on the set! Mr. Fuc to the set, please."

To create Vietnam in Georgia, Wayne populated the location with crowds of "Vietnamese" extras dressed as peasants or Viet Cong guerrillas in black pajamas. During a break, I happened by a cluster of village women in coolie hats chatting in the shade of a pile of sandbags in what sounded like Japanese. Vietnamese peasants conversing in Japanese? I stopped and talked with them. I discovered that most of the women extras were Japanese nationals. They had married American G.I.s in postwar Japan and were now living near the base where their husbands worked. Under those coolie hats and Vietnamese guises, they were charmingly incongruous Japanese ladies.

Before I knew it, I had a dinner invitation at the home of one of them, Yoko Collins.

She and her husband, Calvin, who was retired from the Army and ran a local gas station, had a lovely family: good-looking son Wayne, who it turned out was named after John Wayne, and two beautiful daughters, Nova and Shani. Yoko had also invited her fellow extra friends, all of whose names combined the story of their lives—names like Yuriko Gustafson and Midori Jones. The dinner, too, was a delightful combination of Japan and southern America—chicken teriyaki with corn bread.

After dinner, Yoko and her friends brought out their samisen, a three-stringed Japanese banjo, and sang Japanese folk songs. Then Calvin dragged out his guitar and regaled us with his songbook of country music. Yoko occasionally joined in and harmonized with her hubby in her Japanese-accented country sound. You haven't heard real down-home country until you've heard "Country Road" sung by the sweet duo of Cal and Yoko.

The aftermath of a world war was creating a new kind of people in Columbus, Georgia. Cultures, instead of colliding, were combining to make musical harmony and beautiful children. America was evolving again. It made me wonder what the country might be like another generation from now after this current war which we were re-creating on film ended.

Those evenings I spent at the Collins home were wonderful respites from the ferocious Captain Nim, who was now living and crawling under my skin. In some ways, I was foreshadowing the dark, Gestapo-like, parallel universe Sulu of the "Mirror, Mirror" episode of STAR TREK's upcoming season. Always, even while I was on the Vietnamese battlefields of Fort Benning, Georgia, a part of my mind was on the new season of STAR TREK starting up back in Hollywood.

The scripts that Gene had given me were getting dog-eared with anticipatory readings and rereadings. But as summer turned brown with wear and our shoot was making slow progress, my anxiety started to mount. *The Green Berets* was already behind schedule. I had to be back in Los Angeles to begin work on the new season of STAR TREK. I asked Wayne if some accommodation could be made to get my scenes done earlier so that I could leave. He was quite understanding and agreed to move my scenes up.

Then, that proverbial rain that falls on a blessed life began to fall. It started to fall and it continued to fall—day after rainy day. Not quite forty days and forty nights, but to me it seemed like forever. And as the rain continued to pour, I sat looking out the window of my motel room. With each rain-soaked day, I watched my hopes gushing right down that muddy Georgia gully into the raging Chattahoochee River. The rain continued and washed away whatever chance I had of making it back to Hollywood in time for the start of filming the second season of STAR TREK.

16

Return to Tomorrow

I RETURNED TO LOS ANGELES HEARTSICK AND RESENTFUL. THE scripts I had taken with me to Georgia had all been filmed, save for "Mirror, Mirror." The lines I had so anxiously committed to memory had already been spoken by someone else; the spirited lobbying I had mounted to enhance Sulu's role had all been for naught. I had gained nothing but a new competitor—the person to whom I had lost all my lines, an actor named Walter Koenig. I was prepared to dislike this interloper, this thief of my efforts. All right, I'll admit it—I hated him! Sight unseen, I churned with venom for this Walter Koenig!

Jealousy is an ugly emotion. I knew that. I wanted to think I was a better person than one who coveted another's success. But this was something that belonged to me. I was the one who worked for it. I was the one who cultivated the opportunity for a whole season. And yet, this Walter just sailed into our second season on the wings of fate, wearing that silly Prince Valiant wig, and plucked off the fruits that rightfully belonged to me. It was so unfair.

The show that I returned to was titled "Return to Tomorrow." Tomorrow indeed! It was like returning to the dinner table after briefly excusing myself only to find my meal cold and half eaten by someone else. At least the production people showed some good grace and consideration for my feelings by not including Walter in this script. Or was this the same capricious fate trying to spite him now? Whatever the circumstances, I gloated. I was as petty as I could be.

Walter was in the next show, "Patterns of Force." However, Sulu was not! This was alarming. Were they trying to keep us apart? Were we going to be alternated from one show to another? My worry increased commensurate with my growing dislike of Walter.

The following show, "The Ultimate Computer," was a morality tale about the machines man creates and how they come to embody both its creator's weaknesses as well as his strengths. If a machine were to be made by me at this point, it would have been boiling internally with the greenest of jealousy, lubricated by the black grease of malice, and bristly on the outside with the most lethal of assault weaponry. I couldn't guess what kind of machine Walter might have built. Probably a sleek, slippery, high-tech burglary device. Both Walter and I were together in this script. In dramatic structure, this would be called the obligatory confrontation, the showdown.

I walked into my dressing room that morning and was greeted by a puzzling display. There were two sets of uniforms hanging in the closet. There were two pairs of boots placed by the couch. Why would the wardrobe people leave two sets of costumes in my dressing room for me? Greg Peters, the assistant director, happened to be rushing by. I asked him about the double costumes.

"Oh, sorry we didn't let you know," he apologized. "We're short of dressing rooms, so we'd like to have you and Walter double up just for today. I'll let Walter know. He's already in the makeup room." And with that abbreviated advisement, he was off.

Insult upon injury! The veins in my scalp started to swell up. Were they deliberately trying to inflame the hate that was already raging within my all-too-human soul? Now were they trying to incite mayhem? My blood was boiling, when I heard soft mutterings outside my door.

"I hate it. I hate it!" someone was mumbling. The door opened, and there was Walter Koenig, lips curled with animosity, his eyes glowering with loathing. When he saw me, he repeated again, looking right into my eye, "I hate this!"

"Well, I don't like it any better either!" I shot back, glaring right at him. He seemed startled by the intensity of my response.

"You do, too?" he asked, his eyes suddenly wide with innocence. He seemed puzzled.

"Of course I do. I don't like it any better than you do." I repeated fiercely. He looked embarrassed and smiled sheepishly.

"Well, at least you don't have to wear it," he said. Then with renewed intensity, he added, "I feel ridiculous with this on!" Now he sounded fierce, and I was puzzled. What was he talking about?

"Wear? Wear what?" I asked. This conversation was getting bizarre.

"This stupid wig! I thought you said you hated it too." I looked at the big, shaggy mop on his head, framing that baby face with a pageboy hairdo. He looked so juvenile, so cloyingly precious, and also absolutely mortified. I couldn't suppress a smirk. "I hate this!" he wailed. "I feel like a walking joke!"

Even in my hatred, I couldn't help but feel a bit sorry for Walter. He looked so pathetic. All the bile that churned inside me began to dissolve at the sight of another actor reduced to public humiliation every time he stepped in front of the camera. It was a sad and pitiful plight.

Walter, I learned, was to be the bait for the young teenaged girls' viewership. The character of young Ensign Pavel Chekov had been created for that purpose. Actually, Chekov was a copy of a copy. The pop group the Beatles was the single biggest phenomenon in show business, then at the peak of their celebrity. Replicating their teen popularity on series television was another mop-haired musical group known as the Monkees.

The teeny-bopper heartthrob of this bunch was a talented young English boy named Davy Jones. Ensign Chekov was supposed to be the futuristic, Russian-accented version of Davy Jones, who was himself replicating the Beatles right up to the crown of his thickly thatched head.

As Walter told me of his plight, I saw that under that silly wig was a man damned by his sensitivity and his intelligence. If he were dumb and thick-skinned, he could probably have breezed through it. But unfortunately, he had the judgment and taste to know that he looked totally preposterous. As he continued talking, I discovered that he was also quite articulate. He went on and on comparing the shaggy helmet he wore to a dust mop, a rag-doll wig, a bird's nest, a Shih Tzu lapdog perched on his head, et cetera. I realized that this was a man equipped with a true gift of kvetch. Walter was the quintessential poet-bellyacher.

As I listened to him complain, I learned that he, too, had gone to UCLA and that he, too, had a brother in medicine; we had things in common, and I saw that he was an ambitious actor excited by the opportunity of being part of a quality television series, just like me. The hate that had tempered down to pity, then tolerance, was now softening to a recognition of our matching lives and shared ambitions. We were in this together. Walter was now a part of the team. He was fact, a given that I had to live with whether I liked it or not. I decided to accept that reality. Besides, he seemed to be an interesting guy. He probably would complain long enough and hard enough and get that stupid wig taken off his head. Sure enough, it wasn't long before he was providing his own, very ample hair for Ensign Chekov.

We were all ambitious actors, every one of us, each elbowing the other for our own place on the set and in the script. Walter may have gotten Sulu's lines by fate, but he got his wig off by his own kvetch. Leonard was constantly inventing new aspects of Spock, like the neck pinch and the Vulcan greeting. Jimmy was coming up with ideas and lines for his character, Scott. Nichelle reminded me of Thelma Oliver from *Fly Blackbird!*

always easing herself slightly past her chalk mark, toward the camera. De seemed to be the only one not overburdened with driving ambition. He was the old pro who came in, did the work, and went home to his wife in the San Fernando Valley.

But for the rest of us, the competition was always lively and healthy. This was part of what kept us on our toes and made life on the set interesting. Except for one irritant—a problem that grew with each new episode but about which we were powerless to do anything.

Dorothy Fontana, that sweet lady I had met as Gene's secretary when I went in for my first interview, had been promoted to the position of script consultant. She would occasionally give us an advance peek at an early draft of a script, which might contain a wonderful scene for our respective characters or even a fun line or two of dialogue. Our minds would rhapsodize privately in anticipation as the script was being developed.

But when the final shooting script was delivered, the eagerly awaited scene or line would now be in someone else's mouth, and invariably, it was Bill's. He was the star of the series. There would always be reasonable justifications for the change. And reasonable arguments could be made to counter them. But Bill was the star. That was the one inarguable fact. Even if an idea had originated with one of us, if Bill wanted it, he got it. Even if I tried to ad lib an entirely appropriate "Aye, sir" to a command, he would nix it, claiming it would take away from the rhythm of the scene. This despite the fact that some of us had precious little to do in so many of the scripts. But Bill seemed totally immune to the sensitivities or the efforts of those he worked with.

And gallingly, he always managed to keep up that smiling, charming facade; as if nothing out of the ordinary had happened, he joked and giggled and bantered. Always that sunny, oblivious smile, that smile as bright, as hard, and as relentless as the headlights of an oncoming car. You just had to get out of its way.

* * *

Hollywood is located in a region of geologic instability. The earth moves periodically. The big seismic shake-up is followed by a series of smaller quakes called aftershocks that keep things unstable, and people on edge.

Hollywood is also a place of great corporate instability that keeps people on edge. During our second season, Desilu Studios went through another one of these periodic corporate shake-ups. The studio that was started up as RKO Radio Pictures, then bought and sold by Howard Hughes, and then bought and built up by Lucille Ball and Desi Arnaz as Desilu, was again bought—this time by a giant conglomerate called Gulf and Western, led by financier Charles Bluhdorn.

The studio next door on Melrose Avenue, Paramount Pictures, was also acquired by Gulf and Western at the same time; there was only a high wall separating the two film factories. An aftershock of this corporate commotion brought that wall tumbling down in a huge cloud of dust, and when the air finally cleared, it left one gigantic studio lot. This combined facility was rechristened Paramount Studios. The name Desilu was now a part of the dust of Hollywood history.

The big boon for us on the old Desilu side was that, with the wall down, we now had access to the legendary Paramount commissary for lunch. With our blue terry-cloth robes covering our Starfleet uniforms, Nichelle, Jimmy, Walter, and I would march over to enjoy our newly acquired perk. The high-ceilinged art deco room was redolent with the glamorous history of the studio. And the food was much better than at the old Desilu greasy spoon. We could just imagine Gloria Swanson dining in a room of such suave elegance.

In fact, we didn't have to imagine one personification of Hollywood history who dined there regularly, the ninety-one-year-old founder of Paramount Pictures, Adolph Zukor. Thin, bald, and frail, he still turned heads, and his name was still spoken in whispers when he entered the room. The founder of old Hollywood was still watching over his factory and his flock. But a year after we got access to the Paramount commissary, another corporate aftershock brought this elegant building tumbling down. The commissary, too, was now only a memory.

One afternoon following lunch at that commissary, Nichelle and I were walking back to the set. Even with our plain blue terry robes on, people could tell that we were doing an unusual episode. I was wearing a savage fencing scar over my right eyebrow, and she was made up with intense severity that gave her soft beauty a barbaric look. We were filming the parallel universe sequences from "Mirror, Mirror." But our appearances were deceptive. Our conversation was schmaltzy with nostalgia.

We were discovering that our own lives had faint parallels. She was telling me about her early days as a singer with Duke Ellington, and I shared with her the fact that the father of my opponent for student body president in junior high school was a musician in Duke Ellington's band. She told me she had understudied Diahann Carroll in the musical *No Strings*, and I told her that Josie and I had bought standing room tickets to see that musical in New York—but alas, not with her performing. We tantalized ourselves with the poetic "ifs" of life. It was while we were walking back from that lunch break that something flashed on me.

I had been putting together a Japanese-community benefit dinner at the Biltmore Hotel and was searching for a headline performer for the event. Here was Nichelle, a friend and a colleague, who had been a singer with Duke Ellington, whom I had almost seen in a Broadway musical! What a great coincidence! I asked and she graciously agreed. During this dinner at the Biltmore I was to discover an even more personal connection to Nichelle.

Daddy and Mama were to be at my table, as would Nichelle and her husband and accompanist, Duke Munday. I was the master of ceremonies of the dinner and knew I would be getting up and down a lot, with little time to be with them to ease the flow of conversation. I worried that there might be awkward stretches of silence and uncomfortableness.

My mother has all the outward behavior of a proper Japanese lady. She bows on meeting people and punctuates conversations with small, refined nods. Polite Japanese discussion is one of subtlety and indirection. Everything lies in the nuance.

Nichelle is a grandly glamorous lady of overflowing affection for the people around her. She enchants with her openhearted love and unconcealed emotions. She can be luxuriantly demonstrative, at times, exaggeratedly so. To me, the combination of Nichelle and my mother was perturbing. I loved them both, but the thought of leaving them together filled me with anxiety.

On the night of the dinner, I was in the foyer of the Biltmore with my parents, greeting the arriving guests. Suddenly there was a flurry of excitement and a ripple of whispers. "That's her." "She's here." "That's Uhura from STAR TREK."

I looked toward the commotion just as the crowd parted to reveal Nichelle and her husband approaching us. She was resplendent in a midnight blue velvet gown glittery with sequins and partially covered by a full-length mink coat draped off her shoulders—the very picture of a glamorous movie star.

"Nichelle. Thanks for coming," I greeted her. "Nichelle and Duke, I'd like you to meet my parents." My father shook hands with Duke, and Mama bowed. Quite unexpectedly, Nichelle bowed also.

"I'm so pleased to meet you, Mrs. Takei," Nichelle murmured delicately. Then Mama offered her hand! When Nichelle took it, Mama clasped with both hands and bowed again still clutching Nichelle's hand. Then she looked up and said to Nichelle, "You so pretty! Your face so pretty." Mama let go and discreetly covered her giggling mouth.

"Oh, Mrs. Takei, you're so sweet." Nichelle blushed modestly. She reached over and gently kissed my mother's cheek. Then, as I watched with astounded eyes, my mother reached over and hugged Nichelle in a cheek-to-cheek embrace! Mama and Nichelle! I couldn't believe it. How little we know the people we love. How little we trust those we think we know. Mama took Nichelle by the hand and led everyone over to our table.

During the course of the dinner, Mama inspected the construction of Nichelle's gown and Nichelle explained the complexity of getting into it. Mama and Nichelle carried on like soul sisters. When Nichelle took the stage and dazzled everyone with her artistry, Mama led the applause of a wildly ecstatic audience. By the end of the evening, they were on first-name basis. "Ni-shalu," Mama called her. And Nichelle was calling her "Mama."

It was subtle. Quietly, almost unconsciously, Daddy's sense of financial prudence had seeped into me. I was in the midst of a steady, regular career "feast," but my thoughts were on the potential "famine" that might follow. I had lived through my struggle in New York and knew what that could be like. Now, while STAR TREK was providing a stable cash flow, was the time to prepare for that contingency again.

My apartment building near the hospital had appreciated in value, at least on paper. Now might be a good time to turn it around again for a bigger property. I began a search for the next investment. I found it near the fabled Brown Derby Restaurant on Wilshire Boulevard. It was a twenty-unit luxury apartment building. What had started out as an investment in a few cemetery plots, with a boost from STAR TREK was turning into a sturdy shelter against any famine that might blow across my career.

Life is impermanence, philosophers have said. But Hollywood is impermanence at twenty-four frames per second. And the set of STAR TREK was Hollywood at warp speed. We felt highly impermanent. The insecurity was rampant.

My contract guaranteed seven shows out of thirteen, barely more than half. In the last season, out of twenty-six episodes filmed, I did eighteen—better than the guarantee, but still I had missed eight shows. It really wasn't a consolation that I did two more than Jimmy. Nichelle had five more episodes than I did. And this season, we had Walter in the mix to make the situation

263

worse. I had already lost five shows to him because of my absence filming *The Green Berets* on location in Georgia. But we all had an even greater, collective insecurity.

The nervousness we felt was not because of the corporate reverberations from the New York offices of Gulf and Western. Ours came from the Rockefeller Center headquarters of NBC. The ratings for STAR TREK were not what the programming executives considered acceptable. Our future was in jeopardy. On the set, rumors began to fly that we were about to be canceled. My prediction of two seasons seemed to be coming true.

But Gene Roddenberry, I discovered, was not just an artist and a visionary. He was a fighter. A former Los Angeles police officer, he could become as fierce as an enraged lion protecting his cubs, as cunning and full of guile as a fox scheming to outwit a pack of baying hounds. He had to convince the powers-that-be that the so-called ratings were not truly representative of the viewership. He decided to discreetly launch a plan to save STAR TREK with a letter campaign. Critical to this scheme was an Oakland, California, couple who had become ardent fans of the show, John and Bjo Trimble. Gene had befriended them and extended periodic invitations for them to visit the set.

I first met Bjo and John during the hurly-burly between setups on one of their periodic visits. She was vivacious, enthusiastic, and full of curiosity. He was quiet and composed with a scholarly air. They reminded me of the truism, opposites attract. I didn't realize then what a dynamic combination this set of opposites was.

Gene confided to them the threat that STAR TREK faced. But to avoid the obvious conflict of interest, he couldn't be seen as the spearhead of the effort to generate the letter-writing support. Just the suggestion of the urgency was all Bjo needed to get going. She was galvanized. The Trimbles moved down to Los Angeles and bought a home not too far from the studio. With the surreptitious support that Gene was able to provide, she gathered mailing lists, contacted science fiction organizations, organized a telephone network to spread the word, and literally became the national campaign manager of the "Save STAR TREK" crusade. If her passion had been politics, I'm sure she could have gotten a United States President elected.

The result was astounding. It was immediate, and it was massive. The mail rooms of NBC on both coasts were inundated. The letters were passionate; they were literate; and some were angry. But all recognized STAR TREK as an extraordinary oasis of engaging, intelligent science fiction on television. The fans of STAR TREK, we discovered, were not people who merely sat back and absorbed entertainment. They were activists who took what they got from their television sets as stimuli for action. And when they were alerted to the threat, they acted. We received letters of support from an amazing diversity of people, ranging from engineers, architects, university professors and students, all the way to housewives. The response was enormous—and the letters continued to pour in.

Among them was a letter from my father. Daddy was honest about his personal interest in seeing the show renewed. But he also talked of his pride in seeing his son on the screen as a part of a larger picture. At a time when people were identifying themselves with smaller social units, with ethnicity, with class, with gender, when society seemed to be breaking down into a new tribalism, he wrote that he took more than parental pride in seeing the greater human family so glowingly depicted. With STAR TREK, he observed, television was making a vital cultural contribution. He urged NBC to keep this positive picture continuing on the air.

Many, many such letters came in to NBC. The numbers alone, not considering the content, were persuasive. NBC capitulated. The executives decided to renew STAR TREK for a third season. But the letters continued to stream in; the fans were relentless. Finally, NBC was forced to announce the renewal of STAR TREK over the end-title crawl of the show in order to put a halt to the flood of letters.

STAR TREK was boldly going on to another season, a third season. Thankfully, my prediction was proved wrong. And the time slot was great! Monday nights at 7:30. An ideal time for college students, our primary base of viewership. Everything augured well for the future of our show. And I was determined to make this a good season for Sulu, as well.

17

Mission: Impossible

IT WASN'T SUPPOSED TO BE LIKE THIS. STAR TREK WAS SUPPOSED to be slotted for Monday night at 7:30, not Friday night at 10:00 P.M. That was the morgue hour! All the college kids would be out being college kids that late on Friday nights. Hardly anyone would be watching television.

Gene Roddenberry dickered with the NBC executives to regain the promised slot. He was the executive producer, but had offered to return to the line producer position he had held during the first season if the Monday night slot would be reinstated. With Gene in that position, we could recapture the first-season magic.

They refused. This betrayal by NBC was the last straw for Gene. To have the ideal time slot snatched away and replaced with the worst possible one was a double cross that he could not take without a dramatic display of outrage. He announced that he was keeping the title of executive producer but that he was leaving STAR TREK. He was going off to another office at M-G-M Studio to work on a feature film project starring Rock Hudson. He would be available to us only sporadically, he stated. And Dorothy Fontana, our story editor, was also leaving.

Their departure was a serious loss for our show, but for me, it was dismaying. Gene and Dorothy were the ones who knew of and understood my ideas and aspirations for Sulu. This was the season I had hoped would see Sulu come into some prominence. Again, all the work I had done to develop the character and enhance my role was washed away. I would have to start all over again with our new line producer, Fred Freiberger.

What reenergized me, however, was the professionalism of my colleagues. Despite our setback, despite the poor time slot, and despite the low rating numbers that started to come in confirming our worst fears, the cast members threw themselves into each script with the same dedication as before. The scripts may not have been what they were the previous two seasons, but the integrity of the performances remained unchanged, episode after stressful episode. If anything, we worked harder under this more arduous condition. I felt proud to be a part of this cast.

Though we worked hard, we also managed to squeeze some pleasure into the crowded shooting schedule. One night, after a particularly long day, Jimmy and I were walking back to our cars.

"What're you doing for dinner?" he asked.

"I didn't have anything particular in mind," I responded, too exhausted to feel really hungry. "Do you feel like sushi? It's light."

"What? What's light? What's this . . . su—su . . . ? What'd you say?"

"Sushi. It's a light Japanese delicacy that you eat at a bar. Or if you want, you can make a more substantial meal of it."

"Okay, let's try this . . . su—su. What'd you call it?" Jimmy seemed to have an enthusiastic appetite . . . for whatever it may have been.

"Sushi," I repeated as I got in my car. "Follow me down the Hollywood Freeway to Little Tokyo."

As I drove, keeping an eye on the rearview mirror to make sure Jimmy's car was with me, it slowly dawned on me that sushi was not a well-known Japanese dish like teriyaki. Maybe I should have described it more fully to him, I thought. I hadn't told Jimmy that sushi was made with slices of raw fish. It was probably the idea of eating at a bar that caught Jimmy's fancy. I wondered if Jimmy might be drinking more than eating his dinner tonight.

As we stepped into the small, convivial restaurant, we were immediately greeted by a chorus of loud shouts. *"Irashaimase! Irashaimase!"* Jimmy seemed startled by the assault of good cheers, but when I told him that it was a traditional greeting of Japanese restaurants that meant "welcome," he relaxed. Instantly, he was smiling and beaming as if he were in his favorite neighborhood pub. The air was rich with the aroma of good whiskey.

"What's all this decoration in the glass case?" Jimmy asked as we sidled into our seats at the sushi bar.

"Well, Jimmy," I began confessing tentatively, "it's not decoration. It's actually our menu. They're chunks of raw fish." I was prepared for Jimmy's eyes to pop wide with shock.

"Okay, let's try some then," he chortled eagerly. "You order for me." Now the shocked one was me; I didn't know that Jimmy had an intrepid palate. First I ordered the least exotic of sushi for him, the hybrid California roll. Surely avocado and cooked crab on rice balls wouldn't challenge his taste too much. He lapped the two tidbits up in a breath. I next ordered raw tuna. Jimmy loved it! My shock grew with each new morsel I ordered for him. Raw yellowtail. Vinegared mackerel. Sea eel. Salmon egg roe. He gobbled them all up! Jimmy's appetite seemed to be more than hunger. He had a connoisseur's eagerness for new sensations, a palate as curious and venturesome as his inquiring mind. Jimmy ate up practically the whole glass case of raw flavors.

The following morning around the coffee urn, Jimmy was unstoppable. He waxed rhapsodic on the exotic delights of sushi, transporting himself by reliving each delectable discovery of the night before. If some crew person overhearing his ecstatic ravings had not known that sushi was a food, he might have thought that Jimmy was describing some obscene act.

Jimmy carried on like the poet laureate of sushi. His sensuous descriptions made the experience absolutely irresistable to Majel and Nichelle. A few of the guys on the crew also wanted to try it.

That Friday night after work, a caravan of cars headed down the Hollywood Freeway to Little Tokyo. The Paramount party took over the entire sushi bar. It was a raucous and ravenous party, and when we left, it was because the restaurant had run out of fish. We had eaten them out of house and business for the night. By the end Nichelle and Majel were new converts.

The following Friday night, an even longer caravan started off from Paramount Studios for Little Tokyo. Walter and his wife, Judy, a classmate of mine from UCLA, were a part of our sushi safari this time. He was curious about the experience that by now everyone on the set was raving about. But Walter was also a bit apprehensive. I told him, "Just imagine lox on rice." That gave him some frame of reference but apparently not much comfort. Ultimately, though, his desire to know and be a part of the experience prevailed over his needling trepidation.

"Irashaimase! Irashaimase!" The greeting was as explosive as always. Now, Jimmy, the expert, was explaining to the startled new members of our sushi group, "That means 'welcome' in Japanese." He seated himself at the far end of the bar from me so that he could order for some of the newcomers to our party. Jimmy was a keen student and now knew his sushi like a connoisseur. Majel and Nichelle were also becoming confident enough to start pointing at a glistening orange chunk and asking, "Salmon?" Walter and Judy stuck very close to me.

Of all the sushi, tuna is my favorite, and I think it is also the most palatable for first-timers. Like a cut of the best rare beef, it is mild and very digestible. For Walter's first sushi, I decided tuna would be the best introduction. I thought he should experience the toothsome cool of the raw meat combined with the soft, fluffy neutrality of the rice.

"Maguro wo kono kata ni onegai shimasu," I ordered, showing off. Walter eyed me skeptically.

"What did you say to him?"

"You'll love what I ordered for you and Judy. But I want you to discover the flavor sensation for yourself. I'm not going to tell you what you're eating. Just keep an open mind and receptive taste buds," I suggested to him.

"I'm not eating it until you tell me what I'm eating." He crossed his arms stubbornly and glared at the two delicate but alien-looking morsels that were set down in front of him. A pair of similar creations, thick, red cuts of meat artfully placed on bite-sized balls of rice, was put in front of me. I picked one of mine up with my chopsticks and savored the aroma. Then I dipped it lightly in the tiny dish of soy sauce and gently bit into it. I closed my eyes in exaggerated sensual bliss. Walter was studying me from the corner of his eye through every step of my delectation. Then I took a sip from my tiny cup of hot sake and let out a euphoric sigh.

Even Walter's headstrong intransigence couldn't resist that final sigh. He took his chopsticks and started to fumble around with his sushi. I suggested that, as a first-timer, it wouldn't be improper for him to use his fingers. With wary apprehension glistening in his eyes, he picked up his sushi with his fingers and bit in. His mouth closed and remained unmoving. His eyes took on a distant searching look. His face remained frozen in that questioning close-up for a long time. Then he started to chew, gingerly, suspiciously, very cautiously. Suddenly, he stopped. His eyes began to widen in shock, his nostrils flared; abruptly, with panicked urgency, he wrapped his mouth with the napkin from his lap. In wild-eyed frenzy, he reached for his glass of water and started pouring it down his throat.

Immediately, I knew what had happened. I had forgotten to tell him about the fiery, hot green Japanese mustard, *wasabi*, tucked inconspicuously under the slice of tuna. He hacked and he coughed. His eyes watered, and his nose ran. He looked dazed and disoriented. Poor Walter trembled uncontrollably for the rest of the evening. And he never again joined us in what became our regular Friday night sushi caravans down the

271

Hollywood Freeway to Little Tokyo. To this day, the burden of guilt for Walter's sushi phobia weighs heavily on my conscience.

De Kelley never joined us on our after-hours outings. He always went straight home from the studio to his charming wife and best friend, Carolyn. They were homebodies who enjoyed life with their dog and hundred-year-old tortoise. Somehow, an unhurried, steady, conscientious tortoise seemed the perfect metaphorical pet for De. He was the senior veteran of all of us and the old hand at Paramount.

De had been a Paramount contract player in the heydays when studios kept a "stable" of them. Thus, he knew the lore and the history of the lot. I loved wandering around the studio with him during some of the long breaks between scenes, having him point out the old landmarks like the chorus dressing room buildings, and the star "dressing rooms," which really were sumptuous town-house suites. All of them had now been converted into office space.

"This was a real lively place back in those days," he would drawl nostalgically. "We really used to churn them out then."

"Well, we're doing that today with STAR TREK, aren't we? One show every six days." I reminded.

"Yeah, but it was different then," he insisted. "We said words that we understood. None of this high-tech gobbledygook. It was different. As different as oranges and kiwifruits." What an interesting comparison, I thought. Kiwifruits were the trendy new exotica of the avant-garde. My farmer cousins in Sacramento grew them and were campaigning to popularize them.

"For a guy wistfully strolling down memory lane, you sure seem hip to the newest in fruit," I observed.

"What? Kiwifruits? Carolyn and I love them," he revealed.

"Really?" I answered, making a mental note. "So we are kiwifruits, and your old movies are oranges, huh? Well, infinite diversity in infinite . . ." I didn't have to finish the phrase. De chuckled merrily as he continued his narration.

When my cousin sent down a box of newly picked kiwifruits shortly after a harvest, I took a bag of them to the studio for De and his wife. I included a note that read, "Infinite thanx for the orange tour."

The orange tours continued. And the kiwi thank-yous went to De whenever I got a box from Sacramento.

The soundstage next door to ours was the home of the hit international espionage series *Mission: Impossible*. Martin Landau, Barbara Bain, and Greg Morris—stars of the series—dropped in occasionally on our set, and we visited them. On a film-studio soundstage the mixing of futuristic Starfleet uniforms with other actors in contemporary suits and dresses didn't seem incongruous or at all peculiar. We were just being good neighbors. These visits one day turned into an invitation for me to do a guest role in one of their episodes, titled "The Plague." It was the role of a bacteriologist who joins the M:I team to foil a horrifying germ warfare plot by international terrorists.

For me this meant the comfort of the same familiar studio lot and the same parking place, but the bracing difference of a new character, a different rhythm, another time frame, and easy contemporary clothes. If I got a little homesick for the future, I just strolled next door. I had the best of tomorrow and today.

But "today," for our STAR TREK company, had the nerve-straining tension of a mission: impossible. The ratings continued to be low, and the network compounded our difficulties by slicing down our already reduced budget. Even a visit to the set by my brother, Henry, and his wife, June, who had returned to Los Angeles from Milwaukee with baby Scotty, contributed to my distress during our time of adversity.

I had taken them to lunch at the commissary, and then we strolled back to the soundstage so I could show them the set of the *U.S.S. Enterprise*. We entered a soundstage that was empty because everyone was still off at lunch. I walked them through the corridor set, pointing out the many details. Henry had never been on a movie set before and seemed rather perplexed by the tangled clutter of cables snaking all over the floor, the forest of supports holding up the backsides of the flats, and the general absence of the sleek and gleaming futuristic world that he had expected to see. He rapped on the corridor walls with his knuckles. There was the dry, hollow sound of painted plywood.

"Hunh! Plywood. Is this all it is?" he sniffed.

I demonstrated the way the doors that whooshed open automatically on approach really operated. They were actually opened by stagehands hidden behind the walls, drawing back the door panels manually when a little red cue light lit up. Henry pushed the painted wooden doors back and forth, and they rumbled noisily on their rollers.

"Hunh! Is this all it is?" He sneered in disappointment.

I led them to the bridge set of the *Enterprise*, thinking that this surely should impress my skeptical brother.

"Henry, we had consultants from that think tank, the Rand Corporation, advise us on the design of this set," I told him, thinking that this kind of technical background for the set would score with his science-disciplined mind. He poked at the buttons on my console suspiciously. They just lay there soundless, unlit and inert.

"Hunh! Is that all they are? They look like plastic gum balls."

"Henry," I exclaimed, more than a bit peeved. "If you're going to keep saying that, I won't introduce you to any of my colleagues. I don't want you to look them up and down when you meet them and then say, 'Hunh! Is that all you are?' I won't let you do that!"

Just then, Nichelle entered the soundstage returning from her lunch. Seeing me with visitors, she approached us smiling. With great apprehension, I introduced Nichelle to my cynical brother and his wife.

"Oh, so you're George's brother." Nichelle exuded genuine delight at meeting him. "I've met your mother already, and now I meet another handsome member of the family. What a wonderful pleasure this is."

I looked at Henry and felt my tension ease. He was smiling sheepishly. Nichelle was working her own patented enchantment on him. Just then, through the corner of my eyes, I saw Bill enter the soundstage. Nichelle did also. With gracious nonchalance, she took Henry and June by their elbows and turned them away from Bill.

"May I show you my console and how I operate it?" She eased them away and focused their attention on her work station as Bill strode across the stage to his dressing room. Nichelle guided them all around the bridge and even explained the workings of the captain's chair to Henry and June. Henry was glowing. De walked in, and I introduced them to him. His easy affability charmed them. Then they met Jimmy and Walter. Henry and June were beaming with no assistance from Scotty's transporter. Leonard walked in and courteously greeted them. As I escorted Henry and June out of the soundstage, he said to me in a confidential tone, "The set was kind of fake. But you work with some pretty nice people." I heartily agreed with him on that. And I didn't hear any more "Hunhs" from Henry after that.

Bjo Tremble was working on her "Save STAR TREK" campaign like a woman possessed. She had made it happen once, and she was determined to get us renewed again after the third season. Her goal was to see us through to the finish of our announced "five-year mission." For that, we needed a fourth season. Bjo wrote, she telephoned, she organized, and she schemed. Her campaign to generate support for STAR TREK's renewal was heroic.

On the set, life for us was like walking on needles of cold anxiety. We had been plucked from the jaws of cancellation once, so there was always that hope, that almost taunting expectancy of something coming out of the dark soundstage air to save us—a deus-ex-renewal descending from the catwalks. But we were also aware of the clear reality evident all around us. The ratings numbers week after week continued to be bad. Gene was no longer with us. His periodic visits became fewer, then almost nil. Even Bob Justman, the coproducer who had been with us all three seasons, couldn't take the strain anymore. He left the show as well.

One afternoon, I happened to be near the soundstage telephone when a call came through for Greg Peters, the assistant. I had an unexplainable premonition about that call. I watched Greg's face listening, stoic and silent. Then he said softly, "I understand," and he slowly put the receiver down. He looked at me, and I could feel the chill in his eyes. Very quietly he said, "Well, it's final. We're off." Greg didn't tell anybody else on the set. I understood why—there was work still to be done. He waited until the end of the day, and he made the announcement. "Ladies and gentlemen, thank you for a good day's work, but I have sad news. We are canceled." It was not unexpected, but there was still a gasp.

"Turnabout Intruder" was the last episode filmed. After "That's a wrap!" was called announcing the finish of the final scene of the very final STAR TREK episode, we partied.

We ate too much. We drank too much. And we kissed and hugged a lot. Over the last three years, we had shared the joys and the stresses, the highs and the lows of working together on an extraordinary project. From early morning makeup calls to late night shoots, we had shared a unique adventure. We may have been canceled prematurely, but we had everything to be proud of in what we had achieved.

Our years spent together had made us more than just professional colleagues. We had struggled together against great odds and innumerable adversaries. At times, we even struggled amongst ourselves. Yet, through thick and thin, our lives had become deeply and intimately intertwined. Through adversity and good fortune, we grew to admire the talent we each possessed. We came to enjoy each other as friends—to love each other, each with our own individuality, with our very own peculiarities.

As I stood there at our final party listening to the laughter and the tears through the tinkle of ice in glasses, watching my friends share the last hours we would be spending together, I noticed Bill, in the center of everything as usual, laughing, joking, and slapping backs. Of everyone there, Bill was the merriest, the most strenuously ebullient. And I couldn't help feel a wisp of sadness for him. In his boisterous gaiety, I wondered if he really felt any genuine sense of loss.

The last three years had given me a wonderful gift of shared experiences and rich relationships. Colleagues had become synonymous with friends. But Bill in his single-minded drive for personal success had made himself oblivious to the human riches surrounding him. With his shining armor of charm and wit, he had only taken and not experienced. His unrelenting determination to protect what he had gotten had only isolated him and made him the poorer.

An actor not without inconsiderable talent, he probably would go on to the next series or the next film. He would probably continue to "succeed." And yet, I couldn't help hearing a faint sound of melancholy in his raucous merriment and loud hilarity.

LIFE
AFTER
CANCELLATION

18

Political Animal

I DROVE DOWN TO THE BEACH AT SANTA MONICA. IT WAS A COOL spring weekday, and the beach was nearly deserted. Only the most devout sun worshippers lay on the sand in isolated prostration. It was a perfect morning for a run on the beach. I started running as fast as I could across the ocean-saturated sand as the waves receded. The cool give of the wet underfoot felt good. I ran hard and fast along the beach all the way up to the palisades and gradually slowed down to a jog. Finally, I stopped and turned around on the desolate beach. I had left behind me a long trail of footprints on the wet sand. A gentle wave came tumbling in over them, then slowly pulled back, leaving only a row of tiny swirling pools where my imprints had been only seconds ago. Another wave came churning in, then receded, and my prints were almost gone; only barely noticeable dents remained on the smooth, wet sand.

The last three years had seemed like dreamy halcyon times. They were my most memorable professional years. From them had come colleagues who became treasured friends. STAR TREK had been an uncommon contribution to television, and I

281

was proud of my role in it. Now, in reminiscence, those years were all taking on a golden glow.

But as personally memorable as they were, those three years would probably be only transient little blips in the short memory span of television. The next season would come rolling in as inevitably and as relentlessly as the waves erasing my fast-fading footprints on the sands of Santa Monica.

But in 1969, there were other, unerasable footprints being imprinted in the annals of time. Neil Armstrong, U.S. astronaut, had left his print on the lunar surface, the first human footprints off our small planet. But on the other side of earth, in a tiny Asian nation, America was leaving the muddy prints of an ugly war all over a tortured landscape. That war in a far-off land was at the same time tearing up our own country, leaving bloody footprints all across our land from college campuses to the arenas of politics. Wrenching battles were being waged, doves against hawks, Americans against Americans, in Vietnam and right here at home.

STAR TREK had been a part of that struggle. One episode, "A Taste of Armageddon," was a clear metaphor for the Vietnam War, although, as with so many of our scripts, references to controversial contemporary issues apparently sailed right over the heads of the myopic NBC "program practices" executives.

In "A Taste of Armageddon," two neighboring civilizations had been at war with each other for centuries. Yet, both still had great cities untouched by the destruction of war. This war was a "clean" conflict, fought with computers, and "casualties" were surrogates sent off to be destroyed in disintegration chambers. The physical structures of the two warring civilizations remain untouched; only the people were ravaged. The story presented a science fiction parallel to the Vietnam conflict. Two great civilizations, the Communists and the West, were locked in a cold war; yet with great cities intact, they sent their surrogates to the "destruct machine" of a tiny country in far-off southeast Asia.

With the character of Sulu, however, STAR TREK was reversing a pattern in America's images of Asians. Throughout our theatrical history, Asians had been visible on American stages and screens from the time immigrants first began arriving from Asia over a hundred and fifty years ago. In times of prosperity, the depiction of Asians had been benign—usually as quaintly charming or romantically exotic. In times of stress—of economic hard times and social tensions—Asians and other minorities became scapegoats. The images became darker, depraved, dangerous. Chinatowns were transformed from quarters of captivating exotica to ominous places of white slavery and opium dens. Quiet, servile Japanese became inscrutable and shifty. At times of war, with Japan, in Korea, or in China, Asians were transformed into deadly, omnipotent foes —the personifications of evil. The images of Asians were reduced to politically incited, media-manipulated stereotypes.

We were again engaged in a hot war in Asia. Vietnam was raging. Every night on the six o'clock news, we saw the enemy—deadly, black-pajama-clad threats in the jungle. It was kill or be killed. These cunning foes had to be destroyed. Bomb them! Burn them! Napalm them! They had to be wiped out. These enemies in black pajamas . . . looked like me!

But every night, a little bit after the six o'clock news, the STAR TREK reruns came on. There on the bridge of the *Starship Enterprise*, we saw our heroes, the good guys. And there at the helm console we saw Lieutenant Sulu, a crack professional, a dashing swashbuckler, one of our good guys— one of us. And he was Asian; his face looked like that of those wearing the black pajamas on the six o'clock news. For the first time in the history of the American media at a time of war in Asia, there was a regularly visible counterbalance to the pervasive image of Asians as evil, of Asians as nemeses. That counterbalance underscored the complexity of this conflict. Sulu was on "our side," he was one of our heroes. And his face was mine.

When STAR TREK was born, I had been pursuing my own career ambitions. I wasn't seeking an emblematic image. Fate and Gene Roddenberry had conspired to make me that symbolic visage. But I was proud to be able to play the role. As an Asian in the craft of images, I knew the attendant responsibilities that came with my career choice. I was always mindful of the fact that, when I was seen on stage or screen, I represented more than just myself individually.

I had, however, my own statements to make on the course of events in our country. To do that, I couldn't remain behind the guise of my fictional character. I had to step away from the studio lights and become politically engaged. The memory of my father from almost thirty years ago was always with me. He had been pursuing his own goals in the early forties, but when the course of events and the forces of the times changed around him, he threw himself into the work of the community. He took on public responsibilities for the greater good. I had to become engaged with the challenges of my time.

There was a loosely organized group of antiwar activists in Hollywood called the Entertainment Industry for Peace and Justice, or EIPJ for short, of which I was a member. Jane Fonda and Donald Sutherland were among the most active members of the organization.

In the Asian American community, I had been discussing the issues of the war in Vietnam with many friends and knew there were strong emotions about it. But the voices that were audible from the community came primarily from the youth. Among the rest there was an uneasy quiescence that did not represent their distinct feelings of opposition to the war. There were reasons for this reticence. They had stinging shrapnel fragments from history still embedded in their minds, memory scars from persecutions past that were prickly and sharp. These people, for understandable reasons, were reluctant to identify themselves with controversy.

This concerned me. The lesson that my father had taught me kept coming to mind. "A participatory democracy is dependent on participation. Without it, democracy fails." We had to find a comfortable way for Asian Americans still bearing the scars of history to be able to express themselves and be a participatory voice in the process.

I began working with three friends—art dealer Marj Shinno, civil servant Toshiko Yoshida, and law student Mike Murase—

to put together events that would be easy and reassuring for the community but also become part of the effort to bring an end to the war. We organized theater parties to attend plays, like *The Trial of the Catonsville Nine*, that were about the antiwar movement but presented at the establishment downtown cultural center of the Mark Taper Forum. These events were a great success.

But we felt the visibility of Asian Americans was somewhat diluted in a big theater mixed with others. We now felt we wanted to make a purely Asian American statement. And we wanted to make it big—a strong, clear voice for the Asian American community. But these people would not come out to demonstrations or a rallies, which were usually too strident. Yet a rally was the best way to make the statement. How could we stage one that would be comfortable to the greater Asian American community? That was our challenge.

After much discussion, we decided on a rally held in the elegant Biltmore Bowl, the largest ballroom of the dignified downtown Biltmore Hotel. We would have Asian actors like France Nuyen, who had appeared in STAR TREK as Elaan of Troyius, participate by reading poetry. We would have Asian professors talk about the history of our involvement in the war. We gave the event a soft, uplifting name, "Peace Sunday." And we decided to make it free, not wanting cost to be an inhibitor to peace.

Now, our challenge was to finance this big, costly event. We were all willing to make some contributions to the cause, but they weren't enough to cover the great expense of this production. I went to Jane Fonda for help. I explained to her the importance of a big statement against this war in Asia coming from the Asian community. I explained the history and unique sensitivities of Asian Americans. I found however, that explanations weren't necessary with Jane. She understood immediately and quickly wrote out a very generous check that assured the financing of "Peace Sunday."

We use the word "extraordinary" too loosely. Especially in Hollywood. That Jane Fonda is an extraordinary actress has been amply affirmed. But too often, I have found extraordinary actors to be rather common, uninteresting people. Jane Fonda is an exception and an extraordinary human being. On the surface, her biography reads like a fairy tale about a princess touched by the magical wand of Hollywood. Daughter of a legendary superstar, blessed with wealth, talent, beauty, and opportunities, she seemed to have everything one could want in life.

Yet, I consider her a self-made woman. Instead of a having blessed existence, Jane began life as a deprived child with an emotionally troubled mother and an absent father. In spite of that, with a questing, active mind, the turmoil of the times engaged her intellect and her energies. And as a public figure, she spoke and conducted herself with courage and integrity, for which she received denunciations as well as applause. Undaunted by either, she remained a seeker—inquiring, learning, and constantly reinventing herself. Jane Fonda is a person who has lived through adversity, maintaining an insatiable appetite for life and emerging smarter and more supple, stronger and more sensitive.

Jane is also a kindred soul. I continued working with her in the political arena on issues such as the farm workers and the environment. Later, when she called to announce to me that her then-husband, Tom Hayden, was declaring his candidacy for the California state legislature, I threw myself into the campaign. He was elected, then reelected to the California Assembly.

Jane is a person of extraordinary substance. That she is a brilliant artist is abundantly clear. How extraordinary she is as a person continues to amaze me.

My city councilman, Tom Bradley, had been the first black man elected from a mostly white district. Now he was the first black politician to run for Mayor of the City of Los Angeles. After the anguish of the Watts riot that ripped the fabric of our city, Tom Bradley would be a conciliating force, a healer of our civic wounds. He would be important for our city. I headed up the Japanese Americans for Tom Bradley committee. Marj Shinno and Toshiko Yoshida from the "Peace Sunday" project were again with me on this effort. The campaign was hard fought, but it was dirty. Even in 1969, racism was a factor. Tom Bradley lost a very close race.

Undaunted, I next threw myself into a larger political arena, the statewide race for the seat of U.S. Senator. Congressman George Brown of California was the first member of Congress to vote against the Vietnam war appropriations. Now he was throwing his hat into the ring for the Democratic Party's nomination for a seat in the U.S. Senate. I wanted to help him in this quest. Working in the Brown campaign headquarters one day I encountered a familiar face, Leslie Parrish, who had been a guest on one of our STAR TREK episodes, "Who Mourns for Adonais?"

I became the chair of the Asian Americans for George Brown committee. Brown's opponent was John Tunney, the son of heavyweight champion Gene Tunney. He was youthful with movie-star good looks, and he was a friend of Senator Teddy Kennedy. It was a formidable combination. When the last vote was counted, Tunney took the Democratic nomination and then, in the general election, the U.S. Senate seat from California.

Every candidate that I had supported, from Adlai Stevenson for President back in 1960 to George Brown in this most recent race, had gone down to defeat. I was starting to feel that I was a curse on any political aspirant who should be so unfortunate as to have my support. Maybe I should start working for the opponent of the candidate I actually supported to help mine get elected; maybe I should look for political enemies.

Actually, it was to old friends that I returned. Josie Dotson, Jack Jackson, Elaine Kashiki, and Jeanne Joe had been building while I'd been losing elections. The Inner City Cultural Center was not only presenting production after production on the stage of a resurrected movie palace on West Washington Boulevard, but was offering classes in all areas of performing in a nearby building as well. Their dream of a multicultural performing arts center had become an exciting reality. But to keep it going, to continue feeding its ravenous appetite for cash, meant the constant pursuit of grants and the raising of funds. I wanted to support this project, but with more than money. I became a volunteer teacher at the center two nights a week. In a way, I was fulfilling my father's old hope that I would, at some point in my life, teach. I discovered again how his dreams for me and my own choices eventually crossed. I found teaching to be enormously satisfying.

I taught American Theater History from a minority vantage point. My students were black, Hispanic, and Asian, as well as white. Their general attitude toward the subject of history was that it was something past—remote and irrelevant. All they wanted to hear was Mr. Sulu talking about STAR TREK. I seized this as a wonderful opening—to go from the teeming pluralistic universe of Gene Roddenberry's future back to the mystery of our own multicultural past. I made the exploration of our history more like a probe into the dark unknowns of space. Did they know that there was a great black Shakespearean actor named Ira Aldredge, back in the nineteenth century? This was a fantastic discovery for them, opening up possibilities that they hadn't considered.

I was broadening horizons and options, but my job, at the same time, was to make them aware of the challenges they faced. The great Ira Aldridge had to go to England to win his greatest acclaim. Another black actor, Paul Robeson, of our century, also had to go to Europe to shine as Othello.

But in the future society of STAR TREK, we, too, had to confront beings who couldn't see the substance beyond the surface and were deprived of richness as a result. Our challenge was to act, to do something about it, to change things so that in our own times we contribute to building a better world. That's our great adventure. That's the enterprise of the Inner City Cultural Center. The kids loved it. The STAR TREK metaphor always seemed to work.

The primary enterprise of the Inner City Cultural Center

was the main stage productions. I acted in a thriller, *Monkey's Paw*, playing an old seafarer, and in Shakespeare's *Macbeth* I played Ross, who appears only in the first act. After the glory of storming onstage in my heavy, flowing cape and my scene of alarm, came the tedium of the long wait downstairs in the green room until the curtain call. But I loved it. This was my first opportunity to play Shakespeare before a paying audience. I would peek out at the audience from a crack in the heavy velvet curtain and survey the house every night. It looked good. We were getting the pluralistic audience that Josie had talked so wistfully about. Now we were making it happen.

One night, I spotted Henry and June out there. I guessed that Scotty was being baby-sat by his doting Grandpa and Grandma. But I was surprised to see June; she was heavy with her second baby. In fact, she now claims that the birth of their second child and first daughter was induced that night by the bloodcurdling screeching of the three witches as they incanted their dire predictions to the warrior king. My niece, Akemi, was born two days after Henry and June came to see *Macbeth*.

The blood from the fury of Vietnam was spattering all over—not only across the burning jungles and fields of that Asian land but here on college campuses from Kent State to Berkeley, on city sidewalks from Boston to Los Angeles.

From the outlands far beyond the sound and fury—the plain state of South Dakota—came an unexpected standard-bearer of opposition to the war, a straight-speaking senator, George McGovern. He was running for President, and the political animal in me was again aroused. But rather than work once again as a campaign volunteer, I decided to go a step farther to support the presidential candidacy of George McGovern. I decided to run for a seat on the California delegation to the Democratic National Convention. I would run as a delegate pledged to Senator McGovern.

The junior high school auditorium where the election of district delegates was to be held was a tumult of frenzied electioneering. Smiles flashed everywhere. Flesh was pressed with eager purposefulness. If there were babies to be kissed, we would have kissed them. We did everything we could, save the one thing forbidden. We couldn't leaflet. Only the basic biographical information printed by the election board was allowed. My political credentials read: member of the Democratic State Central Committee for four years; volunteer in the Stevenson presidential campaign, 1960; chair of the Japanese American committee in the Tom Bradley mayoral campaign, 1969; chair of the Asian American committee in the George Brown senatorial campaign, 1970.

The most important part of the process was the speech each of the candidates would make. We had five minutes to give our qualifications, why we could best represent the district and the candidate we supported. It would be a long morning; there were at least two dozen candidates for only six seats. Among them were labor leaders, grizzled campaign war-horses, schoolteachers, and students. After the speeches and the hurrahs, after the voting and the long anxiety-filled wait, when the result was finally announced, one of the six delegates to the Democratic Nominating Convention was an actor. I was elected an official delegate who would play a role in the selection of a candidate for President of the United States.

I wasn't the only actor in that vast convention hall in Miami Beach, Florida. Shirley MacLaine was there vigorously advocating women's rights. Her little brother, Warren Beatty, was also there, a dashing figure involved in the behind-the-scenes machinations of the convention. He seemed perpetually to be in a huddle with the youthful McGovern campaign manager, Gary Hart.

This was a historic convention. There had never before been more women, minorities, youth, and nonpoliticans as delegates to a presidential nominating convention. The democratic process was slowly but ever so surely being opened up. It was becoming, as my father would have put it, "more participatory."

And for this first-time participant, it was a heady experience.

To rub shoulders with Senator Ted Kennedy on the convention floor one moment and in the next to hear his ringing voice from the stage remembering his assassinated brother; to shake the hand of the senator from Hawaii, Dan Inouye, the first Japanese American elected to the United States Senate, and to be offered his left hand because he had lost his right arm on a World War II battlefield in Europe as an American G.I.; to raise my own right hand in casting my vote for George McGovern as the Democratic nominee for President of the United States, remembering that just three decades ago I was a boy on a train taking me to a barbed wire camp in the swamps of Arkansas. Experiences and memories tumbled in on each other in a kaleidoscope of emotions.

On the final night of the convention, to the deafening thunder of the delegates in the hall and a shower of balloons and confetti from overhead, our standard-bearer for President, George McGovern, took the stage to accept the nomination. "This land is my land, this land is your land. This land was made for you and me," he quoted from the folk song. I looked around at the ecstatic faces that surrounded me. I saw snowy-haired seniors and dewy-skinned youths, flinty-eyed politicos and bead-wearing idealists. I saw black auto workers, Hispanic housewives, Native American attorneys, and Asian schoolteachers. I saw the faces of an America of infinite diversity in infinite combinations all looking up with hope glistening in their eyes to the senator from South Dakota. I felt a stirring in my heart and a pride beyond words. I returned to Los Angeles inspired and determined to elect our next president.

I organized an Asian American committee for George McGovern. We opened a storefront McGovern headquarters in Little Tokyo, and that popular Asian celebrity, Walter Koenig, helped us on its gala opening. I arranged for my niece, Akemi, dressed in a colorful kimono, to greet Mrs. Eleanor McGovern at the Little Tokyo headquarters. We organized a big fund-raising dinner in Chinatown. We had small coffee klatches in people's homes. We worked feverishly in the business of this participatory democracy. It was an exhilarating and exhausting campaign. But early on election night in November 1972, Richard Nixon claimed a massive landslide victory. The curse of George Takei had struck again.

Over the years, Councilman Tom Bradley had become a good friend. We crossed paths often on the political hustings. We worked together on many issues. I had come to admire his quiet, low-key consensus-building skills.

One day, he told me he was thinking of making another try for mayor of Los Angeles. Would I help him? My immediate response was, Of course. He had come so close to winning in 1969. Over the last four years, he had built up a lot of goodwill and respect. It was good timing. But I had to be frank with him about my sorry political record and the jinx I brought with me. Did he really want to stay in my not-so-exclusive club of Adlai Stevenson, George Brown, and now George McGovern?

Tom laughed and said, "George, I'll do you a favor. You campaign for me, and I'll break that curse for you. I'll free you of that ugly dead albatross hanging from your neck." We shook hands right then and there to seal the compact. And I threw myself with gusto into another wild and woolly campaign.

It was election night 1973, and Bradley for Mayor supporters all converged on the Los Angeles Hilton Hotel. The main ballroom was crammed with nervously expectant campaign workers, political junkies, and celebratory revelers. They spilled out into the bars, lounges, and corridors of the hotel.

I was with Tom and his lieutenants in his top-floor suite. All eyes were glued to television sets scattered about. The numbers were looking good. But tiny, needlelike memories of the mayoral election night of 1969 still prickled at me incessantly. We had mounted a strong, vigorous campaign again. We were clear and forceful on issues. And most importantly, the people of Los Angeles had gotten to know Tom Bradley. And yet, I was nervous. I couldn't shake those tiny stabs of guilt. Despite my compact with Tom, I didn't feel I would shake my jinx this time. I still felt the weight of that dead bird hanging on me. Could my curse strike another election?

As precinct after precinct reported in, the numbers became better. More precincts reported, and the numbers continued to improve. A phone call came for Tom. He took it and all eyes shifted from the television sets to him. He listened and than broke out in a great, sunny smile. He kept smiling, then started nodding at all of us. As he hung up, he announced, "He just conceded. Let's go downstairs!" To a burst of wild applause, he led our jubilant group to the elevator and down to the roar of the ecstatically cheering crowd waiting in the ballroom below.

May 29, 1973, was a history-making evening. Tom Bradley became the first black mayor of a major American city. And even more momentously, George Takei had come up with a winner! At long last, the curse had been broken. I was freed of my onerous, stinking burden.

Miracles happen in threes, they say. The first two had now happened. I wondered if there might not be that proverbial third.

After the cancellation of STAR TREK, I had returned to the rat race of guest appearances on series television. A month after the last STAR TREK episode was finished, I was toiling among stars, not the galactic stars of the future, this time, but the tinseled stars of modern-day Hollywood, as a hippie film studio photographer in an episode of a new series called *Bracken's World*.

STAR TREK was behind me, I thought. It would enjoy a reasonable extended life on the rerun circuit for a few seasons and then gracefully fade away—like all canceled series. But with this one, something strange was happening. The ratings for the reruns were better, relatively speaking, than when we were on first run. And the numbers were growing.

The early warning signal was sounded by a phone call from Walter Koenig.

"Guess what I heard!" Walter's voice was excitedly conspiratorial. "You won't believe it, but . . ."

"Well, if I won't believe it, why are you telling me?" I teased.

"If you don't want to know what's happening with STAR

TREK, then I won't tell you," he retorted. He knew well I wouldn't be able to resist.

"All right," I conceded, "please tell me what I won't believe."

There were rumors, he told me, that STAR TREK was being considered for revival back on television because of the great ratings in syndication. That sounded interesting but highly unlikely. I told Walter that I'd believe it when I saw it actually happen. I told him that, but in the back of my mind, the thought of the two miracles that had already happened began to stir. Perhaps? Maybe? Could it be? I couldn't help wondering.

But those rumors were like spring wildflowers; they bloomed enticingly only to fade with the heat of summer. As the season turned, they bloomed again. I became cynical about revival rumors. While STAR TREK was on prime time we had been put on a psychological roller coaster ride, hanging on for dear life, and expecting death on the other side of every hairpin turn. I refused to be put through that again, this time grasping every wispy ghost of a rumor for our resurrection from the graveyard of cancellation. But Walter continued to feed me those wisps with excited updates on every fresh hope as well as every new disappointment.

"Guess what? It's definite!" This time Walter's excitement was unreserved. "They're definitely going ahead with the revival as a series! It's definite!" My cynicism couldn't resist his enthusiasm. I caught his fever.

"That's fantastic! You know, I've actually been expecting some kind of miracle to happen. And this is it!" I told him about my anticipated third miracle. This one wasn't in the political arena, but it was a miracle nevertheless, I exclaimed.

"Guess what?" Walter continued, "we're coming back as a cartoon series!" Immediately, I realized I had been had. Walter loves to tease and abuse my trusting nature, and usually I don't fall for it. But my secret wish this time had made me take his bait. I was mortified that I had shared my third miracle hopes with him. I expected his mocking, high-pitched laughter as he reeled in his gullible victim. But it didn't come.

"I think it's an interesting approach," Walter persisted dead seriously. "Animation will allow STAR TREK to handle all sorts of science fiction concepts without an astronomical effects budget." I silently refused to be suckered in further. I didn't respond. "Well, what do you think, George?" he finally asked.

"Walter, I don't think it's funny. I really believed you." I frowned.

"No. It's really true," he insisted earnestly, "STAR TREK is coming back as an animated series through Filmation!" His impassioned persistence seemed credible, but I had been taken in by his act once too often. I told him that I'd check around to verify his words.

After a few calls, I discovered that Walter was, indeed, telling the truth. We were, in fact, coming back as an animated series for the Saturday morning youngster audience. Then, another call from Walter followed.

"Guess what?" His voice sounded crestfallen.

"What is it?" I asked. I hadn't heard him sounding so dejected before.

"We're not in it. They're only going with Bill, Leonard, De, Jimmy, and Majel. They've got a tight budget. We're not going to be doing the voices for our own characters." It was shocking news. But it was also typical. Our emotions were shot up and then plunged down just like that roller coaster ride during the filming of the series. So although STAR TREK was taking off again in another guise, we were not going to be a part of this ride. I learned that Jimmy was going to be doing Sulu's voice and Majel was voicing Uhura. I finally began to reconcile myself to the fact that STAR TREK really was going to be in our past.

My third miracle, however, was yet to happen. Leonard Nimoy was doing something few actors have done. First, he was taking a position on principle. Secondly, he was standing up for other actors. And astonishingly, he was putting his own job on the line for them.

Leonard had learned of our not being included in the cast of this revival of the show, and he took action. STAR TREK, he argued with Filmation, was at its core an affirmative vision of our future. That vision was based on the idea of drawing our strength from our diversity. Nichelle and George were the personifications of that statement in STAR TREK. If Filmation did not recognize that, then he was not interested in being a part of the project. They would have to go ahead without him.

It was a bold stand. It was a stand of integrity. And it was a stand an actor didn't have to take. He could have done the voice of Spock under the guise of a mere hired hand . . . or voice, in this case. But Leonard represented more than actor as mere hireling. An actor, in the truest sense, is an artist who bears the values and the ideals of his culture. Leonard Nimoy is such an artist. I will always be grateful to him for having kept Nichelle and me connected with STAR TREK, and I take great pride in my association with him for who he is as a man.

Unhappily, Walter was not on the final cast list. But, ever the enterprising man, he continued his association with this version of STAR TREK by sharing with us another of his many talents, this time as a writer. He wrote the script of the animated episode "The Infinite Vulcan."

19

The Campaign Run

TOM BRADLEY, MY OLD CITY COUNCILMAN, WAS THE NEW MAYOR of Los Angeles. His council seat was now open. Friends in the political arena began suggesting something I had never considered. They began urging me to run for that vacant seat on the city council.

I had been active politically because of issues and the principle of participation in the process. I was a citizen-activist. I knew I would always be involved in supporting the good candidate or contributing to the important causes, but I had never envisioned myself running for public office. But now here were friends and people I had worked with in the political campaigns who were strongly encouraging me to run. It was a unique opportunity, they pointed out. This was a special election to fill an unexpired term, so there would not be a runoff, only a "sudden death" election where the candidate with a plurality of votes would be declared the winner. Already there were about a dozen potential candidates indicating their desire to throw their hats into the ring.

But I loved acting. The council seat was a full-time job that would require me to forgo my career. The political arena was a calling that meant relinquishing private pursuits for exclusively public service obligations. I was hesitant about forfeiting all that I had worked for up to this point in my life.

But, my friends countered, there had never been an Asian on the council. This was a unique opportunity to bring diversity to the civic body. As far as I knew, there had never been an actor on the Los Angeles City Council either. Both were constituencies that deserved representation, my friends argued. And besides, added a savvy politico, I had a shining image from STAR TREK. I was eminently electable.

There are points in life when unique circumstances demand equally singular decisions. This was an opportunity to contribute in a previously unimagined way in an unexpected arena. I enjoyed the excitement and the engagement with the issues of our times. I believed in the idea of citizen participation in government. I felt that part of the problem with our system was professional politicians who were disconnected from the people; I felt I had that linkage to offer. Like Tom Bradley, but as an Asian American, I could also be a coalition builder. But however attractive the opportunity, I knew that it came with a big price tag. It was a high cost—but the opportunity was equally big. I decided to pay the price and declared myself a candidate for the 10th District seat on the Los Angeles City Council.

I put together a crack campaign team. Marj Shinno was my campaign manager. We had worked intensely together in many political wars. Jerry Zanelli, a sharp political professional, was my consultant. Mike Yamaki, a dynamic young law student, was the campaign coordinator. Al Green and Bill Collier, friends from the Democratic State Central Committee, were my advisors and advance men. Les Hamasaki, an urban planner and an old friend, was a close confidant. And I called on friends from STAR TREK: writers Dorothy Fontana and David Gerrold, who had written that delightful episode "The Trouble with Tribbles," which I had lost to Walter Koenig because of my absence filming *The Green Berets*. The group also included Bjo and John Trimble, activists extraordinaire, and their two little girls, as well as fans from all over southern California. They stuffed envelopes, built a telephone network of supporters, and leafleted the entire district.

A campaign moves on its stomachs, and my mother kept the volunteers well fed. David Gerrold told me he was a volunteer not because of me, but because of Mama's sushi—and I don't think he was just kidding. I did notice he didn't show up on the hot dog days.

My father pitched in wherever he was needed. He phoned, he stuffed envelopes, he walked precincts, he even swept the headquarters after everyone had gone home for the night. There wasn't enough he could do. I worried that he might overwork himself, but he brushed aside all such concerns with a smile and a breezy "There's a lot of work to do till election day." Seeing him bustling around the office exuding pride, watching the joy he took in every detail of his son's candidacy for elective office—for this alone, I was glad I had made the decision to run.

Walter Koenig was indefatigable speaking on my behalf at every street rally and any coffee klatch. Nichelle Nichols sang for me at the drop of a request. A letter from Leonard Nimoy helped cinch the important endorsement of the Democratic County Committee. And at my first fund-raising dinner, the guests of honor were Gene Roddenberry and Majel Barrett, who had recently returned from their Shinto Japanese wedding ceremony in Tokyo. His keynote speech was warm, gracious, and very Gene. It was not stirringly flag-waving. It was not electrifyingly political. It glowed with generosity. It was suffused with love. It was just the right note for my candidacy.

I loved campaigning. The old pros told me that one of the first rules of running for office is not to let the people see you sweat. I broke that rule profusely. In the blazing midsummer sun, I walked the precincts, going from door to door, talking to the voters in their homes. It was exhausting but enormously fulfilling. Talking with neighbors about the concerns of the neighborhood is the basis of our democracy.

The candidate's nights in the neighborhoods, where all the

aspirants for office engage the voters in a question-and-answer session at gatherings in community halls or high school auditoriums, were tremendously stimulating. This, the old tradition of town hall meetings, was what participatory democracy was all about.

But town meetings were updated, Los Angeles style. At one of these candidate's nights in the east side of the district, where the people were primarily Hispanic, I got a leg up on the other candidates. A question was asked in Spanish. As I started to respond in Spanish even before the translation was begun, the stunned expressions on the faces of my opponents amused me no end. I was the only candidate who spoke Spanish.

I was living, sweating, and enjoying the fundamentals of what I had studied in my American civics class in high school. And always, there was my father's beaming face, standing in the back of halls, on street corners leafleting, or back at the headquarters busily stuffing envelopes.

Ironically, STAR TREK became a major problem. The Federal Communications Commission's so-called "Equal Time" ruling unexpectedly intruded as a giant obstacle. This rule required, in essence, that if any candidate for office appeared on any medium, then that station would have to offer equal time to all other candidates for the same office. STAR TREK was airing on a local channel every night in reruns. I was visible nightly on television. But, of course, this was not as a candidate; it was as an actor . . . playing Mr. Sulu, the helmsman of the *U.S.S. Enterprise.*

Yet, when my opponents all claimed their equal time based on my speaking fictional lines as a fictional character in fictional situations, they were able to campaign as themselves, as candidates for office, on issues relevant to the contest—on crime, on education, on taxation. It was the most preposterously unequal interpretation of the notion of "equal time" conceivable. And the "offending" station had to offer each of the twenty-eight candidates running against me, individually, free time equivalent to the amount of time Mr. Sulu was on the air.

Whether a viable candidate or one that could garner only a dozen or so votes, they all got "equal" time. The loss to the station was staggering. After complying for one interminable night of electioneering by my opponents, it prudently began airing only those episodes in which Mr. Sulu did not appear.

To further compound this bizarre turn of events, the cartoon STAR TREK series was about to premiere nationally on Saturday mornings. Except that in Los Angeles it was blacked out for the duration of the election campaign, simply because the cartoon drawings were accompanied by my voice. It was madness. But it was madness we could do nothing about. There seemed to be more intelligence in the cartoon characters than in the rigid minds of the bureaucrats in Washington.

Spirited exhaustion—that was the feeling on election night, September 18, 1973. All the speeches had been made to the point of raspy hoarseness. The precincts had been walked till my leg muscles ached as much as the smile on my sunburned face. And yet, I felt a zest, a hunger for the unknown that awaited us. I felt an appetite that actually seemed to be fed by the fatigue, like the second wind that energizes a long-distance runner.

We gathered in the banquet hall in the back of a coffee shop near our headquarters. Volunteers, staff, campaign advisors— we had worked together intensely, passionately, and we wanted to be with each other to share the hours as the vote counts came in.

The polls were encouraging. They said it was a two-man race between David Cunningham, a political consultant who identified himself on the ballot as a "businessman," and me. When the first votes were announced, we were in the lead. As the numbers flowed in, the race began to seesaw. We traded places in the lead. He was ahead at one point, then I was. It continued like that until about nine-thirty. Then the tide turned. He continued to maintain a slim lead. By eleven o'clock, it was clear that I would not be the councilman of the 10th District. I conceded the election. I had lost the race by a heartbreaking 1,647 votes. The curse of George Takei struck again! It had not been broken. And this time, my curse hit me!

Running for elective office was exhausting, and it was, at times, tremendously draining. I saw venality; I experienced meanness; I had to deal with manipulators. But this was a part of society, and in a hard-fought race, inevitably these elements surface. But I also saw massive dedication to the ideals of this system in the many volunteers of so many different backgrounds who gave so much of their time, energy, and funds. I experienced our American electoral process as personally as a citizen could, and I found it bracing. My experience of running for public office was deeply satisfying.

With the campaign we mounted, we were able to demonstrate that a hard-fought race can be rooted in issues, be broad-based, and still be focused on common ideals. We built a coalition that reflected the diverse rainbow of our district and the richness of our ideas. We demonstrated that principles do not have to be forfeited in the name of political expedience. I was proud of the campaign, for while we lost in the race for the office, we succeeded as a testimony to the vibrancy of our American electoral process.

And personally I won on two counts. First, I won political credibility. I demonstrated that I could be a significant vote-getter and a builder of coalitions. And more personally, I won back my career that I cherished. The STAR TREK reruns resumed. The cartoon series began airing in Los Angeles. And shortly after the election, I was back in the recording booth at Filmation doing the voice of Sulu for the animated STAR TREK series.

A few years later, I was approached again to run for office—this time for a seat in the state legislature. The incumbent assemblyman from my district, Mike Roos, was entangled in a struggle involving the majority leadership position. His base was factionalized, and the people urging me to run against him felt I could oust him. Again, I was confronted with a fork in the road. I wanted time to consider the proposal.

Somehow, rumors of my possible running for the seat reached the ears of Assemblyman Roos. He called to ask me in for a meeting. I was happy to oblige.

The assemblyman greeted me with wary formality in his district office. When we shook hands, only the faintest hint of a smile creased his face. Were the rumors true? he wanted to know. I responded that I indeed had been approached but that I had not made a decision. I was thinking it over. He hinted that, among the things I should be thinking about, perhaps I needed to consider the Federal Communications Commission's "Equal Time" rule.

Again, that outrage against the meaning of the word "equal"! That affront to rationality! I left Assemblyman Roos's office livid at even the suggestion that this absurd bureaucratic nonsense would be made a factor in the electoral process again.

This so-called "Equal Time" rule is a discriminatory law against a category of citizens who happen to be in a specific business—film and television. I did not become an actor in order to gain visibility to run for public office. Acting had been my established means of livelihood for over fifteen years. Offering oneself for consideration as a candidate for public service is both a citizen's right and responsibility.

Every candidate gains recognition from the voters via his or her work professionally and in community service. A businessman with his name attached to his business is not required to remove that name from signs and other advertisements for his business when he campaigns for office. His business identity is part of his credentials for his candidacy. Only those in film and television are penalized for their professional work and visibility by this federal ruling.

In Los Angeles, those in the film and television business make up a significant portion of the population. It is a sector of the community that warrants a voice in the arenas of government. As a member of that community, I felt that I could articulate its interests as well as others. To run for public office, I, as an individual, might be willing to forgo my residual fees when shows are not aired in response to the "Equal Time" rulings. But if by my candidacy I should cost my colleagues—other actors, writers, and directors—their residual revenue, which for some is not an insignificant part of their annual income, then I could not be a very credible voice for their interests. A candidate for public office from the film and television community would penalize that very community he or she represented.

I decided not to do it. I decided against running and provoking Assemblyman Mike Roos into calling up the madness of the "Equal Time" ruling again. As my example demonstrates, this ruling of the Federal Communications Commission is not only an unequal and unfair dictate, it is the single most effective inhibitor of the exercise of a citizen's right to run for public office. It flies right into the face of the ideals of participatory democracy.

20

Rapid Transit

MAYOR TOM BRADLEY WAS CALLING. HE NEEDED MY HELP, HE said.

"Tom, you know I'm available to you. I'd be happy to help you in whatever way I can." I thought he might have wanted me to serve as an MC for some function.

"George, I'd like to ask you to represent me on the Board of Directors of the RTD," he said. I didn't think I had heard right. The RTD was the agency of government charged with public transportation for the southern California area. It ran the comprehensive bus operation for the entire metropolitan district. During the mayoral campaign, Tom had vigorously advocated as a top priority the need for improved public transportation and the construction of a subway system for Los Angeles. All this would fall into the province of the RTD, whose full name was the Southern California Rapid Transit District. What could he have meant asking me to represent him on such a board? I was an actor. I must have heard wrong.

"Did you want me to represent you at some dinner of the RTD?" I asked.

"George, I'm asking you to be my appointee to a seat on the

Board of Directors of the RTD," he repeated, chuckling at my confusion. I hadn't heard wrong.

"But, Tom. I'm an actor. I don't have any experience. . . ." I started to demur.

"If I remember your bio, George, you're an actor who has studied architecture and urban planning. And if I know you, you're a citizen-activist who is a good quick study. You've got political smarts, and you're articulate. You're just as qualified as the businessmen, lawyers, and other politicians that sit on that board, and you just might bring more background than some of them. Let me send you some material for you to look over. Then let me know." This was an astounding and totally unexpected offer. And it was tantalizing.

I call myself a city kid. I love cities. I love visiting many cities to savor their urbane pleasures but also to study the unique qualities that give them each their individual character. What is it that makes a charming city charming? What makes one city more alluring than another? Even failed cities, urban basket cases, I find fascinating. An understanding of the causes of urban disaster areas is as necessary to building a successful city as knowing the manifest delights of great ones.

One of the basics to building a healthy city is efficient circulation of people and goods—it is the civic artery that carries energy to the body of the city. And essential to that healthy circulation is an efficient, affordable public transportation system. Public transit, whether buses, trolleys, subways, or ferries, is vital for a dynamic city. It provides mobility and access to the diverse work, service, and cultural locales of a metropolitan area. And a vibrant city sparkling with urbane spirit is unimaginable without the pedestrian life that public transit creates.

Mayor Bradley was offering me the opportunity to be a shaper of policy in this vital area of urban planning. My city, Los Angeles, despite our history of a fine network of trolley car transit, was known more for private automobile dependence. It was an enticing challenge I couldn't refuse. I called the Mayor and accepted.

The press had fun with the Mayor's appointing an actor to the transit district board. Did the Mayor think he was casting a movie with his appointments? Maybe the campaign had made him too "spaced out." "Earth hailing Mayor Bradley: Beam back to planet Hollywood," they teased.

But the media-savvy Mayor knew just how to play their game. When he was needled about his choice of a member of the Screen Actors Guild as his representative on the RTD Board, he responded, "All America has been watching George Takei drive a public transportation vehicle called the *U.S.S. Enterprise* all over the galaxy. Now you're going to see how he can get the people of Los Angeles from downtown L.A. to Van Nuys, from East L.A. to Culver City. Stay tuned."

The joking stopped—but I knew I had to prove myself. I had a lot of homework to do.

The Mayor had made a priority commitment in his campaign to the building of a modern heavy-rail rapid transit subway system. I agreed wholeheartedly. It was essential to making Los Angeles not only a strong urban center, but also to addressing the air pollution, traffic congestion, and land use issues.

The real challenge, however, lay in building the political consensus to support a tax that would be the local matching fund needed to secure federal funding. We knew that if the current traffic congestion continued, it would start adversely impacting the local economy, job growth, and the quality of life. We campaigned long and hard and finally in 1980 succeeded in the passage of Proposition A, a half-cent sales tax dedicated to transit improvement. We were halfway there.

Now we had to secure the federal match. To accomplish this, it was useful to participate on the national transit scene. We needed to build alliances with other cities planning public transit projects and support each other's efforts. I had become active with the American Public Transit Association headquartered in Washington, D.C. In 1978, I was elected Vice President of Human Resources of the Association and served for two years.

In 1980, a Californian was elected President of the United States. Ronald Reagan, former actor, former president of my union, the Screen Actors Guild, and former governor of our state, was going to the White House. We were optimistic that we would have one of ours in Washington to move our project along. I even went to the gala send-off luncheon at the Biltmore sponsored by the Los Angeles Chamber of Commerce, hopeful of the President-elect's support for our subway project.

But we were to be sadly disappointed. The Reagan administration's "supply side" economists would not supply the full federal matching funds. Instead, they whittled them down even more. We had to lobby strenuously to be able to announce in 1983 the completion of the funding package for the Metro Rail system for Los Angeles.

It was a Herculean effort that involved the dedicated labor of hundreds of people, from legislative advocates, elected officials, transit staffers, to a host of concerned citizens. In this process, I came to understand the essential role of leadership in a project of this magnitude. The Metro Rail could not have become reality without the foresight, political skills, and impelling drive of Mayor Tom Bradley and Congressman Glenn Anderson. They were the dynamic political duo that led the campaign for building the funding base of the project. It was a gigantic task successfully accomplished.

But not a spade of dirt had yet been turned on this, the biggest public works project proposed in southern California. The building of the system itself was the next challenge.

During the time that I served on the board, I had decided to place my commitment to the Rapid Transit District as a high priority and had passed on many television guest appearances —save for one. In 1974, I took time out from my transit duties for an offer that was impossible for me to pass up. It was a drama entitled *Year of the Dragon* by an extraordinary talent, Frank Chin.

I had seen the play months before when I was in New York for a transit conference. After a wearying day of meetings, I looked in the theater listings in the newspaper and found a play that had an interestingly Asian-sounding title playing at the distinguished theater company American Place Theater. I went to see *Year of the Dragon,* and that night, for the first time in my years as an inveterate theater-goer, a play spoke to me viscerally as an Asian-American.

It was the story of a Chinese-American man, Fred Eng, living in Chinatown, San Francisco. Not old but no longer young, still single, still living in his father's house, working as a tour guide in his father's business. Shaped by the forces of his culture, conflicted by the values of American society, and feeling that he had sacrificed his life to the exigencies of family circumstances, Fred was an angry man on the verge of a breakdown. It was a potent drama with insinuating resonances for Asians in America. The role of Fred was brilliantly brought to life by actor Randall Kim.

I went backstage after the performance and was introduced to Frank Chin. We went out for a drink. And from that after-theater get-together, I got to know an artist churning with ideas, a man of explosive emotions and a blistering personality. I went back to the hotel exhilarated, not only by one of the most powerful and at the same time personal dramas I had experienced, but by having met Frank Chin, an enormously gifted dramatist who understood the experience of being Asian in America so deeply and so intensely.

So when the offer came to play the role of Fred Eng in the television adaptation for the *Theater in America* series on Public Broadcasting, I was not conflicted. I made arrangements with the Rapid Transit District to take a leave of absence for about six weeks.

The time I spent in New York rehearsing and then filming *Year of the Dragon* with Pat Suzuki, Tina Chen, Conrad Yama, and Lilah Kan was deeply fulfilling. Sinking my thespian teeth into a chunk of dramatic red meat for the first time in my professional life served only to remind me of the meager fare I had had to nibble on in my acting career. The difference was in the writers—the chefs who can prepare such rich, savory fare, such solid nourishment for the soul. When we were finished, rather than being satisfied, I was hungry for more. I was convinced that we needed to encourage good writers who understand the unique American experience of Asians.

I returned to Los Angeles revitalized as an actor and ready to continue my work of moving people, not so emotionally this time, but from one place to another. The Metro Rail project still had a long way to go.

21

Ventures and Enterprises

"HEY, GEORGE, YOU WANT TO MAKE SOME MONEY?" IT WAS JIMMY Doohan calling with a business proposition. "There's a seminar at the L.A. Hilton downtown. Meet me there, and you'll hear about something fantastic. You're going to be thanking me for the rest of your life." With that ebullient but cryptic invitation, he hung up.

I went to the seminar and discovered that it was a women's cosmetics pyramid scheme. It worked this way: Jimmy bought a supply of cosmetics from his supplier, then he was to find other people to supply. Those people would, in turn, find their customers to supply, and so on and so on. If everyone continued finding new customers to supply, then the person at the top of the pyramid would be, as Jimmy put it, "fabulously rich." The trick was for us to build such a pyramid under us. He wanted me to be the first under him.

Jimmy was uncontainably optimistic. Californians are beauty conscious, he enthused. We lead the rest of the nation in trends. And these cosmetics were going to be the next thing in a nationwide craze. These were all purely organic; made with real fruits and vegetables. We were getting in on the ground floor of a giant new empire of organic beauty products. I bit. I "invested" in a few hundred dollars' worth of women's cosmetics from Jimmy.

But I found it difficult to find people with the same entrepreneurial spirit that we had. They were busy at other things, they didn't have the time or the money, or they weren't interested.

About a year later, rather than selling my supply of cosmetics to dozens of other buyers and counting my profits, I found myself giving them away as gifts to Josie, my mother, and my sister. I wondered what Jimmy did with his? I didn't have the heart to ask him.

The starship that transported us through the galaxies was called the *Enterprise*. The name suggested boldness, a readiness to challenge uncertainty, to take the initiative. The word also means an undertaking for profit, an industrious effort at moneymaking, a plain business venture. And STAR TREK did indeed spawn a whole galaxy of entrepreneurial brave spirits.

I first got an inkling of this a year after the cancellation of the series. The telephone rang. A young female voice was inviting me to come to a downtown Los Angeles hotel for a gathering of STAR TREK fans. Could I join them for coffee and conversation?

How sweet, I thought. The show was dead and resting in the cancellation graveyard, but these dear people were still gathering to reminisce over the embers of glowing memories. I agreed to drop by.

The gathering was indeed a small group—at most, about three dozen people—mostly women, who wanted to talk about STAR TREK and ask some questions about the making of the show. They were also offering for sale mimeographed collections of essays, poetry, and short stories they had written. I thought they were rather dearly priced, but they were selling. The profit margin had to have been substantial, and I'm sure they did quite well that afternoon. This was my first introduction to the great ship of fan entrepreneurs. It was still only gently warming up for the big blast-off.

STAR TREK conventions were the mother vehicles for these bold entrepreneurs. A prime component of the STAR TREK conventions was the "hucksters room," usually a large ballroom of a hotel where everything from T-shirts to tricorders with blinking lights were displayed for sale.

My nephew, Scotty, saw a phaser gun at one convention I took him to. "Uncle George, I want that," he announced. It was a handsome mock-up of a phaser gun. It weighed, felt, and sounded more realistic than the painted balsa-wood props that we actually used on the set. And incredibly, it was priced at five hundred dollars! But Scotty wanted it. And Uncle George, ordinarily a hardheaded bargainer in business, became a mush-brained soft touch. Scotty was the first kid on the block—and, as it turned out, the only kid in the neighborhood —to have one.

This was how the ship of enterprise was fueled and gained momentum—collectors and doting uncles buying the output of enterprising people. It wasn't long before it was cruising along at warp speed.

In the wake of the entrepreneurial ship, however, were more than a few casualties of this explosive new development. Fired up, more by fan fever than by prudence, and forgetting the first rule of entrepreneurship, which is to venture only after thoroughly studying the market, some fans attempted staging conventions with their family savings or even mortgaging their homes. Las Vegas might have been a better bet. Among the flotsam and jetsam of the soaring STAR TREK entrepreneurism are some tragic stories. The success stories, however, are as remarkable as the STAR TREK phenomenon itself.

There were two teenaged fans in New York who even at that tender age displayed keen business savvy. Adam Malin was the promoter-planner and Gary Berman the financial brains. They combined their talents and began putting on conventions, first in the New York area, then venturing out to other major cities. Soon, they were staging more than one convention each weekend all over the country, and they built their company, Creation Conventions, into a mega-operation that today includes licensed STAR TREK products as well as other merchandise. They also created a remunerative sideline for the actors of STAR TREK, as convention speakers, and provided me, in the bargain, with visits to cities that I probably never would have seen otherwise.

Like most entrepreneurs, Adam and Gary have been accused by their competitors of unfair flexing of their now well-developed financial muscles to maintain their dominance in the hucksters marketplace. But ambitious risk-takers are constantly emerging to keep the arena spirited and competitive. And the convention phenomenon continues to wham across the country.

The man who brought forth all this venturesome activity, Gene Roddenberry, was himself one who did not overlook the business definition in the name of the starship he created. He called the company he shared with his wife, Majel, Lincoln Enterprises and, initially with the help of Bjo and John Trimble, built the company into a major supplier of STAR TREK memorabilia.

Enterprise is the fuel of civilization. Entrepreneurship creates something out of nothing. An idea turned into action can create products, jobs, and whole industries. It can combine with a vision of society and change the world.

Enterprise, however, cannot thrive without two vital elements. It cannot survive without freedom; the freedom to think original thoughts, to experiment, and to innovate—to take risks with something that has never been thought or done before. Freedom is the life breath of enterprise.

But freedom cannot flourish without another element—ethics. Freedom without a common subscription to ethical values is chaos, a wild, dog-eat-dog abandon. Inevitably, this will bring on the backlash of controls, inhibiting that energy. Essential to protecting and strengthening the muscle of free enterprise is a solid framework of ethics.

Gene demonstrated both. He changed people with ideas,

with an optimistic view of our future that instilled confidence in our present, sparking so many to entrepreneurial action. And he did it advocating shining ideals—a respect for diversity and differences, integrity in oneself, and honor in the bold spirit of venture. He made enterprise a powerful and profitable idea.

I had been following my own enterprises long before STAR TREK entered my life. From the cemetery plots that my father had first invested in for me with my earnings from *Ice Palace* long ago, I had moved on to small apartment buildings and then into a number of larger apartment complexes. I parlayed my small pieces of land for the dead into a growing real estate holding for the living.

I may have been entrepreneurial before STAR TREK, but it was my earnings from the show that provided me with the resources with which to be really venturesome. My STAR TREK money allowed me to play in the stock market, invest in publishing, in development projects, and in banking. It also gave me the daring sometimes to invest with my heart instead of my head.

They say that a person in show business should never invest in show business. I broke that rule, more out of friendship than shrewd business sense—and, sure enough, paid the penalty. Nichelle's then-husband persuaded me to invest in his little theater production. Duke was a charming and ambitious man with ideas, energy, and enthusiasm, the very personification of the spirit of enterprise. The play was a musical comedy. It seemed like a good bet. Unfortunately, the production never came to life.

Some of the rides that my investments have taken me on were as spine-tingling and as heart-stopping as any episode driving the *U.S.S. Enterprise*. I did well on most, some not; others are still bumping along. I've learned a few things—namely, no more women's organic cosmetics or little theater productions —and I've repeated a few mistakes. Stay away from gold futures. But always, I've tried to guide myself by the star of ethical values. I'm still intact and still driving the ship of enterprise. The ride has been exciting, fun, and generally profitable. So far, so good.

It was dark when I got up. Dawn was still hours away, but I couldn't sleep. I had a long drive ahead of me to Rockwell International Corporation's space division facility, up in the high plains desert of Palmdale. My heart was filled with an overwhelming sense of moment. We had an invitation to history. It was September 17, 1976, and Gene Roddenberry and the cast of STAR TREK were guests at the "roll-out" ceremony of the first space shuttle.

I arrived at Rockwell International's facility to find a crush of humanity. A staff member of the National Air and Space Administration greeted me and pulled me through the excited horde, past a chain-link security fence to a small bungalow warm with the welcoming aroma of hot coffee and doughnuts. Gene was already there smiling, a cup of steaming coffee in hand, chatting with the people from NASA. Then De staggered in looking disheveled and traumatized by the gantlet he had to run. Nichelle also stumbled in, her wide-brimmed hat askew on her head but still smiling and waving to the people outside. Walter came in complaining, "The traffic in the Valley was incredible! And then this mauling here! Can't we get some of this NASA intellegence down here on earth?" The doughnuts in the cardboard container were disappearing fast, so I grabbed an extra one for Jimmy just in case. He'd be hungry when he got here. Gene's coffee was no longer steaming, but his cup was still full. The NASA people kept him continuously chatting and wouldn't let him get in a sip.

Where were Jimmy, Bill, and Leonard? It was almost time for the ceremony to begin. Quick phone calls were made, and we learned that Leonard had already arrived but was sequestered in another bungalow. But no Jimmy or Bill. We had to go; the time had come. I returned Jimmy's doughnut to the cardboard box and filed out with the others escorted by the NASA ushers.

On the vast runway of the space facility, a sea of folding chairs had been set up almost a mile out. Facing it was a wide temporary stage with a podium and a row of folding chairs for the speakers. The control and decorum on this side of the security fence was in stark contrast to the wild bedlam outside. We were ushered to a row of seats designated for the STAR TREK people.

The speakers began filing onstage and seated themselves. Most prominent of the group was the keynote speaker, Senator Barry Goldwater. Just then, flushed and breathless, Jimmy Doohan was ushered over to us. He stumbled over our knees to his seat, mumbling something about the terrible traffic. There was only one empty seat in our section now. Where was Bill?

People from all walks of life had gathered here on this desert runway in Palmdale: politicians, actors, engineers, teachers, and space buffs, all bound by a shared vision of our future. People with beliefs, expertise, and dreams that ranged across a wide spectrum were brought together by a common recognition of the significance of this morning. A new era was dawning. The keynote speaker was introduced.

Senator Goldwater, the blunt-talking Arizonan, former presidential candidate, and spearhead for the space program in Congress, was a politician on the other side of the fence from me. I had campaigned against him in the last presidential race, and so had Leonard. Yet we converged on some basic principles. He was a libertarian, a rugged westerner who stood for the ideals of freedom and respect for the rights of others. I, too, hold those values dear. We both believed in free enterprise. And we shared a common vision of space as the great challenge of our time. Barry Goldwater and the people gathered on the runway represented the breadth and complexity of support essential to this project. Politicians, technicians, entrepreneurs, and artists had to work in concert; we collectively represented the unity vital to its success. Senator Goldwater was an eminently appropriate speaker.

He spoke of the historic moment of this occasion. This morning, humankind was beginning our venture out into space. With the craft that was about to be introduced to us, we

317

were about to begin our transportation linkage to the entrepreneurial adventure "out there." We had made a great investment of our resources in the question, "What will we find out there?" An even greater question was, "Can we make this venture carry a payload?" We had the spirit and the will to seek the answers. We were ready to take on the challenge of innovation, invention, and creation that lay before us. Our great undertaking was just beginning. Senator Goldwater's voice rang powerfully through the crisp morning air.

Then the Air Force Band that waited below the platform began to play. Immediately, we recognized the melody. They were playing Alexander Courage's theme from STAR TREK. As the stirring melody soared through that brilliant September morning, out from behind the giant hangar emerged a huge, glistening white craft. This was the very first space shuttle built by the National Air and Space Administration. And on the side of its fuselage was imprinted its name. It read *Enterprise*. It was a profoundly moving moment.

A legion of fans had taken the action. They had lobbied to have this historic craft named after the Starship from their favorite television series. But the name also embodied the spirit of initiative, to boldly venture forth, to challenge the unknown, and to make it profitable. The fans' initiative was inspired. And because of it, we television actors were privileged to be a part of this momentous event in human history. I felt a deep gratitude to the people who had made this possible for us.

STAR
TREK
LIVES

22

The Motion Picture

DURING THE SERIES RUN OF **STAR TREK** ON TELEVISION, WE encountered strange and wondrous fictional experiences via the imaginations of gifted writers. But none of them, no matter how fancifully inspired, could have imagined the fantastical reality that was to descend on us almost a decade later.

Ever since the unexpected ratings success of the series in the rerun circuit, rumors about a revival of STAR TREK had continued to surface. Walter Koenig was calling me regularly with the latest version circulating.

"Guess what? We're coming back on television as a weekly series again." This was totally unexpected. My spirits soared. Then another call from Walter.

"The series project is off." My spirits plunged.

Walter again: "We're going to be a monthly series of two-hour *Movie of the Month* episodes instead." This was even better. Hope again flew.

"Forget the *Movie of the Month*. It's a no go." Another plunge.

"Great news! We're going to be the flagship series for a fourth television network that Paramount is going to be starting up." This was incredible!

"Bad news. It looks like Leonard won't be in it." This was worrisome.

"It's definite! Paramount's signed a new actor named David Gautreaux as the Vulcan. Leonard is out!"

Walter's usual enthusiastic voice sounded crestfallen. "The whole thing is dead! Paramount has dropped the fourth network project."

Walter kept me well informed on every detail of the twists and turns of STAR TREK's possible future course. So well informed, that, after a few years, I had become immune to the excitement that each new update used to arouse in me. In fact, I was getting downright irritated with the incessant disruptions these rumors were causing to the order I was trying to maintain in my life. A television series would make a mess of my meeting schedule at the RTD. And I would be confronted with another difficult career decision.

So when Fred, my agent, called one morning in 1978 with the information that Paramount had called to begin negotiations for a STAR TREK feature motion picture, it was as jolting as receiving a call from an RTD staffer telling me that a Klingon was patiently waiting in line to board an RTD bus. It seemed surreal. I had put away thoughts of ever encountering those bizarre creatures again except as figments reappearing only in the rumors reported by Walter.

"This is going to be a major production," Fred informed me. "It's got one of the biggest budgets on Paramount's schedule, and it's got one of the biggest directors in town, Robert Wise."

This was amazing! Robert Wise was not only the director of such super hits as *West Side Story, The Sound of Music,* and *The Sand Pebbles,* but he had edited that landmark film classic by Orson Welles, *Citizen Kane.* What an extraordinary opportunity! To work with a legendary director and to get together with friends from a fondly remembered part of my past, all in the same project—in STAR TREK! It was a fantasy coming true. Even the rumors hadn't been this fantastical. After nine long years of hope and disappointment, gossip and letdown, raised and then dashed expectations, STAR TREK was returning, not as a television series, but as a big-budget, major feature film with a giant of the cinema directing us!

"Fred, I'll make whatever arrangements I need to make with the RTD to do this film," I said decisively. "You do whatever you need to do on your end."

It was glorious being back on the bridge of the *Enterprise* at Paramount Studios. But there were striking differences. The set had the same circular configuration as before, but it was sleeker, more streamlined, more luminous with a steely shine. And it was larger, much larger.

Our uniforms were completely changed. Bob Foster had designed body-hugging one-piece outfits as sleek and streamlined as the set. Even the shoes were attached to the single-unit ensemble. An Italian custom bootmaker had measured our feet and had molded and fitted the footwear part of the costume to the uniform. It looked expensive—and it was.

In fact, everything about the production was bigger and more expensive. The schedule was astonishingly luxurious. We, who had toiled at breakneck pace during the television series, squeezing in as many setups per day as possible, were aghast to note on the breakdown sheet that a whole week had been allotted to film some single scenes. That was almost the time it had taken us to complete one whole television episode!

What was unchanged were my friends. Walter was quite unsuccessfully trying to disguise his happiness by kvetching, saying that the glossy new console at his changed position as the weapons officer was tucked off to the periphery of the bridge. I saw, though, that shiver of joy from him as he discovered that the buttons on this console really worked.

Jimmy was unabashedly jubilant. "I knew it. I knew it from the first day," he boasted. "There was magic in STAR TREK. Magic! That's what it is. I knew we'd be coming back. Didn't I tell you that, George?"

I pretended agreement. But I remembered that he had, in fact, agreed with me back on our first day of filming the pilot, when I made the prediction "I smell quality with this show.

And quality doesn't last on television. I give this show, at best, two seasons." Jimmy had concurred with me then. But my prediction had been wrong. Jimmy's altered memory was happier, more auspicious, and I fully shared in his joy. I quietly agreed with his rewriting of history.

Nichelle was the most ecstatic. She kissed and hugged everyone many times over. Even crew members completely new to us were rapturously greeted as she embraced them with a puzzling "It's lovely to be back working with you again!" They didn't seem to mind, though. By the time they were smooched by Nichelle a third time, I'm sure they believed they had worked with her before.

It was good to see De again. Of all the cast members, he was the one I had encountered the least since cancellation. We had been like the proverbial ships in the night at a few conventions, and that was about it. Dear, sweet De. We will have to renew old acquaintance, I thought. I watched him as he sat smiling in his set-side chair, calmly smoking his cigarette, just like before, the relaxed and assured professional waiting to be called into action.

Curiously, Leonard seemed to have aged the most. His complexion looked more weather-beaten than before, his lines deeper. Vulcans were supposed to age slower, I remembered. But then, they were also supposed to be more long-lived, and Spock's age was never revealed. So perhaps a Spock much older than any of us was starting to finally show his wear and tear. What hadn't changed, however, was his driving professionalism. Leonard was still the intensely focused, detail-oriented perfectionist. He was studiously checking out his new work station.

And Bill was in the center of it all—just as before. He was laughing, joking, giggling, and reveling in the joy of commencing a project undreamed of by any of us.

As Nichelle kept repeating, it was wonderful being back together again. It was great being back in the circular form of the set, back with good colleagues, surrounded by the noise and hurly-burly of the grips and technicians as they prepared for the first shot on this first day on the set of STAR TREK: THE MOTION PICTURE. Bob Wise sat set-side in his high director's chair, his sage white hair and discerning spectacled eyes reflecting everything; he looked like a smart old owl surveying his domain, taking in every detail, just as the action was about to begin. We were all sublimely happy.

There were many notable changes. Color—or the lack of it—was one of them. There was a monochromatic tone to our new environment. Shades were subdued. Where we had obsidian black and bright orange in the rails of the bridge before, it now sheened with a muted steely luster. Where our uniforms had ranged in shades from pale green and electric blue to vivid crimson, now we wore softer hues: beige, powder gray, and creamy white.

But all this restraint couldn't mute the presence of a striking new actress who was joining us on the *Enterprise*, Persis Khambatta. A former Miss India who had gone to London and become a successful fashion model, she was now making her Hollywood debut as the alien navigator, Ilia. She was stunningly beautiful. She had the finely sculpted bones of a top model, skin like alabaster, and the grace and elegance of a ballet dancer. But what made her beauty so transcendent—so shockingly exotic—was her head. It was as perfectly sculpted as her elegant cheekbones and totally hairless. She was bald!

Our perception of beauty is so stereotyped. The ingredients and proportions that go into forming our conventional notions of beauty are based more on tradition than genuine experience. When I first saw Persis, I was startled by her baldness. That's all I saw—a shining-pated, hairless woman. When the shock receded, I saw her beauty. Eventually I came to see her whole—her baldness as a part of her radiant loveliness. And she had an exquisitely formed head. Somehow, her baldness made her beauty closer to perfection. She seemed more alluringly pristine, more sensuous, more nude.

I realized that Gene, in his artfully foxy way, was again challenging another hidebound old conceit. Hair as the "crowning glory." Beauty can be found in limitless guises and inconceivable conditions if one is open to discoveries. I chalked another one up for Gene's credo of "Infinite diversity in infinite combinations." And the clever rascal was demonstrating this with a glamorous foreign woman. Ilia's gorgeously unadorned head, as a matter of fact, inspired more than a few surreptitious soundstage jokes about leading men who couldn't go as boldly as Persis did.

Persis was as beautiful a person as she was a beautiful-looking woman. She was eager to share her Indian heritage with us, inviting Nichelle, Walter, Jimmy, and me to her apartment near the studio for delicious Indian pastry and tea after work. She hosted a sumptuous Tandoori dinner for us at a West Los Angeles Indian restaurant. On the set, she tried to teach me a few basic phrases from her language, Parsi. But, since Persis was the only Parsi-speaking person I knew, I couldn't retain any of the phrases she so graciously tried to teach me.

There was so much that was different and wonderful about coming back to do STAR TREK. But some things hadn't changed. With each passing day, memories of the tensions from the days of the television series started to "ping" back. It was like going back home after a year away at college, looking forward to the return with nostalgia-clouded anticipation, only to come home and be reminded of the reality that Daddy and Mama bickered. We remembered only the good; time had faded the bad. Now those faded memories came rushing vividly back to life.

Walter came up with a clever bit of business for Chekov in a shot. I saw Bill go into a huddle with Bob Wise. An intensely whispered exchange ensued. Shortly thereafter, the camera placement was changed. Walter was no longer in the shot.

Nichelle had her close-up to do. Although she had diligently delivered her off-camera lines for Bill's close-up, Bill was not available to do his for her close-up. The script supervisor droned Bill's lines lifelessly off-camera for Nichelle.

Rewrites on sheets of changing colors would be delivered, and we'd find our lines cut. The cuts usually favored Bill. Perhaps Bill had nothing to do with the excisions. But our history-conditioned sensibilities couldn't help suspecting.

Bill's almost ingrained behavior troubled and puzzled me. He was the star of the picture. Why was he so insecure about any of us getting even a brief chance to shine? None of us were threats to his position. A confident actor would relish being surrounded by a full company of actively contributing players to bounce his performance off. Bill was the reminder to me that coming back to STAR TREK also meant coming back to nettlesome irritation.

But there were greater tensions starting to strain nerves on the production. The special effects in this film were on a scale many times grander than anything we had had on television. Many times more complex, and much more time-consuming.

The "blue screen" process required endless hours of waiting in front of a giant, luminous bluish screen while the technicians fine-tuned this knob and delicately tweaked that modulator. When they were set, it was only to play a simple scene that we had to repeat over and over, time after ceaseless time. It was monotonous and draining.

Much more draining than monotonous was the "worm hole" sequence. The *Enterprise* was plunged into a black hole, and all at once, our entire ship was transformed into a trembling, oscillating environment. The illumination fluttered. Our bodies quivered and shook. Our voices ululated with the vibration. From the moment Bob Wise shouted "Action!" and the cameras started to be shaken, we had to start shivering and speaking our dialogue in broken, quavering voices. And this sequence took more than a week to film. Day after day, on the word "Action!" we became animated blobs of Jell-O. By the end of the day, we were a bunch of shaken-up, cross-eyed, and totally exhausted automatons. Even when we were done with the sequence, we had become so conditioned to trembling on cue that every time we heard the call for "Action!" like Pavlov's dogs, we automatically felt the impulse to start shaking.

Almost imperceptibly, black suits from the front office began hovering around the dark periphery of the set. The special effects were taking longer than scheduled. The costs were starting to mount. Frowning faces began whispering in Bob Wise's ear. We were in trouble. But Bob maintained his equanimity through it all. The tension on the soundstage became palpable, but Bob never allowed it to seep onto the set. He continued to keep a calm, creative environment for the cast and crew.

When the picture was finished, we celebrated. Gene, Bob, Bill, and Leonard hosted the catered party on the set. What we had originally never imagined would happen, what had then kept us on the tether of suspense for years hinting that it might happen, had now actually happened. Then it was over. Like a much-anticipated, activity-packed vacation, it was over. STAR TREK: THE MOTION PICTURE was in the can.

But there was no relief from anxiety. The complicated visual effects hadn't been seen by anybody yet except the people at Robert Abel and Associates. They had been contracted by Paramount to produce the magic. But Abel wouldn't show them, claiming that the effects weren't quite ready to be seen. Walter again became my narrator of the unfolding drama of postproduction. His regular phone calls kept me abreast.

"Robert Abel is finally going to show the stuff."

"They canceled!"

"Paramount is forcing Abel to show them."

"Abel finally showed the effects, and it's a mess! We can't use them."

"My god! Paramount fired Robert Abel! Our picture is unreleasable."

"Guess what? Doug Trumbull has been brought in to save the situation. He's starting from scratch!"

"You won't believe this! Paramount is determined to get the stuff from Trumbull in nine months! That's impossible!"

"They're crazy! Paramount wants to release the film in December!"

* * *

While Walter was keeping me apprised of the drama going on at Paramount Studios, I had returned to my work with the Rapid Transit District. But at the same time, I had another drama, a personal heartache to tend. My father was critically ill.

Daddy had been ill for almost a year. He had been in and out of the hospital with an ailment that the doctors could not diagnose. My parents, in recent years, had been traveling extensively. They enjoyed places off the beaten track. They had visited Russia, South America, Iran, Africa, India, and the South Pacific. The doctors suspected my father had picked up a rare virus, perhaps on a visit to one of those destinations. Daddy's condition would suddenly deteriorate, and he would have to be rushed to the hospital, only to recover miraculously and be able to come back home again. The wild fluctuations of the affliction were tearing away at his spirit. For us, it was wrenching. We had to stand by helplessly, watching him progressively worsen.

There was an important September meeting of the American Public Transit Association in New York. I was serving as vice president, and there were sessions I was scheduled to conduct. Daddy was in another of his periods of respite from the ups and downs of his illness. But he knew of my scheduled annual meeting.

"Go to the meeting in New York," he urged me in his reedy, barely audible whisper. It was so much like him. Throughout his life, he disguised his own suffering for the sake of his children. Even when he had to work below his qualifications, he worked cheerfully, untiringly, swallowing the bitterest tastes so that his children could live with the dignity that circumstances denied him. I wondered what pain he must have been masking when he urged me to go to New York. But I knew his desire for his son to be there conducting that meeting was greater than any discomfort from his illness. It was what he wanted most from me—however he might be suffering.

I held his withered hand. This hand that guided me so tenderly as a child, encouraged me through adolescence, worked for me in so many ways, washing dishes in Chinatown, pressing other people's clothes, the hand that took such pride in stuffing my campaign mailers, that loved me throughout his life in so many countless ways and wore itself out for me. I held him for a long time, feeling an unquenchable love. "All right, Daddy. I'll go to New York." Then I said, "Good-bye."

When I returned to my hotel room from a session of the transit conference, the red message light on the telephone was blinking. It was from June, my sister-in-law. "Please call home," it said. I called Mama's phone, but there was no answer. I called Henry's and June's, but there also, nobody was home. I finally called the hospital and learned of Daddy's death.

The five-hour flight across the country was the longest, darkest, loneliest journey I ever made. The black emptiness of the sky, the vastness of the night, almost matched the desolation I felt. Far down there, somewhere in the darkness, was Arkansas. I thought of that golden afternoon when he freed us from barbed wire confinement for a magical jeep ride through the swamps. He loved driving us places. He loved showing us new things. He loved opening our eyes. I remembered those drives around Los Angeles when he showed us the great universities, UCLA and USC. He liked pointing the way for us. Even when I decided to become an actor, he still pointed the way. He sent me to England and the Shakespeare Institute. Whatever we did, he urged us to reach for the highest star. This man who became my biggest STAR TREK fan also became an inveterate RTD bus rider. He loved coming downtown on the bus to meet me for lunch. This man, even when he slowed down, always urged me to keep moving. To go to New York. Always to keep participating, keep contributing. And now he was gone, and I was flying through this darkness. Flying across this vast night country for my last good-bye.

STAR TREK: THE MOTION PICTURE premiered as scheduled on December 7, 1979, in Washington, D.C. Douglas Trumbull had pulled it off. His team produced the special effects by working frenetically day and night and taking turns sleeping at a motel across the street from the studio. What they delivered was visually gorgeous. But dramatically, I thought, the effects had an unvarying sameness and became wearisome. There seemed to have been more drama and suspense in the Trumbull team's race to complete the effects in time for the scheduled opening than in the results themselves.

The movie seemed to have successfully attained the Vulcan condition of *kolinahr*—the shedding of all emotions—a state Spock was striving for at the beginning of the film. STAR TREK: THE MOTION PICTURE seemed cold, detached, dispassionate. Despite the awesome force the *Enterprise* confronted in V'ger, there was a strange absence of any sense of jeopardy.

When the end credits started to roll, I turned to Walter, who was seated next to me. His expression was as nonplussed as mine. With so much creative and technical energy expended, with so much money invested, with so much hope and anticipation riding, what had happened? The crafting of drama was still a mysterious coming together of talent, chemistry, and fortune.

But the premiere was a gala affair with politicians, space people, and fans galore. The postscreening party at the National Air and Space Museum of the Smithsonian was a rare combination of Hollywood glamour and Washington pomp, fused with the dynamism of high technology. We celebrated, mingling and wandering among the artifacts of our real space adventures: a chunk of the moon rock, the actual space capsule, the moon suit worn by astronauts. We toasted the first model of the *Starship Enterprise* that was now a permanent part of the Smithsonian's collection.

All through this festive evening, however, I couldn't suppress a secret wish, a wish that seemed to arise nowadays whenever I was happiest. I kept wishing that my father could have been here with me in Washington, D.C. I wished he could have seen STAR TREK: THE MOTION PICTURE. I wished I could somehow have shared this happiness with him.

23

Wrath of Khan and Other Demons

STAR TREK: THE MOTION PICTURE WAS A GIANT SURPRISE success. As the box office revenue continued to climb, rumors again started to circulate about a sequel. Again, Walter kept the phone lines buzzing.

"Guess what? It looks good for STAR TREK, but not too good for Roddenberry. Paramount wants to make a sequel. But because of the budget overruns on *The Motion Picture*, it looks like they're trying to take the sequel project away from him."

The film had taken its toll on Gene in many ways. The stress from the tensions of that film had caused his weight to balloon alarmingly. I started swinging by Paramount Studios on my morning runs to invite Gene to join me. I succeeded only a few times in getting him to jog easily around the studio lot with me. On these short and all too infrequent runs, he told me he was trying to control his diet also. But I could see that he was struggling with it. I sensed, as well, the difficulties he was having with Paramount. STAR TREK was really his baby, and he was battling to keep it. I hoped he would prevail; I wanted him to keep STAR TREK. But I also wanted him to lose some of his added weight. Somehow, he never seemed to be able to lose what he had gained.

"Guess what? We're going back to television. The next STAR TREK is going to be a TV miniseries."

But Walter called back a few weeks later.

"Change course. We're back to a feature again. But it's going to be produced by Paramount's television division instead of the feature films unit."

A few weeks more and he called again.

"It's a definite go. They've signed an executive producer, a guy named Harve Bennett. He has a rep for holding to a tight budget. Gene's only a consultant!"

Harve Bennett was a name I recognized. I had worked for him a few years back when I did a guest appearance on an episode of *The Six Million Dollar Man*. I had played a Tibetan Sherpa who guides Lee Majors up the Himalaya Mountains. At the time that I was cast, I told him that I was a runner and that I'd also done some rock climbing. He was delighted that I would be able to bring some reality to the climbing scenes. But like a prudent producer, he scheduled my risky rock climbing sequences at the very end of the shooting schedule. I could fall and be incapacitated, but the production would be all right; he'd have all my other scenes safely in the can by then. And like a frugal producer, I noticed when we shot the climbing scene, he had saved on the cost of one stuntman. No other actor was hardy—or foolish—enough to be dangling from the side of a cliff but me.

Harve Bennett was a new decision maker coming on board, but we already had a working relationship. Here was a new opportunity to improve my situation on STAR TREK. I decided that an early-on campaign to enhance Sulu's role in the next film might be productive. I called and invited him to lunch at an elegant Japanese restaurant at the New Otani Hotel in Little Tokyo for some sushi and gentle lobbying.

It was a sparkling bright day when we met. Our table overlooked a serene Japanese garden with a wide, glassy waterfall slipping into a shallow pool. When we settled into our conversation, I sensed that Harve had an agenda of his own. He seemed anxious to allay any feelings of disquiet we might be having about a new producer taking over Gene's baby.

"I have great respect for Gene Roddenberry and what he has created," he stated. "I consider him the father of STAR TREK. He has done a fantastic job of nurturing his child. But the child grows and reaches a point where it needs a different kind of nurturing. I see myself as the teacher who takes that child from the father and guides it to the next stage of growth. I love STAR TREK just as much, and I can contribute to its development just as much, but in another distinct way. I hope you'll help me do that." Harve was eloquent, charming, and most persuasive. I felt I could comfortably talk with him.

"You can count on me," I affirmed. "You're right about STAR TREK, Harve. I agree about its having reached a point where visible new growth is timely. You know that the officers on the bridge are supposed to be outstanding professionals, some of the best in Starfleet. So far, though, this fact hasn't been evidenced in their career development." I guided the conversation to the point I wanted to make with Harve. "Now, Sulu is supposed to be a top graduate of the Academy. He's highly capable and ambitious. But he's been stuck at that helm console for a decade and a half! If Starfleet is a true meritocracy, Sulu would have had his own command by now. He's earned it, eminently. And by promoting him to his deserved captaincy, it would speak volumes for the vigor and health of Starfleet itself."

Harve smiled in agreement as the clear soup in a classic black lacquer bowl was served. Three lavender chrysanthemum petals floated in artful simplicity. The sushi that followed were delicate morsels of beauty to the eyes and to the palate. We had a delectable and amiable afternoon.

"Guess what?" I knew by now that this wasn't really a question with an answer expected. It was Walter's usual exclamatory punctuation to any exciting new development. "We've got a director for STAR TREK II. He's the guy who directed *Time After Time*. Remember that one? His name is Nicholas Meyer."

Now I had the other person I wanted to lobby. But I didn't have Meyer's number. So I called Harve and invited both him and Meyer for another lunch. A week passed, and Harve didn't call back. So I called him again.

"George, sorry I haven't gotten back," he apologized. "But Nick's deep in perp work and seems not to be able to find time."

"Well, can you arrange a meeting for me with him at his convenience? Any time. I'll work around his schedule." The director was a key person in my campaign. I was determined to move heaven and Harve to talk to Nick Meyer in the early stages of preproduction. The next day Harve called back.

"Nick is really pressed for time, George," he began. I braced myself. I was determined not to take no for an answer. "But I've got a meeting with him here in my office at ten-thirty tomorrow morning. If you can make that, George, I'm willing to give up half an hour of my time with him."

"I'll take it," I said immediately. "Thanks a lot, Harve. I really appreciate this. See you in the morning."

When I walked into his office promptly at the appointed hour, Harve rose with a welcoming smile from his desk to introduce me to Nick Meyer. I looked at the person slouched in a big leather wing chair. A thick, unruly shock of jet-black hair cascaded down his forehead. He was surprisingly young. I had expected someone more mature. And he was unexpectedly short. The tall, grand formality of the wing chair seemed only to emphasize his smallness. But his smoldering intensity was palpable. His dark eyes were penetrating, probing, almost hostile. I walked toward him with my extended hand, and he took it perfunctorily . . . still seated. Maybe he didn't want to get up to reveal his full height, I thought. Undaunted, after Harve's prefatory pleasantries I launched into my spiel. Starfleet was a meritocracy. Sulu was an exemplar. A captaincy for Sulu would burnish Starfleet's star as well as Sulu's.

Nick just watched me with a detached, analytical stare as if he were studying a performance. Harve had probably told him already about the aim of my lobbying. His eyes just bored into me, but at the same time, I could almost feel him calculating, thinking, plotting what he was hearing into some grand scenario. In an unexpected way, I felt I was reaching him. I sensed Nick, ignoring civilities and any pretense at Hollywood cordiality, getting right to the core business, taking in new information, evaluating it, scheming, and arriving at some conclusion—all while listening to me make my case. He was compressing all this into the brief time we had allotted to us.

After my half hour was up, I left Harve's office with a hopeful sense that I had persuaded him and Nick to the conclusion I wanted. At least, I felt I had been given a fair opportunity to present my case.

"Guess what?" I didn't have to guess. My keeper of the chronicle had another exciting update for me. "Khan is returning! Harve has decided to extend the story from the television episode "Space Seed" for STAR TREK II. And he's bringing back Ricardo Montalban." This was exciting news. "Space Seed" was one of our most fun episodes, and Ricardo had made Khan a magnetic antagonist. But Walter's good news was usually followed by the bad. I steeled myself for the next call.

Sure enough, it came. "Bad news! Leonard doesn't want to do Spock. He's insisting he be killed off in the movie. Can you believe it?"

As a fellow actor, I understood Leonard's dilemma. The character he had portrayed had become immensely popular. His face had become synonymous with logic and laser-keen rationality. All this recognition was a tribute to his powers as an actor. Leonard had succeeded eminently as Spock.

The flip side of all this acclaim, however, was that Spock had become all-consuming. The actor was being devoured by the character he had played. It was destroying opportunities for him to truly practice his craft. This plundering popularity was stealing the most visible tool of his art—his face. Leonard Nimoy the actor, his visage, and the man himself were being

336

turned into a walking, talking, living version of his character. I guessed that he had made the hard decision to reclaim his own face and his life by killing his creation.

"Guess what? Gene doesn't want Spock killed. He's resisting. But, you know what? Now, Leonard is insisting that his death be written into his contract! He really means it." This was turning into a life-and-death struggle, but with the oddest twist. One of the combatants was battling for his own demise, the other for his adversary's survival.

I understood Gene's position as well. This was another dilemma of artists. As the author, Gene had a deep, indeed paternal, interest in his creations. Spock was a singularly inspired character. Naturally, the father would not want his child to die off. And yet, in the collaborative art of drama, a myriad of sometimes conflicting interests come into play. I wondered whose interest would prevail in this drama.

The answer came with the delivery of the script. I read it immediately, and I was blown away. It was powerful. The drama was the classic confrontation of two strong forces relentlessly, inevitably driving toward each other to a startling conclusion. And there was a poignant subtext, the awareness of loss—of change, of aging, and of the ultimate loss . . . death. Spock did die after all. What was Gene's loss, though, was Leonard's gain.

For all my determined lobbying, I had gained precious little. Sulu was still little more than an animated part of the technology on the bridge. My only consolation was a brief scene where Sulu achieved the goal for which I had so strenuously argued. Sulu received his promotion! On a shuttle craft with McCoy and Uhura, Kirk tells Sulu of his advance in rank to Captain in command of the *U.S.S. Excelsior*. It was a short sequence, but this was what I had so doggedly campaigned for. Sulu's advance in rank was a part of the generational changes taking place. It was a part of the subtext of the film—with every loss, there was another gain. I had lost in my drive for a bigger part, but I had gained a captaincy. It would be a strategic advance if there should be a follow-up to STAR TREK II. I was eager to begin filming.

Ricardo Montalban was, as they used to say in Hollywood, bigger than life. The early morning hour in makeup is usually a calm and subdued beginning to the day. We shuffled in quietly, many of us still rubbing the remnants of sleep out of our eyes. Ricardo, however, was from another age of Hollywood . . . the golden days of Metro-Goldwyn-Mayer contract players. They didn't shuffle in quietly. They were M-G-M stars. They made "entrances" wherever they went—including into makeup.

"Good morning, everybody," his voice boomed in that musical Mexican accent. He stepped in brisk and bright-eyed, perfectly groomed save for makeup. "Good morning, Walter. Did you sleep well?" Then turning to the next chair, he would effuse, "Nichelle, darling, how do you do it at this hour? You look stunning!" Then soberly, "Well, Leonard, that's going to be a tough scene today. But we'll get it." And he'd punctuate his certainty with a light, firm punch on the shoulders. *"Buenas dias, Jorge. Que tal?"* he would acknowledge me in Spanish and with a courtly nod of his head. After he had greeted everybody in the room with his full-chested morning salutations, no one could pretend sleepiness without risking another robust cheer-up from Ricardo. He had "star presence" from the moment he entered the makeup room in the morning.

Ricardo had had one of those storied Hollywood careers. Beginning in the heyday of the splashy M-G-M musicals starring the likes of Esther Williams, he became the leading Latin lover for a generation of moviegoers. His star undiminished, he was enjoying resurgent popularity with another generation as the star of the hit television series *Fantasy Island*. His was a uniquely long-lived career. Legends with this glowing luster oftentimes have a tendency toward the prima donna. They are accustomed to having their way. Ricardo was unique even in this regard.

STAR TREK II was being produced in the television division of Paramount rather than in the feature film unit, making the schedule much tighter than that of THE MOTION PICTURE. The hours were long and intense, but Ricardo toiled uncomplaining. In fact, when things got tense, he was the uplift on the set, always ready with an interesting anecdote to share or a hearty laugh for a lame set-side joke. He was a disciplined, professional, and vivacious star.

Most uniquely, however, there was a magnificent bigness about him as an actor. Ricardo felt he was there to serve the script. If an angle that favored another actor made sense, he deferred. If a scene needed to be tightened and his line of dialogue was slowing the action, he considered eliminating it. Actors usually come up with reasons why their dialogue shouldn't be cut. But with Ricardo, with grand magnanimity, he would give up the line. He called it his "contribution" to making the scene work. Walter, who had many scenes with him, would come off the set marveling.

"I can't believe it. Ricardo Montalban, this legendary star, is so generous! He's incredible!"

Ricardo was a big star in every sense. There was size to his presence. There was grandiloquence in his speech. And there was bigness in his spirit.

My anxiously awaited, hard-won promotion scene was coming up. How many times in my sleep had I mumbled my lines from this scene? How often in my waking hours did visions of a follow-up Captain Sulu role haunt me? The disclosure of Sulu's advancement was a short moment in a larger scene, but to me, this was the payoff point for Sulu. This was what I had won with all my hard campaigning; I had to make the moment vital and alive.

We began rehearsing, and immediately a cold queasiness started to seep through me. Bill was breezing through his lines, telling me of my new commission as if it were only an aside . . . just an offhanded throwaway. I felt like asking, "That's not the way you're going to do it, are you?" But I bit my tongue. This was still a rehearsal.

The second rehearsal was even more indifferently played. Bill didn't even look at me. I couldn't play my joy, my elation, my sense of attainment against nothing.

"Bill, this is an important moment for Sulu. Can we have some eye contact?" I asked. He looked at me with the most innocent expression. "Of course, George," he answered in a tone insinuating that I had made a patently obvious request.

In the third rehearsal, he gave me a quick, perfunctory glance in passing. Almost begrudging. His line reading was equally offhanded. I went to Nick and whispered my concern to him. "Don't worry. I know how to fix it," he assured me. And he called for the take.

When we shot the scene, Bill played it as he had rehearsed it, disinterested, murmuring some trivia about my captaincy, looking straight out into the void. There was no eye contact. No emotion. No relationship. Nothing. A few other takes followed. He played them as before. He wasn't going to change. Nick called for the next setup. And we moved on.

I didn't know which I felt more strongly, the crushing ache in my heart or the fury raging in the pit of my stomach. Bill's giggling and bantering with the crew after the shot only inflamed the rage and the sting of impotence that burned inside me. Nick said he could "fix it." But I knew he wasn't a magician. I knew what could and couldn't be done. I had a cold foreboding . . . the scene for which I had struggled so long, so doggedly, and with such great hope—was not usable. I was not surprised when I later learned that the scene was cut.

Working with Nick Meyer, however, was great, classy fun. He was a compact dynamo of energy, erudition, and effervescence. The smoldering, intense man I initially met, I discovered, was only one of the large cast of characters that inhabited his body.

There was, very obviously, the talented director. But a director is really a jack of all arts. He has to be a good storyteller. And Nick was a compelling raconteur. He regaled us with set-side tales as well as outspoken commentaries.

A director has to be a writer. And Nick was a published author of two best-selling novels, *The Seven Percent Solution* and *The West End Horror.* He had also written *Target Practice*, coauthored *The Black Orchid*, and been lauded with the Golden Dagger from the Crime Writers' Association.

A director also has to have a bit of the actor in him. And Nick was an energetic and multifaceted performer. At the drop of a cue, he could become Groucho Marx charging maniacally around the set brandishing his giant cigar with all the schticky verve of the great comedian himself. Or he could transform himself into a devastating comparative drama critic, reciting *Hamlet*, first as Laurence Olivier would, then reinterpreting the same speech as John Gielgud might. And he was dazzling as both.

When we were filming Spock's funeral scene, he told me that the phrase "the undiscovered country" from Hamlet's "To be or not to be" speech was his title for this movie. I thought on it as I listened to Jimmy's mournful piping of "Amazing Grace." Death, "the undiscovered country, from whose bourne no traveller returns . . ." How apt and how artful, I thought.

Alas, that title died in the battle with the marketing department of Paramount. But Nick, I discovered, was a tenacious man. He wasn't going to give up. He said he would find another movie to grant that title to. I decided I needed to be just as determined. I wasn't giving up on my captaincy either.

We were right in the middle of a take when somebody charged onto the soundstage excitedly, and suddenly, people were rushing for the exit.

"What's happening? What's going on?" I asked.

"Somebody said there's a fire in the old New York street," one of the crew said as we joined in the mad exodus.

We pushed out the small exit into the alleyway between soundstages and looked up at the slot of sky. Billowing black clouds of smoke churned up from the direction of the back lot.

"Oh my God! It's a fire! The studio's burning!" The hairdresser gasped in horror. There was alarm in everyone's eyes.

"It's all right, folks," shouted the assistant director. "The fire department has been called. It will be under control soon.

Please stay calm and return to work." His voice was reassuring, and it was a relief to know that the back lot was all the way over on the far side of the studio. We milled around a while longer gaping at the ugly swells of smoke; but when the assistant shouted again, this time with more firmness than reassurance in his voice, the crowd started to move back in.

I loved that old back lot. It was nothing more than the false facade of a typical New York streetscape, only plaster and canvas and cheap lumber propped up by scaffolding—my brother, Henry, had "hmphed" at them—but to me, they were a wonderful part of our movie heritage. So much history took place on those streets; so much of our collective memories were recalled in those plaster stoops and painted canvas brick walls. One STAR TREK television episode, "A Piece of the Action," was shot there. Billy Wilder's classic film noir *Sunset Boulevard* was filmed there. So many Paramount memories were recorded on celluloid on that make-believe street. The studio back lot was as important a part of our Hollywood heritage as covered bridges were to New England or boat landings were to the communities along the Mississippi River. Now, all this was going up in that dirty black smoke, our memories consumed and churned up into the sky as charcoal bits and sooty fumes. After one final gaze, I turned back into the soundstage.

The crew and technicians were beginning to pound and bellow as the set roused back to life. The assistant directors were trying to restore some semblance of order on the set. The actors began reassembling. Then, something at once extraordinary and so very typical happened.

The soundstage door burst open, and a couple of people from the publicity department rushed in. They ran excitedly to Bill and then to Nick and went into an urgently conducted huddle. Quickly resolving the situation, the publicity people hurried off with Bill in tow. Nick announced that he would rehearse another scene while Bill was briefly excused from the set. I wasn't involved in that scene, so I thought I'd jog over to the back lot to see how the fire department was controlling the fire.

I stepped out the stage door and looked up. The smoke was still murky but appeared somewhat less threatening now. Thank God! The fire department must be there. I started trotting across the lot with the other people hurrying toward the back lot. The smoke was thinner but still moiling. As I got closer, I could see licks of orange flame leap out through the churning smoke. Blackend scaffolding loomed up out of the conflagration as long streams of water were being poured into the now subsiding billows.

As I approached the fire area, I saw a boisterous horde of photographers snapping away. But rather than focusing on the fire, they seemed to be centered on something else. I peered over to look, and who should I see in the center of all this press attention but our very own firefighter, Bill Shatner, poised with a fire hose held heroically high.

"Point your finger up toward the fire, Bill," shouted an excited photographer. Jaws firmed, chest puffed out, with the hose in one hand, Bill courageously pointed with the other. Cameras snapped eagerly.

"Look this way with the hose, Bill," yelled another. Bill boldly turned toward that photographer with firm determination in his eyes. Snap. Snap. Snap.

"Bill, move closer to the fire," barked another. Bill edged a bit toward the fire. But the real firefighters would not allow an actor to get beyond a certain point of safety. Undaunted, Bill continued posing gallantly as the smoke churned behind him and the cameramen snapped away. After a few minutes, the publicity people shepherded him back into the car that had brought him over from the soundstage and drove off. I thought I'd better be getting back to the set myself. The fire seemed well under control.

That evening, as I was driving home from the studio, the news on the car radio was reporting a major fire on the Paramount Studio lot. Fortunately, it reported, Captain Kirk of STAR TREK leaped to the rescue from the set of the *Starship Enterprise* and single-handedly directed the firefight. I could already imagine the photos that would be illustrating this story in tomorrow morning's newspapers. If it hadn't been for Captain Kirk, the radio continued breathlessly, the fabled studio could well have been lost.

STAR TREK II was released with the subtitle *The Wrath of Khan*. After *The Undiscovered Country* was nixed, Paramount had set our title as *The Vengeance of Khan*. But 20th Century-Fox's third *Star Wars* installment was coming out with the subtitle *The Revenge of the Jedi*. The two titles, directed at similar audiences, sounded too much alike. So Paramount again changed ours, this time, and finally, to *The Wrath of Khan*. By that time, of course, 20th Century-Fox had also changed their title to *Return of the Jedi*. Such are the capricious workings of fate in Hollywood.

STAR TREK II: THE WRATH OF KHAN exploded at the box office. It became a megahit. And the mounting revenues dictated our return with another STAR TREK film. It seemed there was to be further continuity to my association with the show.

That continuity was to surface rather unexpectedly and in a novel form. In April of 1983, I was invited to participate in the welcome-home ceremony for the aircraft carrier *Enterprise*. It was returning to its home port at the Alameda Naval Air Station in San Francisco Bay after an eight-month tour of duty around the Indian Ocean and the South Pacific. The tie-in between me and this *Enterprise* was obvious.

I was flown up to stay overnight at the Naval Air Station and, bright and early next morning, taken out by helicopter to board the *Enterprise* still many miles out at sea. It was awe-inspiring to see the giant floating airport churning its way toward home as we approached it from the air. We landed and immediately I was taken for a tour of the ninety-thousand-ton nuclear-powered vessel. It was huge. The hangar below was as vast as any on land. It carried a crew of five thousand on board.

Of course, my tour ended up on the bridge. From the jaded perspective of an actor used to a starship bridge, this one looked

downright antique. Nevertheless, it hummed with the anticipatory activity of a ship nearing home port. I peered out the view
window, but all I could see was the swirling mass of early
morning fog. Of course, cameramen were waiting. Photos were
taken of me at the helm with my twentieth-century counterpart.
As we were going through this obligatory ritual, without warning the Golden Gate Bridge emerged out of the fog. It was a
spectacularly theatrical moment. The grace and power of the
structure loomed out of the mist like silent poetry in steel and
vapors. As we slid under the bridge, as if on cue, the fog parted
and the City by the Bay, San Francisco, greeted us sparkling and
elegant, all alabaster and obsidian in the sun. The *Enterprise*
was almost home.

I was with the bridge crew, a twenty-third-century guest on
this *Enterprise*, looking out the window across the bay toward
Alameda Naval Air Station. I could see banners and balloons, a
musical band, a crowd of more than two thousand people—
wives, children, and friends. It looked like a festive welcome
awaiting the *Enterprise*. We were just outside the breakwater,
about three quarters of a mile from the pier, when we felt a
slow, ugly, upward swell like the sickening surge of nausea. We
seemed to stay poised and unsure at this crest for the longest
time, and then, slowly, lazily, the ship listed over to one side.
The giant aircraft carrier was stuck in the mud in the middle of
San Francisco Bay. With a sizeable crowd and the bay area
media waiting to greet us, the *Enterprise* was aground for all to
witness.

I was shepherded down to the captain's quarters with the
other guests to wait out the rescue effort. Navy and civilian tugs
were sent out to bump and pull at the beached behemoth. But
to no avail. It would not budge. Navy public relations officers
came aboard and explained to us that we had unfortunately
entered the Golden Gate at low tide, and compounding the
problem, the bay bottom had been built up with sand, silt, and
other materials from the heavy runoff of the past winter's
unusually heavy rainfall. We waited and worried, but the vessel
could not be moved. The bar was opened, and drinks were

served. We waited for over five hours before the tide came in again and we were able to move. When we finally inched into the pier at Alameda Naval Air Station, all the bay area media was gathered in ravenous frenzy.

I came down the gangway well briefed on the reason for this embarrassing accident by the Navy public relations people and ready to face the press. Immediately, I was surrounded by a pack of shouting and pushing journalists. I responded to them with facts, data, and background—just as I had been advised. I think I even handled it with aplomb. That is, until one reporter asked me a fatal question. He yelled out, "What did you do during the time you were waiting to be loosened?" Wit lubricated with a wee dram of the libation from Scotland can be a disastrous combination. Despite all the substantive information I had given the press, the only response of mine that they ran with was my smart-aleck answer to the last question.

"We spent the time sipping a new drink we invented. We call it *'Enterprise* on the rocks.'" That embarrassing comment was played ad infinitum on radio and still haunts me on the most unexpected occasions.

There was another kind of continuity running through my life. Distant echoes from forty years ago gradually began to sound with clarity. At first faint, the sounds became stronger and more insistent with the passage of time.

Japanese Americans too young to have comprehended the experience of the internment camps, and those born after all the camps were closed down, were entering into the mainstream of American life. With the dawning understanding of the ordeal our parents and grandparents endured, our sense of anger increased. The silence of the older generation was the mute stillness of the violated. But we were not going to be victims. We were American citizens. The barbed wire that had encircled our internment experience was not just a violation of the dignity of our parents but an outrage to our American ideals as well. A movement arose to press the government to formally acknowledge that ugly blemish on American history and to recompense the victims for the wrong that had been done. It was in the best tradition of our country—citizens petitioning their government for redress of wrongs.

The movement began at the grass-roots level. Information was disseminated. Funds and support were gathered. The national civil rights organization Japanese American Citizens League joined in. As the movement grew, the campaign was spearheaded by Japanese American congressmen, the personifications of our maturity in the political process. The two U.S. Senators from Hawaii, Daniel Inouye and Spark Matsunaga, Hawaii Representative Patsy Takemoto Mink, and California Representatives Norman Mineta and Robert Matsui built the legislative support in the halls of Congress. In 1980, Congress created the Commission on Wartime Relocation and Internment of Civilians to investigate the records, hold hearings, and to make recommendations.

On August 5, 1981, I testified at a hearing before that Commission. As I sat in the large hearing room waiting my turn, I looked around me. Seated in a row, high on a dais, was the august body of commissioners. Surrounding them with a glare brighter than any studio kleig lamps was a blazing bank of media lights. Below the dais was a long table lined with microphones for those testifying. The people shuffled to the table in groups of five. Many were elderly now and leaned on canes or were assisted down the aisle. When they began speaking, their voices were thin and parched. Some spoke with the distinct chop and breaks of the old provinces of Japan. Others sounded as if they came from Kansas.

As they spoke, I listened to the tremulous memories that hadn't been given voice in decades. I heard the dust of the desert in dried-up voices that couldn't forget. I heard the fatigue from swamp humidity in the slow, stumbling recollections too long kept mute. But I also heard the resilience in voices battered by the cold, gritty winds of the high plains, still remembering the sting of that experience. I heard voices that had been silent for four decades, remembering lives spent behind barbed wire in Wyoming, Utah, Idaho, Arizona, California, and Arkansas. For the first time I was listening to the background of my life. The voices of the injured, after forty years, were being heard at last, not only by Japanese Americans like me, but now by a Congressional Commission.

Then another group of elderly people replaced the speakers. They, too, had snowy hair and shuffled unsteadily. But these speakers were Caucasians. And when they spoke, they talked of Pearl Harbor and their brothers and husbands killed by the Japanese in the Pacific war.

My blood started to boil as they testified. They still didn't understand! We were Americans. We fought and died alongside those very same brothers and husbands they remembered.

"Wartime necessity," they insisted. "Questions of loyalty," they claimed. But America was at war with Germany and Italy as well. Did these people not know that German Americans and Italian Americans were not interned? The hearings of the Congressional Commission also brought out these other elderly people who could not forget. They, too, were a part of the context of my background.

When I gave my testimony, I must confess, my blood was churning from the preceding testimonies. I was moved by the painfully given statements of the elderly internees. I was hot from the reminder of the mentality that had interned us in those camps. My testimony was that of an American who grew up with a unique background and a certain context to my citizenship. And because of that, I grew up with an understanding of the fragility of our democracy. I grew up mindful of democracy's total dependence on its ideals for survival. But those ideals, however shining, however noble, are only as good, as true, and as real as the people who participate in the process. And so I testified and contributed my childhood remembrances for the records of the Congressional Commission on the Wartime Relocation and Internment of Civilians.

Another personal tragedy severed a longstanding friendship and professional partnership. My agent, Fred Ishimoto, died after a brief illness. Ours was more than a business association, for Fred was a confidant and trusted advisor. He represented me through the rebuffs and the accolades, through lean times and fat. We were connected by shared tribulations, common history, and mutual aspirations. And now Fred, too, was gone. One by one, my sources of strength were passing on.

24

Don't Call Me Tiny

I HAD TO FIND A NEW AGENT, BUT I DIDN'T KNOW HOW. I HAD BEEN with Fred for almost twenty-five years. Ours had been a professional marriage, and now I was like a widower. I called around various agencies and made appointments, interviewing a number of agents. Blind dating again. They all were interested, but their interest, I suspected, was because of STAR TREK, because Sulu had made me an easily salable commodity to Paramount. My interest, however, was in expanding my career as an actor. Yes, I wanted to do the next STAR TREK film. But I also wanted to practice my craft, which meant extending my reach beyond Sulu. I wanted an agent who could recognize that and was willing to seek out those opportunities for me aggressively.

One afternoon, I bumped into Jimmy Doohan on the Paramount lot. We stood chatting for a while, and then he suggested we go across the street to Oblath's for a beer. Over a mug of cold draft, I told Jimmy of my frustrating search. He understood my difficulty right away.

"I know just the person," he declared. "I have a great agent. He's been fantastic for me. You should talk to him."

On Jimmy's recommendation, I decided to meet his agent,

Steve Stevens. His office was in the Valley, way out in North Hollywood, on the second floor of a rustic, timbered building. I stamped up the well-worn stairs, opened the wooden door, and met a man who couldn't have been more different from Fred than night is from day.

Where Fred was big and heavy, the man half hidden behind a huge cluttered desk was small and compact. Where Fred was low-keyed and conservatively dressed, the man who got up and came around the desk to greet me was a staccato-talking, gesticulating, rugged-looking cowboy. On the back of his chair perched a huge ten-gallon hat, and on the knotty pine walls were rodeo posters and autographed photos of cowboy actors like Chuck Connors, Slim Pickins, and Dale Robertson. He wore a western-style shirt with dark piping and a giant silver belt buckle atop tight, well-washed jeans. On his feet were a pair of elaborately tooled cowboy boots.

"Hi, I'm Steve. I know who you are." He welcomed me with an extended hand. "Sit yourself down right there." He pointed to a serape-covered couch. I felt like I was auditioning for a rodeo.

But when we sat down and started talking, I knew that Jimmy was right. Here was a man who connected with our situation. Immediately, he understood my frustration with the limited scope of Sulu's role in STAR TREK, having been an actor himself.

Steve began sketching out some strategies. During the negotiations with Paramount, we could leverage their need of Sulu for opportunities in Paramount films. With different production companies, we could parlay my popularity as Sulu into other rules.

Steve was bursting with ideas and game plans. I realized that this man whom Jimmy had recommended to me was a savvy and artful career planner unexpectedly masqerading as a cowboy. I knew I had found my agent. I decided to go with a buckaroo deal maker to represent me.

* * *

Steve half delivered with his first deal. The contract he negotiated for STAR TREK III included an option for STAR TREK IV. It assured work continuity, but it was still confined to Sulu. I didn't yet have that reach beyond Sulu that I so hungered for as an actor. But I heard about an intriguing arrangement being crafted by Leonard that I thought could be instructive.

Paramount recognized that Spock was vital to the continued success of STAR TREK. He was the insurance that guaranteed the colossal box office receipts, and they wanted him desperately. Leonard was in a powerful bargaining position, so he leveraged for an interesting gain and reached for another challenge as an artist. In order to return as Spock, Leonard got Paramount to agree to hire him to direct STAR TREK III. Leonard was as creative a manager of his career as he was inventive as an actor.

Colleagues like Leonard continued to spur me on my own campaign for Sulu. I again began bombarding Harve with ideas for Sulu in the new film. How about a fencing duel in a gravityless environment? Wouldn't that be exciting? And so uniquely Sulu? How about another go at the captaincy—this time granted by an admiral or somebody like that from Starfleet Command? Harve was graciously receptive to the suggestions but remained enigmatically noncommittal.

One day, he called to give me tantalizing hints about the new script. I could hear the enthusiasm in his voice.

"George, the script will be on its way to you soon. But I just wanted to call to tell you that there is a scene in it that you're going to love. I can't wait to hear from you after you've read it."

I was in suspense. When the script arrived, before reading it in orderly fashion from the first page I flipped through to those pages indicating Sulu's dialogue and marked them with a red pencil. But once again, there wasn't much of a speaking part. I noticed, however, that I seemed to be in the script throughout. Then I began reading only those scenes that I had marked, and I came to the scene where Sulu confronts a tall, burly guard and eliminates him with a single, superhuman judo throw. It was awesomely heroic. But something else jumped out at me. There was a confounding reference made to Sulu. Immediately, I got on the phone. Harve was waiting for my call.

"Well, George, isn't it charming? Don't you love it?" His voice sparkled, eager with anticipation.

"Well, that scene where Sulu throws the guard—it does give me something active to do, but there's a serious problem with it."

"Oh? A problem? I thought you'd love that scene." He sounded puzzled.

"It's a strong scene, but there's one big mistake in it. The gaffe is in the reference to Sulu as 'Tiny.' Harve, he's not tiny. We've got to cut that." I was firm and emphatic.

"But, George," he protested after a bewildered moment, "that guard Sulu throws is a huge giant of a man. From the guard's vantage point, Sulu is small." Then he quickly corrected himself. "I mean, Sulu seems smaller." But I was adamant.

"Harve, that may be. But Sulu is a hero in the eyes of our fans. We can't shatter that by derisively inferring that he is small. We just can't do that."

"George, I'm totally thrown. That's a delightful scene. And it plays wonderfully because of the stark contrast between the two. It's not a disparagement of Sulu at all. In fact, it makes him that much more admirably heroic."

"Harve, I respect your pride of authorship. I truly do. But I have to ask you to trust me. I go out to the conventions. I know the fans. We can't do this to them. They look up to Sulu as a hero. We absolutely must cut that reference to Sulu as 'Tiny.' Please trust me on this."

Back and forth we went. We agreed that the scene played well. We saw eye to eye on the size contrast. The only sticking point was that contemptible epithet "Tiny." We just couldn't convince each other. We finally agreed on a compromise. We would film that scene as written and make a judgment after seeing how it played on the screen. I hated the prospect of having to humiliate Harve in this way. But it seemed the only way to resolve the dilemma.

Months later, however, when we sat in the screening room at Paramount and saw the scene played, no one was humiliated. I may have been a bit sheepish, but that was more than smothered by my absolutely amazed discovery that, without that snipe from the overgrown lug, the scene would not have played even half as heroically for Sulu. My back smarted from all the congratulatory slaps I received. And Harve was gracious enough simply to smile magnanimously, never mentioning our telephone compromise.

Leonard's work as director was impressive—sure, disciplined, and indefatigable. He was acting, as well, albeit in an abridged role, so the energy demands on him for his two functions were killing. Where he found the strength to wake up in the middle of the night for his predawn makeup calls, remain so vital and creative on the set during the day, and still be able to do his homework after leaving late at night was an amazement to me. But he was always prepared and thoroughly organized. Uncannily like Spock.

But he was the polar opposite of Spock in the infectious joy he brought to his directing duties. I never saw Leonard smiling and laughing more. The work seemed to energize him. He used his relationship with each actor, built up over the years, as a special directorial asset. He communicated in a time-saving shorthand that comes only with years of professional rapport.

When I began one rehearsal by rushing onto the bridge, flinging off my leather cape with the flourish of a musketeer, he merely said quizzically, "George?" and subtly raised one eyebrow. That was all he needed to do. In the next one, I walked in briskly, slipped off my cape, and smartly slid into my seat at the console. Leonard smiled and nodded. On second thought, perhaps there was something Spockian about his directorial style after all. Minimal energy expended; maximum result gained.

He seemed to be enjoying his dual role so much that it was

hard to believe he had once so vehemently opposed continuing as Spock.

"Leonard, I sympathized with your insistence on Spock's being killed off," I said to him during a break, "but I've got to say, that funeral really seems to have revitalized you as an artist."

Leonard's response to my casual observation shattered a few myths about him. One of those myths had almost kept him from gaining this director's chair.

"I wasn't opposed to Spock's death," he stated flatly. "Though I was opposed to an early draft of the script. Harve was the one who first told me about the death; the idea may have come from Nick. But it came early in the plot. I thought that was dramatically wrong. I was definitely opposed to that. But as it was finally written, I thought it was a moving dramatic scene." So Walter's gossip network had been off. But as Leonard continued to describe the saga of Spock's demise, the story became even more intriguing.

The success of STAR TREK II had prompted Paramount to begin exploring the prospect of another sequel. Leonard was insurance essential to the project. When Gary Nardino, the Paramount executive charged with overseeing the work, approached him about returning as Spock, Leonard broached the idea of his directing the next film. This led to a meeting with the president of the studio, Michael Eisner. Leonard again proposed directing the third STAR TREK movie. Eisner was noncommittal. The meeting was followed by a disquieting few weeks of silence. Leonard's agent called, but the call was not returned. Finally, Leonard himself called.

It seemed Eisner had problems with an actor directing a film in which he didn't like his own character. Leonard tried to assure him that this was not the case. Eisner countered by asking, "But you yourself insisted on having Spock's death written into your contract, didn't you?" Even the president of the studio had bought the myth. Leonard urged him to have the legal department send up a copy of his contract and examine it for such language. The clause was nonexistent. Reassured,

Eisner approved Leonard's directing of STAR TREK III, ensuring the future of the series and the flowering of a great talent resource for STAR TREK.

Since I wasn't involved in the shot being filmed, I had gone for a long stroll around the studio lot. I was just getting back to the soundstage when, suddenly, the door burst open with explosive force. Jimmy Doohan came flying out in a wild rage. "That bastard. He'll never do that to me again! Never!" He was livid.

"What's the matter? What happened, Jimmy?" I could almost feel the heat of his fury.

"It's that bastard," he sputtered. "I'll never let him do that to me again! I mean it!" He stormed off toward his dressing room.

I thought I knew then what had happened. I went in to find Bill basking in the center of the set, the object of Leonard's and the crew's rapt attention. The camera was directly focused on him, and the script supervisor was reading Jimmy's off-camera lines. It wasn't hard to guess what had transpired. Sure enough, I learned that the shot had originally been on Jimmy, but after a whispered conversation from Bill, the camera angle was changed to center right on Captain Kirk. And Scott was now off-camera. I knew so well how Jimmy felt; I knew that rage. Now, it seemed, it was Jimmy's turn to have his temperature turned up by Bill. At least Bill's ego was egalitarian in whom it burned. Or, rather, was his self-absorption simply indiscriminate in its voracious appetite for fuel with which to shine brighter? To me, more than ego, it looked like some deep-seated insecurity was driving Bill's congenital need to be "the star."

STAR TREK III: THE SEARCH FOR SPOCK was big. Leonard had delivered an epic film—our biggest in its sweep and grandeur. For the first time we saw the full scope of the Vulcan civilization. The beloved *Enterprise*, the real star of the series, met its gallant and fiery end. But, fulfilling the title, we found Spock. Our friend, whom we had grieved over in the last film, was supernaturally returned to us. The "family" was again

356

complete. It was a joyous ending, with the enticing promise of more to come.

At the conclusion of filming, we, Leonard's colleagues of almost two decades, wanted to do something to applaud his accomplishment helming his first film. We decided to host a catered luncheon on the set for him and the crew. This would be a festive way to celebrate the end of production and pay tribute to Leonard. We all agreed to share the costs—Nichelle, De, Jimmy, Walter, and me . . . all except Bill. He demurred, saying he was doing something separately. We all wondered, but decided that's Bill.

El Cholo Mexican Restaurant, one of the oldest established in Los Angeles, catered the luncheon. We invited everybody to our tribute to Leonard, including Gary Nardino, the executive overseeing the production. He was a hefty man who obviously enjoyed food and people. Gary was table-hopping with a smile that shone with satisfaction both with the Mexican dishes and the way the filming had gone. He came up to Bill. Assuming that he was one of the hosts of this party for Leonard, he said graciously, "Lovely lunch, Bill. Thank you." Bill smiled back amiably and answered, "You're welcome." And he kept on smiling.

Nineteen eighty-four was a halcyon year in Los Angeles. It was the year of the XXIII Olympic Games, and the city was radiant. The futuristic new Tom Bradley International Airport Terminal opened its welcoming doors to the world; commissioned murals of athletes on freeway walls dashed, leaped, swam, and vaulted in competition with the speeding traffic; pastel banners flapped in the breeze, heralding the games. Even the much maligned Los Angeles air celebrated by purifying itself for the occasion into startlingly crystalline clear atmosphere. It was a glorious time in Los Angeles.

The journey of the Olympic flame from Athens to Los Angeles was the prelude to the commencement of the games. The flame was carried by runners across the country to it final destination, the great torch above the turnstiles of the Los Angeles

Coliseum. For a contribution of one thousand dollars, a runner would be granted the privilege of carrying the flame for one kilometer on its route. It would be a lifetime experience to carry the Olympic flame to the games in my hometown. I wanted to do it.

I happened to mention this wish to Harve Bennett. He knew I was a runner and immediately his mind started to turn. What makes Harve such a good producer and showman is his flair for taking a simple idea and transforming it into something fabulous. He called me a few days later with the gift of a lifetime.

"George, how would you like to carry the Olympic flame?" Of course I would; he knew that. "How would you like to carry it in five cities?"

"I'd like to do it five times as much. I'd be ten times happier. I'd be fifty times more ecstatic. Why do you ask me this?"

"Well, get ready to do it. I just got Paramount to agree to buy you five kilometers in five different cities in the United States." I was speechless. Harve did something that few people have done—he literally had me at a loss for words.

Harve was an inspired producer. STAR TREK III: THE SEARCH FOR SPOCK was about to open. Having me run in five different cities would generate publicity for the film worth many times more than the five-thousand-dollar contribution to the Olympics by Paramount. And he would have a euphorically happy actor.

To my disappointment, the rules of the Los Angeles Olympics Committee allowed one person to run no more than one kilometer; they wanted to spread out the number of opportunities. I suggested to Harve that, if I couldn't run the other four kilometers, we might offer these opportunities to STAR TREK fans who were runners. I had run with many of them on my convention rounds. Harve loved the idea, so I chose fans in Washington, D.C., St. Louis, Chicago, and Denver. Of course, I kept Los Angeles for myself.

Mine was a dream route for an Angeleno. I received the flame at the Old Plaza, the birthplace of Los Angeles. This venerable district is a State Historic Park, and I had been serving as

358

the chairman of the board of the conservation organization charged with the historic area, the El Pueblo Park Association. My course ran down the namesake Los Angeles Street, over the Hollywood Freeway, and past City Hall, where Mayor Bradley waved from its steps. Finally, I passed the flame on to the next runner at the gateway to Little Tokyo, my ethnic community.

It was only a short run, but that one kilometer was rich with symbolism. It spanned the history of my city, encompassed the ethnic diversity of my hometown, and reflected my political involvements. And I was running with a flame that had been carried all the way across the country by representatives of the spectacular diversity of America; from youth to age, powerful to poor, handicapped to athlete, now that flame had been passed to me. It filled my enraptured heart with a thousand emotions as I ran past the cheering crowds. I will never forget that Olympic flame relay of 1984.

I had been working with the Rapid Transit District for over a decade. We had secured the funding base and the alignment of the route. We had hired the construction firms, the engineers for the system, and the architects for the stations. We had even made provisions for works of art in the stations. Not only would the artworks enliven the stations, but their style and flavor would reflect the character of the neighborhoods in which they were located. We wanted the communities above to feel a proprietorship over the stations, to consider these public facilities as extensions of their neighborhoods. At long last, construction was ready to begin.

As eagerly anticipated as the commencement of this major public works project was, there was for me a troubling flip side. Now the streets would be torn up. There would be detours. Noise, dirt, and commotion would be thrown up into the air. The short-term disruption would be significant. But this was another price that had to be paid for a massive public infrastructure improvement.

I knew, though, that public patience would take only so much. There would be confusion, protests, and demonstrations with irate fists raised. The blame inevitably would be placed on the politicians and public officials—in other words, on people like me.

But I was still an actor. My career rested on public acceptance or, at least, a modicum of public support. I thought the better part of prudence and career conservation meant I should tie a bow on my eleven years on the board of the RTD. The vital work of the transit district would continue but it would have to carry on with other people to meet new challenges. Regretfully, but with a feeling of accomplishment, and not without some sense of relief, I handed in my resignation to Mayor Bradley. I brought to a close my hectic but very exciting tenure of service with the Southern California Rapid Transit District.

It was a wonderful accolade for a respected colleague. Leonard was receiving a singular Hollywood tribute—a star on the Walk of Fame. It was a fitting honor for a multitalented artist who had distinguished himself as an inventive actor and as a fine film director as well. Fans thronged Hollywood Boulevard. Officials of the Hollywood Chamber of Commerce were there to preside over the ceremonials. And we all gathered to praise and applaud Leonard: Gene and Majel, De, Nichelle, Jimmy, Walter, and me. But . . . where was Bill?

Eight months later, Gene was also honored with his star. Indeed, 1985 was a bumper year for stars on Hollywood Boulevard for members of the STAR TREK family. But in his usual pioneering way, Gene was boldly going where no one had gone before. Although there was a galaxy of stars on the Walk of Fame, he was the first writer—a breakthrough distinction. When the star-shaped covering was flung off at high noon to reveal a terrazzo star with the name "Gene Roddenberry" embedded in it, all of us from the STAR TREK cast were there to celebrate this happy occasion . . . all except one. Where was Bill? Again, he was absent. He only sent a message congratulating the man who had helped make him a star.

25

Trek Wars

I HAD BEEN PLAYING SULU NOW FOR ALMOST TWO DECADES. Throughout the television series and the big-screen adventures, I had been struggling persistently to enhance the size and quality of my character. I wanted to give him more dimension, to flesh out his character, to make him a more active participant in the plot. I had lobbied, prodded, campaigned, and cajoled— all without notable success.

"George, in this town, what gets respect is money. Pure and simple, money is muscle." Steve Stevens was laying out for me the power mechanics of Hollywood. "Go for the money. You're valuable to them. Use that as leverage to get the money, and then they'll start giving some weight to your campaign for Sulu."

I knew I was worth more to STAR TREK than what I was currently being paid. Paramount was raking in a bonanza from all the many forms of STAR TREK: The television series was still running all over the world generating revenues for the studio exchequer; the first two feature films were providing a bounty; and now STAR TREK III: THE SEARCH FOR SPOCK had opened as an enormous popular hit, and it seemed to me that the associated merchandising was generating good earnings.

Bill and Leonard were receiving huge seven-figure pieces of the action. They were worth it. But I was being paid only a modest five-figure amount. I thought I was worth more.

"Sure you are, George. You've been doing more to promote the show and enhance its worth than the two of them put together." Steve had a point.

"That's true. I think I've done more conventions than anybody except maybe Jimmy," I agreed. "But we've got an option clause from the last contract, don't we?"

"That's just to tie you up for the next picture. But there's no fairness in that money. There's no equity with your worth. Test them, George. Test them, and see how much they value you."

The more I listened to Steve, the more my blood began to stir. I had single-mindedly tried to improve the content of my role with little to show for it. Perhaps now my tactics should change to improve the size of my remuneration. Maybe then I would be more effective with my first goal. I made my decision.

"All right, Steve. Let's go for the money. With STAR TREK IV, let's go for the dollars."

"George, I can't believe this is you." It was Harve calling. "We've always had such a good relationship. I can't believe that this is really you trying to hold us up. Please talk to your agent."

"Harve, I'm not trying to hold anybody up. I think what I'm asking is only fair. I'm asking the studio to pay me my fair worth. If it doesn't think I'm worth it, I'm prepared to pass." I remained firm.

When I reported to Steve on the conversation with Harve, he was outraged.

"He called you at home during negotiations!" he stormed. "That is the most unethical thing I've ever heard. No producer should be talking to the actor and trying to circumvent the agent! I don't want you to let him do that again. Hang up on him!" Now I had my agent angry with me.

I soon learned, however, that Steve's anger and Harve's charm were one and the same. They were tools in the game of Hollywood negotiations. Harve next switched from charm to threats. My phone rang. I picked it up, and it was Harve's voice again. I knew what Steve had told me, but I couldn't just hang up on him.

"Harve, I really shouldn't be talking to you during this time of negotiations. I'd appreciate it if you would talk with my agent."

"I just want you to know, George, that there are legal ramifications to all this." Harve's voice was stern and darkly edged. "A career can be ended with a lawsuit. I'm just warning you as a friend."

I thanked him for the warning and hung up. I wondered if friendship was also only a tool in this business.

If the phone calls I received were ominous, Steve, who had been battling on the front lines, was on the receiving end of an intense barrage of the most sinister anonymous telephone calls. His phone at home would ring in the middle of the night. The voice on the other end would convey brief, cryptic insinuations and then hang up. One of those messages, Steve remembers, was "A smoking gun can shoot both ways." His poor wife was reduced to a traumatized wreck. It was a negotiation of incredible stress and anxiety for Steve and for his family. But he hung tough, and ultimately we prevailed. We got our contract, and my pay was increased to six figures. I wondered if, now, I could better Sulu's role.

"George, my dear, I'm glad we were able to resolve it." Harve was again a transformed person. We were still "friends." "I knew we couldn't take off without Sulu on board," he gushed. I picked up my cue.

"Thanks, Harve. Now, about Sulu . . ." And I resumed my old lobbying campaign.

STAR TREK IV: THE VOYAGE HOME was to be a time-travel story. Leonard had initiated the idea with Harve while he was filming a television version of Ernest Hemingway's *The Sun Also Rises* in France. We were flung back in time to present-day San Francisco. This was a wonderful opportunity to do something with Sulu's heritage, I thought. San Francisco was my father's old hometown and one of my favorite cities. I started throwing ideas at Harve. How about making San Francisco Sulu's birthplace? How about uncovering some artifact from his family's history? What about Sulu fending off muggers with his fencing foil? I inundated Harve with ideas. Walter Koenig joined in and contributed some possible ideas for Sulu. In fact, it was he who suggested Sulu's discovering a family connection with some chance encounter on the streets of San Francisco.

A couple of them took. San Francisco became Sulu's place of birth. And Harve took Walter's idea and wrote in a delightful scene where Sulu happens across a little Asian boy and discovers to his delighted amazement that he is his great-great-grandfather as a child. It was a terrific scene. I couldn't wait to get up to the City by the Bay to begin filming.

San Francisco is storied in song and romance as the place where people leave their hearts. But when clinging to a cable car for dear life in that jammed traffic, I worried if other parts of the anatomy, like arms and legs, might not get left behind as well.

During our location filming of STAR TREK IV: THE VOYAGE HOME, the thousands of tourists in town had another special attraction—us. Wherever we went, the STAR TREK company filming on location was a crowd-gathering magnet. On one location site, however, I was the one treated to a very special attraction.

We were filming in front of an historic saloon, the longest continually operating drinking establishment in San Francisco. Sited near the bottom of a precipitous hill on Grant Avenue, the saloon was a gaudily painted relic of the city's honky-tonk Victorian era. Scotty, McCoy, and Sulu had just been transported to twentieth-century San Francisco. Everything was exotic to them, especially in this most singular of twentieth-century cities. Everything was a discovery. They were awed by the living antiquity that surrounded them.

As we started walking down the street, I decided to peer in the glass front of the saloon. To Sulu, this was a fascinating curiosity. I had been told that the crowd of people inside were not hired extras but genuine regulars of the place. We were not to react to them, or they might try to claim payment as extras. By the window, at the near end of the long bar, sat a blowzy, voluptuously buxom blonde. During rehearsals, each time I cupped my hands around my eyes to peer in the glass front, the woman would try to get a reaction out of me by smiling boozily and giving me a cute little wave or blowing me a seductive kiss. I ignored all her attempts at rousing a reaction from me. After all, I take great pride in my professionalism.

Soon we were ready for the take. This was it. Bells sounded, whistles shrilled for quiet, and we were ready to begin. Leonard called out, "Action!" and the three of us started walking down the hill. Jimmy was smiling away at the children playing on the street; De gawked at the strange twentieth-century buildings, and when we came to the saloon, I cupped my hands to look in as we had rehearsed. The friendly blonde was still there, determined to provoke a response out of me this time. Reaching down, she grabbed the bottom of her disheveled blouse and hefted it right over her face! I stared in startled amazement, smack dab at two spectacularly fleshly, pink-tipped monuments. They reminded me of the tourist brochures' praise of the great Twin Peaks of San Francisco. My boozy blonde succeeded. I burst out in peals of uncontrollable laughter.

"Cut! Cut!" yelled an outraged Leonard. "George, that shot was working great. Why did you do that? You ruined it!"

With tears rolling down my cheeks, I pointed into the saloon and barely choked out, "That blonde flashed me! I just got flashed by a blonde with two big bazookas!"

Assistants stormed into the turmoil in the chaotic saloon, but the woman had somehow slipped out the back way. To this day, I'm not sure if Leonard believed me. But it really happened. Would I jeopardize my professional reputation on such a fantastic story? Could I, in my wildest hallucinations, make up two such gigantic reasons to ruin Leonard's scene?

The scene with my great-great-grandfather was coming up. From hundreds of cute little Asian boys who had been interviewed, video tested, and screened by Leonard, a button-eyed six-year-old Japanese boy had been selected. I was told that his video test was wonderful. And when I met him the morning of the shot, on Columbus Avenue, I found him adorable. But he also seemed shy. Perhaps he was self-conscious because this was our first meeting, I thought. I decided to spend all my off-camera time with him until the shot came up later in the day.

I played games with him; I shared a donut with him; I let him wear my leather cape. I explained the details of moviemaking to him. By the time we had lunch together, he was calling me "Uncle Sulu."

Throughout, his mother hovered solicitously over us. When I was called before the cameras, I noticed that she immediately had the script out and was running lines with him.

By the time we came to my great-great-grandfather's scene in midafternoon, I was worried. The child was beginning to be a bit pouty. He didn't want to wear my cape anymore. He didn't want any orange juice anymore. And he didn't want to be in the bright lights in front of the camera. No way.

Leonard, still wearing Spock's white robe while he directed, hunkered down to the little boy and enticed and cajoled. To the crowd of onlookers, it was the most incongruous sight. Grave, serious Mr. Spock crouched down in front of a little boy, smiling at him, sweet-talking him, almost pleading with him.

"Isn't it fun to playact with all these people looking at you?" The boy just pursed his lips and shook his head.

"Well then, I'll have most of them go away. Would you like to see me chase them away?" Still, he silently shook his head. Every question Leonard asked was answered with a pout and a silent shaking of the head. What really hurt was when Leonard asked him, "But you want to playact with your 'Uncle Sulu,' don't you?" He shook his head mutely. No matter what we did or what we offered, the boy's petulant shaking of his head was the only answer we got. He had decided—absolutely—that he wasn't going to playact.

As we pleaded, implored, and groveled before the stubbornly pouting child, the sun continued its implacable journey across the San Francisco sky. The shadows from the office towers started to lengthen. The streets started to darken. And as the sun slowly slipped behind Nob Hill, my heart sank with it. A scene with such charm, such warmhearted affection—so much of Sulu went down with that sunset.

From San Francisco, we moved to Monterey for the aquarium scenes. Nichelle, Walter, Jimmy, De, and I were finished before Bill and Leonard, so we got on an earlier plane back to Los Angeles. The flight connected through San Francisco, and as usual with that airport, there was a problem. The airline claimed that it would be fixed quickly and requested that the passengers stay on board. But the "short" wait began to drag. Nichelle, my seatmate on the flight, was becoming impatient.

"George, this is getting ridiculous. Why don't we get off and grab a drink?"

"But, Nichelle, they've asked that we stay on," I reminded her.

"Darling," she breathed huskily, leaning over and bringing a limp hand up to her throat, "I'm dehydrating. I've got to have a drink. Please come with me." I was too old to pout and shake my head, so I got up to accompany her out.

As Nichelle was gathering her fox stole around her, Jimmy, from his seat behind us, scolded, "They said they'd be ready to leave soon, you know." Nichelle just gave him a cool glance over her shoulder and flounced off. I shrugged my shoulders and followed her out. I could hear Jimmy behind me grousing to Walter, "That Nichelle—she's going to expect all of us to wait for her, you know. I know that woman. I know her all too well!"

It was great to get off and stretch the legs a bit. There was a convenient cocktail lounge nearby, so we ensconced ourselves in a capacious banquette and ordered our drinks. I chug-a-lugged my beer, but Nichelle was taking dainty little sips of her gin and tonic as if this were a relaxed layover.

"Nichelle, I think we should start thinking about getting back," I hinted.

"You're done with your beer already?" she gasped. "You must have been thirsty. You need another one." And she raised her arm jangling with bracelets to get the attention of the waiter. "Oh, waiter, waiter!"

"No, no, no, Nichelle. We haven't got the time. We really should be going back."

"Another beer," she said to the waiter, pointing at me. "And another one of these." She held up her glass of gin and tonic. She was unyielding.

When I finally got Nichelle to leave, I must confess, I wasn't feeling the urgency to get back too keenly myself. We were strolling leisurely back to our gate. Nichelle was on my arm. When we had passed the row of food vendors and the glass wall gave us a clear view of the runway, she languidly observed, "Look, doesn't that look just like our plane rolling back from the gate?"

"You know," I responded idly, "it's rolling back from the same area as our gate, too."

"Isn't that funny?" Nichelle giggled.

"Oh my God!" I shouted. "That *is* our plane rolling away!" I dashed for our gate like a madman, leaving Nichelle tottering down the corridor after me. But it was to no avail. The door was closed. The jet way had been drawn back, and the plane was rolling down the runway with purposeful momentum. We were left behind. I threw up my hands in angry frustration.

But Nichelle is another kind of determined lady. She trotted up to the counter and appealed to the ticket agent, "Oh, this is horrible! You must stop that plane. My luggage and my friends are leaving without me." But when he hesitated, her tone began to change from beseeching to something quite different. "That's the STAR TREK company on that plane!" she declared.

"You've got to turn it around this minute!" He balked timidly. Then an amazing performance ensued. The fox stole Nichelle was wearing suddenly sprang to life. It leaped. It snapped. It pounced and flailed. That roused animal lashed out at the poor, cowed ticket agent like an angry bullwhip. It fumed and fulminated. But alas, all the huffing and puffing by that irate fur piece couldn't bring that plane back to our gate.

Fortunately, there are hourly flights between San Francisco and Los Angeles. We got back to LAX an hour after the others. But our friends, who had been away from home for weeks, had all gone on.

As Nichelle and I retrieved our bags at luggage claim, I heard her muttering to herself, "It's that Jimmy. I know he's the one that egged the pilot on. That Jimmy is the most impatient man in the world."

I looked at her feisty fox stole. It lay quiet and limp on her shoulders now, completely exhausted from its ordeal at the San Francisco airport. Poor thing. It had a traumatizing flight.

STAR TREK had blessed me with friends and fans all over the world. Their love and support had opened unimagined doors for me, and their generosity had bestowed upon me a bounty of gifts. One of the most appreciated is also one I can share with so many people every day. It is my own star on Hollywood's Walk of Fame. I was joining Gene, Leonard, and Bill.

Karen Lewis, a charming Australian fan who had organized a convention in Sydney, was the one who initiated it. The campaign to get a star for me on the Hollywood Walk of Fame began with her in Australia, then was picked up by my fan club president in Staffordshire, England, Ena Glogowska, and finally coordinated by a dynamo of a woman, Lynn Choy Uyeda, in Los Angeles.

On the morning of October 30, 1986, a month before the opening of STAR TREK IV: THE VOYAGE HOME, Hollywood Boulevard was cordoned off for the unveiling ceremony. A red carpet had been laid out, a speaker's stage and podium set up, and a Japanese Taiko Drum group was beating out a heart-throbbing rhythm. Friends and fans were gathered on the boulevard. Karen Lewis led a group from Australia. Flying in from England were Ena Glogowska, Janice Hawkins and Amy Stevenson. STAR TREK fans from throughout the world and the Little Tokyo community were out in force. Lynn Choy Uyeda had organized the festive event and was hustling about, taking care of last-minute details.

Nichelle rode up in the limo with me and my mother. Gene was there to greet me in a giant bear hug. Harve was there, beaming. Leonard, De, Walter, and Jimmy were all there to share my happy day with me. When somebody from the crowd yelled out, "Where's Bill?" I could only shout back the obvious answer, "He's not here." He had been invited.

Hollywood City Councilman Michael Woo and my own City Councilman Nate Holden read proclamations. Mayor Tom Bradley declared the day "George Takei Day" in Los Angeles.

In my speech, I observed that Hollywood does everything uniquely—even its style of recognizing people. "In most other communities, the honoree's name is carved in stone and put up high for all to see. Only in this town do we put the honoree's name in a star and then embed it right down in the sidewalk so the whole world can walk all over your good name. To begin that parade trampling over my name, I would like the person who helped me with my first step to take the first step—my mother." And with that, the familiar star-shaped cover over the terrazzo square was removed, and a star with the name George Takei was revealed. Mine was just one square away from the one that read Gene Roddenberry. Leonard's was on the corner of the same block. We were still together.

My mother stepped off the red carpet and placed her foot squarely on her son's star on Hollywood Boulevard. Afterward we celebrated with a big luncheon banquet at the Hollywood Roosevelt Hotel that embraced the infinite diversity of our world. It was a heady afternoon.

A month later, STAR TREK IV: THE VOYAGE HOME opened to rave reviews and astounding box office success. Leonard had racked up a gigantic triumph. And STAR TREK V was inevitable.

There were disquieting rumors circulating. STAR TREK was going to be revived on television again—but this time, with different people. The scuttlebutt was that it was to be on the *Enterprise* but with, of all preposterous things, another generation of Starfleet officers.

"That's crazy," huffed Jimmy. "What makes STAR TREK is people. It's the chemistry between people. It's us! If they do this 'next generation' nonsense, they'll kill it! That's it! They'll kill it!"

"Guess what?" Walter's voice was charged with the buzz of news still hot from the source. "They've cast the new captain! It's a bald-headed English guy! Can you believe it? But then, I guess that's nothing new. We've had bald-headed captains before."

To be completely candid, we were miffed. We resented—at the very least—not being asked to do the television revival of the show in which we took a great deal of proprietary pride. We felt STAR TREK was ours, and without our unique alchemy, any reincarnation would be doomed. STAR TREK was and will forever be us! Hubris was soon to be transformed into delighted humility.

26

River Kwai to Edinburgh

WHAT I HAD BEEN STRIVING FOR SO TENACIOUSLY WAS BEGINNING to happen. STAR TREK was opening up other acting opportunities for me. But the inquiry I got in the spring of 1986 was not from another Hollywood producer. This one was from London. It was for an international film!

Kurt Unger, a German-born Israeli based in London, was interested in me for his film *Return from the River Kwai*. It was an epic project based on the chronicles of the evacuation of the Japanese army from Thailand near the end of World War II. Of course, the classic film by David Lean, *The Bridge on the River Kwai*, had given this project its commercial viability; but this new film dramatized events occurring after those depicted in Lean's Academy Award–winning film. This was the story of the retreat of the Japanese from southeast Asia.

Unger had contacted me for the role of the commandant of the prisoner of war camp at River Kwai. It was a juicy opportunity. He told me, however, that he was gathering an international cast of players and was seeking actors from Britain, the U.S., and Japan. That statement gave me some concern. In Japan, there were many fine actors: the great

Toshiro Mifune, Tatsuya Nakadai, Rentaro Mikuni, Tsutomu Yamazaki, and a whole galaxy of others. But he claimed he was interested in me, a Japanese American actor, for the top Japanese role in the film. I should have been more circumspect, but my curiosity didn't stop me from venturing a bold question, "Why me, an American?"

"Well, for one thing," he answered in his heavy German accent, "you speak English. No problem there. But I also need an actor who has popular box-office appeal internationally. You're about the only Japanese actor who has that. I'll stay in touch with your agent."

I realized that what this candid London producer had told me carried more than a grain of flattering truth. The great Japanese actors were not known outside the circle of art house film buffs. It was true that I had done a musical play in England the year before as the Genie in *Aladdin*. But I knew that even the Genie casting was possible because of the wild popularity of STAR TREK in England. The show that so many of my colleagues were fearful would imprison them in their characters was unquestionably opening the doors of opportunity for me to these international projects. The worldwide popularity of STAR TREK was expanding my own professional world.

Return from the River Kwai, however, took almost as long as World War II took to get started. It was to be filmed on location in the Philippines. Problem after incredible problem emerged. To start things off, a government fell. The "people power" revolution against corrupt dictator Ferdinand Marcos erupted and prevented the commencement of production. The victory of the people and emergence of Corazon Aquino, popular widow of the opposition leader, as President brought an unstable peace. Then the construction of the sets began in earnest. But just as the sets were completed, a cataclysmic tropical hurricane struck the Philippines and completely demolished the sets. Undismayed, the crew reconstructed them. Finally, there followed almost monthly coup attempts on the new President's life.

Through revolution, hurricane, coups, and a myriad other

daunting disasters, producer Unger steadfastly forged on. I knew that a producer had to have a multitude of skills. But following Kurt Unger through his trials, I realized that there was a vital core requisite. He had to have the tenacity of a bulldog. Kurt lost major actors because of the delay. His financing was regularly placed in jeopardy. His insurance problems turned monstrous. Yet, Kurt doggedly pushed on.

I stuck with him, and in March of 1988, two years after I was first contacted, I flew into Manila's Benigno Aquino Airport. At long last, filming on *Return from the River Kwai* was about to begin.

From Britain, Kurt cast Edward Fox and Denholm Eliott. From Australia, Nick Tate. From America, Timothy Bottoms, Christopher Penn, and me. And from Japan, the excellent actor in so many Akira Kurosawa films, Tatsuya Nakadai. It was an impressive cast.

But our problems were far from over. The blazing heat of the Philippines was withering. We had to be on guard constantly against sunstroke and dehydration. There was a boy assigned to each of us, carrying bottles of water.

Then we couldn't find enough skinny Caucasian men in Manila to be extras in my prison camp; we needed hundreds. By a stroke of luck, a good friend from Los Angeles flew in to visit me. He was a godsend. Brad Altman, a financial journalist, was a running mate. I had trained for marathons with him. And he had the rail-thin physique of an outstanding runner. Brad was quickly recruited and transformed from a friend into one of my emaciated and much-abused prison camp inmates.

Tatsuya Nakadai was a delightful man. But this actor whom I had admired in so many Japanese films became a problem of some consequence. He had considerable dialogue in English; in fact, he had a major oration scene. The problem was—he didn't speak a word of it!

I was the only one with the company who spoke both English and Japanese, so it became part of my duties to help Nakadai-san with his English dialogue. I had dinner with him at night. During the day, on the set between shots, I sat across from him pursing my lips and contorting my tongue, forming sounds apparently unachievable with his Japanese mouth. When he was on, I stood beside the camera, silently but with great exaggeration shaping the words of his dialogue for him. Nakadai-san agonized on camera, and I suffered off. Even on days when I had no scenes, when I could have stayed back in the air-conditioned comfort of the hotel, if Nakadai-san was on, I made the long, bouncy trek out to that scorching location site.

The tribulations in making *Return from the River Kwai* were compensated for by the pleasure of working with a company of marvelous actors. Under the most arduous conditions, they were gallant professionals.

Proper gentleman Edward Fox always maintained his impeccably amiable speech and concern for the well-being of others. "Are you all right?" was his benign greeting for everyone. A determinedly correct gentleman, his shirt never came off as others' did immediately on the director's cry of "Cut!" When he had to walk into the sun, he made a parasol of a giant tropical leaf and unflappably went from shade to shade.

The English seemed to become even more English under duress. Denholm Eliott was polite even in downright pain. During the rehearsal of his death scene in the jungle, while he lay on the ground, an extra dressed as a Japanese guard unknowingly stepped on his hand. He left his foot on Denholm's hand, probably thinking it was just some jungle foliage. Denholm, although in excruciating pain, looked up at his unaware tormentor and very politely requested, "I would be ever so grateful if you would take your feet off my hand." A few years after the release of the film, I read in the obituary section of the newspaper that this sweet gentleman had passed on.

Robust, blond Australian Nick Tate was pink from the sun, but if the crew needed some extra muscle to help move a piece of equipment, he would plunge into the blazing heat to help out. While this American preferred to confine his assistance to forming English words with Nakadai-san in the relative comfort of the shade, Tim Bottoms was right out there representing the American spirit of lending a helping hand.

It was a wonderful company of actors, and I almost regretted the completion of filming. Almost . . . but not quite. I wanted to get back to the civilized comforts of home. And I had another exciting script waiting for me.

The American Festival Theater Company had invited me to star in their production of Shimon Wincelberg's *Undertow*, to be presented at the celebrated Edinburgh International Arts Festival that summer in Scotland. It was a two-character drama about a Japanese soldier marooned on a Pacific island with an American G.I. near the end of World War II. This seemed to be my year for reliving that bloody conflict.

The two characters were polar antagonists. One spoke only English, the other only Japanese. One was a callow youth, the other a mature man. And they were soldiers in mortal combat with each other. Yet, by the tragic end of the play, they recognized their mutual interdependence for survival and, ultimately, their humanity. It was crackling good drama with powerful acting challenges.

The American soldier was played by a gifted young actor, Andy McCutcheon, who, as it turned out, was also a runner. Early every morning, we would leave our elegant Georgian club residence in the historic "New Town" section of Edinburgh, run across the grounds of regal Holyrood Palace, then up the windswept hillside to Arthur's Seat, so called because the craggy contours of the promontory resembled King Arthur's saddle.

We performed *Undertow* in a restored playhouse in the ancient Netherbow Theater on the Royal Mile in the medieval section of Edinburgh. It was a dream fulfillment for an artist and a glorious holiday combined. To top off an unforgettable summer, the production won the coveted Scotsman Fringe First Award.

The amazing devotion of fans kept the STAR TREK presence vibrant even in this far northern Scottish capital. Ena Glogowska and her daughter Anne traveled all the way up from Staffordshire to be in the audience on opening night, returned in the middle of the run, and once again on closing night. Colin and Freda Boydell of Cornwall, near Land's End in the very southernmost part of the British Isles, took an overnight train all the way up to Edinburgh, attended a matinee, visited me backstage, and then headed straight back to Waverly train station to take another overnighter back home. Their ardent loyalty and amazing support was deeply affecting. STAR TREK friends are a very special breed.

Out of the cool blue Edinburgh sky a bit of American history followed me to Scotland and hit me unexpectedly.

The publicist for the production of *Undertow* had been sending me out regularly to do press interviews to publicize the play. So, like a dutiful actor, I strolled into a pub one afternoon to keep another press meeting that had been arranged with a newspaper reporter.

"So, Mr. Takei," he greeted me as I settled down into a maroon velvet upholstered banquette with my pint of bitter, "what are you going to do with your twenty thousand dollars?" I was puzzled. What a strange way to begin an interview, I thought.

"I'm sorry. You must be mistaken," I corrected. "This play I'm doing is a labor of love. I'm afraid I'm not being paid that much in dollars, but I must say, my artist's soul is being handsomely compensated with every performance." I tried to direct the conversation to the content of the play and not the financial arrangements.

"I can tell you that your pecuniary interest will also be handsomely met," the reporter answered in his heavy Scottish burr. "Your President just signed the bill paying Japanese Americans imprisoned in those American prison camps redress of twenty thousand dollars. I just got it off the wire."

"What! You're telling me that he finally signed the redress bill?" I was shocked and thrilled. Shocked because I hadn't expected the bill to be signed by President Ronald Reagan.

It had been so long since that day I testified before the Commission on Wartime Relocation and Internment of Civilians. The Commission had concluded its hearings in 1983 and had recommended to Congress for monetary redress and a formal governmental apology for the internment. Congress in turn had passed bill H.R. 442, so numbered in honor of the most-decorated military unit to emerge from the Second World War, the all-Nisei 442nd Regimental Combat Team. The bill provided for the apology and a token redress of twenty thousand dollars per individual. This monetary redress had been the sticking point with President Reagan. He agreed with the provision for the verbal apology but not the monetary recompense. The President had been stridently resisting signing, but the news from home that the reporter conveyed to me was that President Reagan could no longer resist the conscience of decent Americans and had finally signed. I was elated. At long last, that dark chapter of America's history was reaching closure. It was August 10, 1988: forty-three years after the end of the war; almost seven years to the day after I had testified to the Congressional Commission; and nine years after my father had passed on. It was a very much belated apology.

I spent that afternoon explaining to the reporter my history as an American. In describing to him the complicated process of gaining redress within our system, I found myself explaining the workings of our democracy. I told him that our ideal is of a government of the people. People, of course, are often not as ideal as we would like to be; but we keep reaching for that perfect star. I sensed myself echoing, unconsciously, words that Daddy had spoken to me so long ago. I told him that the news from America that he brought was testimony to the vibrance of that ideal. And I said to him that I would be donating my twenty thousand dollars to the place where I thought it truly belonged . . . to the Japanese American National Museum in Los Angeles.

I settled myself in my British Airways seat with enough reading material for the eleven-hour flight from London to Los Angeles. I had given myself a week of theater-going in London after the high of the Edinburgh run with *Undertow*. When I'm not on one side of the footlights, I can usually be found on the other side in the audience. The 747 started to roll out, and as always, I got a bit melancholy leaving London. The British Airways personnel helped prolong the lingering memories.

After about an hour up in the air, I needed to stretch my legs. As I got up, I happened to glance over to my seatmate, who was quietly reading a book. He was a distinguished-looking gentleman with a fine aquiline nose and a slight fringe of hair around his smooth, clean pate. I thought the profile looked familiar. But the coincidence seemed too bizarre. No, it couldn't be, I thought, and got up.

When I came back to my seat, I sneaked a good look at the man seated next to me. It really was a remarkable resemblance, I thought. But I sat down and buried myself again in the *London Times* that I had been reading. I tried to read, but my curiosity nagged at me silently. I surreptitiously rolled my eyes toward him for another confirmation of my suspicion. It was truly uncanny. Then I noticed that he was reading Dickens.

I reached over and gently placed my hand on his arm. I started to ask, "Excuse me, but aren't you . . ." The man turned to me, startled by the unexpected intrusion. Then I saw the flash of recognition in his eyes.

"Why, aren't you . . . ," he blurted out. And I knew with certainty that he was who I thought he was—Patrick Stewart, the new captain of another generation of STAR TREK.

"Why aren't you . . . George . . . Sulu!" he stammered.

"George Takei," I corrected. "Pleasure to meet you, Patrick."

This was our first meeting—some thirty-five thousand feet up in the air, somewhere over the North Atlantic.

"What an extraordinary coincidence," remarked Patrick.

I, who had been doing STAR TREK now for over two decades, suspected that perhaps this was not such a fluke. I said to him, "Let me tell you, Patrick, we have fans in the most unexpected places. I have a pretty strong hunch that there is a Trekker with British Airways someplace who had access to the passenger manifest and very thoughtfully made these seating assignments for us."

Patrick Stewart was a charming man and a pleasant seatmate. He told me he was returning to Los Angeles to begin the second season of *The Next Generation* television series. I was returning for the beginning of negotiations for the next film. We chatted amiably about generalities.

I avoided, however, the subject of *The Next Generation* series. I saw no need to make Patrick feel uncomfortable. "Our" generation had, at first, been miffed by the notion of another generation supplanting us. But, despite our resentment, our intense curiosity compelled us to keep an eye on these trespassers. And what we saw the first season had actually given us some unexpected secret pleasures. Not because we thought the shows were good—quite to the contrary—we felt an evil gratification because their opening shows were so disappointing, delightfully disappointing. Their third aired show particularly filled me with glee. It was called "Naked Now," and its very title betrayed its naked imitation of us. The show was an exact redo of one of our most successful episodes and my favorite, "The Naked Time." The contrast was cruelly obvious. "Naked Now" was so unoriginal, such a faltering paraphrasing, it was like children putting on their parents' clothes and trying to be grownups. This pale carbon copy was supposed to carry on the legacy? Their future looked bleak indeed.

As I continued to watch the series, something else about *The Next Generation* troubled me. There was a very conspicuous void. Our *Enterprise* was a good metaphor for the diversity of starship Earth. Our crew personified the pluralism of the people of this planet. The bridge of their *Enterprise*, however, may now have had a Klingon on board as a symbol of galactic coexistence, but at least a third of the population of our world and certainly of the twenty-fourth century was absent. There were no Asians on their bridge. There were occasional background people or guest visitors, but—even less than aliens— there was no continuing Asian presence with this STAR TREK. I mentioned this to Gene Roddenberry one night at a party at his home.

"Gene, I don't see any Asians in the finite diversity of the *Next Generation*. How come?"

"You know, you're right about that. We'll work on it," he said.

Perhaps this conversation was what gave birth to the charming combination of the names Keiko with O'Brien. But, as charming as she was, she still seemed a combination of the traditional Asian scientist and the traditional Asian wife. And the bridge still had a conspicuous void in the world of their brave new future.

All this I didn't discuss with Patrick as we flew westward toward our differing missions. The helmsman of the twenty-third-century *Starship Enterprise* sharing a flight with the new captain of the twenty-fourth-century *Enterprise,* both returning to Hollywood for different chronicles of the same enterprise— STAR TREK.

27

Trek Wars,
the Sequel

"GUESS WHAT?" I HAD NEVER HEARD WALTER'S VOICE SO HEAVY with foreboding. "Bill is going to be directing STAR TREK V!"

"Oh my God," I intoned. "What are we going to do?"

"I don't think Jimmy will do it. For all the money in the world, he won't work with Bill as the director."

"What're you going to do?" I asked.

"I don't know. I'm willing to keep an open mind . . . but they'll really have to pay me for it."

We all feared the prospect of working with Bill as director. It was difficult enough to act with him, but just the thought of having him so totally in control of our artistic lives as director was utterly dispiriting. We would probably be reduced to even less significance in his version.

I fantasized the opening scene with all of us at our usual stations on the bridge. The *Enterprise* moves through a rare energy field and suddenly we all start popping out. The mysterious power of the energy field has made us vanish—all of us, that is, except Bill. Then, astoundingly, figures start to pop back into position! Something amazing is happening. At the stations where we had been—helm, navigation, communication, even down in engineering—the figures that are popping back all look like Bill!

"Warp three, Mr. Sulu," commands Captain Kirk, and a figure that looks just like Bill acknowledges, "Aye, sir, warp three."

Kirk calls down to engineering, "We need more power, Scotty!"

And Bill's voice doing a Scottish accent responds from the intercom, "Ah canna do it, sir."

Kirk calls out, "Communications," and another figure that looks like Bill with a gizmo in his ear swings around in his seat and answers, "Hailing frequencies open, Captain."

Every one of the characters are played by Bill! He would be in seventh heaven directing this STAR TREK. It would be the worst, most horrific nightmare for us! And after all our struggles, over all these years, were we going to be brought down this low? Do we want to do STAR TREK that badly?

Apparently, Jimmy got all the money in the world he needed to work with Bill, because he signed on to do STAR TREK V. Walter signed also. Nichelle did as well. As did De and Leonard. I was the only one who hadn't signed.

I had decided that I would do it in order to work with my friends and colleagues again—but only if Paramount matched the fee I had been paid for *Return from the River Kwai*. Kurt Unger had remunerated me commensurate to how he valued me as, to use his phrase, "an actor who has box office appeal internationally." Steve, my agent, and I had agreed that a price level had been set by Kurt, and we should have Paramount meet it. And thus began the sequel to my Trek wars from the last film.

A good sequel should have all of the familiar elements of the preceding hit with just enough new twists and turns to surprise and shock anew. In that sense, the negotiations for STAR TREK V, and then STAR TREK VI, were crackling good sequels.

Steve Stevens made our proposal to Paramount. Match the figure I had earned from *Return from the River Kwai*. Steve advised the studio of our position, and we waited. There was dead silence from the studio. We waited longer. We didn't hear from them for weeks. I had just about resigned myself to not doing STAR TREK V, when Harve called. His voice was cordial—even affectionate.

"George, my dear. I'd love to have lunch with you at Le St. Germain next week. I have some thoughts I'd like to share with you. Can we get together?" I responded as charmingly as I could. I knew how to play the game also.

"Of course, Harve. I'd love to. But Wednesday is the only lunch I have open on my calendar next week. Is that okay with you?" It was. Actually, I was free any day that week.

Le St. Germain was one of the most sophisticated—and expensive—French restaurants in Los Angeles. It was on trendy Melrose Avenue not too far from Paramount. When I walked into the posh foyer of the restaurant on the appointed Wednesday afternoon, Harve was already there sitting at the bar.

"There's my darling," he called out, getting up. "I have a table waiting for us." We were escorted to a sunny, bricked patio, luxuriant with fresh-blooming greenery. The air seemed scented with perfume.

"George, I'm very concerned," he said to me after our Evian water had been poured. "I want you with us on STAR TREK. It won't be the same without Sulu on board. Can't we work it out?"

"I feel the same way, Harve. My heart is with all my friends. They're all doing the film, and here I am. It breaks my heart that Paramount doesn't value me as my last producer did. It's simply a matter of maintaining what I've already achieved. You understand that, don't you?" Harve's face turned grave.

"You know we have a tight budget. What I'm hearing makes me very sad. Really, George, STAR TREK will then have to go on without you. I'm telling you this as your friend. You won't be in the next film then."

"I'm prepared for that, Harve. To me it's sad that a big studio like Paramount, with a huge earner like STAR TREK, can't meet the salary paid me by a British independent producer. But if that's it, I'm prepared to live with it. My life will go on—with a void in it—but it will go on."

We maintained an amiable atmosphere throughout our leisurely lunch. In the lush ambiance of Le St. Germain, our conversation was as sweetly confected as the elegant pastries that were displayed on the silver trolley. And both our positions remained as firm as the solid oak antique table we dined on. When we left, we parted amicably but with a definite tone of finality. I said good-bye to Harve feeling that STAR TREK was now behind me.

"Paramount called back," Steve exclaimed over the phone. "They still want to negotiate. They've come up a bit, but they're still not meeting our price."

I had truly made my peace with the notion of not doing STAR TREK anymore. Now I was being jolted back into another cycle of expectancy, anxiety, and frustration. Steve responded. Paramount countered. Steve held firm. Paramount haggled. The dickering continued back and forth.

I saw movie negotiations as a game of unequal players. The producer had the force of power and money; we, the actors, only the talent and the producer's need of it. Fairness and equity played no part in the game, yet that was the basis of our position.

But I had one more weapon in my arsenal. I was willing to walk away. Through three seasons as a television series and four enormously successful feature films, my efforts to enhance my role had been futile. I enjoyed working with most of the members of the cast, but that would be about the only thing I would miss, since other projects had fulfilled me more as an actor. If Harve Bennett wasn't going to respect what I had established professionally outside of STAR TREK, I wasn't going to give up that gain simply to return to a supernumerary role doing another STAR TREK. And this one, directed by Bill! My mind was set—conclusively—to move on with my life.

* * *

My upstairs phone was ringing. Only a few people know that number, so I dashed up and grabbed it on the last ring before the answering machine came on. It was Nichelle.

"Baby, we're all here but you. We miss you." Her voice was grave and concerned. I knew from Walter that they were meeting at Bill's home this morning for the first reading of the script.

"Nichelle, I can't tell you how empty I feel being here at home knowing that you guys are together there reading the next STAR TREK script. But I hope you understand."

"Hang on, honey, let me put someone on." Nichelle passed the receiver on.

"Georgie," the voice cooed sweetly. It was Bill. "Why aren't you here with us?" he asked innocently.

"Bill, I'm sure you've had discussions with Harve about my situation. I really would appreciate it if the negotiations could be regarded seriously."

"But, Georgie," he sweet-talked. "We need you here. *I* need you. What can I do to help change your mind?" I felt like saying he could begin by not calling me Georgie. No one calls me Georgie. Not even my mother. No one but Bill. But I restrained myself.

"Bill, I'm quite serious about this. If there's anything you can do, that would be to convey to Harve just how serious I am about this. I really am prepared to pass." We chatted for a while longer, and then we hung up. I was not a bit ruffled by the call. Did Bill think that one charming "Georgie" call from him would change my mind? But I knew better. I knew that he was only playing the role of the director making a final heroic gesture in front of his cast—the one last try at bringing the stray back into the flock. I was not about to accomodate his glowing self-image.

Steve proved to be the buckaroo deal maker I suspected he was on our first meeting. He can ride out the wildest negotiations, the most rough-and-tumble bargaining, and tame it down to an exhausted compromise. He finally crafted a convoluted deal with Harve Bennett that sort of met the price—but with many complicated qualifications. Fifty thousand dollars of the compensation was to be a "pay or play" deal. In plain language, that meant that fifty thousand dollars of the payment could be applied to any other Paramount project—television or movie —that they could cast me in. They thus hadn't in fact met the full *River Kwai* payment. But Steve also negotiated an option price for STAR TREK VI in the same agreement. This figure was a significant increase over the *River Kwai* amount. So he had established a new price for me—on the next film.

I pondered this offer. Even if it didn't truly meet the straight-out pay from *River Kwai,* the promise of parlaying a part of the money from this STAR TREK over to another project was attractive. In that sense, even if my part as Sulu should turn out to be minimal, at least I had enhanced my prospects as an actor with another "pay or play" project. I decided to accept. The suspense was over. Immediately, I got on the phone to Walter and began our conversation with, "Guess what?"

STAR TREK V: THE FINAL FRONTIER was an unexpectedly pleasant surprise on many counts.

It began sublimely. Location filming in Yosemite National Park was really a one-week holiday with a few hours of light work tucked in. My daybreak runs in the invigorating forest crispness, morning sunlight streaming down through the towering sequoias, were daily communions with the glory of nature. I'd return shining with good sweat to the grandly rustic Ahwanee Hotel, give Walter his morning wake-up call, then step into the shower. When I got down to the dining room, Walter would already be seated at a table next to an expansive window with a heart-stopping vista of the Yosemite valley. After breakfast, we would go for leisurely hikes through sylvan meadows on the valley floor. Then, after a late morning nap, it was time for lunch.

"You know, Walter," I observed dreamily as we gazed out at the majesty of El Capitan, "I think I know now how it feels to be a kept woman. I could get used to this living."

"Yeah," sneered Walter cynically. "And every two years, our 'man' comes and gives it to us." I roared at his extending my analogy to its logical conclusion, but I had to agree—Walter did have a point.

The really unanticipated surprise was Bill. It was not an unpleasant working experience to be directed by him. In fact, he was actually quite good at creating a positive environment on the set, marshaling his considerable reservoir of charm, loading it into his weapon, and placing the setting at "enchant." We were pleasantly taken aback. Even Jimmy remarked, "The man's not half as bad as I thought he'd be!"

I suspected, however, that it was more because he was a clever actor than a genuine director. Bill knew that for him to be successful as a director, he needed our support. And if there is anyone driven to personal success, that was Bill. He tapped all his acting prowess in his effort to triumph as a director. He was supportive, he was encouraging, he was solicitous, and he was accomodating. But I knew he was not a changed Bill. We had a history together. I knew that he had always been vivacious and convivial on the set. His charm was intended, however, always to burnish his own star. I knew I was only watching another acting performance—this time, he was enacting the role of a cheerfully earnest and helpful director.

STAR TREK V: THE FINAL FRONTIER opened the summer of 1989. This one was not kindly received. *The Final Frontier* almost turned out to be a prophetic title. It became the only STAR TREK film to disappoint at the box office.

Yet in a way I wasn't surprised. The script seemed rather a muddle. It was as if three separately interesting plots were force-sealed together into one. Perhaps the mystery of Nimbus III, a planet that began as a paradisiacal world, now reduced to an arid place of gaunt, miserable people desperate for a Messiah, might have been developed into a gripping film. Perhaps the fraternal relationship between Spock and his half-brother, Sybok, might have made for fascinating human/Vulcan drama. Perhaps even the Wizard of Oz–like search for God could have been a whimsical STAR TREK IV type of movie.

But rammed together, they made for a confusing and ultimately tiresome two hours.

And the humor serving as the glue to all this, instead of being light and frolicsome, seemed only mean-spirited. The laughs seemed to be at the cost of the very qualities that made our heros distinctive. Chekov and Sulu were supposed to be the best navigator and helmsman in Starfleet. The first joke was in seeing them hopelessly lost in the forest. Uhura was a classy lady as well as a spectacularly gorgeous woman. For a laugh, her beauty was reduced to a striptease sex object for a gaggle of grunting barbarians in the desert. Engineer Scott was supposed to know every inch of the *Enterprise* like "the back of my hand." And just as he utters this line, the joke happens — he rams his head against a very prominent beam and knocks himself unconscious. This is funny? It was no wonder the fans did not buy it. Paramount learned that merely pasting the words STAR TREK on a movie did not automatically produce fans in mindless droves. STAR TREK V was not another megahit.

I got home from a weekend convention in St. Louis and played back the accumulation of telephone messages. There was a time I remembered, way back in the old days when STAR TREK was just starting up, when we didn't have this device. We were mercifully spared this ritual that we now had to perform after any extended absence. Technological advance wasn't necessarily making life easier. Now "progress" had granted us the burden of returning a weekend's stockpile of telephone calls. There were at least four from Mama. I'll never understand why she feels that she needs to leave message after message when she knows I'm out of town. I was writing down the information on my notepad when, suddenly, a voice that I almost never heard on my machine came on.

"George, buddy, how ya been?" That drawl was immediately recognizable. It was DeForest Kelley. But the voice seemed edged with anxiety. He had a problem, he said, and perhaps I could help. That was it. Nothing more. I was worried. I stopped the machine and punched in De's phone number immediately.

It rang a couple of times, and then his wife Carolyn's voice came on. It was the infernal answering machine! They were out. At times, "progress" can be frustrating. I left my message on their machine. Over the next few days, our answering machines got more intimate with each other than we could. What might be troubling De? I worried. My anxiety increased.

But hearing Carolyn's voice also brought back fond memories of the five-city promotional tour that I shared with them almost ten years ago prior to the opening of the first STAR TREK movie. They were the sweetest couple, and engaging travel companions. Carolyn was an actress who had given up her career to be Mrs. Kelley. They moved out to the Valley as a young couple and had been living in the same house since. And together they built that rarity in Hollywood, a solid and lasting marriage.

My concern for whatever might have been troubling De grew with each passing day. I tried again. It rang a couple of times, and Carolyn's voice came on. This time it was live!

"Carolyn! It's so good to hear your voice. I've been worried about you guys ever since De left that message for me last weekend. What's the problem?"

"Thank you for calling back, George. Here, let me put him on." I could hear muffled voices and other background sounds. Then that familiar, slow Georgia drawl came on.

"George, I appreciate your calling back," he began, and immediately launched into a description of a bureaucratic nightmare in which they had become ensnared. It seemed they shared a surname with their next-door neighbor, but with one difference—their neighbor spelled their name "Kelly," without the *e*, while De spelled his "Kelley." Because of this similarity, their property tax bills had somehow become mixed up in the record-keeping machinery downtown, and interests and penalties were piling up alarmingly on their computer-imposed "tax delinquincy." They had called downtown only to get caught up in another tangled web of bafflingly bureaucratic handoffs. They were at their wit's end, and afraid their home was in jeopardy.

"You know how government works, George," De stated. "Can you help us?" As I listened to De describe his plight, my blood started to boil. I knew how confusing the maze of bureaucracy could be even to those familiar with it. I knew how coldly impersonal some government workers could be to the very people they should be serving. We were getting farther and farther away from the basic purpose of government—to serve people. My friends, who were worried for their home, were getting the worst of remote, unfeeling government inflicted upon them.

"De, this gets me angry. Let me make a few calls." I hung up and got to work. I called the deputy to a county supervisor I knew and explained the problem. I underscored the fact that these people had been run through the mill and been left even more worried and confused than before. Government had compounded its own mistake and was creating unnecessary distress. He said he would get right on it.

A few days later, De called again to tell me that the supervisor's office had called and that the problem now seemed resolved. Then he added, "If you ever decide to run for office again, let me know. You've got our votes."

I got more than the assurance of De's and Carolyn's votes in return for that phone call to the supervisor's deputy. A couple of days later, a messenger brought an enormous basket of fruit, and among the mountainous sculpture of exotica were kiwifruits. They were delicious, but even better was having been given the chance to help out old friends.

There was something strange happening with STAR TREK: THE NEXT GENERATION. It was growing in popularity. The show that had, at first, irked us as an idea, then on its faltering initial run delighted us with a secret sense of vindication, now seemed to be gaining its "space legs." The show's ratings were quite good. At conventions, we started getting challenging questions on why we didn't like the show.

I tuned in again. And it surprised me. The characters had become clearer and stronger. The scripts had become imaginative and thought-provoking. Issues such as euthanasia, society's responsibility to its soldiers, and the inclusion of the infinite diversity of sexuality into our infinite combinations were inventively explored. *The Next Generation* was carrying the torch and running with it quite independently and now quite strongly. These characters on our spin-off series were not our spin-off equivalents. Rather, they each had their own identities. Picard was not a mirror of Kirk. Riker certainly was not Spock. In an advance on us, Dr. Crusher was female, and Worf was from our implacable adversary race, the Klingons. Ultimately, the cast's chemistry was uniquely theirs. Yet at the core of both generations was our common subscription to the ideal of facing the future with confidence in our problem-solving capabilities and our creativity.

Their lack of full diversity on the bridge still bothered me, but the show was remarkably improved. The evil delight we had initially taken now became paternal pride. We had given birth to another extention of the STAR TREK phenomenon. And an offspring's success is claimed by many parents.

We wondered if there would be a STAR TREK VI. The general chagrin following the last picture placed a heavy damper on the prospects for another one. There was, however, a tiny glimmering in the near future. It sparkled tantalizingly for the possibility of another sequel.

Nineteen ninety-one would be the twenty-fifth birthday of STAR TREK. A silver anniversary shone enticingly just two years away. What a gloriously rare achievement it would be for a television series that debuted rather inauspiciously back in 1966.

With the anniversary looming, there must have been a lot of pressure on Paramount, both from the Paramount Licensing and Merchandising department and from the general public, to produce still another film. STAR VI soon started to loom as a distinct possibility.

Harve Bennett was once again assigned to come up with an idea. This time, there would have to be more creative thought invested in the project to avoid the fate of the last one. Instead, Harve came up with an incredible whopper.

"You won't believe what I heard!" Walter's voice trembled with incredulity. "Harve wants to do a flashback story again."

"So?" I replied. "That can work if done cleverly."

"Yeah, but this is a flashback to our Starfleet Academy days. Harve wants to find new, young actors who look like us and recast all our characters. Harve wants to replace us!"

"That's crazy!" I blurted out. "This is supposed to be our twenty-fifth anniversary picture. How can you celebrate twenty-five years with people who were never there at all! It doesn't make sense!"

When I hung up with Walter, my disbelief at this outrageous development started to burn, slowly turning into anger. I felt betrayed by Harve. One of his blandishments enticing me to sign the contract for STAR TREK V was the significant increase in compensation for STAR TREK VI—if the option should be picked up. I was in a fury. I knew that by recasting the story as a flashback, Paramount would not have to exercise the option.

And the "pay or play" part of the contract had not been exercised either. So, as it turned out, the studio had paid me the equivalent of what I'd been paid for *River Kwai*. However, my true interest in signing had been in parlaying STAR TREK V into another role. Even that prospect was now dashed. The rage I felt was not just at Harve. I was furious at myself for being taken for a dupe.

My mood as the holidays of 1989 approached was not very festive. I got grouchier as the year end neared. The more I thought on the betrayal, the more my anger gnawed away at me. It was making things unpleasant for all those around me. It was a self-injuring anger. I decided to act on it rather than let it ruin the holiday season.

I didn't consider Harve to be my boss. He was an employee of Paramount. But neither did I consider Paramount my boss. I worked on STAR TREK for those that kept it so popular. I felt that my real bosses were the STAR TREK fans. I decided to report to them, my *de facto* bosses, about this Starfleet Academy proposal of Harve's. They would be the ultimate judges.

Starting with the first weekend of 1990, I did twelve STAR TREK conventions consecutively. Every weekend, for three months straight, I was out to some convention in some city near or far, reporting to my "bosses" on what their hireling was proposing for their STAR TREK. There were gasps when I first broke the news. Word travels fast in fandom, and very quickly, most Trekkers seemed to know. There were loud "boos" of disapproval by the February conventions.

A short time later I received a call.

"This is Harve," the voice at the other end of the line said. He didn't have to tell me. I recognized his voice immediately. But this time it sounded unusually grave. "I know what you're up to, George. That's a dangerous game you're playing. I'm telling you for your own good."

"You tell me, Harve," I responded. "Am I not telling them the truth? Isn't what I'm saying at the conventions what you're really doing?"

"George!" He cut in sharply. "That's a stupid thing you're doing, and I'd advise you to stop!" I could sense the controlled intensity in his voice.

"I'll stop, Harve, if it's not true. You tell me, is it not true?"

"I'm telling you, George, and I'm telling you so you understand, that's a dangerous thing you're doing." And with that ominous warning, he hung up.

It was a strange feeling to be on the receiving end of a phone call like that. The next few weeks were eerie. The very absence of anything happening seemed fraught with portent. Whenever the phone rang with another invitation to a convention, it made me think twice. But I kept doing them. I knew that what I was reporting was true.

"Guess what?" Thank God for Walter! He contributed to my anxiety, but he also had a way of allaying it with new information. I hoped it would be positive news. "Harve's out! Paramount killed the Starfleet Academy idea. Harve is out of his office and off the lot." The power of the fans had struck again!

28

Captain Sulu at Last!

THERE WERE NO RUMORS, NO ADVANCE INFORMATION, NOTHING. The script for STAR TREK VI: THE UNDISCOVERED COUNTRY was delivered, and there it was. Right on the first page, as bold as day, from the very first scene it read "Captain Sulu is drinking a cup of tea."

I couldn't believe what I was seeing. I had been promoting the idea for so long, so persistently and so fruitlessly, that the campaign had now become an automatic reflex with me. Deep down inside, I was close to being resigned to never seeing Sulu's promotion. I was turning cynical. I read the scene over. Bill was nowhere in it. Good.

As I read on, a tiny electric prickle of excitement was touched off in me. This was a gripping plot! The more I read, the more the prickle increased. The action was driving, relentless, galvanic. Now, the electricity was surging uncontrollably through me. Sulu was an impressive captain! Even when he wasn't in the scene, I was aware of his presence. Captain Sulu was speeding to the rescue of a battered and beleaguered *Starship Enterprise*.

"Fly her apart then," he ordered, to spur on a terrorized helmsman of his ship, the *Excelsior*. "Target that explosion and fire!" he commanded, blasting away the maleficent Klingon general into the dark void of space. "Nice to see you in action one more time, Captain Kirk," he said with tenderness to his old leader at the end of battle. Captain Sulu was intrepid, valiant, a man of grace. He was a classic hero. This was really Captain Sulu, at last!

I had to go out for a run. The excitement in me was about to burst. I couldn't contain myself. I started jogging, but my feet seemed self-propelled. They were springing, scooting, shooting off on their own. This wasn't a run. It was more like a mad sprint. I'm sure my neighbors wondered what hysteria drove me to dash down my usual route like a man possessed. I ran until I was completely exhausted, completely spent. But I felt great. At long last—Captain Sulu!

STAR TREK VI began with new Paramount studio chief Frank Mancuso's desire to do "one more STAR TREK movie." He asked Leonard over for lunch and proposed the project. Leonard suggested a story idea and Nick Meyer as director. Mancuso agreed, and Leonard was off to Provincetown, Massachusetts, where Nick was vacationing. Over long walks on the beach, they discussed the project. Together, they crafted a story that was ripped from the headlines of the day's newspapers.

The Berlin Wall, a barrier of ideology as well as of geography, had come tumbling down. An explosive failure at the Soviet nuclear plant of Chernobyl had precipitated a cataclysmic disaster as well as the crumbling of what President Reagan had referred to as "the Evil Empire." The old world order was breaking down into chaos and uncertainty, into an "undiscovered country"—aha, there was tenacious Nick with his Shakespearean title again. No new authority existed to replace the old. The vile smell of bigotry issued up from the most unexpected sources, and nefarious alliances formed. From events as immediate as the six o'clock news and as eternal as the War of the Roses, Nick and Leonard wrought a rip-snorting space opera.

Ralph Winter was the producer of STAR TREK VI. He had

been with us since STAR TREK III as associate producer and then as executive producer in both STAR TREK IV and V. The title "executive producer," although impressive, is actually below the producer and is sometimes derisively referred to as the producer's nephew. But with Ralph, the title more than fully represented the scope of his work. He was the executive charged with the building, scheduling, shooting, and coordinating of the entire production—all, save the script. Harve Bennett, the producer, who was also a master writer, had been responsible for the dramaturgy.

With STAR TREK VI, Harve was now out of the picture, and Ralph was the producer. Harve, who felt he had mentored Ralph, wanted him to resign and leave Paramount with him. But when Ralph stepped up to the producer's position instead, Harve complained bitterly about his lack of "loyalty." Ralph, however, felt that his first loyalty had to be providing for his wife and young children. As it turned out, we were also the beneficiaries of that familial loyalty.

With this film, I had done practically no campaigning for Sulu's captaincy. Yet, here it was, triumphantly shining off the pages of this script.

Even Sulu's first name was revealed for the first time to a film audience. "Hikaru" was a name that Gene Roddenberry had come across in the classic Japanese novel by Lady Murasaki, *The Tales of Genji*, about an epic war between two adversary clans. One of the heroes was a poet/warrior prince named Hikaru, who ultimately brings about a lasting peace. Gene was taken by this character and decided to give his name to Sulu. So now, Sulu acquired both a first name and a captaincy in one great, wonderful swoop.

I couldn't help musing on how Sulu's promotion had come about. Through the years, Leonard knew of my lobbying on the set, with the producers and with the fans. But I suspected that it was really due to that long-ago meeting with Nick when he first came on board as director of STAR TREK II. There, in Harve's office, I had vigorously advocated for Sulu as well as for the ideal of vertical mobility in Starfleet. The seeds that had been planted so regularly, for so long, so persistently, had finally germinated with the combination of Leonard and Nick.

Sulu's promotion to a command seat had resonances larger than just in my character's development. For me, it showed STAR TREK again echoing society's tribulations and fictionally leading the way. Capable Asian Americans, indeed minorities and women in general, whether in the halls of academia, the corporate corridors of power, or professional passageways to success, were discovering that the stairway to advancement went only so high, when an invisible barrier, a "glass ceiling," seemed to prevent any further upward mobility. They were amply qualified in every other respect, save their minority group status. I had been battling that barrier in fact and in fiction. With STAR TREK VI: THE UNDISCOVERED COUNTRY, fiction again pointed the way to the goal for our own contemporary society. With Starfleet, there was no "glass ceiling." Sulu's breakthrough to his captaincy dynamically portrayed a virile meritocracy.

Everybody wanted to be in STAR TREK. With the first film, Gene Roddenberry had put out an invitation to fans to fill a hundred positions as extras. We discovered that neither distance nor the brevity of their appearance on film deterred aspirants who wanted to wear the Starfleet uniform. Scores of fans flew in from all corners of America to be seen for a brief moment in the motion picture.

Christian Slater, a fine actor and a popular star, was no different. He campaigned ardently to be in STAR TREK VI. Any role, any size. He wanted to be in STAR TREK. It also helped for him to have a mother who was a casting director. Ultimately, Christian was cast in a small role as an apprehensive young ensign who has to wake Captain Sulu in the middle of the night.

On the set of the *U.S.S. Excelsior,* wearing the uniform he had wanted to wear for so long, Christian was like an excited STAR TREK fan. "My heart's pumping like a bunny rabbit." He grinned. To me, he looked more like a frolicsome puppy dog. He bounded about the set, his body wiggling with joy; if he had

had a tail, I'm sure it would have been wagging deliriously. Christian Slater was an endearing young fan who happened to be a celebrated star.

There was only one thing I missed as Captain Sulu of the Excelsior. None of the "gang" from the *Enterprise* were with me. I yearned for their set-side company. I missed the gossip, the gripes, and the good-natured camaraderie. All my scenes were on the *Excelsior*—except for one, the Camp Khitomer sequence. That was my only scene together with everybody, and I looked forward to the four days of location shooting of the peace conference at Camp Khitomer.

This was an elaborate sequence on location in suburban Simi Valley with about a hundred extras, many in complicated alien makeup and costume. The massiveness of the production added to the festive air of my reunion with my friends. It was good to be working with them again.

Jimmy was showing me the plans for the new home he and his wife, Wende, were building in the Pacific northwest.

"This is where the breezeway is going to be, right here. See?" Jimmy was proudly pointing. Nichelle came out of her trailer with a sketch of a costume for her upcoming one-woman cabaret performance.

"Let me show you the dresses I've had designed for me," she gushed excitedly. "This one is really spectacular."

"Will you wait a minute, Nichelle!" bellowed Jimmy. "Can't you see I'm showing George these plans?"

"Oh, Jimmy, you can be so impatient," Nichelle snapped back sassily. "You've been showing your old plans all week long."

"Well, George hasn't seen them yet. Do you mind?"

Jimmy and Nichelle fussed and bickered with each other like an old married couple.

Walter was busy with writing projects on all front burners. We all had projects going immediately after this gig. We were all busy, busy, busy. I loved the gregarious showing off of my fellow actors. All, except De, the self-proclaimed "laziest actor in town." He was enjoying the quiet life with his dear wife, Carolyn.

Then, the glum reminder of the other part of doing STAR TREK hit me. With the colossal spectacle of a hundred extras in alien dress standing around, the production was brought to an expensive and stubborn halt. Bill would not play a scene the way Nick was directing it. Chancellor Azetbur's reaction was the focal point of the scene. Nick had blocked the choreography of actors and camera angles with that in mind. Bill thought differently, and he was determined to have his way—his way or the scene would not be shot. We stood around and waited, as the weary extras hunkered down trying not to soil their exotic outfits, technicians rolled their eyes in bored impatience, and the budget people wrung their hands in dismay. Bill was totally oblivious. His driving determination seemed to blind him to everything around him.

Despite my irritation, I again only felt sadness for him. Bill had changed over the years. He had hurt people and seemed ignorant of the pain he had inflicted. He had denigrated his colleagues and blithely giggled about it. He had taken without feeling. And in so doing, he had diminished himself. Where he could have gained from the relationship of decades, he had only developed a protective thick skin; where he might have profited from the company of talented and engaging people that surrounded him over the years, instead he had become the isolated "star," unable even to sense the mockery he had become to all those around him. Bill had changed. The vibrant young actor radiating star energy whom I met back in 1965 had reduced himself to the sad, stubborn, oblivious butt of derisive jokes.

But Bill provided the only rough texture to a rare and perhaps never-to-be-recaptured tapestry of experiences. I savored all of my time filming my favorite STAR TREK movie.

LIVE LONG
AND
PROSPER

29

Gene

THE PHONE RANG. IT WAS NICHELLE. SHE WAS SOBBING HYS-terically.

"Oh, Gene . . . George, oh, Gene . . ." She was overcome with emotion. Her speech convulsed with weeping. I couldn't make out her words, but I thought I knew what had happened.

I called Ralph Winter in his office at Paramount Studios and learned from him of Gene's death. It was October 24, 1991. Gene passed on in the year of the twenty-fifth anniversary of his creation, STAR TREK.

Death is painful. The loss of a dear friend is always anguish-ing. But when the passing is that of a great man who gave so much to so many, made such a giant contribution to our world, and who also shared his life with you as a friend, the sense of loss is immense.

Gene was my boss, my mentor, my ally, my buddy. He was a life guide who opened so many doors to such uncountable life experiences for me. He was a gentle philosopher who, in more ways than I can know, shaped my life—a man whose mind inspired me as much as his heart had been generous to me. He was a pal whose happy chortle made me happy too. The anguish in the loss was overwhelming. My grief was unbearable.

That weekend, however, I had on my calendar a STAR TREK Convention scheduled in Oklahoma City. I called Adam Malin of Creation Conventions to cancel my attendance. I didn't think I could do it. Adam understood and sympathized. However, he encouraged me not to cancel.

"There are a lot of people grieving Gene Roddenberry's passing all over America, George," he said gently. "Some of them are in Oklahoma. You could comfort them by sharing your personal remembrances of Gene with them. If you cancel, that only intensifies their sense of loss. If you go, you could help allay their pain. Please consider this."

I decided not to cancel. I flew out to Oklahoma City that weekend. I decided to make this gathering of STAR TREK fans my memorial to Gene.

I opened the convention by sharing my good memories of the man I first met back in 1965. I was a young actor hopeful of being cast in a continuing role in a series. I had mistakenly called him "Mr. Rosenbury" then. I told them about the fun we had together—of my attempts to get him to jog with me, of the laughs we shared at the parties he threw, of the help he gave me when I ran for public office. I explained to them how much his ideas and his philosophy had shaped mine. I told them I missed him very much but that he had left us a great, wondrous legacy. Then I invited the fans gathered there to share their thoughts on Gene.

They came up, one by one. A young man in a wheelchair spoke of the inspiration he had gotten from STAR TREK to venture into computer programming. A mixed couple, black and white, said they got their strength from the world of STAR TREK. A young woman physically abused by a violent father found her courage to act through STAR TREK. Another young man aspired to become an astrophysicist. One after another, they came up as personifications of Gene's humanity and strength.

As I listened, with each new testimony I sensed Gene there with us. Gene was gone, but he was still very much alive in these people. They were a part of Gene's living legacy. Such diversity in such combinations, such strength and such glowing optimism . . . way out in Oklahoma City. I stayed listening to them until early evening. I was glad I hadn't canceled that convention.

I donated the appearance fee from that convention to charity in Gene's memory.

The memorial service for Gene was held at Forest Lawn in Hollywood on November first. There was a great outpouring of people who had been affected by Gene. There even were a few in Starfleet uniforms. Patrick Stewart spoke eloquently and movingly. Whoopi Goldberg was earthy and touching. Nichelle sang sublimely. Everyone touched by Gene was there.

We were there to pay our respects. We wanted to be there to share our grief. We were there because we had been privileged to know a very special man. We were there because we loved him.

Gene was a man of ideas and of ideals. In a cynical time, when idealism tends to be derided as something spurious, as bogus morality, Gene embraced a shiningly optimistic, determinedly affirmative vision of the human future. Our human past may not have been all good, and neither had the history of his creation, STAR TREK. But he had the boldness of spirit to go into a medium—television—famous for mediocrity and uplift it and succeed, against all odds, with idealism. Then in a medium of hard numbers—Hollywood feature films—where dollar figures and ticket sales were the driving forces, Gene succeeded again with those same luminous ideals. He reached masses of people with the notion that a combination of imperfect people, in an imperfect world, reaching to the stars together, can prevail. He believed that every human being, imperfect creatures though we may be, each possessed something unique that, in combination with the uniquenesses of others, can create miraculous results. Infinite diversity in infinite combinations, he called it. Sheer idealism! Gene made that ideal an incandescent living force in our times.

All of us who were touched by Gene were there. But, again, where was Bill? We looked around. He was the only one who was not there. As always. But, he, too, was a part of that world that Gene envisioned—that world of infinite diversity in infinite combinations. A world of people with obvious talents and hidden flaws, people with surface defects possessing surprising gifts, people with different histories and different perspectives, all in our magnificent human diversity. Gene had brought us together in our own unique combination . . . Bill Shatner, Leonard Nimoy, DeForest Kelley, Nichelle Nichols, Jimmy Doohan, Walter Koenig, and me.